Designing Paris

The MIT Press
Cambridge, Massachusetts
London, England

Designing
Paris

*The Architecture of Duban,
Labrouste, Duc, and Vaudoyer*

David Van Zanten

© *1987 Massachusetts Institute of Technology*

All rights reserved. No part of this book may be reproduced in any form by any electronic or mechanical means (including photocopying, recording, or information storage and retrieval) without permission in writing from the publisher.

This book was set in Bembo by Achorn Graphic Services, Inc. and printed and bound by Halliday Lithograph in the United States of America.

Library of Congress Cataloging-in-Publication Data

Van Zanten, David, 1943–
Designing Paris.

Bibliography: p.
Includes index.
1. Neoclassicism (Architecture)—France—Paris.
2. Greek revival (Architecture)—France—Paris.
*3. Architecture, Modern—*19th century—*France—Paris.*
4. Architecture—France—Paris.   5. Paris (France)—
Buildings, structures, etc.   I. Title.
NA1050.V36   1987   720'.944'361   87-3994
ISBN 0-262-22031-8

In memory of Ann
and for Clara

ACKNOWLEDGMENTS

This book grew out of my experiences in Paris in 1968–69 as a Fulbright scholar from Harvard completing my doctoral dissertation, "The Architectural Polychromy of the 1830's." That topic was only tangentially French, and my choice of Paris as a place to pursue it was essentially practical, but once there that extraordinary city and its social and architectural tradition impressed itself forcefully upon my mind. French nineteenth-century architecture became the subject of my research for the next eighteen years.

I had been prepared for Paris by my undergraduate advisor at Princeton, Donald Drew Egbert, the first American historian of Beaux-Arts architecture, and by my uncle, Theodore Young, an architect who was once a designer for John Russell Pope. They had always assumed that France was the center of things.

In Paris I met Neil Levine, now a professor at Harvard and then a fellow Fulbright scholar. He was in Paris to study French modern architecture in general and the extraordinary work of the mid-nineteenth-century designer Henri Labrouste in particular. I was already exploring the work of Labrouste's generation, that of 1830, but it was through Levine that I perceived the real complexity and beauty of the subject. He made me especially aware of Labrouste and his close friends Félix Duban, Louis Duc, and Léon Vaudoyer and showed me how subtle, complex, and revolutionary were their conceptions of historicism and rationalism. He made it clear that the turn-of-the-century classical Beaux-Arts tradition at its origin in these men's work was something different and more profound than had been previously pictured. I owe him an incalculable debt: this volume exists because of his ideas, insights, and example.

During that illuminating year in Paris I met the first of a number of European scholars who have been unstintingly kind and helpful: Marcel Brion, advisor to the Fulbright scholars in art history; Mme. Bouleau-Rabaud, then librarian of the Ecole des Beaux-Arts, and her able assistant (and soon her successor), Annie Jacques; Jacques Dupont; Karl Hammer; Bruno Foucart; Françoise Bercé; Michel Gallet. I owe them thanks for favors and suggestions of all sorts over the years.

After 1969 I continued my research, focusing increasingly on mid-nineteenth-century France. Mme. Hautecoeur, librarian of the Institut de France, kindly placed me in contact with the Vaudoyer family in its several branches. They were helpful and kind in permitting me to study the drawings and letters of their ancestor and in answering my questions and guiding my research. I express to them a tremendous debt of gratitude.

In 1971 I began teaching at the University of Pennsylvania. There I was lucky to be near Frank Bowman, with his vast knowledge of nineteenth-century France. During eight years in Philadelphia I had three graduate students working in the field of French architecture from whom I learned a great deal: Robert Bruegmann, pursuing French eighteenth- and nineteenth-century hospital design; Christopher Mead, studying Garnier's Opera; and Ann Lorenz (who finished as a student of Levine at Harvard), working on César Daly and the *Revue générale de l'architecture*.

I married Ann and worked with her and depended upon her in many ways before she was killed on the rue des Rosiers in 1982. This book was a common project; it is dedicated to her memory.

While at Penn I also met several European architecture students in Louis Kahn's atelier who became fine friends and helpers in this research: Marina and Christian Devillers, David Elalouf, and Cornelis van de Ven.

During the year 1974–75 I worked with Ann as well as with Neil Levine and Richard Chafee under Arthur Drexler's direction on the exhibition *The Architecture of the Ecole des Beaux-Arts*, which opened in October 1975 at the Museum of Modern Art. We all learned a great deal from each other. We were aided wonderfully by Annie Jacques at the Ecole des Beaux-Arts (together with her assistants Annie Vallantin and Michelle Bacou), as well as by the Labrouste family and by Martine Kahane, librarian of the Bibliothèque de l'Opéra. Other kind friends were made at this time, among them Gérard Rousset-Charny, Robin Middleton, and Joseph Rykwert.

In 1976–77 Ann and I contributed to the exhibition *The Second Empire: Art in France Under Napoleon III*, conceived by Kathryn Hiesinger and Joseph Rishel of the Philadelphia Museum of Art. Again we learned from working together and with our French colleagues, particularly Geneviève Monnier at the Louvre and Bruno Foucart. Our circle of Parisian friends was enlarged as we made the acquaintance of Mme. Thérèse de Puylaroque and Mme. Marie-Noële de Gary. This experience made me aware that after their first works during the Monarchy of July, Labrouste and his contemporaries produced even finer achievements with their great monuments of the Second Empire, Vaudoyer's Marseilles Cathedral, Duc's Palais de Justice, and Labrouste's Bibliothèque Nationale.

It was only after the opening of the Second Empire exhibition in September 1978 and my contemporaneous move to Chicago to teach at Northwestern University that I commenced definitive work on the manuscript that follows. It is based on the documentation that I had assembled during the previous ten years and synthesizes much of my earlier work, but it is reformulated to respond to the perspective of professional context. Ann and I had become increasingly conscious of how profoundly architecture is beholden to the conceptual and technical means invented for its execution. The bigger the project was, the more elaborate these means—and France around 1850 (as well as Chicago around 1900) provided one of the most remarkable demonstrations of architectural organization in Western civilization. We not only became sensitive to all the procedures and tools developed to do so much work so well, but also started to explore how the architects themselves reacted to their social and professional situation, how they tried to make some small space for personal, speculative art. The first expression of our enterprise was Ann's essay "John Lloyd Wright," published in 1982, immediately before her death.

In carrying this volume to completion I have enjoyed the kindness of many other friends, especially Marthe Bernus and François Durand and his family in Paris. I have also profited tremendously from discussions with and advice from many younger scholars: Meredith Shedd and Michael Driskel, Katherine Taylor, Barry Bergdoll, Susan Siegfried, Anne Wagner, Richard Etlin. I have come to owe a great deal to several colleagues at Northwestern far more knowledgeable than I in the matter of the social history of art, especially Karl Werckmeister, Marco Diani, and Hollis Clayson. I have also learned a great deal from my graduate students, especially Tom Rowlands, working on Quatremère de Quincy; Sharon Irish, examining the professional situation of the Beaux-Arts architect Cass Gilbert; John Stamper, elucidating Chicago real estate development; and Steven Moyano, exploring Schinkel's work as Prussian Oberbaudirektor during the 1830s.

I also acknowledge, with warmest appreciation, a 1977 summer stipend from the National Endowment for the Humanities and especially a large research grant from the Graham Foundation for Advanced Studies in the Fine Arts, which made my research possible. The University of Pennsylvania contributed six months' leave, at half salary, and Northwestern a year's leave on the same terms.

Having written a manuscript, of course, the problem has been to make it a book, and here I have been kindly aided by Susan Lorenz, who provided time to travel and write; by Christopher Mead, Richard Etlin, Fannia Weingartner, and Danielle Pickard, who read the manuscript and gave editorial advice; and by Pat Persaud, who produced a beautiful typescript.

Last, but by no means least, I owe thanks to my daughter, Clara, who has been patient these last four years, who cheered me up and left me alone when the manuscript seemed too long and too unwieldy to ever be transformed into the volume the reader now holds.

INTRODUCTION

Around the year 1830 there emerged in Paris a group of architects who studied the history of architecture with a new, precise method of spatial and structural analysis. This permitted them to grasp the subject in terms of its organic principles and thus to be at home with history and not be controlled by its forms. Their method permitted them to project new buildings freely, in terms of their functions and meanings, and to create relieved ornamented surfaces of exquisite freedom and effect. Their emergence brought about a revolution in French architecture. Great opportunities were offered them by the development of Paris, first, tentatively, during the Monarchy of July of Louis Philippe between 1830 and 1848, then pell-mell and splendidly during the Second Empire of Napoleon III, proclaimed in 1852 and overthrown in 1870. They rose to this occasion. They, their students, and their successors largely produced the Paris of the mid-nineteenth century as well as the so-called Beaux-Arts system of training and design that eventually emerged from it. After 1870 the architects of the world flocked to Paris to imbibe this system and went home to create little Paris's all over the earth.

The leaders of this group were four friends: Félix Duban (1796–1871),[1] Henri Labrouste (1801–75),[2] Louis Duc (1802–79),[3] and Léon Vaudoyer (1803–72).[4] They were always seen as a group. They had won the Grand Prix de Rome in four successive years (1823–26) and had consequently studied together as *pensionnaires* at the French Academy in Rome, where they joined their sympathetic predecessors Abel Blouet and Emile Gilbert. The four returned to Paris around 1830 to lead the Romantic movement in architecture during the Monarchy of July. These Romantic *pensionnaires* went on to become the old masters of Second Empire architecture, producing three of its most impressive monuments: Vaudoyer's Marseilles Cathedral, Duc's Palais de Justice on the Ile de la Cité, and Labrouste's Bibliothèque Nationale. Three younger men also emerged during the Second Empire—Hector Lefuel, with his New Louvre; Charles Garnier, with his Opera; and Eugène-Emmanuel Viollet-le-Duc, with his campaign of medieval restoration—but they were individualists responding to the coordinated impetus of the Romantic *pensionnaires*. Both Garnier and Viollet-le-Duc claimed to be carrying on their enterprise, with Garnier claiming Duban and Duc as his precursors and Viollet-le-Duc citing Labrouste.

It is the work of the first four—its principles, its innovations, the professional reorganization that accompanied its emergence, and the complexity and subtlety of its architectural products—that is the subject of this book.

The participants in and descendants of the Beaux-Arts tradition always dated the definitive formulation of their system to the *pensionnaires'* return to Paris. In 1863, in the essays on architecture that were to constitute part of his *Grammaire des arts du dessin*, the editor, artist, and critic Charles Blanc noted enthusiastically:

How can one now despair of our architecture when one remembers that knowledge of the exemplary models is very recent and that the real Renaissance dates from only thirty years ago? Guided by penetrating study and criticism, possessing all the necessary tools, our school today has before it the most promising future.[5]

Again, and more specifically, in 1889 the architect Lucien Magne wrote in his *L'Architecture française du siècle*:

Reason and truth finally penetrated into the domain reserved for the arts; one realized that the work did not depend on an empty formula, but rather on the rational expression of an idea: an artistic reform was rising, and in the first rank among the innovators figured the students who between 1821 and 1826 represented the school at Rome, Blouet, Gilbert, Duban, Labrouste, Duc, Vaudoyer.[6]

Julien Guadet, an occasional student of Labrouste named to the prestigious post of Professor of Theory at the Ecole des Beaux-Arts, cited this reformation in a famous passage in the introduction to his course of 1894:

At the beginning of the century, the only aesthetic was to conceive a Roman building a priori. . . . *A little later, a violent reaction substituted for the Roman* a priori *the medieval* a priori, *architecture of a culture even more different from our own.* . . . *Happily, several proud artists—our masters—perceived and made others perceive that independence does not consist in changing one's livery, and our art slowly freed itself from this paleontology. Everything has not been equally successful, but all the efforts toward this end have been fertile, and today we know and we proclaim that art has the right to liberty, that only liberty can assure it life and fecundity, we might even say, salvation!*[7]

Finally, in 1922—the year of Le Corbusier's "Ville contemporaine pour 3 millions d'habitants"—the last great spokesman for the tradition, Georges Gromort, wrote:

A whole group of artists evolved whose works were to dominate the middle of the [nineteenth] century and prepare for the advent of an architecture totally new in its character, variety, and vitality, seemingly despite its traditional sources. The generation born with the century, that in fact of an age with the great romantics . . .

was fated to illuminate with the compositions of its maturity the eighteen years of the reign of Louis-Philippe and to sustain, for twenty years more, the architectural art of the second empire with examples of the authority of its old age. Four artists of the first rank successively won the grand prix: they were Gilbert in 1822, Duban in 1823, Labrouste in 1824, and Duc in 1825.[8]

For all the precision with which they date and attribute this architectural revolution, each of these authors modifies what it introduced. Blanc, a younger contemporary of the Romantic *pensionnaires*, sees it as a new clarity in the study of history. Magne, the son of an architect of this generation, depicts it as rationalism per se, in structure as well as in style. Guadet sees it as freedom from stylistic restrictions through eclectic selection of sources. Gromort perceives it even more abstractly, as broad compositional elasticity. All are partially right, as we shall see. This was a multiple phenomenon unfolding over time: the works of the Romantic *pensionnaires* were, in turn, historicist, rationalist, eclectic, and compositional. But these were not entirely individual contributions of four men incidentally contemporary: each of these qualities was present in each man's work, making it always experimental and complex.

Their enterprise was to find principles so basic that they could embrace the entire history of architecture and remain valid for the nineteenth century as well. They wished to understand the whole of the world's architectural speech and discourse in a universal language. They tried to do so by simultaneously studying structure, space, and decoration. It was an impossibly comprehensive program—one that could only have been seriously undertaken in the positivist 1830s. It produced various results in the individual works of these men, even more divergent results in that of their successors, and finally academicism when, with Guadet and Gromort at the turn of the century, its comprehensiveness was mistaken for a system that was all-inclusive and eternal, but that in fact proved to be out of date.

By the end of World War II this tradition and its century were history. Until recently the historical study of nineteenth-century France has largely avoided the Romantic generation of 1830. They had been appropriated by the Beaux-Arts tradition and thus were deeply suspect to the emerging modernists of the 1920s. Sigfried Giedion, first in his *Bauen im Frankreich, Eisen, Esenbeton* of 1928 and then in his *Space, Time and Architecture* of 1941, turned attention to engineering rather than design and initiated a long series of explorations of nineteenth-century French technology—often in its utopian aspect—of which Paul Dufournet, Françoise Bourdon, and François Loyer's *Hector Horeau* (1980) and Bernard Marrey's *Les Grands Magasins* (1979) and *Vie et l'oeuvre extraordinaire de M. Gustave Eiffel* (1984) are the most recent examples. Similarly, the anti–Beaux-Arts

Gothic rationalist tradition in France, that personified by Viollet-le-Duc and carried on by Anatole de Baudot and Louis Bonnier, has maintained its reputation as a protomodern movement and has been the subject of continuing research: Françoise Bercé's *Les premiers Travaux de la commission des monuments historiques* (1979), J.-M. Leniaud's *Jean-Baptiste Lassus* (1980), and the 1980 exhibition and catalogue *Viollet-le-Duc*. A third area of research has also emerged from the continued philosophical definition of the nature of modernism and the exploration of the events in economics, politics, and thought accompanying the French Revolution of 1789. Starting from the work of conceptualists like Michel Foucault, this has produced Tony Vidler's studies of Ledoux, Richard Etlin's *The Architecture of Death* (1984), Joseph Rykwert's *The First Moderns* (1980), Alberto Pérez-Gómez's *Architecture and the Crisis of Modern Science* (1983), and, more narrowly, Werner Szambien's *J.-N.-L. Durand* (1984).

All of this has stepped around the central tradition, that which came to be called Beaux-Arts. Even Labrouste, for all his technological innovation and the respect he enjoyed from the Gothicists, seemed tangential to Giedion and his successors.[9] The only exceptions were the most distanced and conservative historians, such as Louis Hautecoeur in the sixth and seventh volumes of his magisterial *Histoire de l'architecture classique en France* (1955 and 1957) and Donald Drew Egbert in his posthumously published *Beaux-Arts Tradition in French Architecture* (1980). Recently this has changed, however. Commencing with Arthur Drexler's exhibition and book *The Architecture of the Ecole des Beaux-Arts* of 1975–77 and continuing with the series of exhibitions and catalogues of nineteenth-century student work produced by the Ecole des Beaux-Arts itself, a broad documentation of the subject has begun to appear. The projected exhibitions of the new Musée d'Orsay in Paris will carry this further.[10] But this interest stems less from historical regard for the subject than from a contemporary, postmodern hope that the Beaux-Arts encapsulated a smooth, consistent system—like the turn-of-the-century American classicism of McKim and Burnham— that might be appropriated to balance the exclusiveness and utopianism of modern design.

The realization that at least at its origins, in the work of Duban, Labrouste, Duc, and Vaudoyer, the Beaux-Arts tradition was something infinitely more complex, personal, and difficult was the doing of Neil Levine in his doctoral dissertation "Architectural Reasoning in the Age of Positivism: The Néo-Grec Idea of Henri Labrouste's Bibliothèque Sainte-Geneviève" (1975) as well as in his contribution to the Drexler volume. Levine's work has given historical value to the central Beaux-Arts tradition by delving into the subtleties of its foundation. Robin Middleton in England and Bruno Foucart in France have been working along similar lines, as are a number of younger scholars in the United States—Chris-

topher Mead, Katherine Fisher Taylor, Barry Bergdoll, Alice Friedman—
and researchers in France who are pursuing the careers of Labrouste,
Alfred Normand, Gabriel Davioud, Paul Abadie, Victor Laloux, Jacques-
Ignace Hittorff, and Charles Garnier.[11]

This volume is a contribution to that project. It seeks to analyze the
intentions of Duban, Labrouste, Duc, and Vaudoyer in the immediate
context of architectural evolution during the Romantic years of the second
quarter of the nineteenth century. But, more specifically, it seeks to
approach their work as a manifestation of the centralized government
bureaucracy within which it was produced, which gave it an abstract,
classical inflection before 1850, and which made it profoundly expressive
of the Second Empire during the two decades after. The designs that resulted were Romantic in attempting to be of their time and place by re-
specting the materials, climate, and social character of nineteenth-century
France. But these designs were also classical in imposing a particular traditional Parisian abstract logic upon each problem as well as in adopting one
or another version of the classical architectural vocabulary. They were
never bohemian, Gothicist, or futurist. Such qualities were ultimately un-
appreciated by Duban, Labrouste, Duc, and Vaudoyer, whose enterprise
was the inflected expression of an institution and a tradition. As a result,
what they created was an elastic, diagrammatic art that could be sys-
tematized, taught, and exported all over the world as the basis of the
Beaux-Arts movement in late-nineteenth-century architecture. The origins
of this art were complex, however, and in that complexity lay the elasticity that made it such a powerful and pervasive idea.

Designing
Paris

One

THE STUDENT WORK: THE *ENVOIS* FROM
THE FRENCH ACADEMY IN ROME

The seminal episode in the story of the Romantic *pensionnaires* is their coming together at the French Academy in Rome after winning the Grand Prix in four successive years.[1] Held every year since 1720, the competition bestowed upon the winning student in painting, sculpture, and architecture a five-year state pension for study in Rome. Duban, the oldest of the four, won in architecture in 1823 and arrived in Rome at the end of that year. He was the son of a Bordeaux *quincaillier* and the brother-in-law of the Parisian architect and academician François Debret (1777–1850). Debret trained Duban in his atelier and shepherded him through the Ecole des Beaux-Arts. Labrouste, who followed the next December, was the son of François-Marie-Alexandre Labrouste, Premier Commis des Finances and an important government official during the Revolution, Empire, Restoration, and Monarchy of July. Duc, who trained in the atelier of André-Marie Chatillon (1782–1859), arrived in 1825. The son of a fashionable sword-maker in the Faubourg Saint-Honoré, he had his roots in the upper level of the artisanal class. Vaudoyer arrived at the end of 1826. He was from the heart of the architectural profession itself: son of the academician Antoine-Laurent-Thomas Vaudoyer (1756–1846), in whose atelier both he and Labrouste trained, and cousin of the academician Hippolyte Lebas (1782–1867). For two remarkable years, 1827–28, the four *pensionnaires* were in Rome working together.

The Académie des Beaux-Arts (which administered the Grand Prix competition and the French Academy in Rome) required the *pensionnaires* to execute studies of details of "les plus beaux monuments antiques" during the first three years of their stay, the study of an entire "monument antique d'Italie" together with a reconstruction and a historical note during their fourth year, and, during their fifth year, "le projet d'un monument public de sa composition, et conforme aux usages de la France." Study was to be concentrated in Rome itself; travel was to be authorized by the Director and supposedly was restricted to the last two years of work.[2] The yearly projects, or *envois,* were exhibited in Rome, then sent to Paris for exhibition and criticism by the Académie. A formal (and usually polite) report on them was prepared by the Secrétaire Perpétuel and read at the Académie's annual *séance publique* in October, while a more lengthy, specific report was sent by him to the Director in Rome.

Though Duban, Labrouste, Duc, and Vaudoyer started with the mandated examination of Roman architectural remains, they were soon studying the whole span of architectural periods and types. From this they derived a vivid sense of history and a specificity and richness in their conception of modern architecture that they would at times permit to be labeled "Romantic." Where their old Neoclassical teachers in Paris had expected them to see an array of eternal, paradigmatic forms, in the monuments of Rome they saw functions, lives, and stories producing an infinite number of ephemeral shapes whose continuing transformation would produce a modern architecture consistent only in its generative principles.

Vaudoyer's thinking was already beginning to focus during the trip down to Rome through Turin, Milan, Bologna, Florence, and Siena, and the terms in which it was focusing were far from those of conventional Neoclassicism. "The cathedral gave me infinite pleasure," he wrote his father on January 6, 1827, of Siena. "A harmony reigns between the exterior and the interior and everything is decorated with colored marbles, paintings, etc. . . . and in no way resembles our white, cold churches in Paris." In Florence Vaudoyer had been unimpressed by the Pitti Palace, "the character of which I do not find appropriate for the habitation of a prince," but admired the Duomo and the Baptistry, "of which one cannot have any idea until one has seen them." Of San Miniato he remarked, "As Labrouste wrote me, it is a very beautiful thing." Labrouste, breaking the rule forbidding *pensionnaires* to travel during their first three years in Rome, had visited Florence in 1825. His enthusiastic discovery there of pre-Raphaelite architecture, embodied in a meticulous study of the Duomo and communicated to Vaudoyer by letter, had clearly already begun to influence the latter's thinking. "I will be very happy," Vaudoyer concluded of Florence, "when I return here to work."[3]

Settled in Rome, he was pleased to form tight friendships with the other *architectes pensionnaires*. "We are extremely close," he wrote in January 1827, "people find us haughty. I don't know why. . . . Labrouste and Duc have conducted me around all the ruins."[4] Soon he was helping Duc measure the capitals of the Temple of Jupitor Stator, learning important lessons about the close reading of monuments, as we shall see.[5] On May 18 Vaudoyer left for Florence in the company of Duban, Duc, and A.-A.-F. Decraëne (1797–1859), a Belgian friend from his father's atelier.[6] They traveled through the Etruscan, Early Roman, and pre-Raphaelite cities of Narni, Terni, Spoleto, Assisi, Perugia, and Arezzo and returned in early

July with a detour to Bologna.[7] The three *pensionnaires* would remember this trip as the moment when they began to understand how they could make use of what they had studied.[8] The next year, 1828, was spent in a strenuous program of travel. In May and early June, Vaudoyer walked through Latium with Duban, Duc, Labrouste, and Labrouste's older brother Théodore (1799–1885), who had arrived in January. They saw the Etruscan and Early Roman monuments at Ariccia (the Tomb of the Horatii), Veletri, Cori, Segni, Palestrina, and Tusculum and visited Renaissance Frascati, where they found time to see only the Villa Aldobrandini.[9] In July Vaudoyer traveled with Henri Labrouste to the Adriatic coast, visiting Loretto, Ancona, Fano, Rimini, and Ravenna, and returned alone through Assisi.[10] Rimini proved a disappointment both in the Roman bridge and in Alberti's San Francesco, but Ravenna was exciting, especially for the wonderfully cut stone cupola of the Tomb of Theodoric. Finally, in September, the group headed south—Vaudoyer, Decraëne, and Felix Wilhelm Kubly (1802–72), a Swiss student from his father's atelier, to Naples and Pompeii; Duc and Labrouste on to Sicily; then all together to Paestum.[11] The remains at Pompeii were more extensive than Vaudoyer had been led to expect; he found them immensely illuminating. Of Paestum he wrote, "The appearance of this beautiful ruin ravished me. It was one of the things that impressed me the most."[12]

Now, it seems, the work of discovery was over: the *pensionnaires* ceased their frenetic traveling. In 1829 Labrouste had only his fifth-year *envoi* to execute, an original design on a modern program; Duc's archaeological fourth-year *envoi* was a reconstruction of the Colosseum, which was near at hand; and Duban had returned to Paris that January. Vaudoyer wrote his father that he would stay in Rome to gather his thoughts.[13] Aside from short side trips to the Etruscan and Early Roman sites around Rome—Tivoli and Cori again with Théodore Labrouste in April;[14] Palestrina and Tivoli in late summer;[15] and, most notably, Tarquinia, where the celebrated archaic Etruscan tombs had been discovered, with Duc and both Labroustes in October[16]—Vaudoyer stayed put until April 19, 1830. Then he commenced one last major trip, a six-week journey to Naples and Sicily with Théodore Labrouste and A.-F.-F. Fries, a student of Huyot sent by him to Rome to measure Hadrian's Villa.[17]

Something exciting happened among the *architectes pensionnaires* in 1827–28. Together they formulated a new way of understanding architecture inspired by the study of the monuments of pre-Raphaelite Florence, of the Greeks in Sicily and at Paestum, and of the Etruscans and Republican Romans in Tuscany and Latium. It made the *pensionnaires'* former work at the Ecole des Beaux-Arts in Paris seem academic and worthless. Already on July 26, 1827, Vaudoyer wrote his father, "In general we disown what we have produced in Paris and count on our future productions to efface the errors of the past."[18] The way to this rejection of the Ecole's teachings was led by Henri Labrouste—the first to go to Florence, the first to do a Greek *envoi*—and seemed to lose some of its impetus when Labrouste returned to Paris in early 1830. What exactly led to the *pensionnaires'* change of heart? Some answers emerge in Vaudoyer's letters.

One of the first notes of what was to become a sharp discordance in the father-son correspondence is struck by Léon's disparagement of the accuracy of earlier studies of Italian monuments. He had carried with him Charles Percier's folio *Choix des plus célèbres maisons de plaisance de Rome* (1809), and on January 22, 1827, shortly after his arrival, he remarked that "all the villas that I see prove the charlatanism of the work of M. Percier." By February 16 he was lecturing his father: "The drawings of M. Thibault [1757–1826] prove that in this time one made something of nothing. That fashion is passé and we think more seriously. One does not pass one's time . . . in making sketches by the bushel." The elder Vaudoyer's response that Léon might enjoy the convenience of a camera obscura occasioned an even louder detonation:

Is it with a camera obscura that we have drawn the entablatures and capitals we have sent back to Paris each year? I measured that of Jupitor Stator and I can judge how much effort it represents to measure, to restore, to trace, and to render. Is it with a camera obscura that Labrouste and Duc made their trip to Pompeii, from which they returned, not with sketches and picturesque views, but with plans and sections measured and redrawn? One no longer makes sketches as before which one never redraws and which repose in a portfolio without ever being consulted. One arrives in Paris today with [the record of] a complete tour, as much of ancient [monuments] as of modern, which one can utilize immediately; our manner of working today is not a fashion; it is scientific and incontestably superior to that of our predecessors.[19]

Vaudoyer ends by complimenting the one member of the former generation whom the *pensionnaires* respected (at least initially), Jean-Nicolas Huyot (1780–1840), professor of the History of Architecture at the Ecole des Beaux-Arts and author in 1811 of the first painstakingly accurate archaeological *envoi*, a study of the Temple of Fortuna at Palestrina.[20] Jacques-Ignace Hittorff (1792–1867), however, having raced through Pompeii and Sicily in two months in the winter of 1823–24, is disparaged by Vaudoyer—"Did nothing, remaining at Pompeii a single day"—and charged by him with "charlatanisme."[21]

What Vaudoyer and his fellow *pensionnaires* were seeking to accomplish was demonstrated in their *envois*. We have Vaudoyer's explanation of his second-year project, executed during the frenetic year of 1828, and his third-year study of 1829.[22] The first was a parallel study of the temples of Minerva at Assisi, of Fortune at Tivoli, and of Fortuna Virilis at Rome. "I sought in my second-year *envoi*," he wrote his father on July 20, 1829, "to direct my attention to a more primitive architecture, to that simple architecture which owes its beauty only to its forms and proportions without distracting the attention to some frieze or *raye de coeur* more or less well executed." Thus in reconstructing missing parts he sought to work in the particular spirit of these primitive, simple productions, not in terms of modern taste:

The moderns have denatured this order [at Cori] because they did not study its principles. It is thus that one Attic sees bases attached to Doric columns. . . . I have not tried to make a beautiful door (in my reconstruction of the temple of Fortuna Virilis), but to make a door in the character of the rest of the monument, which has obliged me to use somewhat crude moldings. . . . I have not made what one calls beaux dessins, *that is of ornamental details, friezes, etc. . . . but I have made good studies (*bonnes études*).*[23]

The Académie des Beaux-Arts, which was confronted in this same dispatch of *envois* by Labrouste's Paestum and Duban's *temple protestant*, was not sympathetic. It criticized the poverty of Vaudoyer's models and especially the fact that they were built of limestone rather than smooth, sculpted marble.[24] In response Vaudoyer sent his third-year *envoi*, a parallel study of four ceremonial arches, again in stone: those at Fano, Ancona, Benevento, and the Porta Maggiore in Rome. His intentions, he wrote his father, were to show how the same arched form (indeed, three of the four from the same, Hadrianic period) took on subtle inflections when applied in different situations. The arch at Fano was a city gate built into a defensive wall, that at Ancona a freestanding monument, that at Benevento the entrance to a forum, and the Porta Maggiore the passage of an aqueduct over a major avenue.[25] He explained, "I am seeking to make it understood that I do not wish to make a comparative study but instead separate studies of monuments that nevertheless have some analogy of form and of construction; that is, the architecture of arches and vaults."[26] This sensitivity led him to dismiss Charles-Edouard Isabelle's *Parallèle des salles rondes de l'Italie* because the buildings illustrated were arranged by shape and not by function.[27] He changed his mind about a favorite project by Huyot for the Arc de Triomphe because it was based on the gate at Fano, with its pilastered gallery for passage along the city wall, and thus was inappropriate for a freestanding monument.[28]

Finally, in a lengthy letter of November 28, 1831, to his cousin Hippolyte Lebas, Léon tried to make a general statement of his new principles:

*Ideas have changed; the constitutional system has arrived and brought with it the spirit of examination, logic, and economy. One has begun now to think that it does not suffice to have an excellent taste for arrangement, to adjust ornaments perfectly, to draw to perfection, to encumber monuments with statutes, reliefs, etc. in order to make architecture. One has come to comprehend that our social and political institutions impose a considered architecture, logical, easily constructed, simple and economic. I do not make it my business to decide whether this is good or bad, but I think, nonetheless, that there is more merit in the monuments of the [Roman] Republic than in those of the time of Trajan; that it is not the richness of material nor the immensity of monuments that constitute true beauty, but rather a clear idea of propriety (*convenances*), of the needs of the period, and finally the nobleness of forms and the expression of a character appropriate to each thing. The Temple de la Paix [Pantheon] in brick and stucco is a masterpiece that is in no way inferior to the richest monuments in marble. I thus think that in order to satisfy the needs of our time, one must by preference study the rudimentary architecture (architecture radicale) of the ancients, that is, that which had to satisfy basic functions and was not corrupted by luxury. It is in this rudimentary architecture that one best perceives the reasons for forms, the skeleton in fact, which later conceals itself under rich garments. It is in order to strip the rich monuments of the Empire of all their adornment and to discover the nude that it is necessary to engage in the study of these Republican or Greek monuments which have only the purity of their forms and their simplicity for ornament. . . . So, this architecture that one calls Romantic, I don't know very well why, is an architecture which seeks to discover true principles, which demands that each form be determined by reason and necessity, which seeks to submit itself to the nature of materials, which tries, finally, to set this art in harmony with its century.*[29]

Later, in a letter of January 29, 1832, one of his last from Rome, Vaudoyer told his father of a conversation between Huyot and Duc: "After a long architectural discussion . . . they parted, saying: one, Duc, was a partisan of what was determined by reason and necessity and the other, Huyot, was a partisan of what first of all pleased the eye despite these two considerations." Vaudoyer concluded, "Thus you have two completely incompatible systems and no hope of ever seeing them changed."[30]

With Vaudoyer, however, we are only working around the edge of the problem. The central figure was Labrouste and the pivotal *envoi* his study

1

Henri Labrouste, Temple of Neptune (Hera II), Paestum, reconstruction of facade. Fourth-year envoi, 1828–29. Ecole des Beaux-Arts, Paris. (Photo: H. d'Espouy, Fragments d'architecture antique)

2

Henri Labrouste, Temple of Neptune (Hera II), Paestum, reconstructed cross section. Fourth-year envoi, 1828–29. Ecole des Beaux-Arts, Paris. (Photo: Bulloz)

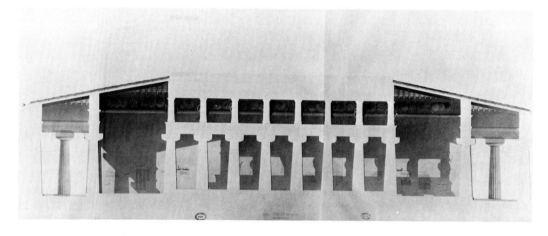

3
Henri Labrouste, Basilica (Temple of Hera I), Paestum, reconstructed longitudinal cross section. Fourth-year envoi, *1828–29. Ecole des Beaux-Arts, Paris. (Photo: Bulloz)*

of Paestum executed in the *annus mirabilis, 1828* (figures 1–3).[31] Everything
Vaudoyer explains—along with a good deal he does not—appears here,
but more decisively and subtly. The Paestum study was later regarded as
the first clear proclamation of the architectural revolution and was, at the
time, the target of the Académie's bitterest criticisms.

The controversy over Labrouste's *envoi* centered on charges of archaeological inaccuracy (compared to the 1793 *envoi* of Claude-Matthieu
Delagardette [1762–1805][32]) in the review sent privately from the
Secrétaire Perpétuel, Quatremère de Quincy, to Horace Vernet, the Director of the French Academy in Rome. So unjust did Vernet find these
charges that he visited Paestum himself with Louis Duc to check the disputed details and then wrote the Académie a vindication of Labrouste's
project.[33] When the academicians refused to withdraw their criticisms,
Vernet tendered his resignation (September 7, 1830), which was refused.
At this point the coincidence of Labrouste's return to Paris, the outbreak
of the revolution of July 1830, and the agitation leading to the creation of
the Commission des Beaux-Arts (January 25, 1831) to review the conduct
of the Ecole encouraged Vernet and the Romantic *pensionnaires* (falsely as it
turned out) to believe that the Académie had been bridled, and the crisis
faded away.

Examining Labrouste's drawings, one wonders what could have been so
upsetting. The buildings are primitive stone monuments, like the temples
Vaudoyer made the subject of his second-year *envoi,* but they are Greek,
not provincial Roman. These were among the best preserved of the Greek
temples in Italy; there was very little to restore. In 1878 Henri Delaborde
spoke of the boldness of Labrouste's reading of the interior colonnades of
the Temple of Neptune as supports for a closed roof and the garishness of
his reconstruction of the painted terra-cotta gutters.[34] The former, however, was a logical solution to a recognized archaeological problem;[35] the
latter conservative indeed when compared to the polychromatic reconstructions of Greek architecture being displayed in Paris during the late
1820s by Hittorff.[36] (In fact, the conservative critic Etienne-Jean Delécluze,
reviewing the 1828 *envois* in the *Journal des Débats,* praised the "perfection"
of Labrouste's reconstructions but asked why he did not show *more* polychromy.[37] Compared to Emile Gilbert's fourth-year *envoi* of 1826 restoring the almost completely destroyed Temple of Jupiter at Ostia—of which
the Académie itself remarked that he had restored a great deal from very
little—Labrouste's Paestum seems singularly judicious and precise. Was
Labrouste merely being made to pay for the aggressive radicality of
Duban's accompanying fifth-year *envoi* because the archaeological project
could be disputed on familiar documentary grounds?

There was, however, something quite frightening in Labrouste's *envoi,*
something more evident in the text accompanying the studies than in the

drawings themselves, as Neil Levine has pointed out. The chronological
ordering of the monuments previously established by Delagardette (and
since proven by archaeological exploration) placed the so-called Basilica as
the oldest, followed by the Temple of Ceres, then the Temple of Neptune.[38] Delagardette's rationale for this ordering was the progressive light-
ening of proportions documented elsewhere in Greek architecture.
Labrouste proposed a reversal: the Temple of Neptune first, then the
Temple of Ceres, and finally the Basilica. He justified this by pointing out
that Paestum was a Greek colony established in Italy far from Hellas and
that this separation might be a more profound determinant of form than
any progressive refinement imagined taking place everywhere simultaneously in the Mediterranean. Labrouste saw the Temple of Neptune as
the earliest structure because it was the truest to the Attic paradigm represented at Olympia and Aegina. The Temple of Ceres he placed next because it had started to deviate from the Attic model (in proportions and in
the placement of half metopes at the corners) and because it was made of
two kinds of local stone, not one like the Temple of Neptune, indicating a
greater familiarity with local quarries. The Basilica Labrouste placed last
because it deviated the farthest from the Attic model. These last two structures, he stated, are no longer truly Greek, but "d'une architecture autre."
But as they deviated from the Greek model, they became more organic to
the Tyrrhenian coast: "Ces deux monuments seules offrent le type de
l'architecture de Posidonia."

Labrouste found confirmation of this sequence in the local designation
of the monuments. It would be logical, he observed, after the perilous sea
journey from Greece, for the colonists to erect their first temple to the god
of the sea, Neptune. Then, after the colony had set down roots and
brought in fertile crops, a temple to the goddess of fertility, Ceres, would
be appropriate. Finally, when the colony had become a strong political and
military force, a civic meeting hall, the Basilica, would be necessary. Thus
Labrouste depicted the group of buildings not as a microcosm of the evolution and refinement of the Doric Order, as they had been envisioned by
Delagardette, but as a piece of history, revealing the specific state of mind
and society of a colony of Greeks thriving two thousand five hundred
years earlier. Labrouste's is a piece of Romantic historical writing in which
monuments, like documents, are made to speak. Labrouste perceived a
moving, personal story in the ruins of Paestum, just as his contemporary
Augustin Thierry had found one in the historical documents of England
and France.[39]

This personal story becomes most palpable in the details Labrouste
added to his cross section of the Basilica (figure 3): inscriptions and symbols painted on the walls and shields and spears suspended from the exposed ceiling beams. This clothing of solemn ancient monuments in

anecdotal dress emerged as one of the chief motifs of the *envois* by the four *pensionnaires* who succeeded Vaudoyer, starting gently with Théodore Labrouste's second-year study of the Temple of Vesta at Rome of 1829 and becoming impishly exaggerated after the Revolution of 1830 in the successive fourth-year *envois* of Théodore Labrouste (figure 4), Marie-Antoine Delannoy (1800–60) and Simon-Claude Constant-Dufeux (1801–71). Delannoy's (figure 5), appearing the year Victor Hugo's *Notre-Dame de Paris* was published, seems to envision the Tiber Island in terms of the cramped, overbuilt Ile de la Cité, in defiance of generations of French classicists who had tried to project Paris as if it were Rome.

Labrouste accomplished this resurrection of the whole by reading ancient monuments closely, by training himself to see distinctions between structures apparently similar (just as Vaudoyer did with his *envoi* of arch forms). He could see one of these buildings at Paestum as not necessarily a temple at all. He refused the testimony of the conventional signs of meaning, the column and the pteripteral layout, to accept instead that of nuances of structure. He raised a new set of signs to consciousness and set aside the received vocabulary of Orders as meaningless (at least, outside Greece). What is amazing—and, to the Académie, enraging—is how much Labrouste was able to extract from the close examination of three nearly identical stone boxes.

Labrouste's Paestum *envoi,* then, was a different kind of reconstruction than the Académie required or expected. But beyond this it had a general message that no one could have missed: the pure Attic style could not be removed from its natural soil in Greece without decaying into the ill-formed if practical architecture of the Paestum Basilica. The larger question Labrouste's drawings posed is clear: If Greek colonists at the apogee of Attic art could not meaningfully reproduce the Doric temple form once removed to a foreign place, how could a Frenchman in the nineteenth century hope to do so in Paris? If the Doric Order decayed so far in the short span of the history of Paestum, how much more utterly must it have evaporated by 1828?

It is clear, then, that Labrouste is declaring that the Doric Order could not survive out of its original time and place, but it is also clear in his rendering of the Temple of Neptune that he agreed that the Attic ideal of form did, at one moment, exist. In the Temple of Ceres and the Basilica he showed the effect of the cultural and structural forces enumerated by Vaudoyer. What forces, however, did he imagine produced the elegantly adjusted forms of the Temple of Neptune? One might reply that, though more subtly here than in the Basilica, structural forces are at work. Thirty-five years later Viollet-le-Duc would analyze the Doric temple in his *Entretiens* to show that it was essentially a rational structure in stone. Labrouste's suggestion that the interior two-storied colonnades did not

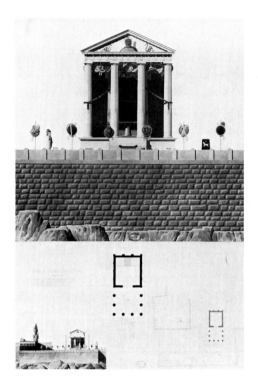

4
Théodore Labrouste, Temple of Hercules, Cora, reconstructed facade. Fourth-year envoi, *1831–32. Ecole des Beaux-Arts, Paris. (Photo: Bulloz)*

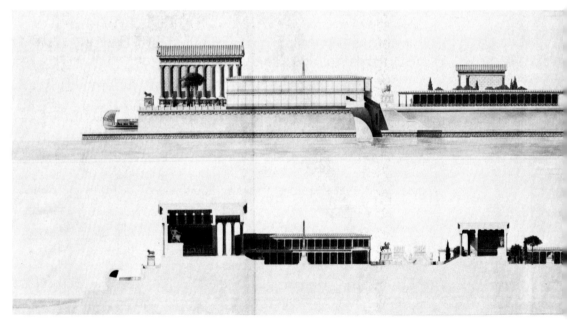

5
Marie-Antoine Delannoy, Tiber
Island, Rome, reconstructed view
from the south. Fourth-year envoi,
1832–33. Ecole des Beaux-Arts,
Paris. (Photo: James Mathews)

support balconies, but were instead a clever way of reducing the wide span of the roof members, has been depicted as structurally rationalist. But Labrouste's solution was that the tall supports were divided into two tiers of columns so that the ceiling could be reached without changing the proportions of the shafts or making them of excessive girth. A structural solution this is, but one to solve an aesthetic problem: how to maintain proper proportions in a difficult situation. Just such elegancies defined the mainstream of classical architectural thought from Ictinus to Palladio to Percier. Labrouste also expressed a preference for the adjustment of the triglyph at the corners of the entablature, a Greek refinement controverting the more regular but less elegant Renaissance and Roman practice. When in 1902 Hector d'Espouy made a selection of the most "classic" *envois* for his *Fragments d'architecture antique,* he devoted three plates to Labrouste's drawings of the Temple of Neptune and, not surprisingly, none to those of the Basilica.[40]

Should we read Labrouste's study as a factual history or as a mirror of a personal state of mind? Might we suppose that Labrouste, examining these evocative remains, deciphered not so much the history of Greek architecture in Italy as the evolution of his own conception of design? That is, the Temple of Neptune—beautiful in form but impossible to sustain by reason and necessity—is the Neoclassical ideal Labrouste himself imbibed in Paris at the Ecole des Beaux-Arts, which he embodied in his Grand Prix project, and which he went to Rome in 1824 to pursue. The Basilica, by extension, is the expression of the collapse of that ideal in Labrouste's mind by 1828 as a result of his experiences in Rome.

This personal interpretation would explain Labrouste's fifth-year *envoi,* a *pont frontière* crossing a stream on the French-Italian border. The Académie intended that this *envoi* should be a large and elaborate composition, but Labrouste sent almost nothing: "un joli sentiment," to quote Vaudoyer.[41] In 1840 Labrouste stated the academic expectation of a fifth-year *envoi* to be "something that . . . was made for France but that appeared to be inspired by travel and the study of Antiquity."[42] To an artist like Labrouste, believing in the fundamental importance of local character (and himself a Frenchman exiled for five years to Rome), the question must immediately have been: What do France and Italy have in common? The simplest answer would be their border, their point of distinction. But of slight distinction, for the two realms do meet, if only along this edge. This border even has an architectural tradition embodied in the Roman bridge at Saint-Chamas and the arch at Aosta, upon which Labrouste's *envoi* is modeled: displaced, provincial Roman designs efficient in structure and simple in details like the Basilica at Paestum. Once again the Académie was moved to criticize his study of a debased, provincial model.[43]

Is one justified in interpreting these *envois* symbolically? They purport to be serious ancient and modern designs. Paestum certainly seems scrupulously archaeological in its details—all but one, however, and the most important: the extrapolation of the function of the buildings and thus of their chronological sequence. In reaching these conclusions Labrouste stated simply that he accepted the designations of local tradition. How could he place such faith in mere local tradition? Obviously because he felt his purpose to be the same: to explain monuments poetically, to reveal what they suggest to the intuitive, common mind.

Since Vico and Herder had been brought to the attention of the French intellectual public, first by Cousin in 1816–21, then by Michelet and Quinet in 1827, art in general and the great works of the Greeks in particular had come to be viewed as communal productions of Hellenic culture and history and as symbolic rather than factual narratives. Quinet and especially Michelet developed in their subsequent writing a "symbolic" reading of history.[44] Labrouste imposed a poetic chronological structure on the monuments at Paestum, concluding that its justness had already been recognized in the spontaneous tradition that designates them as temples to Neptune and Ceres and a basilica. These structures are not, in the end, envisioned as historical facts, but rather as inscrutable artifacts that are valuable for the poetic aperçu they suggest: the sudden glimpse of the Greek colonists in Italy losing their faith in the Doric ideal just as Labrouste himself, twenty-five hundred years later, was losing his.

It is obvious in Vaudoyer's long letter to Lebas that his commitment to archaeological precision was more than just a fixation on correctness; it was the reflection as well of a new point of view—of "the spirit of examination" introduced by the new century of the "constitutional system," producing something called "Romantic architecture." Parallel to his development of the idea of precise reading of historical monuments are general remarks attempting to place his and his friends' enterprise in cultural context—most particularly to link it to what appeared to be Romanticism.

The first murmurs came in June 1827. "Lord Byron, and not Biron," Léon exasperatedly chides his father, "was never an admiral, but a very distinguished poet and a defender of the liberty of the Greeks. . . . To get an idea of his character one must read the *Dernier Chant du Pèlerinage de Chil Harolde* [sic] by M. A. de Lamartine. It is a masterpiece of French poetry."[45] By October of that year Léon was asking for copies of Lamartine's *Méditations* and *Pèlerinage de Childe Harold*. "Don't go to Merlin, a rococo bookseller who doesn't even know who Lamartine is, go to Gosselin."[46] In October 1828 Chateaubriand arrived in Rome as French ambassador to the Holy See in the short-lived Liberal ministry of Martignac.[47] To the pleasure of the *pensionnaires*, Chateaubriand dined with them at the Villa Medicis on December 12. The literary diplomat commissioned

Vaudoyer, at his own expense, to design a small monument to Poussin for the church of San Lorenzo in Lucina. The two met frequently and talked about art.[48]

In late 1829 the Académie's harsh critique of the 1828 *envois* arrived at the Villa Medicis, and Vaudoyer's mere mentions of Romanticism became straightforward declarations. In January 1830 he wrote:

I persist in my opinion that we need no more mythology [in the programs formulated by the Ecole for the student competitions]; we live in the century of the practical [positif]; I do not criticize the virgins of Raphael; on the contrary I cite them as [the work of a] painter who represents the ideas of his time. As for modern subjects, I think one can paint them very well. I need no other examples than the plague of Jaffa and the battles of Aboukir and Eylau of M. Gros, the Sacre *of David, and his* Sermant du Jeu de Paume *[as well as] the battle of Austerlitz and the* Henri IV *of Gérard, and to make my ideas clearer I tell you that the* Famille malheureuse *of M. Prud'hon impressed me more than all the Narcissus's in the world. It is what I would call a scène morale. I do not exclude Greek or Roman subjects nor allegory but it is time . . . to paint our own history. . . . We need no more mythology. That is finished in the arts as it is in theater and in literature.*[49]

By March he was calling for a mild architectural revolution:

I do not have the ability to make myself understood. . . . The war of which I speak is not dangerous. Here it is only a matter of taste. You know that in the matter of taste it is difficult to prove who is right; thus this war in architecture is nothing more than what exists in literature between the Hugoans and the classicists and the same in painting. Why shouldn't architecture also have its little revolution? That is completely natural; the force of events is leading to it. The architecture of a people should derive its character [from] 1. the institutions, 2. the customs, 3. the climate, 4. the nature of materials, etc. . . . Thus the architecture of 1830 cannot be that of 1680 when one built Versailles while making the people die of hunger and misery. The luxury of a despot is superb [and] amazing, but the happiness of an entire nation wisely governed is much more satisfying. Thus it is great wisdom which influences us today to return to architecture an expression truer and more in harmony with the ideas of our century.[50]

(The real, political revolution was to break out three months later in July, and the tone of Léon's letters was to become more menacing, as we shall see.)

The *pensionnaires'* most forceful declarations of Romanticism, nonetheless, were their fifth-year *envois*, original designs envisioned for modern France. Again the first decisive blow was struck in 1828 by Duban's *temple protestant*. Like Labrouste's Paestum series, which accompanied it to Paris, it is a difficult project to grasp immediately; but if placed carefully in context, it emerges as a most striking statement.

The original drawings of the project are lost, but the basic layout is recorded in two sets of sketches made after it, one by Labrouste and one by Joseph Lecointe (figures 6, 7).[51] The latter are particularly precise and give the plan, section, and details with dimensions and with the liturgical furniture depicted and identified. The little that we know about the project is, in fact, what is most important.

First, what kind of Protestant church is this? Duban identifies it only with the subscription, "Temple consacré au culte protestant." It does not resemble in layout or scale any of the impressive Protestant churches erected in Europe after 1800: Weinbrenner's Stadtkirche in Karlsruhe (1807–16), von Hansen's Vor Frue Kirke in Copenhagen (1811–16), Schinkel's Berlin parish churches (projected and built from 1827). Nor does Duban's design in any way resemble the model Protestant church that Wilhelm Stier, a friend of Hittorff and a student in Paris of Lecointe, had produced in Rome for Baron von Bunsen in 1827.[52] Instead, it is a simple double-cubic volume (figure 8) without balconies or interior complexities of form. Seats tier up on three sides, and the altar table, pulpit, and organ are set vertically one above the other on the axis of the fourth. Behind is a bell tower and a room for the minister and the consistory. Around it is a walled cloister, probably the congregational cemetery. The Académie shook its head in dismay at this simplicity. The fifth-year *envoi* was to be the highest display of compositional *virtù*: a big plan accommodating a complex function, like the "Collège de France" Blouet had sent back in 1826 or the "Bourse" Gilbert had sent in 1827, or like the senate building or the public library that A.-L.-T. Vaudoyer had suggested to Léon in a letter of February 8, 1828. But all Duban sent was this little puritan preaching box. "This building admits neither sculpture, nor painting, nor richness of ornament—one regrets that M. Duban . . . has not found, in the obligatory simplicity of the subject he has chosen for his composition, the opportunity to apply his preceding studies," intoned the Académie (in the person of Quatremère de Quincy) at the *séance publique annuelle* of October 3, 1829.[53]

Besides disappointing the Académie's expectation of a striking plan— what Léon Vaudoyer called a "pétard"—in a number of details Duban's project shows that it embodied ideas even more worrisome to the architectural bureaucracy of the Restoration. This particular plan, with everything in a single space arranged for ease of hearing and seeing, is Calvinist, and

6

Félix Duban, Temple protestant,
plan. Fifth-year envoi, *1828–29.*
*Sketch by J.-F.-J. Lecointe. Ecole
des Beaux-Arts, Paris.*

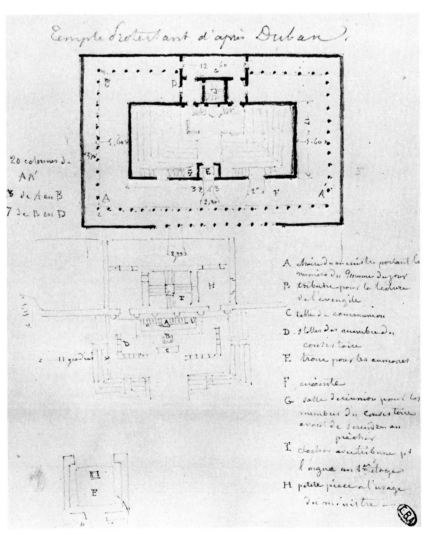

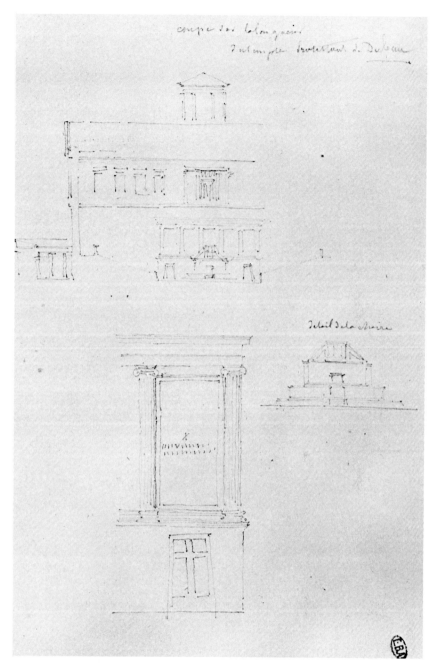

7
Félix Duban, Temple protestant,
cross section and details. Fifth-year
envoi, *1828–29. Sketch by J.-F.-J.*
Lecointe. Ecole des Beaux-Arts,
Paris.

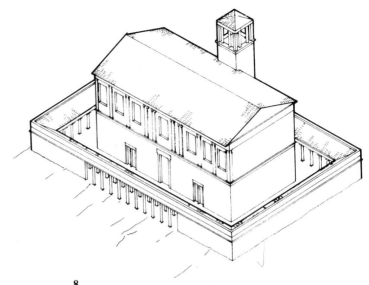

8
Félix Duban, Temple protestant,
reconstructed isometric view by
David Van Zanten.

9
Felix Wilhelm Kubly, Protestant
church, Heiden, Switzerland,
1838–40. (Photo courtesy Benno
Schubiger)

more specifically Swiss Calvinist, a type established in Switzerland in the seventeenth century and manifested in Duban's day in Conrad Stadler's parish church at Uster (1823–26) and in Felix Wilhelm Kubly's at Heiden (1836–40, figure 9).[54] Kubly we have already met: he and Decraëne were part of the Romantic *pensionnaires'* circle, both having studied with La-brouste and Léon Vaudoyer in A.-L.-T. Vaudoyer's atelier in Paris before coming to Rome. Duban's *temple protestant* is the middle term between Uster and Heiden. Nor was it done merely from books or from conversations with Kubly and Melchior Berri, who, besides being Duban's friend and a student of Huyot, was the son and son-in-law of Calvinist pastors from Basel.[55] On his way back to Paris from Rome in 1829, Duban studied Calvinist church architecture in Geneva (as well as, perhaps, elsewhere in Switzerland and Germany).[56] He redrew his *envoi* as a result and replaced that done in Rome with that shown in Lecointe's sketches.

Presenting a design for a Swiss Calvinist church for a fifth-year *envoi* in 1828 had several implications. First, it flouted the expectations of the Académie, which conducted the Academy in Rome specifically so that the ancient Mediterranean tradition might be thoroughly inculcated in its prize students. A Swiss Calvinist type is neither ancient nor Italian in any sense. Second, it was inimical to the policies of the restored Bourbon government. Technically, it presented a model for French Protestant church building (a tradition that had been forced into Switzerland in 1685 by the revocation of the Edict of Nantes). This was an appropriate gesture in 1828 due to the liberalization introduced by the ministry of Martignac that included, on January 11 of that year, the naming of the Swiss Lutheran Baron Georges Cuvier as Conseiller d'Etat for the newly upgraded division of Cultes Protestants et Isréalites. But Martignac's year-long ministry was only a moment in the absolutist, clericist Restoration government, preceded by the repressive ministry of Villèle and followed by that of Polignac—which finally incited the revolution of 1830. Protestantism was otherwise a catchword for Liberalism and resistance to the Bourbon monarchy. Protestants led the Liberal opposition in parliament: Guizot, Benjamin Constant, de Labrode, Delessert, Cuvier, Stapfer. Protestantism was presented as the philosophical ingredient that would regenerate French culture by Rousseau, de Staël, Sismondi, Constant, Mignet, and Quinet.[57]

The historian and Liberal journalist François Mignet—famous as the author of the first popular history of the Revolution—had been very clear indeed about how Calvinism might be Liberalism in politics in his articles and in his popular lectures at the Paris Athenée of 1822 ("De la Ligue et de protestantisme en France") and 1823 ("Histoire de la révolution d'Angle-terre et de la restauration des Stuarts"). Formulating his ideas definitively in "Etablissement de la réforme à Genève" (1824–34), Mignet shows how Calvin, using the ecclesiastical government he created in the consistory, established a democratic counterforce to the existing feudal authority so that in Geneva and subsequently in Holland, Scotland, England, and France the Calvinist church became the instrument of a parliamentary revolution. Calvin "subordinated the State to the Church," Mignet wrote,

civil society to religious society, and prepared in Geneva a religion and a government for all those in Europe who rejected belief and resisted the government of their land. This is what happened in France during the minority of Charles IX; in Scotland during the troubled reign of Mary Stuart; in the Netherlands at the time of the revolt of the United Provinces; and in England under Charles I. . . . This system, which was to extend over a large part of Europe, which prepared the Protestantism of the insurrection against the princes as the system of Luther had prepared by Protestantism the insurrection against the Popes, which put an ecclesiastical government at the disposition of all countries where political power could not sustain itself, which was to agitate for sixty years in France, served to carry out the Reformation in Scotland, contributed to the emancipation of Holland, presided over the revolution in England, which would leave its mark on Coligny, on the Prince of Orange, on Cromwell, this Calvin introduced first in Geneva.[58]

Indeed, this is but the core of the concept of the evolution of postmedieval philosophical history formulated by Victor Cousin in his celebrated courses at the Sorbonne in 1828 and 1829. The Revolution of 1789, Cousin proposed, was but the outcome of the Reformation in Germany and the parliamentary revolution in England. These two phenomena were local and isolated in their time; but when generalized by the philosophers of the great, central nation of Europe, France, during the eighteenth century and when manifested in the Revolution, they were brought to fruition.[59]

Both Liberalism and Protestantism were thoroughly bound up with Romanticism in the late-Restoration mind. In 1825 Ludovic Vitet (founder of the Commission des Monuments Historiques as well as a friend of Labrouste, Duban, and Vaudoyer) wrote, "Romanticism is Protestantism in the arts."[60] The historians whom we have noted exploring the Protestant thread in French and European history were generally called "Romantic" and by the late 1820s were accepted as models for the Romantic writers led by Hugo.[61] In the detail and vividness of their writing as well as in their admiration for the Middle Ages and the early Renaissance (the periods of the communes, the Reformation, and the first parliaments), they seem to complement Dumas, Nodier, and Hugo.

It was not a great step from equating Liberalism, Protestantism, and Romanticism to making anti-academicism the last term in the series. Since

David's campaign against the Académie during the Revolution, that institution had been firmly linked to absolutism. Now, with the royalist Quatremère de Quincy proclaiming a theory of an immutable ideal in the Orders, that charge seemed borne out. Not surprisingly, contemporary critics placed Duban's fifth-year *envoi* in this context. The architect Petrus Borel wrote in *L'Artiste* in 1833:

The temple, perfectly laid out, carefully thought through, of a fine and unexpected appearance, aroused loud cries from MM. the academicians; this design, at least as heretical as the communicants for whose use it was destined, was treated as one treats the Huguenots, and they almost made an auto-da-fé of it, or to speak a more harmonious language, a sacrifice to the God of Good Taste. . . . *At this first and terrifying demonstration, the* belle au bois dormant, *that is the Académie, awoke alarmed and protested as strenuously as possible against this temple, questioning the legitimacy of their architecture of divine right, because there is also legitimacy and divine right in the Académie; because there is a legitimate architecture and an illegitimate one, because there is a revealed art and an apocryphal one, unrecognized, not by the Council of Nice or Trent, but by the council of Fontaine and Guénepin.*[62]

Duban's *envoi* was a rough equivalent of Hugo's *Cromwell* published the year before: an attack on the academic conventions expanded into an historical resuscitation of the age of Protestantism and parliamentarianism. Duban's trip to Switzerland to study Protestantism in its homeland coincided with those of Edgar Quinet and Jules Michelet to Germany (1827 and 1828, respectively), undertaken for the same purpose.[63]

Neither Duban's flouting of the Académie's expectations nor his revolutionary political insinuations, however, are strictly architectural in nature. One can conclude from his *envoi* that he was dissatisfied with the Bourbon monarchy and with the Neoclassical administration of the arts, but can one perceive here the formulation of a profoundly new style of architecture? To look for peculiar ornaments and exotic configurations of the sort that Wilhelm Stier introduced into his Protestant church project of 1827, however, is to miss the basic principle of architectural creation accepted by the Romantic *pensionnaires*. Since, as Vaudoyer stated, architecture is the result of climatic, material, and social forces, to create a new architecture, one must study these forces. The Protestant church type, particularly in the form Duban has chosen here, was the key to the evolution of a new institutional form.

As we shall see in the next chapter, the Early Renaissance, represented in Italy by Brunelleschi and in France by the architects of François I, Henri

II, and Henri IV, was pictured by the Romantic *pensionnaires* as a moment when modern Christian culture comprehended the lucidity and logic of antiquity and was profoundly reanimated by this illumination, before sinking into the academicism of the Baroque and the absolutism of Louis XIV. The *pensionnaires'* objective was to carry architectural evolution forward from this point. Their friend the critic Hippolyte Fortoul later wrote that they "brought back from Rome, with a new and correct conception of the ancient monuments, the necessity to take up the architectural tradition where it had been in France at the beginning of the seventeenth century."[64] A basic component of this Early Renaissance French culture emphasized by every Liberal historian was Calvinism—a French conception gaining strength during the sixteenth century, almost establishing itself with Henri IV, then violently uprooted by Louis XIV in 1685.[65] French Calvinism's architectural masterwork was de Brosse's temple at Charenton, a huge double-cubic space set laterally on its axis. The Swiss Calvinist church type preserved its memory after Charenton was destroyed by a mob and Calvinist church building was forbidden in France.[66] Duban, in his *envoi,* was thus reintroducing the Charenton church type back into France, making good the cultural break brought about by the revocation of the Edict of Nantes.

There is one last knot Duban may have sought to tie with his *envoi.* At least by 1845, when writing of the Charenton temple in his "Etudes d'architecture en France," Vaudoyer recognized de Brosse's church as a materialization of Vitruvius's basilica at Fano (figure 10).[67] That is, he envisioned the church as picking up the thread of antiquity just as de Brosse's other works or Brunelleschi's dome did, but in an importantly different way. Not only was the form of the Fano building absolutely logical—being communicated by Vitruvius almost exclusively in terms of numerical ratios—but it was also specifically designed as a place for legal argument and judgment, a balconied double-cube with the tribune in the center of the long wall. Duban thus would appear to be evoking Fano as well as Charenton—Roman law as well as French Renaissance religion— to make the following historical point: that the Protestant church, like the Calvinist cult that engendered it, was a place of reason and judgment; its reason was Roman logic and its law Roman law (as indeed Calvinist law was). Calvin ruled Geneva as president of the consistory. By submitting this *envoi,* Duban made a series of architectural and cultural links previously ignored by academic Neoclassicism and Bourbon absolutism, ones connecting the Republican qualities of Roman antiquity with Renaissance Protestant France and now, in 1828, with the Liberal effort of Martignac's ministry.

It is interesting to note that the fourth-year *envoi* Labrouste originally intended to submit with Duban's *temple protestant* was a reconstruction of

10
*Andrea Palladio, Reconstruction of
Vitruvius's basilica at Fano.*

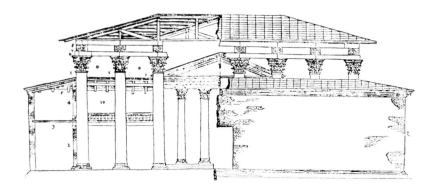

Vitruvius's basilica at Fano. He traveled there with Vaudoyer in July to see whether there were any remains.[68] He changed his mind, however—and Vaudoyer insisted that it was not because he would have had only Vitruvius's written description to work from—perhaps because he wished to make his point personally, not as a reinforcement of Duban's.

After Duban's *temple protestant* came Labrouste's *pont frontière* and several other fifth-year *envois* pointedly political in subject: Duc's 1830 *monument aux victimes de la Révolution de 1830,* Vaudoyer's *beffroi* of 1831 (figure 11), Marie-Antoine Delannoy's *monument triomphal à élever à Toulon en l'honneur de l'armée d'Afrique* of 1833, Simon-Claude Constant-Dufeux's *chambre des députés* of 1834 (figures 15-17), and Pierre-Joseph Garrez's *halle aux grains pour Paris* of 1835.[69] These last could celebrate the new order, however, as Duban's could not (although Constant-Dufeux's and Garrez's were seen as Republican and thus still revolutionary[70]). What is remarkable about these projects is not only their subject but that they all reject the Académie's conception of the last *envoi* as a grand composition and thus carry the revolution in government into the administration of the arts.

The Vaudoyer letters as usual permit an intimate glimpse of these events. In a letter of August 27, 1831, Léon announced his intention of executing a mere belfry, a *beffroi,* for his fifth-year project, already aware that "you will, I think, criticize me for the slight importance of this project." He was too busy finishing his historical studies in Rome, he explained, to execute an elaborate composition of the sort the Académie required, and nonetheless felt that with a *beffroi* "one might make something very monumental and with great character."[71] Vaudoyer *père* responded on September 20:

I admit that this choice has singularly amazed me. Is this, I ask myself, a motif to which one might apply (following the intention, the institution of this last envoi*) all the advanced and excellent studies you made during your four preceding years? Is there here any invention in plan? An occasion for architectural and monumental disposition and proportioning? . . . Do you not fear that one will say of your* beffroi *what they did . . . of the* prêche *(preaching box) of M. Duban, of the bridge of M. Labrouste, and finally of the little* monument de Juillet *of this year on a half-sheet of paper simply in outline without plan or section by M. Duc?*[72]

He went on to cite a list of proper subjects he had suggested in a letter of February 8, 1828—a *chambre des pairs avec salle de trône,* a *bibliothèque publique,* a *campo santo comme à Pise,* etc. But, a loving father, he devoted the rest of his letter to advice about how Léon might make his *beffroi* a good one. "This is your thunderclap," he ended, "try to make it dazzling!"[73]

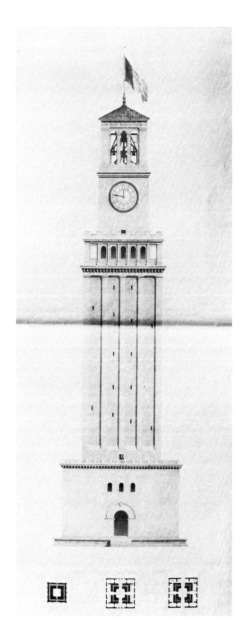

11
Léon Vaudoyer, Beffroi pour une
ville de guerre frontière. *Fifth-
year* envoi, *1831–32. Private collection, Paris.*

Receiving in response only a few remarks about details, interspersed with fierce declarations of adherence to Romanticism, Vaudoyer *père* wrote again on October 15 to suggest that Léon emphasize the decorative rather than the structural in his project. What came back from Vaudoyer *fils,* dated November 17, was this:

I will never compromise my doctrines and . . . I will not sacrifice any of my ideas in an effort to please. I will not make a pétard. *I have neither the time, the means nor the desire. If one insists to me tomorrow that a project of the sort I understand, a vast project, must be made, I would respond that I am not an architect, my studies are not finished, and this is because the arts are not taught in France as they should be.*[74]

Léon also mentioned that he was studying the campaniles at Venice, Cremona, Modena, and Valencia for his *envoi.* His father advised him, in his reply of December 10, "Instead of falling back into the infancy of art, you should seek in the enlightened centuries the monuments which date from the best period of architecture."[75]

With his *envoi* finished and his departure from Rome approaching, Léon made his last declaration in a letter of January 4, 1832:

How can one make architecture like [that of the Temple of] Venus and Rome with the ideas, the needs, the materials of today? There surely is the old school of the antique no matter what . . . and that produced the Madeleine, monument without local character, then in front of it the Chambre des Députés, which is another ancient temple, then the Bourse, and finally the portico of the Pantheon with its infamous lintels. That is how for so long our architecture has been without character; that, to say it more clearly, is why we do not have architecture. . . . Poor France!!! What I wish most is to have a bad report on my project [from the Académie] because then I might believe that it was not too bad.[76]

The Académie duly reported at the annual *séance publique* that Vaudoyer, "having confined himself in a project so slight, has denied himself all his means,"[77] and went on to attack all the fifth-year *envois* recently sent to Paris.

What was at issue? First, the refusal to present a display of compositional *virtù.* But there was more: a *beffroi* is not just its English analogue, a belfry. It is (to quote the dictionary of the Académie Française) a "tower or belfry where one stands watch, where there is a bell to sound an alarm."[78] Again, Quatremère wrote in his *Dictionnaire d'architecture* of this very year: "It is, in fortified cities or in towns within reach of the enemy, a tower, a belfry, or an elevated place, where there is a bell that sounds when one spots the enemy or when one wishes to assemble troops."[79] It is a watchtower, more particularly a civil watchtower, an appendage to the *hôtel de ville* and the very opposite of a church belfry (which has a separate designation in French: *clocher*).

Vaudoyer himself wrote in 1841: "The *beffroi* and the *hôtel de ville* are often interchangeable, and in charters and franchises one bestows on a town the right to a *beffroi* as a sign of liberty."[80] Later, in his didactic fantasy *Histoire d'un hôtel de ville et d'une cathédrale* (1878), Viollet-le-Duc vividly depicted the *beffroi* as the expression of the democratic, communal element in the architectural landscape of his fictive city of Clusy.[81] When in 1099 a commune was established there, the old Gallo-Roman curia was transformed into a *hôtel de ville* by the addition of a massive *beffroi* where it fronted the market square. In this were hung three bells, "the first and the largest for the convocation of assemblies; the second for signaling fires, attacks, disturbances; the third to sound at morning and at curfew."[82] The bishop, however, refused to respect the commune, and his retainers robbed and molested the population. "Often, at night, one heard the bell in the *beffroi* ringing, announcing the attack of a party sallying from the episcopal palace against the richest houses."[83] He forced the king to disestablish the commune. "The abolition of the commune was published in the town [with] an injunction that all the magistrates of the town should cease their functions, deposit the seal and the banner of the commune at the episcopal palace, take down the bells from the *beffroi* without delay, and avoid any assembly."[84] In response the citizens gathered and, to the ringing of the bells in the *beffroi*, attacked the bishop's palace and cathedral, burned them, and slaughtered their inhabitants.

Vaudoyer apparently wished his *beffroi* to be understood in this context, as indicated by the huge tricolor flapping at its roof peak. His initial intention had been to place his *beffroi* on the *terre-plein* at the west prow of the Ile de la Cité in Paris, "supposed to be in front of the city hall, which occupies the space covered by the Place Dauphine and the streets and buildings that surround it."[85] The Revolution of 1830 had been proclaimed at the Hôtel de Ville in Paris, as the Republics of 1848 and 1870 were also to be. It was Vaudoyer's intention to install that institution in the central place of the Parisian urban landscape and mark it with a watchtower visible along the river and from the hills north and south.

Vaudoyer's project, as executed, is isolated, not in Paris but on a "frontière de guerre." It is merely a monument of vigilance, a reminder to the Académie that the revolution is accomplished and that there is a watch for resistance and backsliding. Student demonstrations against the administration of the Ecole des Beaux-Arts and of the Grand Prix competition had followed the revolution of July and had closed the school most of the fall.[86] In Rome Labrouste had already been proposing reforms of these institutions; and on January 25, 1831, the Commission des Beaux-Arts was created by the government to project reforms. Among its members were Labrouste, Duban, and Blouet (as well as Delacroix, Delaroche, and Scheffer). The *pensionnaires* were both excited and aware that from the start the Académie would refuse to acknowledge the commission's authority. In the same letter that Vaudoyer informed his father of his choice of a *beffroi* as an *envoi*, he also blustered, "If the Institut continues to press forward on the absurd course it follows today, I will declare myself in open opposition to it . . . and this opposition will grow so much that it will eventually overthrow this body if it does not desist, just as the Liberal opposition overthrew Charles X."[87] But the Académie did not cede. When the Commission des Beaux-Arts made its report on October 31, 1831, that body refused to respond and by obstinacy (helped by governmental lethargy) rendered it a dead letter. Years later, in 1862, Viollet-le-Duc wrote of the Académie, "It has not had its revolution, poor devil, and it must have it, it will have it, I do not doubt . . . but we will probably not see it in our own time. . . . We need a 1792."[88]

Until recently the Labrouste family kept on the wall a framed watercolor inscribed on the back, "Agrigentum. 1828" (figure 12). It shows a fortified Greek hill town with terraces above a gateway, a temple, a tomb, and perhaps a palace (from left to right), all garishly painted and, in the case of the city gate, decked with battlefield litter to frighten any potential enemy. The first thing one realizes is that this was the real source for the teasing *envois* of Théodore Labrouste and Delannoy (figures 4, 5), not the comparatively restrained section drawing of the Basilica at Paestum (figure 3). One also notices that this model is fiercer and more profound than its imitations. It is not an archaeological reconstruction at all; and despite its subscription, it does not represent any of the six celebrated temples commanding the ridge of ancient Agrigentum. What it shows instead is a jumble of construction quite like the nineteenth-century town of Grigenti, which clung to another less dramatic ridge inland to the north (figure 13). Labrouste, as he did in his Paestum series, has projected back into the past from the real, undignified experience of the site itself with a ragged, humble life still warm within it. He has been blind to "the Roman magnificence, which one would love to see," as Quatremère remarked of Delannoy's *envoi*.[89]

The most striking and peculiar quality in Labrouste's "Agrigentum," however, is that the style of rendering itself is primitive and naive. The scale is wrong; the perspective is exaggerated; the lines are too sharp; the colors are too intense—it exists in an eerie "airless space" (to use Neil Levine's phrase). Duban had also begun executing watercolor fantasies in Rome and continued to do so far into the 1850s, to considerable public

12
Henri Labrouste, "Agrigentum,"
imaginary reconstruction of an
ancient Greek city, dated 1828.
Académie d'Architecture, Paris.

13
*Nineteenth-century view of
Grigenti, Sicily. (Photo courtesy
Northwestern University)*

14
*Félix Duban, "Baja," architectural
fantasy, dated 1835. Musée
Vivenel, Compiègne.*

acknowledgment, but his are realistic reconstructions of ancient and Renaissance monuments that invite one to walk directly into them (figure
14).[90] Labrouste's fantasy, by contrast, is just that: something "other" that
carries the mind across a threshold into a different world. His sketchbooks
from his years in Rome are filled with drawings of naive, out-of-scale,
unperspectival architectural backgrounds extracted from Pompeiian and
quattrocento frescoes. They embodied a way of seeing that he was trying
to study and that here, in the "Agrigentum," he reproduces.

Labrouste's "Agrigentum" is a pure fantasy and as such brings out a
quality underlying the more constrained official *envois*: they were not serious building designs but rather conceptual gestures. It was a pretense of
the *envois* that practice in archaeological reconstruction would increase the
designer's knowledge of canonical form and that the fifth-year exercise in
composition might sharpen his practical ability. But neither the academicians nor the *pensionnaires* had the slightest intention that these designs be
erected. If you were one of the Romantic *pensionnaires* who had ceased to
believe in the conventional worth of these exercises, what could you use
them for? Certainly not for demonstrating a "new style" since they were
not real projects—they offered no field to check expressive proportions
and light effects; you could not calculate the thrusts or finger the moldings
or savor the color and grain of the masonry. The only thing you could do
was make them gestures, either political, like Vaudoyer's *beffroi*, or personal like Labrouste's Paestum, *pont frontière,* and "Agrigentum." The
"Agrigentum" is Labrouste's musing on the hodge-podge town of Grigenti, which transforms itself back into Periclean times before his mind's
eye. Labrouste alone among the *pensionnaires* is personal, rather than political and programmatic. The result is that only in his work are things unre-
solved but continuously resolving. We shall see in the final chapter how he
came back to the "Agrigentum" in his last, greatest design, that of the
Salle des Imprimés at the Bibliothèque Nationale (figure 84).

The culmination of the fifth-year *envois*—intentionally so—was the penul-
timate one of the series, the *chambre des députés* of Constant-Dufeux of 1834
(figures 15–17).[91] In subject, it continues the political thread of Duban's
and Vaudoyer's *envois*, but with greater emphasis. In composition, it develops the boxy reticence of these earlier designs, but now at large scale
and with perverse elaboration. In its use of ornament it applies the accretive, incidental decoration suggested in Labrouste's Paestum basilica reconstruction and its progeny among the fourth-year *envois*.

It is not surprising that such a cumulative statement of the *pensionnaires'*
ideas should come from this hand. Constant-Dufeux was as old as Labrouste and, upon his arrival in Rome in late 1829, the most successful of
all the *pensionnaires*. While still a student at the Ecole he had designed

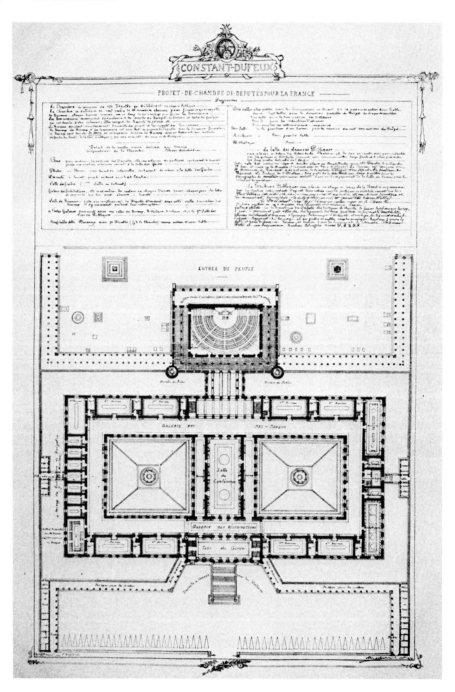

15
Simon-Claude Constant-Dufeux,
Chambre des députés, *plan.
Fifth-year* envoi, *1834–35. Re-
drawn and published lithographi-
cally by A. Joilly, Paris, 1872–75.*

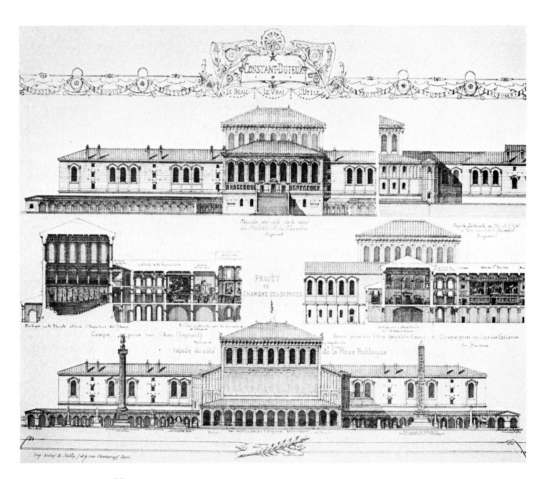

16
Simon-Claude Constant-Dufeux,
Chambre des députés, *elevations.*
Fifth-year envoi, *1834–35. Re-*
drawn and published lithographi-
cally by A. Joilly, Paris, 1872–75.

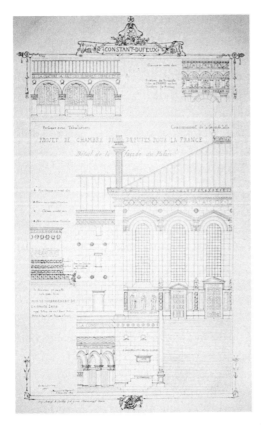

17
Simon-Claude Constant-Dufeux,
Chambre des députés, *details.*
Fifth-year envoi, *1834–35. Re-*
drawn and published lithographi-
cally by A. Joilly, Paris, 1872–75.

important work at the canals Saint-Denis and Saint-Martin and had projected the Galérie Colbert for the architect Billaud and the Fontaine Gaillon for Visconti—this last the finest piece of Restoration decoration not from the hand of Percier.[92] He is said to have had eight million francs of work on hand when he won the Grand Prix. Upon his return to Paris, he established himself as the principal ornamentalist of the group—Labrouste's competitor as the originator of the Néo-Grec mode. But the great opportunities he had received before going to Rome did not again present themselves, apparently in part because of the reputation for radicality he had cultivated with his *envois,* and he never built a major public structure.

Constant-Dufeux's *chambre des députés* was obviously conceived with the existing building, erected by Bernard Poyet (1742–1824) in 1806–10, in mind (figure 18).[93] The first thing evident in comparing the two facades is that the monumental columnar temple front that constitutes the whole elevation of the Napoleonic building has, in a sense, slipped down Constant-Dufeux's facade to become a series of short Doric half-columns embedded in a low, arcaded portico. The majestic file of statuesque shafts topping a high cascade of steps has been transformed into a functional cloister set at street level to keep rain off visitors arriving at the building. And as that colonnade has slipped down, it has revealed the blank, boxy volume of the chamber itself; the exposed surface bears a lengthy inscription headed "CHARTE CONSTITUTIONELLE." The chamber's walls are pierced with a ring of large arched windows and crowned with a corbelled cornice enframing painted porcelain plaques bearing the arms of all the cities of France. The roof is a tall, hipped covering built to cast off the rains and snows of the North; the windows are expansive to admit an ample flow of the feeble Northern light.

Behind the chamber rises a second larger, less open and decorated volume divided into suites of committee rooms. Constant-Dufeux rephrased and regularized the 1830 constitution of France as his program, and this layout is its consequence. It divides the legislative process into a public, deliberative function and a private, analytical one carried on by committees in secret.[94] The chamber enclosing the deliberative function faces outward; porcelain emblems of the cities of the nation sparkle around its crown, the constitution rests on its brow, a cloister opening upon a public square filled with political memorials sits at its foot. This last includes a column "à la mémoire des victimes de la Révolution," the Monument Desaix, a "Sepulture aux citoyens mort en juillet, 1830," the obelisk of Luxor (set up in the Place de la Concorde in 1836), and is surrounded on three sides by a "tabularium" of written inscriptions. The private committee block of the structure faces inward, away from this square, with a private members' entry at the back.

In the public square or in the cloister around it, the public might wait

18
*Bernard Poyet, Chambre des
Députés, Paris 1806–10.*

for the opening of the session, then flow into the building through the broad corridors surrounding the chamber and climb the spiral staircases to the two tiers of galleries. The inner wall of this annular corridor steps forward in a series of four tall benches. In a detail sketch, Constant-Dufeux shows that these benches are decorative bands inscribed with all the names of the deputies of the Constituent Assembly, the Legislative Assembly, and the Convention—the three original Revolutionary legislatures of France. The chamber literally, physically rests upon the memory of the Revolution and of the first representatives of the people. Constant-Dufeux's building thus embodies the history and organization of a French Republican government, as a Gothic cathedral once embodied that of the Christian doctrine: in its pattern of volumes it states the structure of the political system; in its decorative dress it communicates its spirit. Founded upon the legislators of the Revolution, its constitution is open for all to read, while the names and history of its people gather about it in memorial and increase year by year.

In an important sense Constant-Dufeux's monument is a manifestation of and the key to everything going on in the *pensionnaires'* minds. Labrouste's basilica at Paestum, Duban's *temple protestant*, and this *chambre des députés* were all public assembly halls. They were simple boxes in plan and structure, but they were potentially the type of modern democratic architecture. Already in 1836 Vaudoyer had ended his entry "Basilique" in the second volume of the *Encyclopédie nouvelle*, "It seems to us that the activities of a government based on national representation, on public discussion of certain matters, and on the election of magistrates will bring about the creation of a new edifice, the function of which might have some relation to that of the ancient basilica."[95] Writing in César Daly's *Revue générale de l'architecture* in 1846–47, Constant-Dufeux himself was more categorical:

Today when every capital, every city, even the smallest village, must have their assembly halls, why do we not seek here the motif for a new architecture? Why do we not make these buildings the object of particular study and research, in order to constitute a new type, because they are now so important and new as well? . . . Will we be powerless to conceive an architecture représentative?[96]

He continues, making specific suggestions about procedure:

Have more confidence in our institutions and in our future, and especially have more confidence in ourselves. Consider that in order to make good architecture, it is necessary first to imagine the layout of spaces and the method of construction, without any preoccupation with style, *having in view only* the satisfaction of material and moral needs, *as generally as will permit a* prudent economy of the means at our disposal. *This first operation of the spirit, which we call the ART OF BUILDING, should be followed by that which constitutes what we call the ART OF SCULPTING, that is, the art of conceiving and of giving to the work the most appropriate and expressive form, so that the work may finally receive the ART OF PAINTING, the indispensable complement for perfecting the work so that it is worthy of being called a monument of art.*[97]

The architect, the *pensionnaires* seem to have agreed, is the student and servant of his society. His responsibility is to house and make expressive its primary institutions, which around 1830 meant the public assembly hall. The architect's method is to study this problem functionally and historically, to distinguish an abstract, practical core, and then to dress it up with an accretive, meaningful decoration.[98]

Two

THE FORMULATION OF THE APPROACH:
THE THEORY OF
REYNAUD, FORTOUL, AND VAUDOYER

Between 1829 and 1832 Duban, Labrouste, Duc, and Vaudoyer all arrived
back in Paris. Within their narrow circle upon their return were several
thinkers and writers who formulated a concept of architecture that articulates their basic concerns. It was a clear, if limited, concept, which pre-
dates and informs the design of most of their buildings. This particular
group embraced Duban, Duc, and Vaudoyer as well as the architect
Léonce Reynaud, his brother the engineer and philosopher Jean Reynaud,
and the critic Hippolyte Fortoul. Labrouste was conspicuously absent.

Léonce Reynaud (1803–80) had been trained at the Ecole Polytechnique
(from which he was dismissed in 1822 for Carbonarism, falsely alleged but
as a result enthusiastically embraced) and at the Ecole des Beaux-Arts from
1825 to 1829 in the atelier of Huyot.[1] After a trip to Italy, he settled in
Paris, where from 1833 he worked in the administration of the Ponts et
Chaussées while pursuing theoretical matters with his brother's friends,
Fortoul, Edouard Charton, Pierre Leroux, and Sainte-Beuve. In 1834–39
he erected the lighthouse at Heaux de Bréliat, and in 1843–47 he designed
and erected the Gare du Nord, the first monumental railroad station in
Paris. He was appointed Professor of Architecture at the Ecole Polytech-
nique in 1837.

Reynaud's younger brother, Jean (1806–63),[2] also studied at the Ecole
Polytechnique, where he met the Saint-Simonian Prosper Enfantin, and
later at the Ecole des Mines, where he became close to Michel Chevalier
and Charles-Joseph Lambert. He traveled with Chevalier in the summer of
1828 and subsequently became an adherent to his Saint-Simonianism.
Indeed, during 1829 and 1830, he was an itinerant proselytizer. After the
Revolution of 1830 he became involved in the sect's publishing efforts,
first on the *Revue encyclopédique*, then from 1833 as editor, with Pierre
Leroux, of the *Encyclopédie nouvelle*, which engaged him until 1848. When
Hippolyte Carnot was appointed Ministre de l'Instruction Publique et des
Cultes in the first provisional government of the Second Republic, Rey-

naud and Edouard Charton were each named Secrétaire Général. Reynaud also lectured at the Ecole des Mines and served in the Constituent Assembly. He lost his post in the administration upon Carnot's ouster in July, however, and finally had to flee to Nice after Napoleon III's coup d'état of December 2, 1851. Thereafter he occupied himself with emigré Republican agitation and philosophical writing, and in 1854 published a well-known volume, *Terre et Ciel.*

Fortoul (1811–56), born in Digne near the Alps north of Aix, worked as a critic in Paris from 1830 until his appointment as Professor of French Literature at the University of Toulouse in 1841.[3] In 1842 he summarized his ideas in an important volume, *De l'Art en Allemagne,* and in 1846 he was made dean of the Faculty of Letters at Aix. A meteoric and controversial political career began in 1849 with his election as a deputy, followed by his appointment as Louis Napoleon's Ministre de la Marine before the coup d'état, which he helped to arrange. On December 3, 1851, he was appointed Ministre de l'Instruction Publique et des Cultes specifically to tighten state control over the professoriate and priesthood. His old friends Léonce Reynaud, Carnot, and Charton had already noted suspicious tendencies when he returned to Paris after the revolution, and by 1851 Fortoul was firmly in what had come to be the anti-Republican, enemy camp, along with certain other Saint-Simonians like Michel Chevalier. Nonetheless, in his ministerial position he was well placed to help his old friends the *pensionnaires* (Vaudoyer, for one, did not hesitate to ask his aid[4]) and passed on to them a series of major commissions before dying of a heart attack in 1856 at age forty-five. His importance to them in the 1830s, however, was as a link to the mainstream of the new philosophical history represented by his friend Edgar Quinet and Quinet's mentor, Victor Cousin.

The Reynauds and Fortoul were all Saint-Simonians around 1830, but subscribed to the nonceremonial doctrine summarized in the *Exposition générale de la doctrine Saint-Simonienne* by Carnot.[5] (Vaudoyer appears to have been sympathetic to the movement as well.) They were among the dissidents who abandoned the sect upon Enfantin's assumption of leadership in 1831, but they remained faithful to the movement's basic tenants: the inevitability of evolution and progress in all human institutions; the primacy of science and industry in the modern age; the need for society to reorganize itself in response to these developments.

The pivot of the group seems to have been the encyclopedia project. In 1833 Jean Reynaud and Pierre Leroux commenced work on the *Encyclopédie pittoresque* (later *nouvelle*) in belated response to Saint-Simon's request for a new encyclopedia to update Diderot's and to lay the foundation for the rational, scientific society of the future.[6] Léonce Reynaud was assigned the architecture entries and he, in turn, solicited the aid of Vaudoyer for volumes two (1835) and three (1836–37). This led to

Vaudoyer being asked to contribute his "Etudes d'architecture en France" to Charton's *Magasin pittoresque*, beginning in 1839, and to Jean Aicard's *Patria* of 1846, while Léonce Reynaud expanded his ideas into the course he taught at the Ecole Polytechnique from 1837 and published as his *Traité d'architecture* (1850–58), which became the principal architectural treatise of mid-century France.

Fortoul, one of the *Encyclopédie's* major contributors, had been praising the *pensionnaires'* work in his critical pieces[7] and by 1837, if not earlier, had become personally friendly with them. In that year he traveled to England with Vaudoyer,[8] and by 1838 Duc and Vaudoyer were planning a trip with him on the Versailles railroad. Duban, through Vaudoyer, invited Fortoul to visit the recently completed Hôtel Pourtalès with him.[9] On May 19, 1839, Vaudoyer wrote Charton:

Tomorrow Wednesday we dine with Duban Duc Reynaud and one of our friends Boullée who is now at Paris. It would be very kind of you to join us along with Fortoul. . . . It is a picnic. . . .

I forgot to tell you that tomorrow we are going to visit Duc's column. The rendezvous is at 2:30 at his home, rue du Marché St. Honoré 4.[10]

Later that year Vaudoyer and Fortoul traveled to Laon, Rheims, and Beauvais together; and from August 15 to September 24, 1840, they made a study trip through Germany, which both of them depicted later as a profound experience.[11] Fortoul then went off to Toulouse, but kept up a steady correspondence with Vaudoyer,[12] who wrote with regret on April 18, 1842: "No more fine morning discussions in the midst of blue cigarette smoke! No longer any hope of finding ourselves united around a bottle of Curaçao."[13] In 1845 he summarized the news of Duban, Duc, and Reynaud: "Duban continues his Sainte-Chapelle and is beginning his château at Blois, Duc is beginning this year his Palais de Justice, and Reynaud will finish his station for the Chemin de Fer du Nord."[14] But, most important for our purposes, Vaudoyer wrote Fortoul about their shared conception of architecture:

I cannot conceive of a trip without you. Let us see each other frequently to mature our common ideas about art in general and architecture in particular.[15]

You must not doubt the number of occasions on which I have been called upon to defend the doctrines which I share [with you].[16]

One [article by Vaudoyer in the Magasin pittoresque*] has appeared . . . on Renaissance architecture in which you will find a great number of the ideas we share, unfortunately expressed in a very vulgar form.*[17]

When will you return to Paris, and when can we take up again the question of the orders posed in the square at Bamberg?[18]

These letters open a kind of window into the minds of at least some of the *pensionnaires* upon their return to Paris.

This small, tight circle of artists and writers produced a "doctrine" (to use Vaudoyer's term) during the 1830s. Léonce Reynaud led off with his contributions to the *Encyclopédie nouvelle*, most particularly in the entry "Architecture," written in 1833 and published in 1834.[19] In the first paragraphs of this essay, Reynaud declares that architecture is the shell and visible embodiment of social institutions and that its construction becomes more efficient as man's knowledge advances with time.[20] Furthermore, he states, this is the basis of architectural expression; for a building to be beautiful it must physically manifest the institution it contains as well as the technical knowledge of its creators.

It was the principle of Neoclassicism that mere construction is aesthetically mute and that expression comes through a decorative veil of the Greek Orders laid over the functional surfaces. In his basic entry "Architecture" in his *Architecture* (published in the *Encyclopédie méthodique* in 1788), Quatremère de Quincy denies that architecture is merely "l'art de bâtir" and defines it instead as "the art of building following proportions and rules determined and set by Nature and taste."[21] He goes on to depict the Orders as "natural" because they are based on primitive wooden construction and defends the translation of that wooden prototype into stone:

Do not doubt it: it is by fortuitous illusionism that man enjoys the pleasure of imitation in architecture, without which there would not be that pleasure which accompanies all the arts and is their charm, the pleasure of being partially deceived, which makes romances and poetry so treasured, makes veiled truth preferable to naked truth.[22]

Reynaud answers this most pointedly in his entry "Colonne" in volume three of the *Encyclopédie nouvelle* (1836–37).[23] He begins by quoting both Vitruvius's and Quatremère's definitions of the column as a fixed form, taken over from the mythical primitive hut, uninflected by its actual material or function. Reynaud then points out that the arrangement of the shaft and capital make no sense in terms of wooden construction, and he shows that their entasis and profiles, in fact, respond to the exigencies of stone building. In a word, he proves that the Greek Orders were not works of ideal sculpture but rather examples of practical construction, yet no less elegant for their structural efficiency. Indeed, he asserts that their beauty lies in that efficiency. The column imitates the human body, he concludes, in that it is just as neatly and simply made: "Just as, in the case of the human body, nothing capricious or extraneous strikes the eye, so in [Greek] constructions, and especially in columns, nothing is admitted that cannot be legitimated by reason and that does not carry the mark of utility."[24] In this sense the column does indeed recall the human body and has symbolic force—although what is symbolized is not man individually, but the pervasive structural principle of nature into which he is subsumed. The issue, Reynaud writes, is simply whether art reproduces nature's forms or nature's laws, "whether art should derive its effects from the imitation of forms, or whether it should seek them in the observation of the diverse conditions imposed by the means of realization and by the proprieties it is necessary to satisfy; in a word, whether art demands material models or principles for creativity."[25]

Reynaud and his friends did not deny that architectural beauty has a mathematical basis, but they perceived that basis differently. They concluded that these mathematics were founded not on aesthetic proportions but on the scientific laws of structural statics; by extension, therefore, as structural knowledge advances and constructive systems evolve, so do the canons of mathematical beauty.[26] Every culture has a distinct canon based on its particular level of scientific knowledge. Beauty lies not in a form, static and unchanging through ages, but in a principle that manifests itself progressively and differently in each epoch.

The historical development of architecture was very simple to Quatremère de Quincy. Architecture is synonymous with the Greek Orders: these were its expressive organs. The Greeks discovered the Orders; the Romans perfected them; the Middle Ages forgot them; the Renaissance rediscovered them. There was a Golden Age, then a fall, and now an effort to recreate that Golden Age. The task of the modern architect is to reproduce the ancient Orders as accurately as possible; there has been no change or progress in architecture's ideal. Quatremère ends the entry "Moderne" in his 1832 *Dictionnaire historique d'architecture:* "We have established in this whole work that our architecture is that of the Greeks and the Romans, in a word, ancient architecture."[27]

To Reynaud, Vaudoyer, and Fortoul, the history of architecture was far more complex. They saw it evolving step by step, each step a continuation and inflection of the preceding one. The forces that drew it on were social and philosophical; it was the shell of human society in evolution. Thus what they felt to be important was the extrapolated trace of architecture's development, the abstract inner principles that its changes delineated, not its specific external forms. Consequently most of their writings are historical, analyzing how these principles were spun out in time.

They associate the arch and its geometric principle, the curve, with Christian culture and the post and lintel and its principle, the right angle, with Greco-Roman society. Thus they explain the application of the grid of the Orders over Roman arcaded facades as the expression of Greco-Roman humanism, while they see the freeing of the arch—set on top of columns, not within them, beginning in the Constantinian era—as the manifestation of the Christian sense of religious infinity. They see the Renaissance as a new, distinct era, not one in which antiquity was recreated, but one in which a synthesis of the rational principle of Greco-Roman culture was married with the Christian sense of infinity. That synthesis, however, was incomplete; it became unstuck when seventeenth-century academicism resurrected the Roman solution of imposing the Orders over arcaded surfaces. A real synthesis would be the imposition of order on medieval arched architecture in its own curvilinear terms. This has not yet been achieved; it is the modern architect's task to accomplish it and thereby correct the Renaissance.[28]

This is a new reading of architectural history. It celebrates styles formerly denigrated. It combines eras formerly held to be distinct and distinguishes eras formerly seen as homogeneous. Finally, it presents as the great monument of modern building a structure customarily overlooked: the Duomo in Florence.

The core of this reading is the emphasis on Christian medieval architecture and the conception of it as a single style merely inflected to become the Byzantine, Romanesque, or Gothic. Reynaud and Vaudoyer point out that the pointed arch, held to be the distinctive mark of the Gothic, is but a natural outcome of ribbed vaulting, evolving slowly out of the Romanesque as that style developed. The key is thinking in terms of principles instead of forms, as Vaudoyer explains in an essay of 1839, interjected into the narrative of his "Etudes d'architecture en France." "It is necessary to establish a distinction between the *forme ogival* and the *style ogival*; that is, between the pointed arch considered as a form by itself and the pointed arch as constituting a whole system of architecture."[29] Vaudoyer argues that one can find the form anywhere—India, Persia, Mexico— evidently thinking of such authors as Hittorff, who in 1835 insisted upon the Islamic origin of the pointed arch.[30] But the structural system was clearly nothing but a refinement of the Romanesque. All medieval building was but variations on curved arch and vault forms and could be subsumed under the heading "style curviligne."[31] In Western architecture the Romanesque was the basic mode: "truly the primordial type of Christian architecture in France."[32]

In this manner, Reynaud, Vaudoyer, and Fortoul perceived that Gothic architecture was not only a perfect expression of Christian mysticism, but also a structural advance over Roman building. "Never," Reynaud wrote in 1834,

had religious monuments received a character more complete and appropriate; never had they been more wholly identified with the sentiments to which they were to testify; never had they better summarized and made more comprehensible all the poetry of their epoch; and never also had spaces so wide and so high been erected with so few and such light supports. Art and science had progressed together; they had supported each other; and the scientist and the artist both were satisfied at the sight of these admirable creations.[33]

As they conceptually drew the medieval styles together, Reynaud and his friends revised the standard reading of the style's origin and demise. The acceptance of the arch and vault as forms in themselves became a momentous revolution. Vaudoyer gave it a name: "l'affranchissement de l'arcade," the emancipation of the arch.

We attach the greatest importance to this event, the emancipation of the arch: *because it is by this, in our opinion, that one may explain naturally the formation of Byzantine art, of Arab art, of Roman art, and of Gothic art, and in so doing deduce the principles in the name of which commenced the protestations of the Renaissance.*

In taking the ancient basilicas as the model for their first temples, the Christians did not copy the treatment of the Orders. Either because they derived from the constructions of the Late Empire the example of a new system, as one might suppose in examining the ruins of the palace at Spalato; or because they were led to it practically by a different method of construction; or because they possessed within themselves the instinct for a new form giving a distinct physiognomy to the Christian temple, it is a fact that they used columns as the supports for the arches which they substituted for the monolithic lintels of pagan antiquity. At first these columns originated from ancient monuments and were such as had been designed to carry architraves; but soon they felt the need to modify the proportions and to substitute a new form of capital more appropriate to their new function; then later the system of constructing arches, which had been applied in principle only to join isolated points of support, was generalized and gave birth to an embracing system of vaulting. So it is that Byzantine art was engendered while Italy was faithfully preserving its first Latin basilicas, the layout of which she was later to transmit to the West.

It seems to me that in this architecture, thus constituted of completely new elements, one must first coordinate elements and fix principles so as to establish rhythms totally different from pagan rhythms; but this was not the case, and in adopting this architecture, which would be called upon to become the expression of

Christian spiritualism, these medieval artists seem to have paid little attention to everything that might seem a consecration of a material form, and they concentrated simply on the conditions necessary for the stability of their works.[34]

The end of the medieval style was for Reynaud and his friends a more complex event, and a more momentous one since it gave birth to modern architecture. It did not come with the rediscovery and accurate reproduction of the Orders in the late sixteenth and seventeenth centuries, as Quatremère insisted. On the contrary, that was a false turning, a byway in the evolution of architecture. For them the Renaissance in building coincided with that in literature and painting—with Petrarch and Giotto—and began with Arnolfo di Cambio's projection of the Duomo in Florence in 1293–94 as a domical structure announced at the west by a four-bay nave vaulted like the Basilica of Constantine. Retaining a traditional medieval layout, it reintroduced Greco-Roman volumetric elements and proportions, but not the Orders as forms in themselves. It developed a spacious structural organism, broader and more efficient than the Gothic, which was exposed to view as swelling volumes unencumbered by spires and flying buttresses. Reynaud wrote in 1834 of the Duomo and the structures of its time:

These buildings still recalled Gothic structures; they had the same layout and the same proportions; all the considerations that determined them were frankly expressed, all the proprieties wisely satisfied. These were still Gothic buildings, but with more harmonious forms, purer and more gracious contours, and covered, in a way, with a strange veil, a rich and diaphanous veil that decorated without concealing.[35]

Arnolfo, Vaudoyer explains in his "Etudes d'architecture en France," combined in the Duomo the Roman thermal hall and the domical pyramid of the Byzantine church. In so doing he opened interior spaces further than in the Gothic cathedral and encumbered them with fewer supports because loads and thrusts were carried to earth diagonally, within the walls and piers themselves. Brunelleschi, a century after Arnolfo laid out the Duomo, managed to vault its vast east end. He did so, according to Reynaud, through his knowledge of science and through his discovery of the principles of Roman construction. His accomplishment was to understand that structure and form are one: "in his way of seeing, form should be the natural consequence of the necessities of construction; the *beau* could only be the manifestation of the *bien*."[36] Here Brunelleschi established the Renaissance ideal in his art. "It was thus a new principle for his epoch that Brunelleschi felt called upon to proclaim; this was, in architecture, to depend first of all on intelligence and to rehabilitate the imperceptible laws of nature."[37] The building Arnolfo and Brunelleschi produced has not been equalled since. It is the paradigm the later architects of the Renaissance should have developed more faithfully and to which the modern architect should now return: "The key work (*l'oeuvre capital*) of Renaissance architecture, we are almost tempted to say, of the architecture of modern times."[38]

In his *Dictionnaire historique d'architecture* Quatremère speaks well of Brunelleschi (while presenting himself as a bit of a pioneer in so doing at all) but expresses disappointment that he did not emphasize the Orders in his work.[39] That, of course, is just what Reynaud and his friends admired in Brunelleschi: his ability to extract the principles of Roman construction and proportion without the details of Roman form. But, Reynaud wrote in 1834, the idea of learning from Rome had now been broached, and after Brunelleschi it was pressed "jusqu'à dans ses dernières conséquences."

After having borrowed some of the motifs from the monuments of antiquity, one tried to imitate the relationships and the arrangement of these details, and in the end one considered these monuments to be absolute types of beauty. . . . Architecture became something mysterious and fated, which had unchanging rules and prescriptions and which imposed them fixedly. . . . It was thus that one saw open porticos, flat roofs and small windows introduced among us in place of the closed porticos, pointed roofs, and the broad windows of the middle ages. . . . Finally, during the last few years, we have dressed up our churches, our stock exchanges, our theaters, our customs houses, and even our guardhouses as ancient temples. Strangely enough, this was precisely the moment when one removed all character from architecture, all truth, all expressiveness, that is, everything that made it an art; it was at this moment that one wished to see here only an art of the imagination and one repulsed most vigorously any scientific or industrial influence. . . . Thus our modern buildings do not present the expression that belongs to art, nor the layouts demanded by our customs or climate, nor the solidity that our science would permit us to achieve. Far from representing our society in all its aspects, it does not represent it in so much as one.[40]

Fortoul sums up these ideas in a lengthy passage in a notebook he kept during the middle 1830s.[41] He begins by asking: Since Quatremère defines beauty as residing in mathematical proportion, why cannot there be more than one system of such proportions? Why cannot the Gothic cathedral also be beautiful in this sense? (Quatremère contended that the Gothic was irregular and capricious, but during the 1820s researches such as those of Sulpiz Boisserée were elucidating its geometric basis.[42]) Fortoul notes that he has "often dreamed of a new architecture that would be a vaster, more divine realization of earthy forms," but wonders "is not this dream impious, and would it not tend to pull ideas and the arts backward?"[43] This is an important crisis in Romantic architecture: its vision of something as vast as the experience of nature itself—expressed a generation before in the projects of Boullée and the young Schinkel—is checked by the realization that this is too easy, if not sacrilegious. Fortoul goes on to say that such a vision, in fact, is that of primitive man, a kind of fetishism. "The constructions of Asia and India imitate earthly forms and sometimes incorporate them."[44] The Greeks, in contrast, saw architecture as a tool, something created by man to serve him: "Is it not this which brings about its social, communal, civilizing character; it becomes the envelope of man instead of being that of the forces of nature. The Greek temples were only the houses of the gods and not their images."[45]

For architecture to thus cut itself off from the natural world, Fortoul continues, is for it to sidestep its ultimate task, which is to reproduce the universe as it is reflected and transformed in the mind of man. This Christian Gothic architecture alone accomplished:

Gothic architecture appears to me to have progressed in recreating the universe. Oriental architecture is the refuge of man crushed by nature; Greek architecture is the whole man posed on top of nature; Gothic architecture is nature itself— transfigured by human thought; it is the universe where . . . foliage, sculpted figures, songs, images and smells of man, the vault of the sky itself, proclaim with one concerted voice the presence of God.[46]

But Gothic art is not complete: it has to be made rationally expressive by the imposition of some system of proportions equivalent to the Greek Orders. Fortoul asks himself, "What compromise might produce the union of Greek and medieval art? . . . Is a new Dark Age necessary to make them elastic in an unexpected manner?" And he answers, "It seems to me that in the modern conception of nature one might find the source for their transformation."[47] We know from Reynaud's entries "Architecture" and "Colonne"—indeed from many of the entries the Reynaud brothers collected in the *Encyclopédie nouvelle*—that the "sentiment moderne de la nature" was the scientific perception of its inner laws. The way Fortoul proposes that Gothic be made effective is through its synthesis with Greek building, both understood as natural emanations of man's mind. Indeed, in a note at the end of his musings, Fortoul hints at a moment in the history of architecture when such a synthesis of the Greek and Gothic had already been broached: "Edgar Quinet notes in the Byzantine monuments of the Peloponnesus the fusion of all earlier features and the announcement of a Gothic architecture that is going to be a new transformation of these historical elements."[48]

What, then, is the task of the architect in 1830? There is a necessary sense of powerlessness in this "doctrine" that damns pure imaginative expression as caprice and that makes architecture the result of social and technological forces. To this Fortoul, the *literatus*, adds that history and society move to an inevitable but dimly perceived plan. "Peoples, like individuals," he says in *De l'Art en Allemagne,* "are instruments that serve the accomplishment of the general plan of creation; it is this plan which a serious mind should propose to study."[49] Architecture cannot move forward until society and science have evolved onto higher planes. Fortoul wrote in his notebook:

*Architecture is of all the arts the least predictable, because it is a posterior art (*art posérieur*) that presupposes something to satisfy and to envelop. Thus, if such a thing existed today, there is no doubt that architecture would offer it its garment. If one could project the spirit of this thing, one would know how to project its form.*[50]

Fortoul, as writer and philosopher, is bold enough to admit he cannot perceive the modern architect's goal. *De l'Art en Allemagne*—all 1,150 pages of its two volumes—is structured around the exposition of a theory that develops what we have seen in Reynaud and Vaudoyer. The book is ostensibly a tour of German cities and museums. These give rise to general observations that slowly expand and merge to dominate the narrative by the end. The work is divided into a preparatory section, extending to chapter six in volume two, where the discussion of modern German philosophy, painting, and architecture leads to an "idée générale," and a culminating section in which that idea is demonstrated, first in the history of German and Italian painting, then in the history of German medieval architecture. Fortoul ends the book with his prescription for the architecture of the future.

Fortoul's "idée générale" is that historical and artistic phenomena, in all their superficial variety, are united in their inner principle and evolve from each other in a three-part cycle. This cycle is most paradigmatically demonstrated in the Greek Orders—the primitive Doric coming first, followed by the refined Ionic, then the complex Corinthian, which is a synthesis of the first two. This law he sees obeyed in the art of Dürer (a synthesis of the North and the South) and of Giotto and Arnolfo di Cambio (adding Northern, Gothic elements to the Italian classical tradition). "His glory," he says of Giotto, "and the immense step forward that he caused painting to make thus lies in his establishing in Italy the passage from the *Dorian* epoch to the *Ionic* and in his creating the principle of the latter by the fusion of the medieval element with a lesser portion of the antique element, which was bound to dominate, little by little, in Italy and lead imperceptibly to a final revolution."[51] The modern art of Cornelius he sees as successful for the same reason and that of Overbeck as futile because it is exclusively Gothic.

In the culminating portion of his work, Fortoul demonstrates how early Renaissance painting, from Giotto to Leonardo, synthesized the ancient and the medieval, but then in the mid-sixteenth century fell into mannerism. When he turns to architecture, he begins by identifying the inner principle of all Christian building as the arch, whether round or pointed. Proceeding through the monuments of Germany from Trier to Regensburg, Fortoul tries to show that the Romanesque and Gothic were not only chronologically distinct but also national styles—German and French, respectively[52]—and as such were two distinct orders of medieval building, like the Doric and the Ionic. They embodied the first two periods of the cycle of Christian architecture; the third, the synthesis, has yet to come. He concludes that it is a modern architect's task to accomplish this synthesis and to produce a third style of arched building adhering to a fixed system of mathematical proportions:

The mission of contemporary art is to begin the study of curvilinear rhythms. If this effort might ever succeed, which criticism should never prejudge, the semicircular arch and the pointed arch, brought together by fixed relationships and measured by Orders which remain unknown to us, will become, in the hands of our architects, what the Doric and the Ionic were for the architects of the last Greek period, modulations susceptible of being combined into one complex and supreme modulation. Such new and regularly determined relationships will necessarily give birth to an analogous style which will return to sculpture and painting their lost majesty, and which, more and more, will spread the sentiment of order and beauty through all the productions of our society, left [now] to anarchy and bad taste. That is what our architects must meditate and what they alone can accomplish.[53]

This book is thus the answer to the question Fortoul posed himself in his notebook years before, "What result might be produced by the union of Greek and Medieval art?"[54] It also answers the "question of the Orders posed in the square at Bamberg" referred to in Vaudoyer's letter to Fortoul of July 31, 1843.

The basic concept of the "doctrine" produced by Reynaud, Fortoul, and Vaudoyer is that architecture is the structural envelope of a social institution and so expresses that institution in its form, changes with it, and evolves as technical knowledge becomes more sophisticated. A biological analogy was quick to present itself. Indeed, Reynaud ends the introductory part of his entry "Architecture" with the observation, "One may, in a profound sense, compare human monuments to those shells formed by animals who give them the shape of their bodies and live in them: the method of the naturalists makes no distinction between the description of the shell and that of the mollusk."[55] Edgar Quinet in 1839 described architectural remains as the skeletons of perished civilizations.[56] This is more than a literary analogy. Georges Cuvier and Geoffroy Saint-Hilaire were defining the mechanism of natural life during these years, making it common intellectual coin and engaging in a celebrated public controversy in 1830–31 that embroiled even Goethe far away in Weimar.[57] Saint-Hilaire subsequently carried on his side of the polemic in the extensive series of entries he contributed to the *Encyclopédie nouvelle*.[58]

Cuvier, beginning with his *Recherches sur les ossemens fossiles* of 1812, demonstrated with relentless and incontrovertible precision that all the forms of a biological organism are the direct outcome of its function—its locomotion, diet, environment, etc. More impressive to the contemporary imagination, he showed how a complete organism might be reconstructed from a single bone by a process of logic that takes these factors into account. One achievement was the reconstruction of the gruesome pterodactyl of 1809.[59] (It is a cliché that the modern mystery story, a new Romantic literary genre, grew out of Cuvier's demonstrations of reconstructive logic.[60]) It was common to cite Cuvier's biology as an analogy for the system of the Greek Orders.[61]

There is, however, more to Reynaud's conception of architecture as mankind's shell than simple functional determinism. He believed architectural organisms evolved. Cuvier held that, because every organism is perfectly constructed, there can be no change or evolution since these would throw off the balance. Saint-Hilaire, on the contrary, insisted that organisms do evolve; indeed, that all organisms are linked together and descend from one primordial parent, the zoological equivalent of Goethe's *Urpflanze*. In his entries in the *Encyclopédie nouvelle* and elsewhere, Saint-Hilaire spun out his idea that function inflects organic structure— that it is an active force manifesting itself in many ways and degrees—but that a "unité de plan" survives everywhere underneath. It was Saint-Hilaire's analogy that Reynaud adopted (just as it was Cuvier's that a conservative like Ernest Beulé found sympathetic).

Around 1830 the concept of nature—the model for architecture of every generation since the Renaissance—was transformed, and ideal, God-given form was replaced by physical adaptation to function as its basic principle. The last volume of the *Encyclopédie nouvelle* contains a dramatic statement of the biological analogy, here broadened to embrace the conception of the city. Not inappropriately, it is from the pen of Jean Reynaud, although it is quoted extensively in Léonce Reynaud's *Traité d'architecture*.[62] Cities should not be laid out regularly and all at once, Jean writes, but rather should be irregularly adapted to their natural and social environments and be built up slowly.

I imagine a site conveniently chosen, the streets, the gardens, the squares neatly laid out, the position of each building marked, the houses built to the taste of each [resident], and one feels, looking at them, that they are all of the same family. . . . Each street is a harmony of which the various houses composing it are the terms and of which the reciprocal propriety of the inhabitants of each neighborhood is the principle. Each quarter, by an analogous propriety of all the streets that it contains, forms another harmony of a more elevated order. Finally, the city itself, by the composition of all these harmonies between themselves and with the public buildings, constitutes a last [harmony] which can either be seen as a whole from several points of view or divide itself into separate elements, similar to the various but always related phrases of a well-conducted melody, and striking, one after another, the eye which promenades through the interior of the city. And this great monument of architecture which, with so much unity in its ensemble, permits itself nonetheless to be divided without resistance into a multitude of different monuments, is but the symbolic shape of the society which it contains and of which it is, one might say, the garment. . . .

One might thus consider each city an inscription marking on the earth, in sharp and positive letters, the history of the world at the point where it rises. I even remark that as the taste, the spirit, the customs, the political and religious institutions vary from one place to another in accordance with the climate and the dispersion of the primitive peoples, cities, which are properly the expression of these things, vary naturally across the earth in the same way. So that, differing one from another by the character of their construction following a system of variation strictly identical with that of the diverse groups of which the human species is composed, they constitute together a single city which, enveloping the whole globe and increasingly harmonizing with it each day, makes sparkle among the stars this symbolic expression of the human race itself.[63]

Reynaud, Vaudoyer, and Fortoul did not envision architecture evolving merely biologically, but also historically, in stages responding to successive states of human consciousness. In this their "doctrine" parallels that of contemporary historians, specifically the Romantic political and philo-

sophical historians who envisioned the evolution of Western culture in a
new manner.

Traditional history in France had presented the Roman Empire as the
age of enlightenment, with the Greek democracies merely preparing the
way; the Middle Ages as barbarism; and the Renaissance as a slow progress back toward Roman glory, peaking during the reign of Louis XIV.
After 1815 Romantic historians, led by Saint-Simon's old collaborator Augustin Thierry, began to attack these conceptions from three directions.
First, they proposed continuous progress and perfection in history, not
cyclical return to an ideal, original state. Second, measuring with the yard-
stick of popular sovereignty because of their Liberal political orientation,
they perceived in Western history a series of forward thrusts coinciding
with crises in the evolution of democracy: the Greek and Early Roman
democracies; the medieval communes established after the year 1000; the
perfection of parliamentary government, especially in Britain, with the
Reformation and the decay of feudalism in the Renaissance; the French
Revolution. These moments, formerly seen as ages of darkness and chaos,
were now illuminated and depicted as epochs of wonderful popular élan
by Sismondi in his *Histoire des républiques italiennes* (1807–9) and *Histoire des
Français* (1821–44); by Thierry in his *Lettres sur l'histoire de France* (1820,
1827); by Guizot in his *Histoire des origines du gouvernement représentatif*
(1821–22), *Histoire de la révolution d'Angleterre,* and *Histoire de la civilization
en France* (1830); and by Mignet's and Thiers's histories of the French Revolution (1824 and 1823–27, respectively). Third, influenced by Romantic
philosophy, these historians emphasized the two great post-antique crises
in religion as evolutionary epochs so that the establishment of Christianity
at the fall of the Roman Empire was depicted as a moment of advance into
a new theological culture rather than as a decline, and the appearance of
Protestantism not as a regrettable fall from orthodoxy, but as a second
step forward—a step the once-glorified Louis XIV prevented France from
making with the revocation of the Edict of Nantes. The Revolution was
finally the establishment of the principles of a new age. It is upon these
epochs that the subsequent philosophical histories of Quinet and Michelet
would concentrate.[64]

This Romantic structuring of history is, of course, that adopted by Reynaud, Vaudoyer, and Fortoul. Progress is the foundation of their thinking.
The Greco-Roman tradition is admired, but depicted as irrelevant since it
is based on an elementary state of human consciousness. The establishment of Christianity is a step forward, carrying architecture into the "style
curviligne" with the "affranchissement de l'arcade." A more decisive advance, however, comes with the Renaissance, when Christian theological
insight is tempered with scientific reason. In contrast, the age of Louis
XIV is seen as a moment of regression because of the emergence of aca-

demicism. Finally, the task of the modern architect is to return to the moment of the inception of the Renaissance, the Reformation and the perfection of representative government, and to evolve a rational style avoiding the pitfalls of imitation and academicism, the architectural equivalents of absolutism.

Where the influence of Romantic historical thinking becomes most direct and unquestionable is in Fortoul's *De l'Art en Allemagne,* with its hypothesis of dialectical architectural evolution. As we have seen, he proposed that this proceeded in stages, in the case of Christian "architecture curviligne" from the round arch of the German Romanesque to the pointed arch of the French Gothic and finally to a future system of fixed geometric relationships not yet conceived but historically inevitable. Confidence in such a structure is nothing unexpected in a Saint-Simonian protégé of Edgar Quinet who claimed, on occasion, to be an interpreter of Hegel to France.[65] At first glance this theory appears to be a crude application of Hegelian dialectical evolution. But Fortoul need not have gone so far. Saint-Simonism was based on a belief in progress in which evolution was defined as a spiraling alternation between "organic" and "critical" epochs moving forward through three stages of human consciousness: the ancient superstitious, the medieval "theological," and the Renaissance "positive."[66] Nonetheless, the closest parallel to Fortoul's theory in *De l'Art en Allemagne* is the theory of progress enunciated by Victor Cousin, mentor of Quinet and Michelet, in his celebrated lectures at the Sorbonne of 1828–29.[67] Here Cousin draws the strictest picture of historical fatality and dialectical evolution. History consists of distinct cultures, each necessary and characteristic of its time and place, but tread down by its successor. Great men do not emerge by their own powers, but because their qualities are appropriate to their time. Wars are not won by personal valor, but by irresistible movements of historical progress. Consciousness, Cousin states, has passed through two great contrasting eras—the finite and the infinite—and now, in the modern epoch, is about to achieve maturity in the synthesis of the two, when the vision of the infinite will be grasped and held by the sense of the finite.

In the first lecture of his 1829 series, Cousin summarizes his conception and states its implications for modern man. He notes that it is France's task, as the great central power in Europe, to carry the Renaissance to completion. The Reformation had been a local phenomenon in Germany, the Puritan revolution a provincial affair in Britain. In absolutist, Catholic France and elsewhere, the Middle Ages continued down to 1789, when, after the philosophical preparation of the eighteenth century, the old world of religion and politics was finally swept away. But nothing new has been set firmly in its place; these movements were destructive only. It is the task of France in the nineteenth century to construct a new world order, generalizing the advances of the Reformation and the Revolution and synthesizing them with the traditions of the past. (Discreetly, he adds that the constitution of 1814 accomplished this, approbation he would withdraw as soon as the Revolution of 1830 was accomplished and he ensconced in the Conseil Royale de l'Instruction Publique.) This, of course, is precisely what we have seen in Fortoul: that the nineteenth century was to create a general system from the local attempts of the Renaissance, one synthesizing the finite aesthetic of antiquity and the infinite art of the Middle Ages and based on the positive science of the eighteenth century.

In comparison to Fortoul's, Cousin's concept of the expression of idealism in modern architecture is crude: he imagines that it can be imposed by the traditional use of applied Orders. Closer contemporaries of Fortoul, like Quinet, do little better. Their sense of organicism in the relation of the parts of a culture is much sharper, but they follow Hegel in treating architecture as an expression of pre-Hellenic paganism and consequently dropping its analysis in later epochs as if building itself had ceased.[68] What Fortoul accomplished is the considered application of the Cousinian, "eclectic" point of view to Christian, modern architecture. First, in accepting the arch as the basic expressive element, he distinguishes the modern epoch from the Hellenic and pre-Hellenic. Then, by proposing a single system in arcuation itself—one embracing simultaneously the Roman, Byzantine, Romanesque, and Gothic styles—he moves analysis to a plane where distinctions of detail can be subordinated. Finally, in his projection of an architecture in which the abstract ratios of the Greek Orders will be applied to Christian arcuation, Fortoul admits that at a level of abstraction beyond that imagined by Cousin—not that of the Orders but that of the mathematical abstraction of them—all architecture shares a common organ of beauty. Nonetheless, in his insistence on the need to transform and purify arcuated building, Fortoul echoes his friend Quinet, who wrote in *Le Génie des religions* that, while every artist is the product of his time and culture, he is not just a passive product but a conscious individual struggling to reach beyond them to the common ideals of art—in short, is a prophet and a revolutionary.

It is not easy to precisely locate the ideas of Fortoul and his friends among the competing architectural ideals of the 1830s because these were partially and variously expressed. In 1830—and indeed down until the end of the reign of Louis-Philippe—there was no one volume definitively expounding any variety of post-Neoclassical professional theory. Although there were a number of lecture series in the theory and history of architecture being delivered, none had the cogency and radical purpose of those in history and philosophy by Cousin, Guizot, and Villemain at the Sorbonne in 1828–30. Quatremère de Quincy, of course, spoke for the Académie as

Secrétaire Perpétuel until 1839. His *Histoire des vies et ouvrages des plus
célèbres architectes du Xe au XVIIIe siècle* (1830), the revised edition of his
Dictionnaire historique d'architecture (1832)—not to mention his broader essays, *Essai sur la nature, le but et les moyens de l'imitation dans les beaux-arts*
(1823) and *Essai sur l'idéal dans ses applications pratique aux arts de dessin*
(1837)—were the only general treatises of recent publication the unin-
formed visitor would have found to purchase during the decade.[69] L.-P.
Baltard, Professor of Theory at the Ecole until his death in 1846, followed
Quatremère's doctrine scrupulously.[70] Huyot, Professor of the History of
Architecture, was broader in his interests and more advanced in his arguments, but ended up at much the same place conceptually, as we have
seen.[71] There is little evidence that the more inquiring students of this
moment attended the lectures of J.-N.-L. Durand (1760–1834) at the Ecole
Polytechnique, where he continued to teach until 1834, or studied his
Précis des leçons d'architecture données à l'Ecole Polytechnique (1802, 1805,
1817, 1821).[72] In place of the packed, applauding crowds that filled
Cousin's, Guizot's, and Villemain's lecture halls, we should imagine the
enrolled *Polytechniciens* sitting in stiff uniforms (executing the crude, rote
graphic exercises perserved in the school's archives) in Durand's hall and a
half-dozen dutiful stragglers in Baltard's and Huyot's.[73]

Alternatives to Neoclassicism were being formulated nonetheless, but in
less easily discovered places and publications: in the ateliers of Duban
(who began teaching in 1829), Labrouste (opened August 1, 1830),
Vaudoyer (1832), and Constant-Dufeux (1837); in novels and utopian
tracts and journals, especially *L'Artiste* (founded in 1830), but also more
obscure sheets like *La Liberté* (1832–33); and finally in formal groupings
and sects, notably the Fourierists and Saint-Simonians. Also, of course,
there were groups of friends. Petrus Borel lived with Théophile Gautier,
Gérard de Nerval, and the rest of the *petit cénacle* in the rue de Vaugirard
and was slowly being converted from architect to author.[74] Hector
Horeau, François-Alexis Cendrier, and Charles-Joseph Lambert established a small Saint-Simonian foyer on the rue de Seine.[75] Duban's student
César Daly was part of the inner circle of Charles Fourier in the mid-
1830s.[76] In comparison to these groupings, the visits and picnics of Fortoul, Reynaud, Duc, Duban, and Vaudoyer seem rather staid.

There was an important bohemian current among the young architects
in 1830. Borel organized these bohemians as the claque in the orchestra for
the opening of *Hernani* on February 28, 1830.[77] But they had no doctrine.
At first they addressed themselves to Duban and Labrouste for instruction.[78] In late 1828, after the scandal of the display of Duban's *temple protestant* and Labrouste's Paestum series at the Collège des Quatre Nations, the
students in the atelier of Abel Blouet (1796–1853) requested that Duban

serve as Blouet's replacement while he was absent on the Peloponnesian expedition of 1828–29.[79] Duban then joined his brother-in-law Debret in conducting his atelier, but on January 6, 1832, founded his own when their ideas proved incompatible.[80] In 1830 a rebellious group within A.-L.-T. Vaudoyer's atelier broke away and eventually presented themselves to Labrouste, who opened his atelier for them on August 1, 1830.[81] In 1832 Léon Vaudoyer opened his own atelier, succeeding his father.[82] Otherwise the only place the radical students went was to the office of the decorator Aimé Chenevard (1798–1838), who had established himself in Paris in 1829. A.-I.-A. Couchaud (1813–49), for example, did so in the mid-1830s before joining Labrouste's atelier. Chenevard had invented a florid decorative mode combining many historical styles, especially the Gothic and Oriental.[83] Before his unexpected death, he had a high reputation among innovators, being compared positively to Duban and Labrouste[84] and receiving commissions for stained glass for the Louvre and the royal château at Eu. The editors of *L'Artiste* turned to him for their frontispieces during the 1830s.

The students themselves produced the weekly *journal des arts, La Liberté,* from September 1832 to January 1833. Besides pieces by Borel, Vivant Didron, Delacroix, and the Republican painters Gabriel Laviron and P.-A. Jeanron, there were a number of architectural essays by Alfred Pommier (1801–40) and Bruno Galbaccio. Their approach was what the journal's title suggests: bitter criticism of the established system in the arts (especially as it was manifested in the Académie and Ecole) and the call for imaginative freedom. They otherwise proposed no deliberate, positive doctrine. Pommier had been in the atelier Duban took over from Blouet and was considered one of the most brilliant architecture students of the late 1820s, but all that we know from his hand are architectural fantasies shown in the Salons (figure 19).[85] Galbaccio published Hugoian poetry and designed the café-concert Casino Paganini at 11 Chaussée d'Antin, opened in 1837 and received enthusiastically by his friends the radical critics Gabriel Laviron and Théophile Thoré.[86] It was, however, in the late Empire style and displayed nothing not familiar in Hittorff's contemporaneous cafés on the Champs-Elysées. Jean Gigoux remembered Galbaccio in 1885: "This Galbaccio could make the most interesting and varied conversation in the world but he always concluded by negating everything."[87]

As might be expected, from the start there was tension between the Romantic bohemian students and the *pensionnaires chefs d'ateliers.* We know a good deal about the circumstances of the founding of Labrouste's atelier. In a letter of July 23, 1830, A.-L.-T. Vaudoyer huffily wrote Léon of the actions of these "Romantiques à la barbe":

19
Alfred Pommier, Architectural fan-
tasy exhibited in the Salon of 1833.
From G. Laviron, Salon of 1833.

In April there were grave disorders. . . . We [A.-L.-T. Vaudoyer and his
assistant Hippolyte Lebas] decided that those who felt themselves dissatisfied with
our objectives were free to stop following our lessons and that, in order to suppress
the disorders, the atelier would be closed for two days.

One of the ringleaders—there is always one such—gathered the students at a
café or somewhere and signed up those who wished to desert the atelier. He ob-
tained the signatures of seven or eight sheep who have not since reappeared. . . .

Accomplishing nothing during three months, they thought that Labrouste, hav-
ing just arrived, might receive them [as students] and they presented him with a
petition.

M. Labrouste refused them at first, saying that he wished to submit this demand
to us since it questioned our integrity. . . .

Flattered by this action, instead of opposing this proposition which seemed useful
for him . . . we encouraged Labrouste to accept this fledgling atelier.[88]

The facts of the story are confirmed by Labrouste's son Léon.[89] And
Vaudoyer's acerbic tone is reflected, very gently, in a letter of November
20, 1830, from Labrouste to his brother Théodore in Rome. "I work enor-
mously and, what is more difficult, I make my students work."[90] Few of
the initial group stayed long; a second, larger group took their place. Certainly there was no love lost between Pommier, who railed at the *envois* of
1831 in *La Liberté*,[91] and Léon Vaudoyer, who received the news that Pommier was second *en loge* in the competition for the Grand Prix in 1828 with,
"how Pommier could have placed second I in no way comprehend."[92]

By 1833 the younger generation, once united in their resistance to the
Académie, realized that their ideas were becoming distinct and various.
Borel had been the bohemians' leader since the *Bataille d'Hernani* and in
this year he was asked to contribute an article to *L'Artiste*, "Du Mouvement en architecture." Here he reviews the first years of the Duban and
Labrouste ateliers with the insight his experience provided. He attacks
them for importing the architectural vocabulary of Southern, Italian architecture to France. Duban and Labrouste are freer and more imaginative,
he allows, but still Neoclassicists. "Do they make progress? No, because
they turn back to the Etruscans and to Pompeii. Do they make relative
progress? Yes, because they have better intentions than their predecessors
and they are more skillful."[93] Borel asks for a new architecture derived
directly from French society and the French environment. He praises the
propriety of the "style riche gothique" of the thirteenth, fourteenth, and
fifteenth centuries, which is "Roman-oriental" in its intricacy. It is clearly
the work of Pommier and Chenevard that he most admires; in another

article in *L'Artiste* of that year he praised the latter as the only "thinking" architect in France.[94]

In this same year, Fortoul made perhaps his deepest mark as a critic when he published his article "De l'Art actuel" in the *Revue encyclopédique* attacking the "Roman-oriental" Gothicism popular among Hugo and his circle and coining the phrase "l'art pour l'art" to describe it.[95] He accused them of seeking beauty and exoticness of form regardless of meaning, criticisms (which Fortoul expresses by expended architectural analogies) even more applicable to the work of Pommier and Chenevard. This has not taken the form of a program, "code avoué et complète," but "it is the password recognized by the affiliates of certain coteries."[96] He proposes instead a theory of Saint-Simonian social literature.

To Fortoul this group's art was essentially fantastic. "Poetry," he mimics them, "is the glorious fantasy of one man."[97] But he makes no mention of the particular points Hugo proposed in his principal Gothic novel of these years, *Notre-Dame de Paris* (1831–32)[98]: that the printing press has destroyed the cathedral as the "book" of humanity.[99] Another utopian, the Fourierist Victor Considérant, attacked Hugo on this score in his *Considérations sociales sur l'architectonique* of 1834. This widely circulated and often-reprinted volume set the idea and image of the *phalanstère* in the public mind.[100] It described and illustrated the huge palatial structure that was to provide a psychologically balanced community with all the comforts of modern science—gas lighting, running water, good ventilation, fireproof construction—and that was to be the instrument of the perfection of society. This great industrial habitation would become the expression of modern civilization as the cathedral had been of medieval culture. In his conclusion, Considérant cites Hugo and attacks him as a narrow aesthete who cannot comprehend the fundamental importance of architecture as a social mechanism as well as an art:

M. Hugo! M. Hugo! who has put together I don't know what ridiculous theory, who sweats blood for three or four chapters in order to establish in pompous phrases that humanity once created architecture to the unique and simple end of making poetry. . . .

Thus, artists, believe in the genius of humanity rather than in the voice of false prophets. . . . Architecture, which you are told is dead and buried, truly has still to grow several cubits to achieve full stature!—the future is broad, man is strong. The apostles of the scanty and weak, of the poor and the meager, do not take their inspiration from vital sources, and it is not to them that one should listen.[101]

By 1833–34 the Romantic generation had split into the Hugoian Gothicists and the utopians. By 1838 both of these groups had evolved and split.

Gothicism in architecture lost its radical branch and became the serious archaeological and liturgical concern of the Commission des Monuments Historiques. Borel after 1833 turned his attention entirely to literature; Chenevard died in 1838; Pommier was obliged to flee to America in 1833 for political reasons; Galbaccio committed suicide. As these figures departed the scene, a new group appeared in their place. First came Ludovic Vitet, the young *literatus* and journalist who caused himself to be appointed Inspecteur des Monuments Historiques in 1830.[102] In 1831 he produced a forcefully argued report on the condition of historic monuments in France that called for a government bureau to supervise their restoration. In 1834 another Romantic *literatus*, Prosper Mérimée replaced Vitet as *inspecteur* (chief assistant architect) and in 1837 he completed the establishment of the Commission des Monuments Historiques. The original commissioners were principally antiquaries (Vatout, Taylor, Leprevost, Montesquiou), except for the architects Duban and A.-N. Caristie. Slowly, however, there grew up a staff of young architects engaged in restoration work. Among the very first were Viollet-le-Duc, sent to Vézelay in 1839; J.-B. Lassus, the leader of the students who had presented themselves to Labrouste and now Duban's *inspecteur* for the restoration of the Sainte-Chapelle; a Labrouste admirer, Léon Danjoy, sent to Lisieux; and Charles Questel, Duban's student and then his *inspecteur* at the Ecole des Beaux-Arts. As the 1840s, 1850s, and 1860s unfolded, these men became the core of a skillful and influential group of medievalists led by Viollet-le-Duc.

The completion in 1838 of the first major work by one of the *pensionnaires*, Duban's Ecole des Beaux-Arts, occasioned a corresponding split in the ranks of the utopians. Fortoul, representing the moderate Saint-Simonians, considered the building a model.[103] Théophile Thoré, representing a more resolute point of view, questioned it in a pair of articles in *L'Artiste*.[104] He listed three options Duban had in framing his design: doing a historic pastiche in the style of the fragments on the site, inventing a new style of architecture, or following established academic practice. Thoré describes the second option with unmistakable enthusiasm: "It is for a long time now that theory has dreamed of revolutionizing architecture."[105] He is disappointed that Duban has declined to do so. "Why has he not taken the initiative to make a radical reform and thus make a place for his name in the history of art, as the great reformers of the Renaissance did in their time, Bullant, Philibert, and Lescot?"[106] Instead Thoré concludes that Duban has combined all three options and produced an "eclectic" result. This still has a virtue, but a negative one: that of placing the existing system in doubt. "After one has practiced for a while this mixed and rather anarchic architecture, it will no longer be possible to go back to the old orthodoxy."[107] But this is only a first step toward architecture's real objective.

"It is very necessary that we eventually create an art in harmony with the conditions of our time and our country because here are the two relative and variable elements that combine to produce a marvelous unity with poetry, that divine faculty, which is as unchanging and absolute as truth."[108]

Fortoul and his friends Duban, Duc, Reynaud, and Vaudoyer held back from a radical transformation of architecture either in terms of giving themselves up to fantasy, adopting a local style as the archaeological medievalists would do, or accepting exclusively functional and social determinants. They sought some absolute order in the new world of possibilities opened before them by Romantic historicism and science. Fortoul found it in his concept of order without Orders, a modern arcuated architecture controlled by precise expressive ratios. His architect friends had a more difficult task, for they had to materialize this idea in actual buildings. We will watch their efforts in the next and later chapters.

A last note. One can see from this why it is difficult to attach a label to this group. The Romantic architectural students in Paris in 1830 proclaimed them their leaders principally because they lacked spokesmen and goals of their own. The circle of Labrouste nonetheless saw themselves as quite distinct from the bohemians and opened a progressively widening gap between themselves and those whom they perceived unsympathetically as "Gothicists." It was a cliché repeated several times in the necrologies of the *pensionnaires* in the 1870s that they were "Romantiques de la façon d'Ingres."[109] Nor were they utopians either, or "Néo-Grecs," despite important contacts with both these groups. With Charles Garnier's appropriation of the label "eclectic" during the 1860s, even this is denied us today, although originally it was probably the most accurate term for defining their enterprise and the one they themselves adopted between the mid-1830s and the end of the Second Empire.[110] This obliges us to find our own designation. In the end Labrouste, Duban, Duc, and Vaudoyer were the most influential practitioners of achitecture in France between 1830 and 1860, the period of Romanticism broadly defined. Their definition of Romanticism was narrower than ours; what we now perceive as the characteristics of the period apply to their work as well as to that of Lassus and Pommier. Romantics they were, even if "de la façon d'Ingres." They were the generation's Romantic architects, who clarified their ideas in Rome at the French Academy and who henceforth worked in the government system: that is, they were always *pensionnaires*. Thus the label I have attached to them in this book: the Romantic *pensionnaires*.

Three

THE FIRST BUILDINGS: THE ECOLE DES BEAUX-ARTS, BIBLIOTHEQUE SAINTE-GENEVIEVE, AND CONSERVATOIRE DES ARTS ET METIERS

Upon their return from Rome, the *pensionnaires* received the minor appointments usually bestowed by the government upon Grand Prix winners. In 1829 Duban was made *inspecteur* to his brother-in-law, François Debret, for the rebuilding of the Ecole des Beaux-Arts. When Duban was appointed architect of that structure in 1832, Labrouste was named his *inspecteur*. That same year Duc was appointed *sous-inspecteur* under J.-A. Alavoine (1778–1834) for the Colonne de Juillet on the Place de la Bastille. In 1833 Vaudoyer was named *inspecteur* on the staff of Jacques Lacornée (1779–1856) in the erection of the "Palais d'Orsay," a massive block of government offices dominating the left bank of the Seine (burned during the Commune in 1871). They also received some private commissions: Duban erected the Hôtel Pourtalès on the rue Tronchet in 1835–39 and Labrouste won the competitions for the design of an insane asylum in Lausanne, Switzerland, in 1836 and of a prison at Alessandria, Italy, in 1839–40. Far more importantly, however, as the decade of the 1830s progressed each was nominated *architecte-en-chef* of a major government monument. First was Duban when he replaced Debret at the Ecole des Beaux-Arts. Then Duc succeeded Alavoine at the Colonne de Juillet in 1834. Finally, in 1838 Labrouste was appointed *architecte-en-chef* of the new building for the Bibliothèque Sainte-Geneviève, and in that same year Vaudoyer was put in charge of the expansion of the Conservatoire des Arts et Métiers.

The appointment of Duban and Labrouste to rebuild the home of the Ecole des Beaux-Arts (figures 20–28)[1] was itself a challenge to the Académie and the Ecole administration, both Bourbon foundations and staffed with Bourbon appointees. The new Liberal government seems to have intended that. Like the Commission des Beaux-Arts of 1831, a bill of 1832 authorizing 100 million francs to complete the monuments of Paris, and a law of 1832 restricting government architects to one major commission at a time (giving Duban this commission in particular), this was another effort to support Romanticism and to extend the Revolution beyond a mere change of kings.[2]

Duban did his best to carry out his difficult assignment. He pushed his design through despite resistance on the part of the Ecole professors and, to a lesser extent, of the Conseil des Bâtiments Civils, fraying bureaucratic nerves on all sides and producing some of the most emotion-laden documents moldering today in the Archives Nationales—documents no less emotional for the sincere conviction with which Duban defended his principles.

In the end a puzzling building arose. The liberals claimed to love it.[3] The conservatives claimed to hate it. But the uncommitted claimed not to understand it at all. "Have you seen the new constructions at the Ecole des Beaux-Arts?" the *pensionnaire* Mathieu-Prosper Morey (1805–78) confronted his friend Viollet-le-Duc when the latter visited Rome in 1836. "Some say: admirable! Others say: absurd! I do not permit myself to judge in such an absolute manner, but if I must give you my opinion, I admit to you that I don't understand that architecture; some call it Renaissance, others Late Empire, still others Etruscan."[4] What was so confusing was that this new architecture was something other than a new vocabulary of forms, at least as it stood in 1833. It had the elements of a synthesis, but not yet the synthesis itself. Like the *envois* of the years immediately before, it delineated a point of view and made a gesture, but nothing more.

Duban's design of 1833 was for the alteration and completion of the Ecole building begun in 1820 by the Neoclassical architect Debret (figures 20, 21). The three wings furthest from the rue Bonaparte were essentially complete in 1830. The building occupied the garden of the seventeenth-century Couvent des Petits Augustins, the cloister and chapel of which stood along the street, temporarily divided into studios and habitations for the institution. When Debret's building was completed, these vestiges of the cloister were to be demolished to open a suitably dignified open space around it. However, piled in the basements and littering the courtyards of the old monastery were masses of French medieval and Renaissance architectural fragments, including two whole facades rising dramatically above the confusion, that of the château at Anet (by Philibert de Lorme) and that of the château at Gaillon (thought to be by Fra Giocondo) (figure 21). Upon the supression of the religious orders at the time of the Revolution, these fragments had been gathered here by Alexandre Lenoir. Between 1791 and 1814 he created his Musée des Monuments Français, the first intentionally constituted museum of national antiquities and a beloved resort of the Romantic artists of the Empire.[5] Upon the restoration of the Bourbon dynasty (by decrees of September 15, 1815; April 25, 1816; and December 18, 1816), the museum was dissolved and its collections re-

20

Félix Duban, Plan of the Ecole des Beaux-Arts, Paris, before beginning work in 1832. Ecole des Beaux-Arts, Paris.

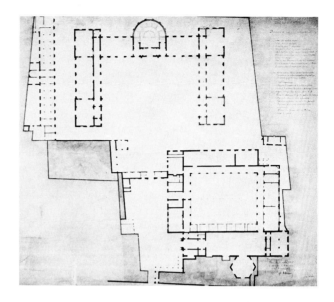

21

Ecole des Beaux-Arts, view across the remains of the Musée des Monuments Français. From Magasin pittoresque 2 (1834): 284.

turned to their former owners—the church and emigré nobility—and the site itself given to the Ecole des Beaux-Arts, which was in the process of reconstitution. Not surprisingly, however, the former owners of the fragments displayed little industry in dragging them away, so by 1830 the Ecole was functioning amid the ruins of the museum.

On July 31, 1832, Duban was asked to draw up a plan to complete the Ecole structure, and he presented a finished project on April 5, 1833. In preparing his design he entirely rethought the problem. He sought to retain the monastery and the museum as well as to complete Debret's block in the garden. Doing so permitted him to divide the functions of the institution into two parts: instruction and research. The instructional spaces—studios for the required course on anatomy, etc.—he put in the old cloister, partly rebuilt. The research collections—casts, the library, the archives, premiated Grand Prix designs—he placed in Debret's half-built block. He opened its interior to make it a museum, simplified its staircase, and suppressed a monumental vaulted hall that was to occupy the center of the courtyard and to introduce the ceremonial hemicycle for prize ceremonies, the Salle des Prix. Duban now called this block the Palais des Etudes and redesigned its facade in an elegant but conventional style, adding an attic story to house the library (cf. figures 22, 23). Duban furthermore proposed to leave the facades of the châteaux of Anet and Gaillon in place and to make them the organizing features of a pair of narrow courtyards leading from the rue Bonaparte. These courtyards would be ornamented with other fragments from Lenoir's collection and thus would constitute museum spaces—an outdoor museum of French national architecture like the original Musée des Monuments Français.

Like all designs for French government buildings, Duban's project had to be evaluated by a board of architects, the Conseil des Bâtiments Civils, and corrected if necessary before being submitted to the Minister for signature and presentation to the Chambre des Députés for funding. This occasioned an illuminating dispute.

On June 18, 1833, the Conseil met with Duban and a delegation of Ecole professors and officials (the latter consisting of the artists Ingres and Cortot and the officials Léonor Mérimée and Charles-Léon Vinit[6]). The body concluded that Duban should be asked to remove the facade of Gaillon—the so-called Arc de Gaillon—from the center of the forecourt to its south wall, to omit the attic of the Palais des Etudes, and to restudy his details. Duban protested, appearing at the June 21 meeting of the Conseil to read a lengthy but carefully reasoned memorandum explaining his intentions in retaining the Arc de Gaillon. "Charged by the Minister with the definitive formulation of a project to complete the Ecole des Beaux-Arts," he commences, "I was first of all obliged to make an account, through careful study, of the state of the buildings."[7] The Arc, he had

22
Félix Duban, Ecole des Beaux-
Arts, 1832–40, view across court-
yards from the rue Bonaparte.
(Photo: Giraudon)

23
Félix Duban, Ecole des Beaux-
Arts, view of inner courtyard look-
ing north. (Photo: Giraudon)

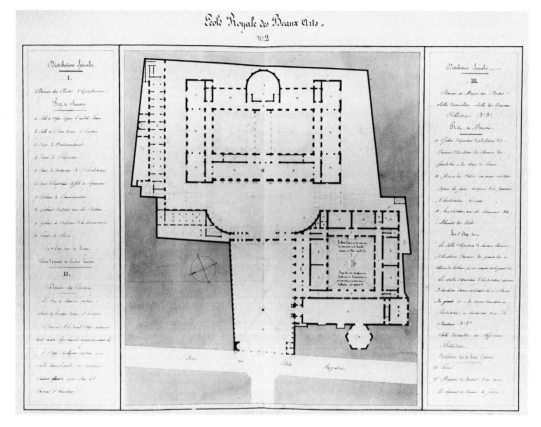

24
Félix Duban, Project for the completion of the Ecole des Beaux-Arts. Inscribed "Vu et approuvé . . . le 1er octobre 1833" by Minister Thiers. Archives Nationales, Paris. (Photo: Bulloz)

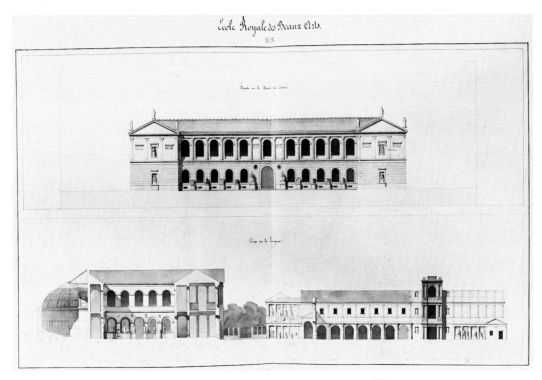

25
Félix Duban, Project for the completion of the Ecole des Beaux-Arts. Archives Nationales, Paris. (Photo: Bulloz)

decided, was both appropriate to mark a school of art and fortuitously sited to articulate the spaces in front of the Palais des Etudes.

Its position facing southeast so favorable for the light and graceful forms that compose it; its parallelism with the street, which permits the eye to grasp immediately the configuration; its open forms, which let the glance penetrate to the Palais which it precedes, which announces, one might say, the boundary it in a sense establishes between the outer court made up of forms of past centuries and that of the Musée des Etudes; the subjects for examination and comparison it offers for consideration—all this, in a word, all this forced me to treat it as the chief ornament of the establishment.

The fragments scattered in the courtyards of the Ecole, the numbered courses of masonry ready to retake their original forms, about which public opinion has so long reproached the administration for the abandon and resulting decay, gave me the idea of erecting two light, open porticos to consolidate the principal monument, realizing an idea conceived thirty years ago by the illustrious Master of all masters [Charles Percier] to define a courtyard where young students might come, if not seeking models, at least to admire what former centuries had produced. Foreigners envy our national riches and everyone—artists, literati, antiquaries—will thank the Administration that saves and protects this storehouse of art confided to it.

Beyond [the Arc de Gaillon] two semicircles will be encrusted with all the fragments that cannot be utilized in the construction of these buildings, permitting the eye to penetrate to and to embrace the whole facade of the Palais. Exiting from the Musée des Etudes this amphitheatrical form will offer an immense surface of fragments artistically arranged, interrupted by the open porticos which define this sort of roofless museum.[8]

He concluded by proving that any fear that the Arc de Gaillon would mask the Palais des Etudes was unfounded because such an arrangement had been adopted in many of the most admired ancient ensembles—the Portico of Octavius (the subject of his fourth-year *envoi*), the Temple of Juno and Jupiter, and the Basilica Ulpia.

This apparently was ineffectual, and Duban prepared a far more passionate document for a third meeting of June 25.

I must state that in this case removal is synonymous with destruction.

No one will dispute that because of the lightness and delicacy of the parts of the building we are discussing, they will not survive a double demolition and a double reconstruction unscathed.[9]

He reviewed again the fortuitous siting and symbolism of the Arc de Gaillon. Then he declared more pointedly than before:

If the architect of a building can raise his voice in favor, not of his own work, but of the work of the great masters of which he asks the preservation, I say here that the facade of the principal building was conceived to be, not masked, but preceded by this elegant portico, by this sign (I dare thus say) of the establishment that he has to restore, that the relief of its details was worked out to make a visually agreeable whole, picturesque without disorder, to be articulated by contrasting the forms of the principal building with the elegant lightness of the open portico which masks the edifice as the Arc du Carrousel does the Tuileries, as the obelisk of Luxor does the Chambre des Députés, as all the basilicas were masked by the open porticos which preceded them, as the Egyptian temples were by their pylons, as all buildings of all periods whose beauty is always increased by the picturesque combination of structures that precede and accompany them.

But what for many buildings is a simple picturesque beauty is here, I dare say, an appropriate enhancement. If this portico did not exist, the architect would have had to propose an equivalent. Indeed, when one thinks about the parts of the establishment—in front, the entrance court [with], to the right, the daily studies, masses of students milling about at all hours on their way to classes, the constant coming and going of employees; beyond, everything is silence and meditation: a museum, a library, exhibition rooms, all places where one goes individually for study and examination. Such different functions demand a dividing wall: a grill in the opinion of the Conseil: *indeed, this grill exists, it is of stone, it exists, it is a masterpiece from the past, it is an admirable fragment of architecture and sculpture, it is a reminder of Giocondo, of Louis XII, of Georges d'Amboise; it exists there, in the Ecole des Beaux-Arts, where the government would have to erect it were it not there already, together with the portico from Anet and the Gothic fragments which would be laid out in front, an admirable summary of our national architecture, and a council composed of the most eminent architects of France ponders its relocation, that is to say, its ruin!*[10]

Duban was then asked by the members of the Conseil to withdraw. The Arc de Gaillon was the central issue and the minutes show that the Conseil reviewed the advantages of moving it or keeping it where it was. They appreciated that it would serve as a neat demarcation between the outer courtyard, opening along the facade of the studio block, and the inner courtyard fronting the Palais des Etudes. But they insisted that its Late Gothic–Early Renaissance style would not be in harmony with Duban's facade and that it would mask the view of it from the street. They also asserted that the use of fragments from several historical epochs was regrettable, and finally expressed doubt: "Perhaps one should avoid, in the museum of the Ecole des Beaux-Arts, placing too prominently works of art whose composition and taste are not entirely in harmony with the principles of ancient architecture."[11] However, in typically bureaucratic fashion, the Conseil finally deferred decision, permitting the Arc de Gaillon to remain in place during construction until its effect could be judged, while demanding the removal of two low loggias linking it to the north and south sides of the outer courtyard. Their injunction to remove the attic and restudy the details was reaffirmed.

Duban drew up a new project (figures 24, 25), which was signed by the Minister, Thiers, on October 1, 1833, and construction pushed forward. When it was completed in 1838, the attic had reappeared (authorized by the Minister during a visit to the site on September 25, 1834) and the Arc de Gaillon, of course, was still in place. It remained there until 1978, when it was abruptly dismantled and sent back to the municipality of Gaillon.

What the Empire architects comprising the Conseil des Bâtiments Civils did not seem to appreciate was that Duban's fragments were, in fact, an ordered museum of French national antiquities meant to train the students of the next generation through the broader lessons of architectural evolution and inflection that Duban and his friends had themselves learned in Rome. Young architects, Léonce Reynaud observed in 1834, "before creating for themselves a new system of architecture, must examine those that were followed by our fathers to determine their worth and to study their laws."[12] This however, was to be a museum of a very particular part of the whole subject, of the Late Gothic and Early Renaissance epochs. In the initial submission of his design, Duban described the arrangement of the courtyards thus: "The objective of this proposal is to offer in the principal court for admiration and study: fragments of Gothic art on the left facade, the architectural forms of the century of Louis XII [reigned 1498–1515] at the back, and those of the reign of Henri II [1547–59] on the right, a summary of our national architecture."[13] Fra Giocondo was regarded as the first architect to design in the Renaissance style in France and the château at Gaillon, still Gothic in many parts, as the first Gallic statement of the new style. Later, in 1844, Duban attempted to have the facade of the Gothic Hôtel Dieu at Orléans removed to the Ecole to face that of Anet across the outer courtyard. The *procès verbal* of the Commission des Monuments Historiques record him explaining, "It will occupy the place he designated for a thirteenth-century doorway, facing the fragment from

Anct."[14] In the organization of his design, quite without any ornamental oddities, Duban had transformed the instruction of the Ecole des Beaux-Arts without removing any of the Bourbon appointees who comprised its staff. As construction was being completed another statement of Duban's message was conceived—the mural occupying the entire curved wall of the semicircular Salle des Prix (figures 26–28). It was commissioned from Paul Delaroche in 1836 and opened to public view on December 1, 1841.[15] Delaroche was a friend of Duban and Thiers and a Romantic in the inclusive sense of that term in the 1830s.

The Salle des Prix was a ceremonial chamber at the culmination of the building's axis used for the annual award of student prizes. "The function of the room in a sense indicated the choice of subject," one critic wrote.[16] What Delaroche chose to represent were the great artists of the Christian Gothic and Renaissance eras—painters, sculptors, and architects—discussing their art (figure 26). Set apart from the two conversing groups and unacknowledged by them are Apelles, Ictinus, and Phidias—the masters of painting, architecture, and sculpture of ancient Greece. In front of them, mediating between them and the Christian artists, are four figures representing Greece, Rome, the Middle Ages, and the Renaissance. The latter two are "like the link that connects the ancient and entirely ideal portion of the painting with the modern and almost living part," Ludovic Vitet explained in an admiring review.[17] A nude genius at their feet throws a victor's crown into the Salle des Prix itself.

There are two things extraordinary about this mural at first glance: first, the spatial composition is not self-contained but rather the illusionistic continuation of the room it decorates; second, the subject is not allegorical but instead the portraiture of historical figures. "M. Delaroche," Ludovic Vitet wrote,

by the temper of his spirit and by the direction of his studies, is a historian more than a poet: his ideas are uncomfortable in the field of symbolic abstractions, they more happily take on the costume of a country or a time, they attach themselves to a place, a date, they make specific and personify. Where others see art, he sees the artist: sculpture for him is the sculptor.[18]

Spatially, Delaroche continues the rings of steps and benches of the hemicycle up into his mural and closes it with a file of Ionic columns supporting an entablature precisely coinciding with that of Duban's room (figure 27). Considering the architecture of the room and the narrow, bending field Duban provided Delaroche, this is the only way it could have been treated. It was meant to be painted this way, as a frieze of figures illusionistically *in* the space, unified not within the painting itself, but by means of the activities in the room, the prize ceremonies. To make this point unmistakable—to create a point of entry into the illusion—Delaroche paints the genius actually throwing the victor's laurels outward, toward the rostrum.

But these historical figures are not merely present, they are characterized: in conversing they are taking positions among themselves and responding to one another. "One thinks one hears them," wrote Charles Blanc, "so great is the precision, the fine intention, the clarity in his characterization, in his pantomime."[19] Delaroche makes the architects act out the history of their art (figure 28). At their center addressing them is Arnolfo di Cambio, the Gothic designer who began the Duomo in 1292. Brunelleschi and Bramante stand immediately to his left and right; the former, Vitet notes, "listens, but with a slightly distracted air; one perceives that he is already considering his dome."[20] Inigo Jones and Pierre Lescot stand next to them, and Lescot, "with the petulance of a Frenchman, advances to listen to the old Florentine and leans familiarly on the shoulder of Bramante."[21] Further away, observing the scene but not participating in it, are Robert de Luzarches and Palladio, standing together as friends in afterlife. Erwin von Steinbach, Jacapo Sansovino, and Peruzzi, all late masters of developed styles, talk together. To the right of Arnolfo's auditors sits François Mansart, elegantly attired and looking bemused. Lescot's elbow, however, blocks our view of his eyes. At the far left Philibert de Lorme sits head in hand, lost in thought. Vignola is cut off from the group at the left. Delaroche has thus not only depicted the individual characters of the historical masters of Christian architecture, but also dramatized their common enterprise. They crowd around and listen to Arnolfo di Cambio, just as their buildings can be seen as responses to his Duomo.

This, of course, is precisely the history we saw Labrouste and Duban formulating in Rome in the 1820s and Vaudoyer, Reynaud, and Fortoul exploring in the 1830s. It is also the history made palpable in the fragments Duban used to organize the spaces of the Ecole courtyards. As the critic Louis Peisse observed in 1840, the public "may [now] traverse with us these rooms and galleries . . . and see with their eyes and touch with their hands this *histoire figurée* of art which M. Delaroche has been able to paint symbolically on the wall of the amphitheater."[22]

The facade of Labrouste's Bibliothèque Sainte-Geneviève of 1843–50 (figures 29–34)[23] also reflects the ideas and events of 1828–40, but in a very different sense. It is the *pensionnaires'* and Reynaud's and Fortoul's reading of history that one sees materialized in the Ecole, while it is their acceptance of structure as the basic material of design that is manifested in the Bibliothèque Sainte-Geneviève. And, most importantly, Labrouste's

26
Paul Delaroche, Replica of the mural in the Salle des Prix, Ecole des Beaux-Arts. Walters Art Gallery, Baltimore.

27
*Félix Duban, architect, and Paul
Delaroche, painter, Salle des Prix,
Ecole des Beaux-Arts, 1840–42.
(Photo: Giraudon)*

28
*Paul Delaroche, Detail of the ar-
chitects, Salle des Prix, Ecole des
Beaux-Arts. Walters Art Gallery,
Baltimore.*

building presents something like a new style of architecture, while Duban's Ecole presents only its materials.

What one encounters set on the edge of the Montagne Sainte-Geneviève is a narrow, rectangular box wedged onto a long, constricted site ringed by a continuous range of arches on tall, narrow piers—a sort of viaduct doubling back on itself—not disrupted by pavilions, projections, or pilasters (figure 32).[24] The interior space is defined and protected by curtain walls filling the lower two-thirds of the arches, but these are set back and distinguished by their ornamentation of names, once picked out in red paint so that they did not blur the expression of the structural skeleton. Lightly fitted inside is an almost transparent floor and ceiling structure of iron and plaster tied together by a row of spindly iron columns down the axis of the single major interior space.

A number of circumstances render such a reticent treatment of the building appropriate.[25] Forming part of the facade of the public square surrounding the Pantheon, one of the principal monuments of Paris, it could neither compete with that structure for attention (indeed, had it done so with a display of pavilions and projections, it would have seemed ridiculous in its comparatively small scale), nor ignore its position as part of the entourage. Furthermore, as a library, it is neither a building that is traditionally a monumental element of the cityscape, nor one that requires a spatial configuration any more elaborate than the long rectangular one suggested by this site.[26] Other architects would surely have proposed designs similar in shape and emphasis.

Labrouste could not have been distressed that these factors obliged such a simple, boxy solution. The whole thrust of his study in Rome, as we have seen, was to distinguish profound differences through details of articulation and ornament read closely where previously only typological similarity had been seen. Thus he had perceived the basic distinction of function between the basilica and the temples at Paestum, regardless of the fact that they all had the same boxy layout. One of the points of Labrouste's Paestum *envoi* is that a simple box, if read closely, can be as architecturally expressive as an elaborate academic composition of contrasting volumes—a point repeated in Duban's and Constant-Dufeux's fifth-year *envois*.

The history of the design of the Bibliothèque Sainte-Geneviève is not as complex as that of the Ecole: the project did not touch so tender a place in the Académie's heart, and the architect's aesthetic intentions harmonized with the bureaucracy's practical objectives.

The institution itself was the former monastic library of the abbey of Sainte-Geneviève, founded in 1624 and housed, until 1850, in a large cross-shaped space occupying the attic of the abbey behind the Pantheon. It had been nationalized in 1791 and by the 1830s had become an important place of study for the students in the colleges surrounding the Montagne Sainte-Geneviève. So heavily used was it, in fact, that in 1838 it became the first library in Paris to be opened at night and illuminated with gas. The government had been concerned about the insufficiency of its old quarters, however, and in 1836 had asked Alphonse de Gisors (1796–1866) to draw up a project for a new building on the site of the Prison Montaigou, nearby on the south side of the Place du Panthéon.[27] The matter lay dormant until June 6, 1838, when Labrouste was appointed to replace de Gisors (who was commissioned to rebuild the Luxembourg for the Senate) and a new project was requested for that same site.

Labrouste presented his design on December 19, 1839 (figures 29–31). It was analyzed and approved by the Conseil des Bâtiments Civils in meetings of January 23 and 25, 1840, and a bill to fund it was prepared for the Chambre des Députés. Delays followed, however, including a further examination of the project by the Conseil on November 21, 1842; and it was only on July 19, 1843, that the funds were appropriated. Excavation was begun on August 1, 1843; the structure was completed in December 1850; and it was opened to the public on February 4, 1851.

The preliminary design of 1839 is very general in its depiction of the building's articulation—which was finalized only as the masonry actually rose during the late 1840s—but the plan and the structure are already clearly set. It is fireproof, gas-lit, and centrally heated and ventilated. The plan is neatly arranged, with a main reading room occupying the whole of its upper story and book storage, special reading rooms, and a vestibule below. Its most conspicuous innovation is the iron interior frame, which is the first use of a consistent, exposed iron skeleton in a monumental public building in the history of architecture.[28] This frame troubled the Conseil des Bâtiments Civils. They suggested that Labrouste study a stone vaulting system instead. He replied that he had considered that solution and had found that the masonry would be so heavy and produce such lateral thrusts that the window openings would have to be eliminated at the two ends of the structure. The iron frame, he pointed out, was not only light enough to permit an even light in daytime, but also could be fabricated off the site while construction of the masonry envelope was proceeding, thus considerably shortening the construction time. The Conseil remained dubious, asking Labrouste to rethink the question in 1842, but in the end it did not forbid his innovation. He proceeded with remarkable success, changing only the profile of the ceiling from the angular shed roof of the project to a barrel-vaulted one, which was less honest to its material but more harmonious with the masonry arches around the four walls.

How is one to read this retiring masonry box? First, through inflections in its structural skeleton; second, through legible symbols integrated into its ornamentation; third, through the actual rendering of the stone sur-

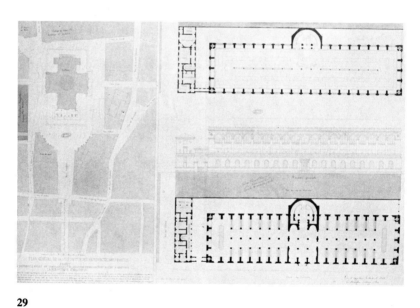

29

Henri Labrouste, Bibliothèque Sainte-Geneviève, Paris, preliminary project. Inscribed "Vu et approuvé, le 10 avril 1843" by the Minister. Archives Nationales, Paris.

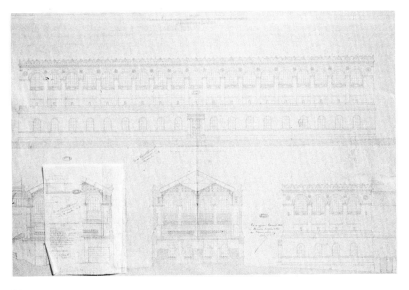

30
Henri Labrouste, Bibliothèque
Sainte-Geneviève, preliminary
project. Inscribed "Vu et approuvé,
le 10 avril 1843" by the Minister.
Archives Nationales, Paris.

31
*Henri Labrouste, Bibliothèque
Sainte-Geneviève, preliminary
project for reading room interior.
Inscribed "Vu et approuvé,
le 10 avril 1843" by the Minister.
Cabinet des Dessins, Louvre,
Paris.*

faces—for everything has been thought through and made to reflect its function in the ensemble. There are no conventions; even the two columns framing the door in the preliminary design were replaced with more specific symbolic motifs as construction progressed.

The upper and lower stories contain the primary (reading room) and secondary (storage, vestibule, manuscripts) spaces, respectively. The predominance of the reading room is made clear by the emergence of the skeleton in the upper story as a tall, arched cage, while it is concealed by a horizontal veil of masonry below. The monumental column-ribs of the reading room have been freed by draping a curtain wall across the inside of the arch embrasures, while their upper thirds are opened into broad windows that signify the continuous space inside and admit a flood of light. Built within this skeleton are secondary structures that show through on the surface: a staircase to the roof in the corner piers, identified by lines of tiny windows; two tiers of bookshelves ringing the reading room, expressed by the curtain walls, which are enriched like bookspines with the names of authors; and a range of small storage rooms below the upper tier of shelves signified by a string of openings. Finally, the iron interior structure emerges in the form of two ranges of tie rods at the top of each story, blossoming into platelike pateras that support a carved garland on the first floor and compositions of ribbons and swags on the second. Thus by the size of the window openings and the degree of relief, Labrouste makes the interior appear through the confining skeletal cage, which becomes a compositional grid organizing and unifying what is a highly varied, emphatic spatial configuration.

The building is decorated with carved stone ornaments, but they are not conventional motifs (figure 33). "This monumental catalogue," Labrouste wrote of the fields of lettering on the curtain wall, "is the principal decoration of the facade, as the books themselves are the most beautiful ornament of the interior."[29] The only other significant ornamentation is the main entrance, which is shown flat-lintelled and flanked with Tuscan columns in the approved design but was executed arched and with two flaming lamps sculpted in the masonry on each side. Henry Trianon, the librarian, explained in 1851 that these carvings commemorated the opening of the library at night for the convenience of students and workers.[30]

All of Labrouste's ornamentation thus simply articulates facts of the building. It functions directly, without any intervening filter of conventional Neoclassical forms or Orders. The primary fact remains the building's structure: externally arched construction in layers of limestone. Even the cutting of the surfaces brings out the structure, through a new reticence of relief and a new expressiveness of curve in moldings. To continue the wall plane and to take emphasis away from the windows of the lower story, Labrouste indents the surface around them, thereby subtly outlining

32
Henri Labrouste, Bibliothèque
Sainte-Geneviève, Paris, 1844–50.
(Photo: James Austin)

33
*Henri Labrouste, Bibliothèque
Sainte-Geneviève, details of
masonry at doorway.*

them with a single, sharp, continuous shadow line. Deeper in the embrasure is a second continuous surface, now made into a broad cymation to vary the shadow. To give emphasis to the upper story arcade, Labrouste carves an elaborate plinth (sharply contrasting with the mere bevels marking the stony, solid base of the lower story), but one composed only of bevels and exquisitely drawn quarter-rounds so that the bands of light and shadow are broad and distinct.

Most impressive and illuminating is his treatment of the carving at the entrance (figure 33). The plane of the lower-story masonry is brought right to the edge of the arched opening but is subtly and perversely "slowed" here by a single thin projection ringing the embrasure like a wave caused by a stone dropped in a pond (all the more so for permitting the swags hung on the tie rods to run unbroken through it). This molding, square on two sides with a cymation on the third, establishes a plane an inch-and-a-half in front of the wall plane that is picked up in the window sills and that defines the relief of the flaming lamps. One is made to feel every millimeter of the wall surface cut back in the *ravalement* from the continuous datum of the molding, sills, and lamps. Further, one is made to sense the coursing of the stone, already clearly stated in the bevels along the top of the lowest course of the wall base, as Labrouste confines each division of the lamp form within each stone field and has the flame just lick the mortar joint of the course above.

The manner in which Labrouste draws forth the moldings reflects his objective in the whole design: to draw art forms out of structure, not impose them upon it. Nowhere is his ornament a veil over the stone surface obeying sculptural rules of its own. Either it emerges from the mass itself, like the lower-story plinth moldings, or it is clearly attached, like the garland of swags. Taking the design as a whole, there is neither a colonnade nor a tier of windows on the main story—that is, neither an ornamental convention nor a series of holes in a passive wall plane—but rather a ring of piers bearing a continuous arcade, truly and unmistakably the skeleton of the building. The strange little capitals that emerge at the pier tops oblige one to read it thus—a colonnade, if you will, transformed into Fortoul's "style curviligne." This, the pier-borne arcade, is the organizing element of the design. Other spaces and elements are subordinated to it, inserted into it. Labrouste even extends its characteristic semicircular span into the ironwork of the interior, knowingly distorting its practical form so that it can echo and reinforce the motif that he, in the spirit of Vaudoyer, Reynaud, and Fortoul, accepts as the quintessential expression of this first design in a purely arcuated style of architecture.

The exterior walls of the Bibliothèque Sainte-Geneviève hold themselves with tremendous firmness, especially when seen from the inside in their full depth (figure 34). They seem to complement and hold in the

34
*Henri Labrouste, Bibliothèque
Sainte-Geneviève, interior of read-
ing room. (Photo: James Austin)*

dramatic iron webwork of the interior. But there is a problem with this intuitive assumption: Labrouste's iron armature in fact applies no thrust against the stone exterior at all. Being of cast iron, bolted together in large sections, the ironwork exerts no live thrusts despite its resemblance to a pair of barrel vaults. It is simply a series of lateral cantilevers balanced on the row of central columns, infilled with a thin plaster webbing.[31] Labrouste even tries to impress this disturbing fact on us by supporting the iron trusses where they meet the girdling masonry wall by nothing more than the slightest corbels. The function of these corbels is merely to stabilize the cantilevers at their ends; as a result, the skeletalized but nonetheless thick and stable stone viaduct enclosing the space supports nothing more than its own weight. And as a further consequence, despite superficial appearances, because of Labrouste's use of iron the Bibliothèque Sainte-Geneviève has no structural relation to the Cathedral at Albi, the refectory of the monastery of Saint-Martin-des-Champs, the Vatican Library, or any other masonry-vaulted historical sources that present themselves.[32]

Why, then, did Labrouste conceal the most remarkable advantage of his new iron system by enclosing it in this thick stone envelope? The answer is, in a sense, very obvious: not only for stability but also because the building is a library, a place illuminated properly for reading, and because proper lighting is difficult here since the site is flattened and oriented along its whole vast length directly toward the southern sun. The only means Labrouste had to provide a diffused, comfortable light was to protect the interior by a light, deep arcade whose thin piers would act as sun screens, breaking the direct rays and diffusing the sunlight by reflection off their flat, unornamented sides. This is also why the windows are set so close to the outer plane of the facade and why the ceiling was altered from the structurally "honest" form of flat panelled planes (figure 31) to the "irrational" one of undecorated, white half-cylinders suggesting vaults. In 1860–67 Labrouste went a step further in his Salle des Imprimés at the Bibliothèque Nationale (figure 84), where he erected nine domes of paper-thin ceramic tile—domes not in the structural sense, but merely hemispheres, reflectors amplifying and diffusing the light admitted by oculi at each peak.[33] (The succeeding architect of the Bibliothèque Nationale, Jean-Louis Pascal, did not understand this and in building the Salle des Périodiques at the turn of the century provided a single large skylight without reflecting surfaces that resulted in an ill-lit hole.) Labrouste was building with light even more than with iron and stone. His approach is indeed functionalist, but not just narrowly that of a structural rationalist.

Vaudoyer's Conservatoire des Arts et Métiers, designed and erected beginning in the 1840s, mixes the qualities of the Ecole des Beaux-Arts and the Bibliothèque Sainte-Geneviève (figures 35–42).[34] It is both a completion and a spatial articulation of a complex of historic monuments

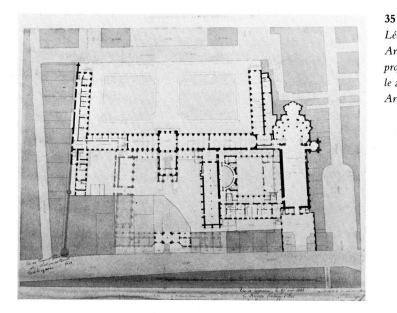

35
Léon Vaudoyer, Conservatoire des Arts et Métiers, Paris, preliminary project. Inscribed "Vu et approuvé le 27 avril 1844" by the Minister. Archives Nationales, Paris.

36
Léon Vaudoyer, Conservatoire des Arts et Métiers, preliminary project. Inscribed "Vu et approuvé le 27 avril 1844" by the Minister. Archives Nationales, Paris.

37
*Léon Vaudoyer, Conservatoire des
Arts et Métiers, Paris, 1847–58,
facade from Square Chautemps.*

38
*Léon Vaudoyer, Conservatoire des
Arts et Métiers, exterior facade on
Square Chautemps. (Photo: James
Austin)*

39
Léon Vaudoyer, Conservatoire des Arts et Métiers, monumental entrance to museum in east wing in first courtyard. (Photo: James Austin)

40
*Léon Vaudoyer, Conservatoire des
Arts et Métiers, north wing in first
courtyard.*

41
Léon Vaudoyer, Conservatoire des Arts et Métiers, details of masonry on north wing in first courtyard.

42
Léon Vaudoyer, Conservatoire des Arts et Métiers, facades along rue Saint-Martin. (Photo: James Austin)

and, in parts, the demonstration of a new, nineteenth-century style of skeletal design. It is elegant and supple but ultimately lacks the concentrated historical reference of the Ecole as well as the constructional toughness of the Bibliothèque Sainte-Geneviève. It is a professional rather than an inspired design.

This is a general characteristic of Vaudoyer's work, which might fatigue us somewhat today but which in the mid-nineteenth century made it the model for progressive professional practitioners. The work of the next two generations of progressive architects—of Charles Questel, for example, beginning in the late 1830s; of Emile Vaudremer beginning in the late 1850s; and of Richard Morris Hunt in the United States—parallels Vaudoyer's at the Conservatoire.

The institution itself was a museum founded in 1793–94 and recognized in 1819–20 and in 1839–40. It's purpose was to foster mechanical knowledge through displays of machines and technical models, through its technical library, and through demonstrations and an expanding series of public lectures. It was envisioned as a "haute école d'application des connaissances scientifiques au commerce et à l'industrie." Jacquard, Dolfus, and Schneider of Le Creusot all studied there during the Revolution.

It was established in the old monastery of Saint-Martin-des-Champs, which had been nationalized during the Revolution.[35] This comprised a large chapel (with an extraordinary Early Gothic chevet and a bald, unfinished Late Gothic nave), a cloister to its north, an exquisite High Gothic refectory (usually attributed to the thirteenth-century architect Pierre de Montreuil) across the north side of that, and finally a large U-shaped dormitory block extending northward from the transept and facing east to the narrow rue Vaucanson, which widens here as a public market square. This last block had been erected in 1742 by J.-D. Antoine (1733–1801) and had a beautiful stone staircase in a pavilion projecting westward from its center. On the back, the rue Saint-Martin, lined with private houses beyond the monastic garden, defined the site.

First A.-F. Peyre (1739–1823) and then Victor Dubois (1779–1850) held the post of architect of the Conservatoire; each presented projects for better adopting the complex to its new function and for its extension.[36] In 1838 Dubois was named architect of the Archives Nationales and resigned from his post at the Conservatoire. As a result, in a letter of June 22 of that year, Léon Vaudoyer received his first serious position, as *architecte-en-chef* of the institution, together with a request for an immediate project to reconstruct it. This he submitted to Jean Vatout, Directeur des Bâtiments Civils, as a sketch on October 21, 1838, and again as a preliminary project in February 1839. This project was analyzed by the Conseil des Bâtiments Civils at their meeting of January 30, 1840.

Vaudoyer's basic scheme appears at the outset, although the details of its articulation are sketchy and far from what, in the end, was actually executed.

Vaudoyer proposed to make a monumental composition of the abbey structures while retaining all its important historical elements: the chapel, the cloister, the refectory, and the Antoine block with its stairway. His plan was to reverse the axis of the complex and set it in a large urban context by erecting an ornamental pavilion around Antoine's stair block, which would have a monumental entrance opening onto its landing, and by sending an axis down a grand flight of stairs and across a *cour d'honneur* made from the abbey garden. This he defined on the north by a new block of classrooms below a display space for machines, which would balance the mass of the refectory on the south. On the west, Vaudoyer proposed to purchase the houses along the rue Saint-Martin and to open the *cour d'honneur* toward it with a monumental gateway on his new axis, thus making the reformulated complex address this more important thoroughfare. Indeed, the urban texture at this point was soon made to respond to and enlarge his gesture, as the opening of the Square Chautemps in 1861 continued the axis, repeated and emphasized the *cour d'honneur*, and provided a place from which to enjoy the view of the ensemble (figure 37).[37] Vaudoyer proposed to block off the eastern axis of the complex by placing a wing of laboratories between the ends of Antoine's wings. The library was to be established in the refectory, which was well suited to this function with its high ceiling, open structure, and large north windows. Display space would be in Antoine's wing and lecture amphitheatres in the cloister.

This was a fairly obvious solution, distinct from earlier projects by Dubois chiefly in the large scale of the elements and in the retention of the chapel. This latter had not originally been part of the Conservatoire property and instead belonged to the Département de la Seine, which used it as a *mairie* and headquarters of the Garde Nationale. The building itself was slated for demolition.[38] Vaudoyer's principal departure from his original assignment was a successful effort to appropriate the chapel as a historic monument, to preserve it, and to rebuild its dilapidated west facade. To this day it incongruously houses a display of automobiles, trains, and airplanes, continuing Vaudoyer's pretense that its retention was a practical necessity to the institution.

Vaudoyer's project was shuffled around in the bureaucratic labyrinth for a half decade. When finally it was funded, the architect wrote Fortoul, "The Chambre des Députés has proclaimed me architect . . . at 43 years old . . . I thus may finally accomplish something."[39] In the report of January 30, 1840, the Conseil des Bâtiments Civils had made some minor suggestions (notably the addition of a covered gallery on the inner, east

side of the west wing of the *cour d'honneur*), and on April 27 Vaudoyer
submitted his revisions. After some glacial progress—principally the preparation of a bill to fund the project, ready in March 1842, but never submitted—the Conseil des Bâtiments Civils asked to re-examine the project.
It approved it again on December 5, 1842, but objected to Vaudoyer's use
of overlays to show modifications and requested a new set of drawings,
which he provided on January 19, 1843 (figures 35, 36).[40] These were
stamped with the Conseil's approval on that same day and with the
Ministre des Travaux Public's approbation in April 1844. The bill to fund
the project was then definitively prepared and passed.

Vaudoyer was told to begin work at once. ("1845" is inscribed on the
eastern attic of the entrance arch.) He began in the cloister, which was
rebuilt to accommodate two amphitheatres and several chemistry laboratories. Meanwhile, he perfected his designs for the blocks around the *cour
d'honneur,* which appear in their final form in a set of drawings bearing the
watermark 1847.[41] Construction began that year. In 1858 the courtyard in
front of the chapel facade was begun, together with the two blocks along
the rue Saint-Martin (figures 38, 40).

Vaudoyer faced three basic design problems as he refined his project
during the 1840s. First, he had to articulate his new axis of approach from
the entrance on the rue Saint-Martin to the pavilion added on to Antoine's
stair block. Second, he had to erect the new classroom and display space,
balancing the Gothic refectory but remaining distinct and not distracting
from the accent points of the main axis. Third, he had to ornament the
wall of the low wing along the rue Saint-Martin as a frontispiece and *jeu
d'esprit.*

Vaudoyer's solution to the first problem, the articulation of the axis, is
excellent in the abstract. The pace and tableaux work perfectly, and the
emphases fall where they should. But it remains disappointing in many
details, as if such a traditional, Baroque problem was not yet sympathetic
to the *pensionnaire's* vocabulary. In the project of 1842 (figure 36) the pavilion around Antoine's stairway is focused at its center by two three-quarter
columns topping the high stair from the court. These support a pedi-
mented attic with a clock and frame a deep archway in which is set the
principal doorway. This arrangement is precisely repeated in Vaudoyer's
contemporaneous proposal for the gate on the rue Saint-Martin. When
imagined in perspective, the gate would have anticipated the pavilion, but
on a smaller scale and with its angular pediment enframed by and contrasting with the round pediment of the pavilion attic. That in turn would link
visually with the rounded roof of the whole stair block, and the little belfry would be the last, topmost term in this compressed composition of
planes in space (figure 37).

It is interesting to watch how between 1842 and 1847 Vaudoyer refined

his detailing and the cutting of the stone to enrich and articulate this pro-
gression of tableaux. His most brilliant refinement (and the one most often
noted and praised) was the replacement of the pilasters at the rue Saint-
Martin gate with caryatids thrust high up at the springing of the arch
(figure 38). They impart a light but clear emphasis here, raise the viewer's
eyes toward the composition of pediments, and, most importantly, replace
the banal, conventional vocabulary of the 1842 project with freer sculptural speech. These caryatids, carved by the sculptor Elias Robert, are actually engaged in the masonry of the wall and seem to push actively
upward, like the voussoirs that spring at their feet. "Caryatids of great
character," said Labrouste's son Léon, they are remarkable because they
"form part of the masonry of the structure."[42] They are an expression of
the construction as well as accents in light and shade, like similar passages
in the carving of the Bibliothèque Sainte-Geneviève, but more richly
sculptural. The historian and critic Charles Blanc later reminisced that
watching the carving of these figures while a young man provided his first
insight into architecture. He recalled:

*One day when I was passing by in the street while a young sculptor, M. Elias
Robert, was working on these figures, I remarked with surprise that, far from
dissimulating the joints, he tried to make evident the superposition of the courses so
that the statue, traversed by the great horizontals of the masonry work, seemed not
an added ornament provided by sculpture to take the place of a column, but an
evolution of the stonework itself, an energetic projection of the construction and,
one might say, a partuition of the building. Not knowing anything more about
architecture than what everyone knows or thinks he knows, that is, knowing nothing, I was struck as by a lightning bolt and in my profound naïveté thought I had
discovered, all by myself, one of the great principles of architecture, namely that
decoration must be engendered by construction.*[43]

This, Blanc goes on to explain, Robert told him was Vaudoyer's precise
intention.

The free play of accents inherent in sculpture is also applied by Vaudoyer to the carving of the moldings surrounding the caryatids—the powerful curve of the plinth, the profile of the brackets holding the figures, the
return of the egg and dart of the pediment cornice on the two end blocks
of the arch entablature. It is thus with disappointment that, upon entering
the gate, one is forced to recognize that the culminating accent, the pavilion facade, is ineffectually sculpted (figure 39). The attic is inarticulate, the
pilasters (replacing the columns of the 1842 project) weak, and the composition of panels, windows, and busts on the side bays ill-proportioned
and overemphasized. The moldings in particular have gotten out of

hand with a multiplicity of deep, round surfaces of the sort that the *pensionnaires* had usually been so careful (and so wise) to avoid. This failure is perhaps understandable because the Baroque vocabulary that Vaudoyer was forced to echo in order to harmonize with Antoine's work was precisely that which he found least sympathetic. Indeed, he was here trying to sidestep the problem by using the details of the French Early Renaissance, Lescot's Louvre, the Hôtel Lamoignon, and the engravings of the Du Cerceaus.

The weakness of the pavilion facade is redeemed by the exquisite treatment Vaudoyer devised for his second basic design, the classroom and machine display block (figure 40). Here is one of the finest Romantic rationalist walls in Paris. It is a long, rectangular prismatic background building like the Bibliothèque Sainte-Geneviève with its skeleton similarly emerging from its surfaces and its ornament sinking into them. Yet spatially Vaudoyer's solution is entirely different, as the lower floor is necessarily higher than Labrouste's and its surface is broken by larger windows. As a result, Vaudoyer's skeleton must emerge from the facade plane as nine buttresses (aligned to pick up the nine similar projections on the Gothic refectory across the *cour d'honneur*). He uses the round arches of the nineteenth century, which leap completely between the buttresses of the upper story and embrace spurs of curtain wall at either side of the tall vertical windows in the medieval style (a lighter structure and more vigorous combination of shapes than the simple arched bays proposed in his 1842 project, figure 36). The buttresses are similarly carried forward in time by the suggestion of Tuscan pilasters on their upper stages. Vaudoyer's adjustment of chiaroscuro in the moldings is perfect (figure 41). At points of secondary emphasis he takes the motif of the beveled moldings on the refectory, repeats these to build by transitional planes around the openings, and brilliantly sharpens their emphasis with narrow grooves, Greek in origin, at their meeting with the facade plane. On the buttress tops and the wall base he uses broader, curved moldings which are kept shallow, strong, and springy in their profile.

Along the rue Saint-Martin, to solve the third of his basic design problems, Vaudoyer carved the surface of the wing closing the *cour d'honneur* in a part-Pompeiian, part-Early Renaissance manner (figure 42). His objective was clearly to render this plane distinct from those of the blocks rising behind it in the tableau presented to the Square Chautemps. His technique was to emphasize the coursing of the masonry construction and to sink a series of pilasters and window frames into that pattern. This passage is characteristic of Vaudoyer's entire design in that, for all its structural honesty, it is closer to its historical sources and more restrained in its decorative fantasy than Labrouste's or even Duban's productions. It remains precise, logical, judicious, and very professional.

The solutions Vaudoyer offered to these three design problems were all worked out in the context of one general objective: preserving and articulating the specific architectural history manifested in these buildings, gathered over a period of seven centuries at this spot in Paris. He has neither imposed a single historical style nor restricted himself to a consistent "modern" style (although he has modified the Gothic and the Baroque in his additions and framed the whole, when seen from the Chautemps, behind a Néo-Grec frontispiece). This is a more judicious and more profound understanding of historicism than that of, for instance, the imposed fantasy in Alavoine's *flèche* at Rouen (1823–77) and was to become the model of professional architecture in Paris.

The principal example in Paris during the 1830s and 1840s of a historic building extended in its original style was the Hôtel de Ville (figure 43). This project was richly funded with fifteen million francs in 1835 and executed between 1837 and 1849 by E.-H. Godde (1781–1869), aided by J.-B. Lesueur (1794–1883), who was "very erudite in the monuments of the Renaissance."[44] They took the system of the building's Renaissance facade, simplified it and stretched it north and south to more than twice its original length, then carried it around the remaining three sides of what became a very large rectangle enclosing three internal courtyards.[45] Fortoul, near the beginning of *De l'Art en Allemagne,* derides Godde and Lesueur because they "applied to the works of the Middle Ages a routine that they could not justify by any example from the best period of antiquity."[46] What he would have preferred was the mixing of styles to bring out the history of the building. He felt von Klenze had achieved this admirably in the Munich Residenz. "My God! What would these people [Godde and Lesueur] say of the palace of the King of Bavaria? . . . The palace of King Ludwig is like a book the four parts of which, created in four different centuries, embrace the history of the art and of the world."[47] It was the enjoyment of this mixing of styles that attracted him to Munich (the subject of most of the first volume of his book), with its recent monuments in contrasting historical styles.

In no other country is it possible to find the variety of systems and the luxury of reminiscences that one finds in the buildings of the capital of Bavaria. . . .

Animated by the political and religious passions of this country, [Munich's architecture] has succeeded in realizing on its surface a living and almost complete history of architecture.[48]

This he contrasts to the situation in France:

In France one generally agrees that art consists primarily in invention; but this great principle, which often encourages ignorance, does not preserve it from either

43
E.-H. Godde and J.-B. Lesueur,
Extended Hôtel de Ville, Paris,
1837–46. (Photo: L. L. Roger-Viollet)

monotony or bad taste. In Bavaria one practices art as if one accepted that it resided above all in memory; but in displaying more knowledge than genius, the architects of this country provide a fascinating field for study and criticism and perhaps prepare for a new epoch when, following the usual course of events, the transfigured forms of previous ages will be blended, with distinctions due to the particular character of each people.[49]

This generation experienced a real excitement in seeing a story told in architecture. It was surely to this that Fortoul referred when he wrote of Duban's Ecole, "I have seen the public struck by a mysterious passion for this building, astonished to find so much pleasure in an art that bored them for so long and so much imagination in what appeared to them, until now, just the science of raising stones upon one another."[50] Yet at the Ecole and the Conservatoire des Arts et Métiers — in Duban's main facade of the Palais des Etudes and in Vaudoyer's entrance and wings on the rue Saint-Martin — and even more emphatically in later buildings by the *pensionnaires,* we find an important passage in the "new style" of the nineteenth century amid the carefully resuscitated ensemble of early forms. This pops out of the composition and dates it. As Duban declared to the Conseil des Bâtiments Civils in 1833, "The monument erected by the nineteenth century should not be denied the means which the contemporary state of the art provides to characterize our epoch."[51] These passages become progressively refined and striking during the Second Empire in Duc's Palais de Justice (figure 64) and Labrouste's Bibliothèque Nationale (figure 84). But one must not see them in isolation and analyze them by themselves. They are merely markers attached to broader and more subtle historical compositions; they are meant to bring the history of these buildings up to date but not to deflect attention from that history. The problem for the *pensionnaires* was always the whole, not the individual decorative parts.

Four

THE ORGANIZATION
OF THE ARCHITECTURAL PROFESSION

We have repeatedly mentioned the broadness and abstraction of the Romantic *pensionnaires'* ideas, and have seen these worked out freely in their *envois* and in their first buildings. There have been some intrusions on their independence—especially in the case of the buildings of the Ecole des Beaux-Arts—but clients or patrons have not been prominent in our history. Why? Who were these men working for and what relationships did they maintain with them? This is a complex and important matter because it brings us to one of the most basic aspects of nineteenth-century French architecture: the fact that it was essentially government building and, as such, part of the distinctive, pervasive, but in many ways anonymous bureaucracy.[1]

The four architects we have concentrated upon were all government architects. That is to say, they had been trained at the Ecole des Beaux-Arts and the French Academy in Rome at government expense and were then employed in the construction of government buildings. Yet the first thing that is striking about their careers is how very little they produced. Vaudoyer and Labrouste both completed two major works during their careers (the Conservatoire des Arts et Métiers and Marseilles Cathedral; the Bibliothèques Sainte-Geneviève and Nationale); Duc, one, the Palais de Justice; Duban, none beyond the extension of Debret's partially complete Ecole des Beaux-Arts.[2] Even this enumeration is optimistic: only two of these buildings, Marseilles Cathedral and the Bibliothèque Sainte-Geneviève, were completely new constructions on unencumbered sites. This is an amazing lack of productivity compared to the eight to ten major public buildings built by each of their German counterparts, Leo von Klenze, Karl Friedrich von Schinkel, and Gottfried Semper, or the approximately 750 structures of all sorts and sizes produced by Sir Gilbert Scott in England. It is amazing too when one realizes that Duban and his friends each received some five years of architectural training at the Ecole and five more as *pensionnaires* in Rome. What was the government paying for? What were these architects preparing themselves to do?

The answers to these questions were by no means clear during the Restoration, and this state of affairs troubled both the government and the *pensionnaires*. Through the 1820s there were a small number of architects favored with most building projects because of royal or noble protection, especially the partnership of Charles Percier and Pierre Fontaine, who were architects to both the King and the Duc d'Orléans and who worked at the Louvre and Tuileries, the Palais Royale, and at Neuilly.[3] Since they often owed their positions to personal influence, thoroughness of training—that is, having been a *pensionnaire* in Rome—was not always a major consideration. Grand Prix winners were often left with little work while, for example, a non-*pensionnaire* like L.-T.-J. Visconti (1791–1853) enjoyed an extensive public and private practice, although he employed apparently bright young Ecole products to actually design his works.[4] In 1827, returning to Rome from Florence, Vaudoyer, Duc, and Duban sat late at Ronciglione near Lake Vico, the last coach stop before Rome, discussing just what would become of them. "Duc glimpsed magnificent horizons," Charles Blanc later described the conversation, "pictured the renovation of architecture, and abandoned himself to illusions of a Golden Age. A man of critical and practical sense, a relaxed and sharp-witted Gaul, so as not to be of the same opinion as his friend Duc, Vaudoyer laughed at him and treated his aspirations as chimerical. He foresaw that after the poetry of dreams would succeed the prose of reality and that soon enough it would be necessary to descend from the Portico of Octavius to the partywall."[5] "When I think of the fate that awaits me in Paris," Vaudoyer wrote his father on December 9, 1828, "I am overcome by moments of discouragement. It seems as if it will be all the same, we learn here that our predecessors are without positions, that that of Labrouste was given to a stenographer in the administration. . . . The Institut acknowledges the zeal of the architects, but where is our recompense?"[6] The founding document of the Société Centrale des Architectes of 1840 specifically cites the disadvantage of winning the Grand Prix, which led to losing connections and missing opportunities.[7]

Upon the establishment of the middle-class government of 1830, a thorough reorganization of the architectural service was put through by decree of July 22, 1832. The old system obviously had been inefficient in utilizing the talents of government-trained architects. Of at least as great importance, however, was a positive inclination to support the young Romantic architects on the part of several of the new government officials: Vitet and Mérimée, of course, but also Adolphe Thiers, who had been an early supporter of Romanticism in his Salon of 1824 and who actually promulgated the 1832 reform.[8] That decree reinforced the division of labor and the hierarchy of posts in the administration of the Bâtiments Civils as well as, perhaps most importantly, restricting each architect in government service to a single project and to employment in a single branch of government service.[9] Places as *auditeurs* were reserved on the Conseil des Bâtiments Civils for former *pensionnaires*. This rigorous antitrust act was later loosened, but the tradition of monopoly had been broken. The immediate result in 1832 was the creation of a number of posts for the younger ex-*pensionnaires*. For instance, Debret as a consequence had to resign as architect of the Ecole des Beaux-Arts since he was also architect for the restoration of the Basilica of Saint-Denis, giving Duban the chance to make the first statement of French Romantic architecture.

Nonetheless, the architects themselves felt the government's actions insufficient. On June 9, 1840, a commission was created by the architects of Paris to report on how the profession might be better organized.[10] Most of its nine members were young (Blouet, Emile Gilbert, Albert Lenoir, A.-M. Garnaud), but its president was Huyot (who died before its work was complete) and the secretary Charles-Pierre Gourlier (1786–1857), Inspecteur Général du Conseil des Bâtiments Civils and that body's defender and spokesman.[11] The lengthy and carefully researched report they submitted to a second meeting of the architects of Paris on November 15, 1840, painted a dismal picture of the profession, especially in comparison to that of the engineer. They objected to the fact that training at the Ecole des Beaux-Arts failed to lead directly to employment in the government architectural service, not only because it left trained designers without work and professional security, but also because it permitted anyone wishing to call himself an architect to function as such. "As soon as they leave school," Gourlier wrote for the commission,

engineers are admitted into the lower grades [of the administration] where they acquire at the same time the practical experience that they lack and the right to [promotion to] the higher grades and to an honorable retirement pension. The actual pecuniary advantages of this system are not great; but, in general, the position of engineers is honorable and secure. . . . Members of a well-run administration, they enjoy the public respect that is attached to it as well as what they might merit individually.[12]

In contrast, the architects had to find a place in the government service as best they could with no assurance of regular promotion, and even when successful, they might remain underemployed while colleagues were buried in commissions. Furthermore, they could expect little employment from the private sector where contractors or young students were preferred.

The commission proposed to ameliorate the situation by founding a professional Société des Architectes with strict rules of admission. The membership would constitute a slate of qualified professionals, like doctors, lawyers, and engineers. The society would also become a forum for the study of matters of professional technique. The architects at the November 15 meeting voted to found this society and to accept the commission's definition of its first members: the architect members of the Académie des Beaux-Arts; the members of the Conseil des Bâtiments Civils; the architect members of the jury of the Ecole des Beaux-Arts; the *architectes-en-chefs* and the *adjoints* of government buildings; the architect winners of the Premier and Second Grand Prix de Rome and the Premier and Second Prix Départemental. These (who turned out to number 135) would then choose further members, up to the number of 500, after careful scrutiny. During the first few years the selection of members was its principal activity.

On January 24, 1841, a *séance d'ouverture* was held at the Société d'Encouragement, 42 rue du Bac, under the presidency of L.-P. Baltard. Albert Lenoir and Constant-Dufeux served as *secrétaires provisoires*. Of the 135 architects eligible for membership, 80 had agreed to join and 59 were present. Labrouste, Duc, and Léon Vaudoyer were among these; Duban joined in 1843. They nominated a committee to write a constitution,[13] which was accepted by the membership at a meeting on May 9, 1843, and authorized by the Ministre des Travaux Publics on May 27. The first regular meeting of what was now the Société Centrale des Architectes took place on June 27, 1843.

The founding of this society was contemporaneous with that of the Royal Institute of British Architects (1836) and with the first (abortive) founding of the American Institute of Architects.[14] Its objectives were essentially the same as theirs, but it always envisioned a close relation with the government bureaucracy and a nervous competition with the engineers. One of the first actions of the Société Centrale was to press the Ministre des Travaux Publics to assign the work regulated by the *Loi compréhensive des Chemins de Fer* of 1844 to both engineers and architects—the former supervising trackage, fills and cuts, bridges and tunnels, the latter stations, shelters, administrative buildings, warehouses, and workshops.[15] The suggestion came from Hittorff, and a delegation consisting of him and Cendrier, Constant-Dufeux, Albert Lenoir, Blouet, Gilbert, Alfred Armand, Pellechet, Gourlier, and Grillon met with the Minister. They were successful; and not only did the work made available immediately profit some of the founders of the Société, but it was also of great importance to their students, especially those of Labrouste. In 1847 three of the five *architectes-dessinateurs* employed by the Paris–Lyon railroad were recent students of his, while Labrouste's friend Cendrier was the *architecte-en-chef*.[16] Armand, like Cendrier, devoted his career to railroad station design (he also did a house for the railroad financier Emile Péreire). Hittorff, the leader of the delegation to the Minister, ended his career with the rebuilding of the Gare du Nord in 1861–64.

Napoleon I, reorganizing the government bureaucracy after the Revolution, had preferred engineers graduated from the newly founded Ecole Polytechnique for most building projects but retained Percier and Fontaine and a few other architects for palatial and decorative work.[17] The architectural profession had been seriously threatened in the early nineteenth century by the evolution of bureaucracy and industry, but during the 1830s and 1840s it carved out a place for itself, partly through its own efforts, partly through the sympathy of government officials in the age of the literary man and the dandy, officials like Vitet, Mérimée, and Thiers. A price was exacted, however, because the architect ceased to be a decorator and became instead a bureaucrat. Bureaucracy, if practiced with freshness, knowledge, and conviction, could accomplish great things, as it did in the mid-nineteenth century in the hands of Mérimée and Labrouste. But it could also become bloated and obfuscating, as it did in France after 1870.

Let us be more specific about the span, scale, and nature of the responsibilities of a French government architect between 1830 and 1870. A young architect beginning his career had at once to choose between private practice and public work, assuming that his ambition was to be more than a *dessinateur*.[18] If he chose the former course—and about fifty percent of the thousand architects in Paris around 1850 did so[19]—he had a second choice to make between being the salaried functionary of a contractor or a large corporation (as Cendrier was, for example, for the Paris–Lyon railroad), or a free agent, principally employed in designing houses and furnishings for the rich (as were Aimé Chenevard and most of the *style troubadour* designers.[20] Although today it is the government architects that we chiefly remember, in the nineteenth century it was these private decorator-architects that were judged the most impressive purveyors of Parisian taste. It was they whom visiting maecenases employed to work back home, as, for example, the Prince von Pless and barons Albert and Ferdinand Rothschild hired H.-A.-G.-W. Destailleur to build their palaces at Berlin, Vienna, and Waddeston, respectively. John Bowes hired J.-A.-F.-A. Pellechet to build his palatial museum-mansion in Barnard Castle, County Durham (1869–75), following the example set in 1848–51 when Henry Thomas Hope had P.-C. Dusillon erect his Piccadilly town house in collaboration with T. L. Donaldson. In this the foreigners were following the example of their Parisian contemporaries.

Destailleur (1822–93) was characteristic of the private architect of the first rank. He was the son of the successful Empire and Restoration architect F.-H. Destailleur (1787–1852), who had been a student of Percier, designer of the Ministry of Finance on the rue de Rivoli, and architect to several of the *grandes familles* of France, including the ducs d'Orléans, de la Trémoille, and d'Harcourt, the Comte d'Haussonville, the Vicomtesse de

Noailles, and the marquises de la Guiche and de Vogüé.[21] The son studied with Percier's most respectful student, Achille Leclère, then joined his father's practice. He carried on after the latter's death in 1852, erecting the foreign mansions already cited, rebuilding the Hôtel Pourtalès (erected originally by Duban in 1835–39), restoring the château at Vaux-le-Vicomte in 1877 (for the de Vogüé), and building Napoleon III's funerary chapel at Farnborough. He assembled an extraordinary collection of prints and drawings relating to architectural decoration, which he sold to the Berlin Kunstgewerbemuseum in 1879, and then assembled another, which was purchased by the Cabinet des Estampes of the Bibliothèque Nationale in 1890. His son, Walter-André Destailleur (1867–1940), carried on the practice in turn, building the Hôtel Wildenstein on the rue de la Boëtie (1900–3) and restoring the Hôtel Crillon. Yet for all the impact this family had upon European taste between 1810 and 1930, its members include no *logistes* in the competition for the Grand Prix de Rome, no academicians, no members of the Conseil des Bâtiments Civils. They were essentially private architects, even more so than such an English contemporary as Charles Barry, who, although he spent only a small part of his time on public work, nevertheless carried out major projects, most notably the Houses of Parliament.

Perhaps the most influential family of private architects were the Rohault de Fleurys, even though they did no work outside France and were remarkable for the justness and reticence of their style.[22] Here there was a military connection: the most eminent of the line, Charles Rohault de Fleury (1801–75) was nephew of Baron Hubert Rohault de Fleury, who was a graduate of the Ecole Polytechnique and had been an officer in the Spanish campaigns of both Napoleon and Charles X, suppressor of the Lyon uprising of April 1834, engineer in charge of the siege of Constantine, Algeria, in 1837, and a Senator. That connection was confirmed by Charles's own training at the Ecole Polytechnique in the footsteps of his father, Hubert Rohault de Fleury (1787–1846), who had become an architect in the government, won the Grand Prix de Rome in 1802, and served on the Conseil des Bâtiments Civils. After training at the Ecole Polytechnique, Charles did start in government service as architect of the Jardin des Plantes, erecting the Musée de l'Histoire Naturelle (1833–37) and the Serres there, but he did not have his father's academic or administrative acumen. He occupied himself with building discrete houses for the rich; for example, the Duc de Gramont's on the rue de Chaillot and the Hôtel Péreire on the rue du Faubourg Saint-Honoré. His son, Georges (1835–1905), carried on the practice and also published an important series of books on late medieval architecture in Italy, including *Les Edifices de Pise* (1862), *La Toscane au moyen age* (2 volumes, 1870–73), and *Le Latran* (1877). Like the Destailleurs, the Rohault de Fleurys were better known to the general public than such important government architects as Labrouste or Blouet. Nor is there any indication from their collecting and scholarship that there was the slightest financial disadvantage in pursuing a private career of the first class. Indeed, in 1838 Labrouste had written in his letter of candidacy for the chair of architecture at the Ecole Polytechnique, "I have not engaged in private construction enterprises, which is the only way of making a fortune available to architects."[23]

If a young man chose to become a government architect, he had to select just what branch of the administration to enter, a choice most often made by chance or personal connection. The broadest path was that of the administration of the Bâtiments Civils, the successor to the Surintendance des Bâtiments du Roi first established in 1664.[24] This was responsible for the major government structures in Paris—the Chambre des Députés, the Arc de Triomphe, the Ecole des Beaux-Arts, the Bibliothèque Sainte-Geneviève, the Conservatoire des Arts et Métiers. There were, however, other parallel services in the central government, like the Administration des Hôpitaux et Prisons, for which Blouet and Gilbert worked most successfully and happily all their careers. There was also the service of the Palais Royaux and, starting in the Second Empire, the separate service of the Ministère de l'Instruction Publique et des Cultes. Outside the central government one could be employed as diocesan architect or departmental architect in the provinces. In the case of the Département de la Seine in Paris, this became a very large and complex architectural service, divided into six sections by building type, each accorded an *architecte-en-chef* with a staff.[25] Victor Baltard, his brother-in-law Paul-Eugène Lequeux, and his uncle A.-M.-F. Jay all worked together in this service, apparently established here by their relative Edouard Gatteaux, modeler and city councilor.[26]

In the government architectural service, a clear hieratic division of responsibility was evolved for efficiency and to create a profession where ability and experience could replace the older system of preferment. The model was the Bâtiments Civils, established in 1793–95 and reorganized repeatedly thereafter, especially by Thiers in his ministerial decree of July 22, 1832.[27] By this document the service was divided into a *service ordinaire*, for the maintenance of structures already erected, and a *service extraordinaire*, for the construction of new buildings. The former was divided into eight *arrondissements* or regions with an *architecte-en-chef* in charge of each, authorized to employ an *architecte-inspecteur*, a *vérificateur*, and a *garçon de bureau*. In the latter, each building under construction had an *architecte-en-chef*, an *architecte-inspecteur*, a *vérificateur*, a *sous-inspecteur* or *conducteur*, and a *garçon de bureau*. Sometimes the subordinate posts were multiple. The *architecte-en-chef* provided the drawings to be executed, signed all documents, and provided weekly, monthly, and yearly reports on the progress of the work. The *inspecteur* was the executant. He was obliged to be on the site all day to supervise the execution of the architect's drawings and to check the quality of materials. The *sous-inspecteur* was the scribe and draftsman, handling correspondence in particular (which, of course, was all handwritten). The *vérificateur* checked the accounts.

Controlling the whole administration of the Bâtiments Civils was the Conseil des Bâtiments Civils, presided over by a bureaucrat, the Directeur des Bâtiments Civils, and consisting of four Inspecteurs Généraux des Bâtiments Civils, a Président, and a variable number of *membres honoraires* and *flottants* or *auditeurs* to help with the analysis of projects. The *inspecteurs généraux* approved all projects before passing them on to the Minister and also made periodic visits to each building site.

A real career was thus possible within this administration. One might start as a *sous-inspecteur* while still at the Ecole des Beaux-Arts at a salary of 1200 to 1500 francs a year (as Labrouste did under Godde at Saint-Pierre-du-Gros-Caillou before he won the Grand Prix), then become an *inspecteur* at a salary of 1500–1800 (as Labrouste did under Duban at the Ecole des Beaux-Arts upon his return from Rome), then be named *architecte-en-chef* of an existing building for 1000 francs a year plus three percent of any work executed (as Labrouste was at the Pont de la Concorde in 1836), then *architecte-en-chef* of a new building at the same rate of pay (as Labrouste was of the Bibliothèque Sainte-Geneviève in 1838), and finally perhaps be named Inspecteur Général at 6000 francs a year (as Duban was in 1857).

The records of the construction of the New Louvre are particularly complete and permit a glimpse of how this system worked in detail.[28] This was one of the largest projects of the Second Empire and was peculiar in being administered directly by the Ministère de la Maison de l'Empereur. For this very reason it shows how a career might be spun out in one corner of the system. First, these documents make clear how many architects might be employed on a project. At the beginning of construction in June 1852, there were twenty-four designers and two *garçons de bureau*; in December 1857, forty-three designers and three *garçons de bureau*; in January 1862, twenty-three designers and two *garçons de bureau*. Second, we see how many grades of promotion there might actually be. At the height of the work in December 1857, there was the *architecte-en-chef* (Lefuel, also Architecte de l'Empereur, paid 40,000 francs per annum), two *inspecteurs principaux* (Jules Thierry and Paul Piot, 5000 francs per annum), one *inspecteur de la première classe* (5000 francs per annum), five *inspecteurs de la seconde classe* (3500 to 4500 francs per annum), eleven *inspecteurs de la troisième classe* (2600 to 3000 francs per annum), eighteen *inspecteurs de la quatrième classe* (2200 francs per annum), and ten *agents de la première classe* (1800 francs per annum). In other years there were *inspecteurs de la cinquième classe* (2000 francs per annum—Richard Morris Hunt was one of these in 1854), *agents de la seconde classe*, and *dessinateurs* employed at a daily rate. Third, one sees how this mass of professional talent was marshaled. In 1859 there was both an office of the *architecte-en-chef*, Lefuel, with a staff of three architects and two *garçons de bureau* as well as an office of the *inspecteur principal*, Piot, with two *gardes* (*garde magasin* and *garde de chantier*). The rest of the *agence* was divided into six divisions, each for a particular portion of the structure and each with an *inspecteur* in charge. The work on the Ministère d'Etat et de la Maison de l'Empereur was overseen by one Bettoise, *inspecteur de la seconde classe*, with five designers under him; the Grands Appartements formed another division, headed by Chomet (*inspecteur de la troisième classe*); the "cour et descentes à couvertes" was another, headed by Paul-Ernest Letrosne (*inspecteur de la quatrième classe*); and the "installation provisoire de la 2ème division" was headed by Jules Frédéric Gunther (*inspecteur de la cinquième classe*). The public rooms, the stables, the library, the Musée Sauvageot, and the barracks of the Gendarmerie Nationale formed other divisions.

Another thing evident in this glimpse into a cell of the governmental bureaucracy is that a career could be pursued within the *agence* of a major building. Because a structure had to be maintained after it was erected, the *agence* itself was deathless—in the case of the Louvre it exists to this day in the Pavillon Mollien with a staff of a half-dozen. In Lefuel's time, although construction was compressed into the five years 1852–57, completion of the interior and the decoration went on until 1870, after which it was partially burned in the Commune and repairs began. Thus in the pay records one can watch men slowly climb the ladder. Jean-François Verel (1814–85), for instance, started with Visconti in June 1852 as *inspecteur de la cinquième classe*; in April 1893 he became *inspecteur de la quatrième classe*; in June of that year *inspecteur de la seconde classe* in charge of the fourth division; in February 1854 temporarily *inspecteur de la première classe*; then finally, in March 1858, he became one of the four *inspecteurs principaux*. He remained in that post until 1870. There were clearly "inside" men and "outside" men in the *agence*. Verel was one of the former, as were about two-thirds of the staff of June 1852, who were still in place in December 1857, although promoted. Mixed with these were bright young men from the Ecole who stayed a shorter period, rose swiftly, and went on to careers as *architectes-en-chefs* in their own right. Among these were Alfonse Girard (in the *agence* from 1854 to 1862) and Alphonse-Nicolas Crépinet (in the *agence* from 1852 to 1860),[29] the two men Richard Morris Hunt looked up when he visited Paris in 1860–61 and 1867.[30]

The system of the Bâtiments Civils was slowly extended to the other branches of the government and was even imitated in the larger departmental administrations and the railroads. In 1837 the Commission des Monuments Historiques was created with a network of architects and

inspectors under its supervision.[31] Many respected architects of the
nineteenth century worked almost exclusively in this administration:
Viollet-le-Duc, of course, and his friends M.-A.-G. Ouradou, Léon
Ohnet, and Emile Boeswillwald, as well as Labrouste's friend Léon Danjoy. Eleven years later a similar administration was projected for the
Edifices Diocésains within the Ministère de l'Instruction Publique et des
Cultes. While previously the *architectes diocésains* had been named by the
prefects and had been answerable only to them and the Bishop, now they
were to be named by the Minister and their projects were to be analyzed
by a board in Paris like the Conseil des Bâtiments Civils.[32] Three *inspecteurs généraux* were to be named who would also make annual tours of
inspection. The older *architectes diocésains*, whose modest talents (not to say
near incompetence) are obvious in the designs preserved today in the administration's archives, were to be replaced by well-informed, well-
trained Parisians. It is enlightening to read the original rationale for this
proposal stated in the *procès verbal* of September 6, 1848, of the Commission de Répartition des Fonds et des Subventions pour les Travaux des
Edifices Diocésains (which at the time included Labrouste, Vaudoyer, Fortoul, Viollet-le-Duc, and Mérimée among its seven members):

*The examination of this project [Catoire's for a seminary at Rennes] leads the
commission to ask itself whether, in the case of a department that does not contain
an architect capable of composing a project for a large building, should not young
architects of good talent at Paris be commissioned, who would also direct the construction. Were this system adopted, it would be indispensable that the architects be
named by the Minister: because the inferiority of departmental architects is especially due to their precarious position, revocable by the Prefects, there are few men
who would willingly accept such a situation. It is thus necessary to give to whom-
ever the administration employs all liberty of action by making them answer directly and absolutely to the central administration. Their number might be twenty:
France could be divided into an equal number of circumscriptions arranged according
to the importance of the dioceses.*[33]

A subcommittee was appointed to formulate this proposal. The result was
implemented in stages over the next five years until, beginning in 1852, all
architectes diocésains were appointed directly by the Minister and their work
was overseen by a Comité des Inspecteurs Généraux des Edifices Diocésains, replacing the Commission de Répartition. Slowly the provincial architects were retired and replaced by Parisians—J.-B.-L. Catoire by Paul
Abadie at Périgueux (1850); Auguste Lejeune at Fréjus, Montpellier, and
Aix by H.-A. Revoil (1852); Vincent Barral at Marseilles by Vaudoyer

(1852); d'Anglais at Rennes by Labrouste (1854); Clouet at Orléans by Boeswillwald (1856). Indeed, the centralization could get a little high-handed. In 1854 H.-J. Espérandieu was appointed architect of Notre-Dame-de-la-Garde in Marseilles on Vaudoyer's recommendation (Espérandieu had been his student and *inspecteur* at the cathedral), but was discovered by the local church authorities to be a Protestant. While having to accept the appointment, they wrote several sharp letters to Paris suggesting that one could not always take for granted the spiritual suitability of the Minister's appointments nor assume his sensitivity to local feeling.[34]

Several questions remain. What was the exact nature of these various activities and how much time and effort did they require? What were the architects' obligations and, under these circumstances, how could they do good work? Let me approach these questions by sketching the responsibilities of the four Romantic *pensionnaires* in three representative years, 1838, 1845, and 1858.

In 1838 they were all in the first decade of professional practice and all novices in the administration of the Bâtiments Civils. What legally occupied the time of Labrouste and Vaudoyer is quite clear: they were *inspecteurs* in that service, Labrouste at Duban's Ecole des Beaux-Arts and Vaudoyer at Lacornée's "Palais d'Orsay," and by the decree of 1832 were present on those sites during working hours—twelve hours a day, six days a week. Considering this fact, it is extraordinary that both were then conducting ateliers (each located very near their building sites, however[35]) that required daily visits and were also holding other minor posts, both public and private. Vaudoyer served as *suppléant* to his father in the post of Secrétaire-Archiviste of the Ecole des Beaux-Arts and actually performed most of the elder Vaudoyer's duties between 1838 and his death in 1845, which consisted, in the former year, of attending sixteen meetings of two to four hours duration each.[36] Labrouste in 1838 was architect of two dormant projects: the Dépôt des Marbres (a warehouse) and the Pont de la Concorde (the latter in partnership with his brother Théodore). He produced two exquisitely drawn projects for monumental bronze lamps on the bridge dated January 30 and February 15, 1838.[37] Though Vaudoyer and Labrouste obviously did not spend all their time on their building sites when *inspecteurs*, they were not extensively engaged elsewhere. (From 1833 Questel worked under Labrouste at the Ecole as *second inspecteur*, but then he couldn't have spent all his time on the site either since in 1835–36 he won the competition to design the church of Saint-Paul at Nîmes.) It must have been frustrating at the age of thirty-five (Vaudoyer) or thirty-seven (Labrouste) to be chiefly occupied in executing other men's designs.

Labrouste and Vaudoyer escaped this grind when on June 18 and July 22, 1838, respectively, they were named *architectes-en-chef* of the Bibliothèque Sainte-Geneviève and the Conservatoire des Arts et Métiers. They thereby joined Duban and Duc in positions that required only weekly visits to the site, the signature of all important documents, and the preparation of designs. At this point in the architect's career, he passed from the workshop to the studio, from hourly and daily labor to the free schedule of the gentleman and artist. Yet this artistic work could be time-consuming in its own way. Duc engaged in absolutely no other activity during the 1830s but the design of the Colonne de Juillet, and Labrouste worked very hard indeed between June 1838 and December 1839 to produce his first project for the Bibliothèque Sainte-Geneviève.[38] Duban, however, beyond his work as *architecte-en-chef* of the Ecole des Beaux-Arts, was engaged in 1838 in the completion of a major private commission, the Hôtel Pourtalès.

By the decree of 1832, Labrouste and Vaudoyer would have received between 1800 and 2400 francs a year as *inspecteurs* in 1838, while Duc and Duban would have received between one-half and three percent of the cost of the work being executed plus 600 to 1000 francs a year and all costs incurred in preparing drawings. In 1834, when 639,142.49 francs of work was executed at the Ecole, Duban should have earned 3195 francs as his fee, but in 1838 when only a last 55,678.87 francs were spent, his earnings should have fallen to 1670 francs.[39]

In 1845 all four of the Romantic *pensionnaires* were mature architects. Duban, Labrouste, and Vaudoyer still conducted their ateliers. Each was an *architecte-en-chef* of a major public building with *inspecteurs* and *sous-inspecteurs* to help him. However, in this year only Labrouste's design, the Bibliothèque Sainte-Geneviève, was actually under construction. Vaudoyer was preparing final drawings and estimates for the Conservatoire des Arts et Métiers, and Duc was engaged in a long controversy about just how the Police Correctionnel block of the Palais de Justice should relate to the Sainte-Chapelle. Duban, upon the completion of the Ecole buildings in 1838, was not assigned a new project and was left to occupy himself with maintenance and with the conception of plans for its enlargement. In 1845 he designed and set in place some very elegant iron columns to support the sagging floors of the second story of the Palais des Etudes and drew up a project to extend the cloister block along the rue Bonaparte. This meant greatly reduced fees for Duban, but by 1845 he had developed an important private practice, including the rebuilding of the château at Dampierre for the Duc de Luynes and projects for the rebuilding of that at Chantilly for the Duc d'Aumale.[40]

Significantly, by 1845 the *pensionnaires* were engaged in a second kind of government employment, membership on commissions. Vaudoyer continued to perform his duties as Secrétaire-Archiviste Adjoint at the Ecole des Beaux-Arts, and Duban was now a member of the Commission des Monuments Historiques and a *membre honoraire* of the Conseil des Bâtiments Civils. These bodies met twenty-six and eighty-eight times, respectively, that year. Such a commitment could be time-consuming, but Duban in fact attended only twelve of the meetings of the Commission des Monuments Historiques and four of those of the Conseil.[41] Furthermore, the real work of these bodies was the writing of reports analyzing projects submitted for their approval. In 1845 all Duban did was report to the Commission des Monuments Historiques on his own work at the Sainte-Chapelle and on a belfry at Peronne, while serving as part of a commission to analyze one of Visconti's projects for the Bibliothèque Royale. On the other hand, Duban was deeply involved in the practical work of the Commission des Monuments Historiques, conducting the restoration of the Sainte-Chapelle and the château at Blois in 1845, both very complex problems in interior decoration. Blois, we know, he visited twice monthly.[42] He also spent much time away at Dampierre and Chantilly. Labrouste also worked for the Commission, beginning the restoration of the cathedral at Mantes in 1841–44, but resigned in frustration at the bad local workmanship.[43]

Duban, the oldest, was the busiest of the four in 1845. Vaudoyer, for his part, considered himself abandoned and was in despair until the Conservatoire des Arts et Métiers was actually funded. In the meantime he occupied himself with writing his articles for the *Magasin pittoresque* (two of which appeared in 1845), a study of the domestic architecture of Orléans for the Commission des Monuments Historiques, and a preliminary report on the erection of a cathedral at Marseilles. The last, which resulted in no further employment or fees until 1851 and which occupied a twenty-one-day visit there plus ninety *vacations* labor (about twenty-five working days), netted him 1025 francs, from which living expenses in Marseilles had to be deducted.[44] He was forty-two years old.

In 1858 all four of the *pensionnaires* were fully occupied, each with a major building actually under construction. The acceleration of public construction during the Second Empire was directly reflected in their experience. Duban was authorized to carry out 100,000 francs worth of work on his new quai Malaquais wing of the Ecole; Labrouste 150,000 francs worth of work at the Bibliothèque Nationale. Vaudoyer, however, was the busiest, with 749,450 francs budgeted for Marseilles Cathedral and 843,297.21 francs actually spent. As one result of this increased activity, both Duban and Labrouste had closed their ateliers.[45]

Besides major construction projects, which required a steady flow of detail and structural drawings from the architect's *agence*, the *pensionnaires'* work on committees had greatly expanded. Duban was now a member of the Académie des Beaux-Arts, attending in 1855 thirty-six of its forty-eight Saturday afternoon meetings and writing the program for the Grand Prix competition in architecture. He was also now an Inspecteur Général of the Conseil des Bâtiments Civils, of which Labrouste was a *membre flottant*. Both attended virtually all of its seventy-eight meetings in that year, and they wrote twenty-two and eighteen reports, respectively.[46] Duban, Vaudoyer, and Labrouste were now all members of the Commission des Monuments Historiques, but Duban attended only one of the six meetings the body was now reduced to holding. Vaudoyer attended five, served on a committee that visited the château at Vivier (Seine-et-Marne), and wrote the report. Most time-consuming of all was the Comité des Inspecteurs Généraux des Edifices Diocésains, consisting in 1858 of Labrouste, Vaudoyer, and Viollet-le-Duc. They did 144, 92, and 95 reports respectively. Besides attending the meetings and writing the reports, the *inspecteurs généraux* each had to undertake an annual inspection tour of a third of the dioceses. In 1858 Labrouste's assignment was Agen, Angers, Angoulême, Nantes, Orléans, Périgueux, Poitiers, Quimper, La Rochelle, Saint-Brieux, Tours, Tulle, and Vannes. He accomplished this grueling task in increments, spending August 4 to 13 on one leg, September 3 to 20 visiting Orléans, Blois, Nantes, and Périgueux, and October 6 to 17 at Rennes (where he also inspected his work on the seminary), Quimper, and Saint-Brieux.[47] He would have needed one or two more trips to finish the tour, meaning that it would have occupied about two months of his year (and left him thoroughly disrupted and worn out).

By this stage in a government architect's career, the importance of private commissions was somewhat reduced. Duban, after his frustration over the rebuilding of the Louvre, is supposed to have turned increasingly to making architectural watercolors.[48] Labrouste, however, was just now embarking on a short but vigorous spate of private building. In 1858 he completed the Hôtel Fould, which led to commissions for the Hôtel Thouret in 1860, the offices of the Paris–Lyon–Méditerannée railroad in 1862, and the Hôtel Vilgruy in 1865. Duc remained satisfied with his one great public commission, the Palais de Justice. He neither built privately (except for a house for himself at Croissy of 1875[49]), nor conducted an atelier, nor was active on commissions (except for serving from 1862 as *chef divisionnaire* in charge of schools in the architectural department of the city of Paris).

The kind of week and year a successful professional architect experienced we can see in the case of Labrouste in 1858. Winter, spring, and summer he was engaged four times a week for most of an afternoon: every Monday and Wednesday from noon to about four with the Conseil des Bâtiments Civils and every Tuesday and Saturday from three to about six with the Comité des Inspecteurs Généraux des Edifices Diocésains. He furthermore wrote and then presented an average of two reports at each meeting of the latter body and a total of eighteen during the year at the former.[50] In the fall he took four or five ten-day to two-week tours of diocesan building. In what time remained—mornings and Tuesday and Thursday afternoons—he oversaw the construction of the seminary at Rennes, completed the decoration of the Hôtel Fould, and completed the restoration of the Hôtel Mazarin, while preparing projects for the rebuilding of the Bibliothèque Nationale.

We also know precisely what Labrouste was paid because his account book survives. In the 1850s his average income was between 25,000 and 30,000 francs, being 24,203.56 in 1855, 30,401.78 in 1856, 22,696.44 in 1857, 33,008 in 1859, and 35,426.49 in 1860. In 1858 he received his fee for the Hôtel Fould in one lump sum, 55,690.35 francs, which raised what would have been an income of 24,341.21 to 80,031.56 francs for that one prosperous year. (The advantage of private practice is obvious. In 1865 Labrouste received a five-percent commission for the Hôtel Vilgruy, 22,828.90 francs on 456,578.14 francs of work, of which he gave two-fifths to his *inspecteur*, J.-F.-M.-J. Thobois and kept 13,697.34 francs for himself.[51]) Otherwise in 1858 Labrouste earned 5,361.27 francs for his work at the Bibliothèque Nationale, 2,969.37 for that at Rennes, and 588.61 and 200.97 for maintenance work at the Bibliothèque Sainte-Geneviève and the Dépôt des Marbres, respectively. Roughly balancing one of the two major items of income was the 3000 francs he received in monthly increments of 250 francs for his work for the Conseil des Bâtiments Civils. Early in 1859 he received his 6000 franc salary as an Inspecteur Général des Edifices Diocésains. Thus, adding in his salary as Inspecteur Général and spreading the Fould fee over the three years the work actually consumed, out of an adjusted income of 48,904.66 francs in 1858, Labrouste earned twenty percent (9000 francs) for his work on government commissions, a little less than another twenty percent (8,330.64 francs) for construction at two major public buildings, one-and-a-half percent (789.58 francs) as architect of two completed structures, and forty percent (18,563.45 francs) from the construction of one major private house. (The remaining twenty percent of Labrouste's income in 1858 was from interest on various securities.)

One can see why in the 1840s Duban had been so willing to slight his government responsibilities for private commissions: if one worked in the right circles, these were at least as remunerative as public commissions. It might be noted that both the seminary at Rennes and the Bibliothèque Nationale were buildings of moderate size erected over many years. Vaudoyer at Marseilles was receiving fees on the order of 21,511.18 francs yearly (1859)[52]—and built himself a house on the rue Lesueur just off the Avenue de l'Impératrice as a result. As Architecte de l'Empereur, Lefuel received a yearly salary of 40,000 francs. One could conclude that a government architect without interest income or private commissions might earn as much as a member of the various administrative boards as he would from the construction of government buildings. One should also note that these boards would consume about a third to a half of his time. Such an architect was, in a word, well on his way to becoming a bureaucrat—a neat piece of the evolving nineteenth-century governmental machine, just as the administrators hoped.

This is significant because it demonstrates that the French architectural profession was very nearly congruent with the government administration. Architects functioned along the edge of the administrative class of *fonctionnaires*—what the Germans gave legal definition as the *Beamtenstand*. In mid-nineteenth-century France this was a fact of immense importance. The administrative class—the employees, *chefs-de-bureau,* and *directeurs* of all the multitudinous parts of the governmental bureaucracy—was one of the central facts of contemporary French culture.[53] Americans are unfamiliar with the idea of government service as a lifetime profession, in part from Andrew Jackson's Tenure of Office Act of 1828, which made such officials revocable. In Europe, and especially in France, however, the status of the *fonctionnaire* brought with it *immovibilité* and immunity from civil law suits.[54] The administrative class was legally, economically, and philosophically a separate estate. It figures as a force influencing French history in de Toqueville's *Ancien régime et la révolution* (1856) and Taine's *Origines de la France contemporaine* (1876–94). It provides a setting for Balzac's *Les Employés* (1838) and a subject for his "Physiologie des employés" (1841).

Architects do not seem to have been precisely and legally *fonctionnaires*—they retained the right to pursue a private practice—but they largely functioned as such. That is to say, their work was produced within the administrative system and their method of proceeding necessarily responded to the *fonctionnaires'* methods and preconceptions. More precisely, these architects were careful to work within clear functional and budgetary limits, were aware of producing models that were both up-to-date and widely applicable, and finally assumed that architecture was an intellectual enterprise—the conception of a system which others might execute—rather than a craft or a technique.

The specific standards of the administration as they applied to architecture are evident in the *procès verbal* of the Conseil des Bâtiments Civils and the Comité des Inspecteurs Généraux des Edifices Diocésains. They were three: fiscal accuracy, functional satisfaction, and aesthetic propriety. The art historian is always mystified and impressed by the tremendous detail in the estimates presented with a project to these bodies. These were carefully criticized in the reports to the Conseil and the Comité and their verification clearly constituted one of the largest parts of the *rapporteur's* work. The architects were expected to keep within these estimates: Labrouste's Bibliothèque Sainte-Geneviève came in precisely on budget, as did most of the work of the Romantic *pensionnaires* during the bureaucratic reign of Louis-Philippe. During the Restoration, Huyot—well connected at Court—had been cavalier about the costs of the Arc de Triomphe, and in 1832 he was investigated and removed from his post.[55] Napoleon III and Haussmann were notorious for overspending on projects like the New Louvre and the Opera, but had to buck the resistance of the administration as well as of the public, as we shall see.[56]

The functional criticisms that fill the *procès verbaux*—suggestions that corridors be widened, staircases be reversed, structural systems be reconsidered—reflect two important aspects of the *fonctionnaire*'s charge: the administration existed to satisfy the public's material needs, and the implements that it used to this end were to be the most technically sophisticated of their type. The second point is important. The primary concern of the Conseil des Bâtiments Civils was the great public buildings of Paris. (Indeed, after the Decentralization Decree of March 25, 1852, these were its only concern, although its advice was often sought on other projects.) In 1891 Maurice Block could list all ninety-six structures involved in his *Dictionnaire administrative française*.[57] But these were no ordinary buildings: they were the prototypes for similar structures in the provinces and the great manifestation of French building science set out in the metropolis for comparison with the best that London, Vienna, or Berlin had to offer.[58] We are used to encountering little cellular prisons like the Mazas in the French provinces and colonies; little Bibliothèque Sainte-Genevièves and Palais de Justices, or, most particularly, little copies of Baltard's Halles Centrales. The great Parisian prototypes were based on exhaustive studies of function by their designers. Labrouste in 1857 traveled to London to examine the British Museum Library (as well as the Crystal Palace at Sydenham); J.-L. Pascal made a more thorough study of English libraries upon succeeding Labrouste at the Bibliothèque Nationale.[59] Earlier, in 1836, Blouet had visited the United States to study prison architecture, publishing a report upon his return, and in 1845 Baltard had traveled about Europe on a government mission studying market buildings, then published a report in 1846.[60] The buildings these architects produced after these studies were contributions to the scientific study of their type and for generations after were analyzed as models.[61]

Despite the time necessarily devoted to estimates and function in the *procès verbaux* of the Conseil and the Comité, the art historian is nonetheless gratified to find that the most lengthy and animated discussions were on points of art. We have cited the Conseil's resistance to Duban's use of architectural fragments in the courtyards of the Ecole des Beaux-Arts because they presented models "impure" to the Neoclassical mind. During the Second Empire, the body was to debate the over-decoration of Visconti's projects for the New Louvre, the oddness of Duc's elevations for the Palais de Justice, and the character of the facade of Garnier's Opera, while the Comité was to find Vaudoyer's first project for Marseilles Cathedral too obscure in its historical references. The length of these discussions, however, also emphasizes their frequent uselessness, since issues of philosophy became confused with ones of quality. This was a problem the administration recognized, and it made efforts to disentangle the two, to define the opposing philosophies of art, and to support the one apparently most sympathetic to the State. A particularly direct, if crude, effort in this direction is found in the fourth volume of C.-P. Marie Haas's *Administration de la France* (1857–59) where for the benefit of administrators and law students, the author, citing Edouard Charton, distinguishes three philosophies of art—the Sensualist, the Catholic Spiritualist, and the Rational Spiritualist (Eclectic)—and summarizes the "doctrines philosophiques," "doctrines morales," and "tendences politiques" of each.[62] Sensualism, we read, "prefers liberty but accommodates itself perfectly to an enlightened despotism."[63] Catholic Spiritualism supports a theocratic monarchy, while Rational Spiritualism (Eclecticism) is not so much defined as warmly praised: "it envisions the education, not the chastisement, of mankind."[64] In implying that Eclecticism might best function as a state philosophy of art, Haas unwittingly echoes the accusation of Pierre Leroux and Hippolyte Taine.[65]

If an administrator really believed Haas's distinctions, he would be obliged to employ adherents to this philosophy as *fonctionnaires* in an art administration. That is what Hippolyte Fortoul almost accomplished when he founded the Comité des Inspecteurs Généraux des Edifices Diocésains with Vaudoyer and Reynaud as members. But Viollet-le-Duc was the third member and was both indispensable because of his tremendous expertise and forceful in his resistance to the *pensionnaires'* Eclecticism. Here, the lines were most clearly drawn, as they were not in the Conseil des Bâtiments Civils, and in the next chapter we shall witness how difficult it was to apply bureaucratic doctrine to the art and industry of building.

As important as the specific standards expected to be maintained by a *fonctionnaire* were the mentality and the ways of working that architects took over as they became more deeply involved in the administrative system. The most basic of these predispositions was how one thought through a problem. An Inspecteur Général spent a great deal of his time judging, and he had to have a general method of analysis in order to do so quickly, effectively, and as the administration expected.

This, of course, is what French architecture students are celebrated for having learned at the Ecole des Beaux-Arts under the rubric "composition." They were trained to read a program critically, to select the salient features, to embody these features in a memorable and expressive form, and, finally, by the elaboration of axes and cross-axes, to spin out a whole complex of secondary spaces around it. Fundamentals were clearly distinguished from details. What came first in the analysis of a design problem was clearly distinguished from what came later. Architecture students thus learned to think quickly and surely in terms of architectural composition. Also, importantly, they could be sure all their colleagues were learning in the same manner, so that their judgments would be understood.

Implicit in the *fonctionnaire*'s method of reasoning was his way of working—the fact that the *fonctionnaire* gave orders to *employés* (architects) and did not execute them himself. We have seen that a man in Duban's or Labrouste's position in 1858 spent a third of his time in committee meetings and perhaps an equal amount in writing analyses of projects. Just as they came to have a sense of generalities in this work, they also had methods for designing less by drawing themselves than by giving orders to be carried out by the staffs of their large *agences*. The *architecte-en-chef*, as we have seen, was only required to visit a site weekly and was provided with a full-time staff of *inspecteurs* to produce drawings and oversee construction. In the provinces, visits were more infrequent, with Duban going to Blois twice a month and Vaudoyer going to Marseilles twice a year.[66] The consistent high quality of nineteenth-century French architectural drawings was largely due to the specialists employed to execute them. We know from his letters, for example, that Espérandieu as a student in 1852 divided his time between drawing an exquisite set of renderings of Questel's Saint-Paul at Nîmes (now in the Musée des Beaux-Arts in Nîmes) and executing Vaudoyer's initial studies for Marseilles Cathedral (figures 44–46).[67] At the Ecole the Grand Prix drawings were already executed not by the competitors but by large teams of "nègres" under their supervision. There thus was a profound tradition of "talking up" a design rather than drawing it out, personally and in detail.

A final aspect of the *fonctionnaire*'s mentality that one might mention is that it was one shared with an entire social class. It was often complained that the government architects were a caste, with ancestors and descendants in the government service.[68] Léon Vaudoyer's father, A.-L.-T. Vaudoyer, was Secrétaire-Archiviste of the Ecole des Beaux-Arts and a member of the Académie des Beaux-Arts, while his son, Alfred, became Architecte de la Ville de Paris and his grandson, Jean-Louis Vaudoyer, a member of the Académie Française. Victor Baltard's father, Louis-Pierre, was Professor of the Theory of Architecture at the Ecole des Beaux-Arts and a member of the Institut. Labrouste's son Léon succeeded him as architect of the Bibliothèque Nationale; his brother Théodore was in 1853 appointed *architecte-en-chef* of the Administration des Hôpitaux et Hospices; while another brother, Pierre-Victor-Alexandre, was director of the Collège Sainte-Barbe. His father, François-Marie-Alexandre, was Premier Commis des Finances in the Ministère des Finances and a very highly respected *fonctionnaire*.[69] In the next chapter we will examine the collaboration between the critic-become-Minister Fortoul and the *inspecteurs généraux* Reynaud and Vaudoyer, and it is important to realize that not only could an *haut fonctionnaire* like Fortoul be particularly well informed about art, but architects like Vaudoyer and Reynaud could be intimately acquainted with administration.

This brings us back to the question posed at the beginning of this chapter: who were the Romantic *pensionnaires'* clients? By now it must be clear that there is no simple answer. Duban, Labrouste, Duc, and Vaudoyer were government architects in every sense: they devoted most of their time to governmental administration and design, they derived most of their income from it, and the best creative work they produced was on the government's behalf. Their bureaucratic titles and commissions were not simply window dressing: they embodied the basic fact of their careers.

With whom, then, did these architects work out their designs? From the administrative standpoint this is perfectly clear: the essence of the French system was centralization, and so the architect was under the orders of those above him in the chain of command. That meant the head of state, represented by his minister, delegating to his directors and *chefs-de-bureau*, advised by professional advisory councils. Of course, in fact, things were not so clear. The head of state could not pass an architectural wish down a chain of command which transformed it into a handsome design. Who, within this system, was really in charge? More pointedly, where in all this were the individuals who would actually occupy the finished buildings—the faculty of the Ecole des Beaux-Arts, the librarian of the Bibliothèque Sainte-Geneviève, the director of the Conservatoire des Arts et Métiers?

In considering the first question, it is clear that the advisory boards usually exercised the most authority in criticizing and approving plans. The middle-level *fonctionnaires*—the *directeurs* and *chefs-de-bureau*—were relatively unobtrusive figures. Most of them were well born and possessed some modest personal competence or pretense, as the careers of the Comte de Montalivet, Directeur of Louis-Philippe's Liste Civil, or de Cardaillac, Directeur des Bâtiments Civils, bear out.[70] Some of this class could be quite forceful, as was the case with Ludovic Vitet and then Prosper Mérimée at the Monuments Historiques. But such forcefulness was usually exceptional. Charles Garnier depicts de Cardaillac as a well-intentioned mediator.[71] Effective leadership within the administration, if it appeared at all, usually came at the ministerial level, as in the cases of Thiers in 1832–33, or of Fortoul in 1852–56. In the parallel administration of the departments, of course, there was Georges Haussmann, Prefect of the Seine from 1854 to 1869.

In considering the second question, it is remarkable how little influence the occupants of particular buildings seem to have had. According to bureaucratic procedure, the architect was to consult with these occupants in formulating his initial design. The surviving records about this preliminary consultation are quite slight,[72] and there is little evidence that the occupants were consulted after the project was sent to the advisory boards, the minister, and finally to the Chambre des Députés for funding. The attitude appears to have been that these were less individual buildings than collective expressions of the state, materialized and coordinated by the responsible boards of professional designers.

It was, then, the advisory boards—that is, the architects themselves—who constituted the consistent, dominant patrons and overseers of French government architecture. They had the knowledge, authority, and patience to coordinate all the building projects of the state. They could and did resist the intrusions of the politicians and the personal desires of the occupants of the buildings. They were a caste—part *fonctionnaire*, part liberal professional—following rules they themselves set. Labrouste's 1852 description of the Bibliothèque Sainte-Geneviève prepared for César Daly ends with the declaration:

I forgot to mention to you the different ministers who succeeded each other in the direction of government works.

M. de Montalivet, who commissioned and had this project studied.

M. Teste, who presented the authorizing bill.

M. Dumon, who set the cornerstone.

MM. Jayr, Trélat, Recrut, Vivien, Lacrosse, Bineau, Magne.

In all, eleven ministers; but there was only one architect.[73]

Five

VAUDOYER'S MARSEILLES CATHEDRAL

We opened the last chapter by asking how eminent architects like the four Romantic *pensionnaires* could produce so few major buildings, especially after receiving the lengthiest and most sophisticated training then available in the world. The answer broached was that as they rose to the pinnacle of their profession they were transformed into *fonctionnaires* who spent much of their time sitting on committees and judging the work of other professional colleagues. Yet their committee work was an extension of their design labors, and vice versa, because each was the painstaking formulation and application of general principles. The designer of a major public building and his various consultative committeemen went through a long process of suggestion and adjustment together—they were, after all, architects of similar background and often close personal friends—to produce a large and serious edifice standing for the new rational, bureaucratic state. Committee work was no diversion; it was where the judgment basic in this sort of design was refined and exercised.

A case in point is Vaudoyer's design of Marseilles Cathedral, carried out between 1845 and 1858 (figures 44–50).[1] It is illuminating, first, because it is an instance of the cooperation of the bureaucracy and the profession; second, because it was a project that brought forward the central Second Empire concerns for the support of the Church and the economic development of the Mediterranean; third, because its response to these concerns was expressed in the great building type of Western culture, the church; fourth, because the final design did indeed acknowledge the complexity of the situation that produced it. The result was one of the seminal buildings of the age.

The stages and chronology of the design and construction of Marseilles Cathedral are complex. By the beginning of the nineteenth century the old cathedral, the Romanesque church of Sainte-Marie-Majeure, was a narrow, dark, partly ruinous fragment—ideally sited, however, on the edge of the cliffs facing seaward west of the Vieux Port. It had become entirely inadequate, especially as Marseilles grew with the railroad to Paris and with the new port. Upon his appointment as Bishop in 1837, C.-J.-E. de Mazenod (1782–1861) began a campaign for the erection of a new structure.[2] The Duc d'Orléans, in a visit to Marseilles on November 17, 1839, promised to push the matter, but bureaucratic obfuscation bore his initiatives to a halt after his death in 1842. In the summer of 1844 Bishop de Mazenod enlisted the aid of the Prefect for another campaign, the tone of which was clear in his first letter to the Garde des Sceaux:

It is to be feared that a longer disillusionment of the hopes given to this pious population might negatively effect the idea it has formed of the good intentions of the government in regard to religion. At the present moment, when passions have been raised to sow discontent on this point (discontent that I certainly recognize as completely without justification), an unmistakable fact like the encouragement to construct the cathedral at Marseilles would render vain this effort at divisiveness and perhaps would attract again to the government of the King those who have not benefited from the other advantages the city has received since 1830.[3]

To their delight, in August 1845 Léon Vaudoyer arrived from Paris to make an initial survey of the situation.[4]

At issue at this stage was the selection of a site. The choice was between that of the old cathedral, a dramatic but peripheral spot necessitating the demolition of that building, or one on the Cours du Chapitre at the end of a projected avenue in the center of town. Vaudoyer remained in Marseilles fifteen days; when he returned to Paris, he drew up his report with three block plans for the building supporting the Cours du Chapitre site.[5] This he submitted to the Ministre de l'Instruction Publique et des Cultes on December 20. A sharp dispute then developed between the Marseilles administration and the ministry in Paris about how to split the five-million-franc cost that Vaudoyer estimated. The ministry insisted the major part should be paid by the city, while the city offered only one million francs (in ten yearly increments).[6] It was pointed out in response that the public treasury was already burdened with the expense of the erection of a new port and the completion of the railroad line from Avignon. "The construction of a new cathedral at Marseilles," the Minister replied on October 16, 1846, "is not called for by the imperious needs of *utilité publique*. It is a project of purely local interest, the expense of which should be first of all and almost exclusively borne by the population that will receive the benefit of it."[7] Finally, on November 27, 1847, Bishop de Mazenod wrote directly to the King, citing the earlier offer of a million francs and begging that work begin at once. The King was sympathetic, as his son had been eight years before, but his reign was prematurely ended by revolution only thirty-eight days after he had written his Minister (on January 18, 1848) to push the matter.

Bishop de Mazenod neither rested nor despaired. The revolution installed a series of vigorous prefects at Marseilles, first Emile Ollivier, then A.-L.-A.-E. de Suleau, and the latter commenced a series of large building projects into which the cathedral was strategically inserted. On January 15, 1850, Suleau sent a lengthy report to Paris proposing the sale of the old lazaret at Marseilles (its functions having been moved to the island of Frioul) and the expenditure of the resulting profit on an extension of the new port, the provision of warehouses and a rail spur, and the simultaneous erection of a new bourse and a new cathedral. He offered three million francs (in addition to the one million already offered in 1846) to defray the cost of the cathedral and requested only two million francs from the state. His balancing of the cathedral with a bourse was not inharmonious with the spirit of the report, which pointed out that other public works in Marseilles were coming to completion so that the "classes laborieuses" would present a peril to "l'ordre publique" if new works of some sort were not undertaken.

The Minister agreed to pursue the matter, and on December 20, 1850, Vaudoyer was asked to review his project of 1845, and in particular to change its site to that of Sainte-Marie-Majeure, overlooking the projected new port extension. Ten months later, on October 30, 1851, Vaudoyer was instructed to start work on a definitive project for the cathedral and to submit it with "le plus bref delai." On January 19, 1852, the sale of the lazaret was approved by the government. Meanwhile, on January 15 Vaudoyer had sent a site and building plan to Marseilles. It was analyzed there at inquiries commencing on February 18 and returned to him on May 14 with the suggestion that the project be set on a high platform extending out over the new port.

This was the moment of Louis Napoleon's coup d'état and Fortoul's consequent appointment as Ministre de l'Instruction Publique et des Cultes. One of the first moves Napoleon made to consolidate his government was to tour the Midi accompanied by the *meridional* Fortoul. He was in Marseilles on September 26, 1852, and signed a decree authorizing the execution of Suleau's bold project and ceremoniously laying the cornerstones of both the bourse and the cathedral.[8] To the city's four-million-franc contribution he promised two-and-a-half million from the state.

For this visit a final project for the cathedral, or at least something convincingly resembling one, was needed in a hurry. Vaudoyer was accordingly instructed to draw up a project, to go to Marseilles (evidently for the first time since 1845), and to be ready to present his work to the Prince-President during the ceremonies. He produced a set of drawings, dated August 15, 1852, which he placed before Bishop de Mazenod for his approval on September 24 and displayed to Louis Napoleon two days later (figures 44–46).

44
*Léon Vaudoyer, Cathedral of
Sainte-Marie-Majeure, Marseilles,
preliminary project, facade. Signed
and dated "le 15 août 1852."
(Photo: Bulloz)*

45
*Léon Vaudoyer, Cathedral of
Sainte-Marie-Majeure, preliminary
project, side elevation. Signed and
dated "le 15 août 1852." Private
collection, Paris. (Photo: Bulloz)*

46
Léon Vaudoyer, Cathedral of
Sainte-Marie-Majeure, preliminary
project, cross section. Signed and
dated "le 15 août 1852." Private
collection, Paris. (Photo: Bulloz)

This way of proceeding was not, of course, in accordance with canonical bureaucratic practice. On February 15, 1853, Vaudoyer presented the project to the Commission de Répartition for preliminary approval as a "projet esquisse." On March 10 Viollet-le-Duc criticized it sympathetically but severely, as we shall see, and the body accepted his evaluation.[9] From then until the spring of 1855, Vaudoyer worked on a second, definitive project (figure 47), which Bishop de Mazenod again signed on April 15 and Viollet-le-Duc reported on approvingly on May 15. Almost immediately afterward bids were solicited for the foundations and construction began.

The design, however, was still only approximate. As late as April 8, 1857, the Comité des Inspecteurs Généraux des Edifices Diocésains approved a revised project moving the facade one bay westward (figure 48),[10] and constant modifications were made in proportions and details. Vaudoyer kept a model of the cathedral in his Marseilles office, upon which he made and studied each change (figure 49).[11] He did not live long enough to design any of the decorative carving of the capitals and cornices; all but the capitals of the west belfries are from the designs of his successors Henri Espérandieu (*premier inspecteur* at the cathedral from 1854 and in 1872–74 *architecte-en-chef*) and Henry-Antoine Revoil (*architecte-en-chef* from 1874 to 1900).[12]

Work on the site had begun in 1854 with the acquisition of the necessary land and continued in 1855 and 1856 with work on the foundations. Construction of the cathedral proper commenced in 1857. By the time of Vaudoyer's death in 1872 the masonry shell was up and twenty million francs had already been spent in increments varying between 650,000 and 200,000 francs yearly.[13] On November 3, 1893, the state officially relinquished the building to the Catholic Church, after spending another million. Work costing 100,000, francs was nonetheless done in 1894; by 1899 this had fallen to 15,325.01 francs and the building was more or less as we see it today (figures 50, 51).

It is gratifying that the Ministre de l'Instruction Publique et des Cultes all through the final development of Vaudoyer's project was his mentor Hippolyte Fortoul. We know they worked on the project together. When the matter was first raised, Vaudoyer wrote Fortoul on May 15, 1845, "It will be necessary to put on the table the celebrated problem of the Catholic [church] type in 1845. Alas, this is not easy and I tremble."[14] In two subsequent letters Vaudoyer tried to arrange a meeting with Fortoul, then a professor in Toulouse, to discuss the matter.[15] Ten years later, when the project was complete, Fortoul wrote in his diary:

I went to Vaudoyer's to see the project for Marseilles Cathedral. I made a few more observations, but I find the plan sufficiently ameliorated to produce one of the

47
*Léon Vaudoyer, Cathedral of
Sainte-Marie-Majeure, definitive
project, side elevation, 1857 or
after. Private collection, Paris.
(Photo: Bulloz)*

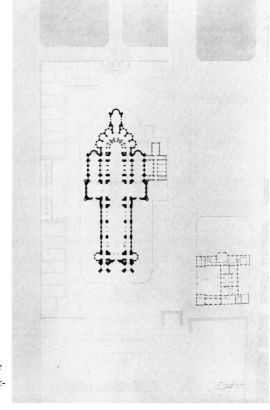

48
*Léon Vaudoyer, Cathedral of
Sainte-Marie-Majeure, definitive
project, plan, 1860. Private collection, Paris. (Photo: Bulloz)*

49
Léon Vaudoyer, Cathedral of
Sainte-Marie-Majeure, 1856–93,
models.

50
Léon Vaudoyer, Cathedral of Sainte-Marie-Majeure, exterior from the harbor. (Photo: N. D. Roger-Viollet)

most beautiful and curious monuments with which France might honor itself. It is a work of which I shall be the most proud. I think that I contributed a great deal even to the first conception.[16]

Here is an important instance of collaboration between a government architect and a high official who was simultaneously a knowledgeable critic. But things are never perfect. Vaudoyer actually became architect of the project quite by chance. While Fortoul was still an obscure professor in Toulouse, Vaudoyer was named architect at Marseilles in compensation for not having been named architect for the restoration of the cathedral at Bourges. In applying for that latter post, Vaudoyer himself, and Vitet backing him, emphasized his knowledge of Gothic architecture—expertise important for Bourges but irrelevant for the Marseilles project.[17] But then, all he was really being hired to do in 1845 was to visit Marseilles and pass upon a problem of urbanism. Only 2000 francs were budgeted and Vaudoyer suspected the whole thing would result in nothing.[18] His suspicion was nearly realized; the ministry did not correspond with him about Marseilles again until five years later; and even when the project came to life again, Bishop de Mazenod and Prefect Suleau proposed, in letters of December 24, 1851, and January 2, 1852, that Léon Feuchère be named architect.[19] What Fortoul did was to reject this suggestion, keep Vaudoyer in this position, and raise him to the more solid dignity of *architecte diocésain* on July 27, 1853, making fruitful the opportunity Vaudoyer had already received by chance.

Vaudoyer's first project, that dated August 15, 1852, was a most elaborate configuration of volumes (figures 44–46). A tall octagonal dome over the crossing is surrounded by three lower domes over identical square bays comprising the transepts and choir. A broad nave in three groin-vaulted bays extends forward with passages (rather than aisles) below narrow balconies on each side (figure 51). Two octagonal towers with tall curving roofs mark the facade with its king's gallery, rose window, and carved tympanum over the main door inset at the back of a porch. At the chevet a huge mosaic half-dome terminates the axis. Below it a double ring of arches opens into an ambulatory and a crown of semicircular chapels. A domed Lady Chapel extends out the rear, and two deep parish chapels stretch back from the transepts.

It is often observed that Vaudoyer's project combines the Roman vaulted hall and the Byzantine domical church. Vaudoyer's *inspecteur* and successor at the cathedral, Henri Espérandieu, wrote Charles Blanc in a letter of February 19, 1875, "The layout of the cathedral derives simultaneously from the halls of the Roman baths and from the Byzantine churches (especially Saint Mark's at Venice)."[20] Liturgically this made good sense. A cathedral was an urban institution, the seat of a bishop and

51
Léon Vaudoyer, Cathedral of
Sainte-Marie-Majeure, nave.
(Photo: N. D. Roger-Viollet)

his chapter serving the city population with their schools and administration of the diocese.[21] During the Renaissance bishops had come to take their duties lightly and the public functions of the cathedral had declined. But in the nineteenth century the institution was reinvigorated, both in France and in England, and, as part of the politics of clericism and legitimism, its functions were emphasized. In the case of de Mazenod at Marseilles, the cathedral was the symbolic core of a worldwide missionary project. Thus a broad practical nave for the congregation became necessary, as well as a dramatic, ritualistic chevet for the bishop and the chapter. In the vocabulary of historical architecture, the type of the unencumbered public space was the Roman thermal hall, while the type of the splendid ritualistic space was the Byzantine domical church. The basilican type that dominated French church building from Chalgrin's Saint-Philippe-du-Roule (1769) to Hittorff's Saint-Vincent-de-Paul (1824–48) had not permitted the expression of this distinction, but it was acknowledged in several of the more important medieval church restorations (Baltard's of Saint-Germain-des-Prés of 1842–47 and Vaudoyer's of Saint-Martin-des-Champs of 1840 and after, for example). It appeared decisively in the first major church designed by the circle of the Romantic *pensionnaires*, Questel's Neo-Romanesque Saint-Paul at Nîmes of 1836–48, where a barnlike nave introduces a richly decorated east end past a tall crossing tower. In his 1852 project for Marseilles Cathedral, Vaudoyer made this distinction between nave and chancel still more emphatic and added a pair of facade towers modeled on those of Sankt Maria in Capitol in Cologne and a crown of ambulatory chapels around the chevet like those at Saint-Sernin at Toulouse.

Marseilles Cathedral can thus be explained functionally and be shown to manifest—to make symbolic—an interpretation of the Christian institution of the cathedral. Its forms are not geometrically abstract, but clearly historical in derivation: the nave from Rome, the chevet from Venice, the chapels from Toulouse, the towers from Cologne. We know from Vaudoyer's historical studies as well as from his design for the Conservatoire des Arts et Métiers how tremendously conscious he was of historical continuity. We also know that Fortoul wished a building to display its history through a combination of forms, like the Residenz in Munich. And we have the basis for a historical reading of Vaudoyer's project in the history of architecture that he, together with Fortoul and Reynaud, formulated during the 1830s and 1840s, in which Arnolfo di Cambio is pictured as founding Renaissance architecture when, "sensing . . . the need to reforge the entire chain of its tradition,"[22] he linked the Roman thermal hall and the Byzantine domical church in his plan of the Duomo (figure 52).

52
Cathedral Santa Maria del Fiore
(Duomo), Florence, 1298–1452.
(Photo: Alinari)

But Arnolfo was a late-medieval architect and Vaudoyer a nineteenth-century one: where does this mean that Vaudoyer places himself historically? Again, there is a hint from Fortoul, whose basic point in *De l'Art en Allemagne* is that when the Orders became explicit in the High Renaissance, architecture went astray, and the task of the modern architect is to get back before that moment of failure and proceed forward again using a system of implicit Orders—coordinated proportions and curves—that embraces both the architectural and the monumental decorative forms. (Significantly Vaudoyer indicates a hieratic Byzantine decorative scheme covering the vaults and domes of his project, a very regular one closely related to the architecture.[23]) Thus it would be illogical to expect Vaudoyer to cite any historical sources later than the Duomo. But he is, nonetheless, here attempting to correct, place, and update the Duomo. Arnolfo included no bell towers in his plan for the Duomo, so Giotto had to erect a freestanding one beside the facade. Vaudoyer sought a more organic solution by consulting a Northern, Romanesque source, the heavily Byzantinizing churches of Cologne, to adopt the facade towers of Sankt Maria in Capitol (which likewise had a Roman nave and a Byzantine chevet). Arnolfo provided only three open chapels around the crossing of the Duomo; Vaudoyer adds an ambulatory and chapels behind his chancel dome. Finally, where Arnolfo is free in his adaptation of historical models, Vaudoyer is precise and accurate so that one can read each part. The only reference that is obscure is that to the Duomo itself, for to Fortoul and Vaudoyer the Renaissance was without form, only marked by memory and intellect, as Fortoul insisted the nineteenth century was as well.

Reading Vaudoyer's project symbolically and historically is still not to read it architecturally, as aesthetic form. Fortoul saw the need for French art to educate itself through the study of German historicism, but nonetheless to retain its native sense of "invention" to produce a new, powerful synthesis.[24] It was this French native skill in the manipulation of forms that he hoped would succeed in creating a new architecture of implicit Orders.

Vaudoyer's problem was that he could not create such a new style out of whole cloth. He had to have some consistent vocabulary and tradition to hold his composition together, and this vocabulary could not be the traditional one of the Greco-Roman Orders. The solution to his dilemma had been broached in Reynaud's writings of the 1830s and again in Fortoul's *De l'Art en Allemagne*: the elevation of the Romanesque and Byzantine styles from the status of isolated historical modes to that of a general tradition continuing that of ancient Rome and preparing for that of the Renaissance. The last ten chapters of Fortoul's book is an architectural tour of Germany (in fact, precisely the trip made in company with Vaudoyer in 1840[25]) in which he everywhere emphasizes the Romanesque style. Even in Cologne Fortoul spends most of his time on the Romanesque churches, depicting the cathedral (following French scholarship) as a foreign intrusion, a copy of Beauvais Cathedral in France, and the beginning of decadence.[26] At Bamberg he wrote:

This is not the first time that antiquity appeared to me to be alive almost on the eve of the century which pretended, after a thousand years, to draw it from the tomb. In all the directions embraced by the expansion of the human spirit, it kept its dominance almost to the end of the twelfth century; in the thirteenth it was momentarily vanquished by a movement that gave birth at the same time to modern languages and to the Gothic style; but swiftly in the fifteenth century it regained all its authority in Italy and was about to impose itself on all Europe more powerfully than ever.[27]

It is only in the context of this belief in a continuous vaulted tradition from Rome to the Renaissance that we can understand a paragraph Vaudoyer inserted at the end of his installment of "Etudes d'architecture en France" of April 1846, immediately after his first trip to Marseilles. Here he states the proper basis of modern church design:

We think that, in order to succeed, the program should be formulated thus:—In layout, the application of all the advantages furnished by the science of vaulted construction; the adoption of the style vertical and of the arcade free and unencumbered by the ancient Orders; introduction of the dome without the exclusion of towers. As to style, take as the point of departure the great principles of ancient architecture while recognizing the contribution of those appertaining to Christian art, and propose in general to create a monument that will be of our times, of our country, and that will be of the same family as those for which other needs might motivate the construction at the same place.[28]

We have noted that Viollet-le-Duc wrote a critique of Vaudoyer's initial project that was adopted by the Commission de Répartition at their meeting of March 10, 1853. This was immediately before Fortoul transformed that body into the Comité des Inspecteurs Généraux des Edifices Diocésains by *arrêtés* of March 7 and May 20 of that year; its members were Duban, Labrouste, and Mérimée as well as Viollet-le-Duc, Fortoul, and Vaudoyer.[29] It is an unusually long report. Viollet-le-Duc begins by noting that his colleague, Vaudoyer, understands the importance of the project, "which, by its scale as well as by its situation in one of the richest and most beautiful cities in France, should attract the attention of all intelligent men in Europe."[30] It is a polite, diplomatic document. (Reports in general, and those if Viollet-le-Duc in particular, were not always so.) But for all its apparent restraint, it is of great importance; first, because it was accepted by the Commission and occasioned a basic revision of the project; second, because, while seeming to imply a softening of its author's Gothicism, it in fact demonstrates one of its subtlest and most profound aspects; and third, because by a gentle and calculated naïveté in its assumptions, it showed Vaudoyer and Fortoul how close they were to a position they wished to avoid and thus forced them to be careful about a matter that, as the 1850s progressed, became the crux of an important controversy. Viollet-le-Duc's document is diplomatic not only in tone but also in intent: by its strategy it put Vaudoyer and Fortoul in a position where they were obliged to respond to important issues.

After noting the importance of the project, Viollet-le-Duc broaches the matter of in what system of architecture such a building should be designed. "There were two choices: either project a monument according to completely new parameters that would summarize the particular taste of our time, or follow traditions and take inspiration from historical types."[31] The first choice, he notes, Vaudoyer has wisely put aside, "for who among us can define the architecture of our times?"[32] Having chosen to follow a historical style, Vaudoyer, in Viollet-le-Duc's opinion, was wise to have selected the Byzantine. His choice was between the Early Christian, Byzantine, Gothic, and Renaissance. Early Christian is too ancient, Viollet-le-Duc judges; a building in that style could not satisfy the needs of a modern cathedral. But Gothic too would have been inappropriate because "to take our great Gothic cathedrals as models would be to erect a monument in disharmony with Southern architecture, with the elements and traditions of these localities."[33] The choice of the Renaissance style, Viollet-le-Duc declares, would not have been so much inappropriate as depraved: "To take inspiration from our Renaissance buildings would be to reproduce a bastard architecture, to risk committing the mistakes so frequent in this architecture."[34]

What is significant about this formulation by Viollet-le-Duc of Vaudoyer's thinking is not only that he prefers the Byzantine to the Gothic because of the requirement that style have local significance, but also that he backs Vaudoyer into an embarrassing dilemma by refusing to comprehend that the project *is* a Renaissance conception—the very sort of thing Viollet-le-Duc calls "bâtard"—and not Byzantine at all.

In the paragraph that follows, Viollet-le-Duc is more blunt:

M. Vaudoyer seems to have occupied himself too much, in the ensemble of his

composition, with the banal citation of sources (accusation banale d'imitation).

He seems to wish to prove that one might combine in a single building forms

appertaining to different peoples and ages. Certainly, if someone were able to

surmount this difficulty, it is M. Vaudoyer, who has patiently studied the styles

that he wishes to combine; but if one can here laud the efforts of the scholar,
admiring his skill in bringing together forms of diverse origin, the artist never-
theless regrets these efforts, which destroy unity without adding effect.

M. Vaudoyer knows better than us that an architecture is not the product of chance;
when one thus decides to adopt a style (and how to do otherwise today?), why not
take it as it is at its purest source? Why seek to create a macronic *language when*
one already has in hand a simple and beautiful speech?[35]

Earlier in his critique Viollet-le-Duc had stated that what constituted "une
architecture" was the perfect harmony of parts and details so that no
others could be imagined in their place. This quality, he asserts, was to be
found in Amiens as well as in Saint Mark's in Venice and was the source
of aesthetic satisfaction to the educated as well as to the general public.

Why is Viollet-le-Duc, the Gothicist, trying to push Vaudoyer into doing a Byzantine design, especially an archaeologically correct one, citing
the example of Saint Mark's? We have noted, like generations of earlier
scholars, that Viollet-le-Duc understood Gothic structurally. We have not
noted, however, that this structural exploration was for him simply the
instrument for understanding the historical and social reality of Gothic in
particular and of the whole history of architecture in general. Structure
was merely a means to an end—the great Romantic historicist end discussed earlier, the resuscitation of the past. To Viollet-le-Duc, it was by
the way in which a society built that it most vividly manifested to the
modern archaeologist (a name he accepted with pride) its particular qualities.

Viollet-le-Duc's discovery in his examination of Gothic architecture was
the multitudinous details of its tremendous structural efficiency. This was
also the source of his delight in it, for he perceived that this reflected a
rational, democratic society. He summarized this in his series of articles
"De la Construction des édifices religieux en France" in the *Annales archéologiques* of 1844–47 and stated it definitively in his entry "Construction" in the fourth volume of the *Dictionnaire raisonné* of 1859. The Gothic
system, he points out, used small, hard, precisely cut stones, cut so that
the least material was wasted and carved at the quarry to lessen the weight
to be transported to the site. The Roman system of construction, in contrast, using masses of concrete poured over forms, had been inefficient and
was possible only because of Imperial Roman centralization and slave
labor. The Gothic was the building system of free, thinking men. Viollet-
le-Duc discovered the elasticity of Gothic structure, the manner in which
each vault thrust is balanced by a counterthrust so that the mass of construction could be reduced to a minimum. The Romans, with their army
and slaves, he imagines, did not worry about such fine-tuning of the structure and grounded vault thrusts with huge inert masses of masonry.

Again, Viollet-le-Duc points out that the Gothic bay system permitted construction to proceed slowly, bay by bay, so that a huge structure could be erected in steps as the money and labor became available. Thus the Gothic cathedral's piecemeal appearance, its changes of plan and decoration from part to part, was indicative of the fact that it was not erected all at one time to a single architect's plans.

But the Gothic builder Viollet-le-Duc envisioned was not just a clever, happy tinkerer. First in the entry "Cathédrale" in the second volume of his *Dictionnaire raisonné* (1856), then again in the sixth and seventh of his *Entretiens sur l'architecture* (1863), and finally in his *Histoire d'un hôtel de ville et d'une cathédrale* (1875), he localizes the invention of the Gothic style in the city cathedrals of the Ile de France begun in the mid-twelfth century: those of Paris, Bourges (which he misdates to 1172), Noyon, and Laon. As any reader of republican Romantic history knew well, this was the time and place of the establishment of the first French democracies, the communes. Augustin Thierry's *Lettres sur l'histoire de France* of 1820 was principally devoted to this topic, and Viollet-le-Duc cites that volume repeatedly. Already in 1845 Ludovic Vitet had published his *Monographie de l'église Notre-Dame-de-Noyon*, where he studies the political evolution of that town in order to explain the interweaving in its cathedral of the Romanesque round arch and the Gothic pointed one. He concludes that the pointed arch was symbolic of republican, civil spirit and the round arch of traditional, centralized Papal authority, but he states firmly that each was merely a geometric form chosen by its supporting party by chance.[36] Viollet-le-Duc, working from his contemporaneous study of Gothic construction, takes a step beyond his friend Vitet when he proposes why the pointed arch was republican and the round arch authoritarian: because one permitted efficient, piecemeal construction and thus presumed political freedom, while the other assumed single building campaigns and thus controlled mass labor and capital.

Using his extraordinary powers of archaeological extrapolation, Viollet-le-Duc reconstructed the first Gothic cathedrals. Peeling away the accumulated chapels and transepts of the later, declining periods, he discovered the model that in 1875 he embodied in his imaginary cathedral at Clusy (figure 53). As at Bourges, there are no transepts; as in his reconstruction of the first state of Notre-Dame, there is only one small chapel in the chevet; as in all the Early Gothic cathedrals, there is a high tribune gallery so that the building would hold most of the city's population at one time. All of these qualities harmonize with the efficiency of its structural system to indicate that the building was conceived as a meeting place for the commune's inhabitants; it is a structure so huge in proportion to the city's population that only the new Gothic system made it possible to build in the first place. Its resemblance to a Roman basilica was thus not fortuitous: these first Gothic cathedrals were at least as much civic monu-

53
Eugène-Emmanuel Viollet-le-Duc,
Imagined Early Gothic cathedral
at Clusy. From Histoire d'un
hôtel de ville et d'une cathédrale, *1878, pp. 82, 86.*

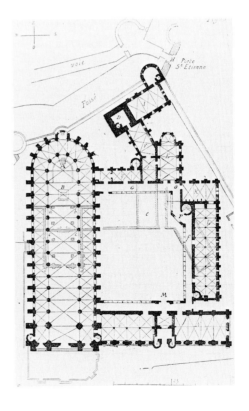

ments as religious ones. With Thierry and Vitet, Viollet-le-Duc envisioned the bishops who built the first cathedrals as consciously making an alliance with the bourgeoisie of the commune to resist the feudal lords and abbots, who still built in the authoritarian Romanesque manner. The communes thus built these new structures on a scale previously unheard of, but with rights to hold festivals in them and to conduct in them business of all sorts.

Where do we find the great cathedrals erected at the end of the twelfth century and the beginning of the thirteenth? In towns like Noyon, Soissons, Laon, Reims, Amiens, which all had, among the first, given the signal for the liberation of the communes. . . .

At the beginning of the twelfth century the feudal system was established; it enmeshed France in a net whose links, strongly forged, would never, it seemed, permit the nation to develop. The regular and secular clergy never protested against this regime; it associated itself with it. . . . It was not the same with the bishops; they had not profited from the exceptional position spiritual power gave them; they began to array themselves, like the lay lords, behind the banners of their sovereigns. . . . It was then that, sustained by the already significant monarchic power, strong from the support of the population, who were rapidly turning toward the openings where they glimpsed the hope of liberty, the bishops wished to give a visible form to a power that seemed henceforth founded on imperturbable bases; they gathered immense sums and tore down the old cathedrals that had become too small, they set to work at once upon the construction of huge monuments built to unite forever around their episcopal throne these populations desirous of freedom from the feudal yoke.[37]

Viollet-le-Duc's vision of structural rationalism led him to two conclusions important for his critique of Vaudoyer's Marseilles Cathedral project: that Gothic architecture, although vaulted in principle, was essentially distinct from Roman architecture and its derivatives; and that such a republican architecture, emanating from the community and conceived with local conditions in mind, must vary from place to place, always reflecting its social and natural environment.

In his writings, Viollet-le-Duc repeatedly equates the Gothic of the communes with Greek architecture, depicting both as structurally efficient and formally rational. This he accompanies with the flat dismissal of Roman architecture as not only authoritarian in its construction but also simply nonsensical in its ornamentation, which is a superficial cladding of the Orders borrowed from the Greeks. In the first volume of his *Entretiens sur l'architecture*, he expands these ideas into a history of architecture embracing two opposing traditions, the rational and republican against the arbitrary and authoritarian. To do this he must solve certain historical problems. The first is that of the Byzantine style which—like Reynaud, Vaudoyer, and Fortoul—he pictures as a more rational form of Roman construction engendered by the frank acceptance of the arch. He saves this style for the party of rationality by insisting that its vocabulary is not a Roman derivative, but rather that of the lost style of the Hebrews.[38] The Byzantine Empire preserved it but was unable to develop it. Viollet-le-Duc's second problem is that of explaining the resemblance of the Romanesque to the Roman style. This he does by insisting on its localization in monastic establishments, which preserved the ancient Roman centralized authority. Finally he explains the collapse of the Gothic and the emergence of the Renaissance as a reflection of the centralization of political power in France from François I to Louis XIV. Not unexpectedly, with this periodization comes a frequently expressed dislike of Italian Gothic in particular and Italian architecture in general, which Viollet-le-Duc describes as being slave to ancient Roman forms and expressive of the political weakness of the peninsula.[39] Arnolfo's Duomo does not appear in his writings.

One of the greatest defects that Viollet-le-Duc decries in Renaissance authoritarian architecture is its destruction of local competence and style. He begins his ninth *Entretien*:

In France during the Middle Ages, even the most modest house, the poorest church, was as artistic as the signeurial castle and the bishop's cathedral. . . . The art of architecture slowly withdrew from the provinces to survive vitally only in the centers of population; and the more that it accumulated immense resources in the big cities and became splendid, the more it was miserable elsewhere. . . .

Today architecture finds itself submitted to a sort of intellectual governance even narrower than that established by Louis XIV; it has never had its revolution of 1789.[40]

Viollet-le-Duc frequently called in his letters and publications for an architectural '89, and here he makes it clear that part of his program would be the liberation of the provinces and the nurturing of local competence and local style in building. In his entry "Restauration" in the eighth volume of his *Dictionnaire raisonné* (1866), he speaks at length of how the work of the Commission des Monuments Historiques has revived provincial architecture. Even more categorical is the compendium *Eglises de bourgs et villages* of 1867 by Anatole de Baudot (identified as "élève de M. Viollet-le-Duc" on the title page), whose plates demonstrate the profoundly different results produced, from province to province, when medieval and medievalist architecture is intelligently derived from local materials and structural devices. The Gothic parish church is not a universal type nor a cathedral model reduced in scale, de Baudot says in the introduction, but always a new, individual piece of thinking. "Each of these is based on a general system of construction formulated in terms of the dimensions of the church and the nature of the materials; thus a small church is not the reproduction of a large one and architectural character varies with the region."[41] To demonstrate this de Baudot parallels Boeswillwald's two churches at Masny (Nord) and Soissons and explains how the brick construction of the first and the cut limestone of the second result in very different configurations. His most striking example is a church by Viollet-le-Duc, that of Saint-Gimer at Carcassonne, built in 1852–59 (figure 54).[42] The generative fact of its design, de Baudot explains, is the use of the local system of tile roofing:

With the system of vaults on pointed arches, the more flat the roof of the aisles, the easier it is to keep down the height of the principal vault and thus that of the building as a whole, and consequently to avoid flying buttresses. Now, fired tile requires only the slightest slope; the architect has taken advantage of this to place the springing of the main vaults as low as possible, while letting it extend above the roofs of the aisles, the rose windows occupying the breadth of each bay and giving full light to the interior.[43]

Viollet-le-Duc's church at Aillant-sur-Tholon in Burgundy (1862–67), also documented in de Baudot's volume, is completely different because of its distinct structural system. Never, however, does de Baudot (or Viollet-le-Duc) mention regionalism as an objective in itself; to them, regional distinctions are the inevitable result of the sensitive, intelligent solution of functional problems. There is no need to conceive some symbolic local nuance: it will appear spontaneously if you work carefully and logically.

The supposed cumulative tradition of Southern round-arched architecture, extending from Constantine to Arnolfo di Cambio, in which Vaudoyer had conceived his first project for Marseilles Cathedral was thus dismissed by Viollet-le-Duc as "bâtard" in one sense or another. Such indeed it must have seemed from his rigorous definition of the organicism of style. The conception of the round-arched tradition, however, was both a legitimate expression of an earlier, Romantic historicism and of an aesthetic. It had powerful attractions. The encounter before the Commission de Répartition was only part of a broad and celebrated controversy that extended to the end of the century.

The dispute centered on the Lombards, a German tribe that ruled Italy from their defeat of the Ostrogoths in Ravenna in 568 to their own conquest by Charlemagne and his Franks in 744.[44] They appear to be a point

54
Eugène-Emmanuel Viollet-le-Duc,
Saint-Gimer, Carcassone, 1852–
59. (Photo: N. D. Roger-Viollet)

of light in the Dark Ages because their history had been recorded by a contemporary, Paul the Deacon, and published in 1514, while the law code of their King Rothari also survived. Their descendants in northern Italy were later to establish the first communes and to become a respected nation of traders. There thus was a strong temptation at the beginning of the nineteenth century to picture the Lombards as the preservers of the classical tradition. In the first volume of his *Histoire des républiques italiennes du moyen-âge* (1807), Sismondi described the Lombard conquest as a "Renaissance": "Independent principalities, communes, republics began to establish themselves everywhere, and order was given to life in this country so long buried in lethargic sleep."[45] Savigny, more emphatically and with weightier arguments and documentation, depicted the Lombard state and legal system as a continuation of the Roman and as the inspiration of the modern in his *Geschichte des römischen Rechts in Mittelalter* (1815–31; published in French in 1839).[46] Finally, Seroux d'Agincourt extended this to the realm of architecture when, in his posthumously published *Histoire de l'art par les monuments, depuis sa décadence au quatrième siècle jusqu'à son renouvellement au siezième* (1823), he depicted the Lombard kingdom as having a sophisticated style of building in the sixth, seventh, and eighth centuries, as represented in the churches of San Giulio and San Tomasso at Bergamo and most particularly San Michele at Pavia. In 1829, however, the Atheneum at Brescia held a competition on the question of whether or not there was such a Lombard architecture bridging the Dark Ages. The proposition was carefully refuted by the antiquary Cordero di San Quintino, who demonstrated that San Michele was actually an eleventh-century successor to the original Lombard church of that designation.[47] Ludovic Vitet reported these conclusions in Paris in his article "De l'Architecture lombarde" of 1830.[48]

There one might have thought the matter would have rested. A number of later archaeologists confirmed Cordero's arguments, beginning with Viollet-le-Duc and ending in our own century with Rivoira and Kingsly Porter.[49] But the idea of a mysterious style bridging the gap between the Roman and medieval times proved to have a powerful attraction, and not just to nationalist north Italian scholars like Luca Beltrami. The Brescia competition had also elicited a defense of the early dating of the Lombard churches, and this proved the more influential of the two documents.[50] Fortoul, as we have seen, accepted the idea. And Léonce Reynaud, in a lengthy discussion of the evolution of church architecture in the second volume of his *Traité d'architecture* of 1858, reintroduced the Lombard style.[51] He dated San Michele at Pavia to the Lombard kingdom, praised the epoch as a renaissance of culture and government, and declared that what henceforth would be the vocabulary of the medieval church—the articulated pier and the colonnette—was its discovery.

These two things, piers with attached columns and elongated columns starting at the floor level, are fundamental in the history of art. They constitute the most characteristic element, the most essential basis of all medieval architecture; they are more important than the pointed arch. It is these which permitted the vaults, the elongated proportions, and the predominance of vertical lines, which brought about, in a word, the special art of Western Christianity. Their invention is a title of glory for the Lombards, which one would dispute in vain.[52]

In 1860 Ferdinand Dartien (1838–1912), a student of Reynaud at the Ecole Polytechnique in the 1850s, then his assistant (*répétiteur auxiliaire*) and after 1867 his successor as Professor of Architecture there, led a mission to study the architecture of northern Italy.[53] He published the results, formulated during nine subsequent visits between then and 1875, as his compendious *Etude sur l'architecture lombarde* (1865–82). He backs Reynaud, step by step, and insists there was a continuous tradition of round-arched architecture in Italy from the ancient Romans to the Renaissance.

The resuscitation of the Lombard style was the crux of a broad movement during the 1830s, 1840s, and 1850s to explore the round-arched vocabulary in the medieval period. Byzantine architecture in particular had been studied in a series of articles in the first volume of Daly's *Revue générale de l'architecture* by Albert Lenoir (1840), then by A.-L.-A. Couchaud, a student of Chenevard and Labrouste, in his *Choix d'églises bysantines en Grèce* of 1842, and then by Debret's student Charles Texier in his *Description de l'Asie Mineur* of 1839–49.[54] In 1851 the antiquary Félix de Verneilh published his *De l'Architecture byzantine en France*, which documents the domed churches of the Périgord, dates their parent, Saint-Front at Périgueux, to 984, and describes it as a brother of Saint Mark's in Venice, not an imitation. (Vitet and Viollet-le-Duc contested this assertion.)[55] The celebrated restoration of the church of Saint-Front by Paul Abadie was projected in 1850 and executed from 1857.[56]

The problem with Reynaud's vision of a continuous round-arched tradition extending unbroken from Rome to the Renaissance was that it could not be documented. Kingsly Porter saw Dartien's massive study as entirely out of date, handling documents with the imprecision of the turn of the nineteenth century.[57] The idea had already been archaeologically refuted by Celeste Clericetti in 1869 and again by Raffaele Cattaneo in 1888.[58] Viollet-le-Duc, in the first volume of his *Entretiens* (1863), dismisses Lombard style out of hand.[59] But an aesthetic objective motivated this illusion of a tradition. We have noted how Fortoul in *De l'Art en Allemagne* depicted this continuous round-arched tradition as more basic and longlived than the Gothic. To a mind like Fortoul's, seeking an orderly yet elastic and characteristic architecture, it was the way to avoid the picturesqueness of the Gothic and still be Christian. It was a vocabulary of architectural forms as eternal as that of the Greek Orders, only needing to be recognized and given expression. Greek architecture, as an ideal, and Gothic architecture, as a threat, show through the fantasy of the Lombard style at many points. One of the recurring themes of *De l'Art en Allemagne* is the rejection of Gothicism.[60] Vaudoyer, in the installments of his "Etudes d'architecture en France," attacks Gothic with increasing vehemence through the 1840s.[61] Reynaud's essay on church design in his *Traité d'architecture* (1858) ends with an outspoken attack on the idea that Gothic might be an appropriate style for the modern church. "Il y a dans l'art ogival une profonde expression de contrainte, de mélancolie, de tristesse, de souffrance même" ("There is in Gothic art a profound feeling of constraint, of melancholy, of sadness, even of suffering"),[62] he writes, and implies that such an architecture is out of harmony with the powerful, progressive society of nineteenth-century France. In place of the Gothic cathedrals, he recommends that the modern architect study the vaulted halls of the Baths of Diocletian and the Basilica of Constantine and the domes of Hagia Sophia and the Duomo.

These last remarks were a challenge to Viollet-le-Duc, who refers to them in a number of passages in his *Entretiens* and answers them directly in an article in the *Gazette des Beaux-Arts* of 1859.[63] He disputes three of Reynaud's assumptions: that one style of architecture might be appropriate for churches and another for other types of building; that the Gothic style elicits such emotions as "mélancolie" and "tristesse"; that there ever was a seminal "Lombard" style. The whole thrust of his *Entretiens* is to refute these points on a general level. Architecture is organic to society—one or another form of constructive logic inflected by function and material—not a vocabulary of a priori forms selected in order to arouse some appropriate sentiment. Thus in the fourth volume of his *Dictionnaire raisonné* Viollet-le-Duc rejects Verneilh's contention that the domical Saint-Front at Périgueux proves that Byzantine architecture is organic to France because its structure was unsound and crumbling (requiring complete rebuilding by Abadie in 1857) and so clearly unnatural to its habitat.[64]

Now perhaps it is clear why Viollet-le-Duc in his 1853 critique of Vaudoyer's project complimented the choice of style but not its eclecticism. In its style he saw an expression of its locality, but in its combination of forms he saw a nineteenth-century architect doing badly what nature and history, manifested in the existing local architecture of the Provence, did subtly and convincingly.

Vaudoyer revised his project in response. The revised design was approved by the Bishop on April 15, 1855, and adopted by the Comité des Inspecteurs Généraux des Edifices Diocésains, upon Viollet-le-Duc's favorable report, on May 15. Except for the movement of the towers and the facade one bay westward, this is the design that was executed beginning in 1857 (figures 50–51).

The composition of volumes has remained the same. It has been greatly strengthened and unified, and a consistent Byzantine style has been adopted in the detailing. In this, of course, Vaudoyer was responding to Viollet-le-Duc's criticisms, and the latter was duly laudatory in his second report:

He has been led to give to the nave a greater breadth, to the masses surrounding the central dome and the sanctuary a simpler arrangement better related to the weights and thrusts, to his elevations and sections a quality of unity lacking in his first project. Considering this system of architecture (and it is perfectly appropriate to the climate and materials of Marseilles), one could not make a more considered and happier application."[65]

Vaudoyer has retained the liturgical system of his first project, but played down the eclectic historical one. And the emphasis upon locality that has replaced the latter has introduced two completely new elements: the broad arch of the facade and the striping of the entire exterior in alternate courses of green and white marble.

As redesigned in 1857, the facade (figure 50) opens southward along the harbor toward the Vieux Port and the city center with a tall arched opening flanked by lower openings, forming a porch across the whole front. Vaudoyer both monumentalized and sanctified the facade by integrating into its composition the twin towers which in his first project had been set on top of the closed facade block like Rhenish turrets added incongruously to the facade of Saint-Denis (figure 44). Vaudoyer was in part responding to Viollet-le-Duc's criticism that the entrance of his first project needed to be widened. More importantly, however, he was making the facade a triumphant entryway by reproducing the configuration of the arches of Titus and Constantine (as well as of Orange, nearby in the Provence) with the tower buttresses in place of columns. Charles Blanc, in his *Les Artistes de mon temps*, explains Vaudoyer's building as a gateway to the Mediterranean.[66]

The basic fact of the cathedral project was its integration into Prefect Suleau's plan to expand the port of Marseilles. After finishing his hurried project in 1852, Vaudoyer must have become profoundly aware of this context, especially since it provided the site for his building on a platform of warehouses extending out into the new harbor. Industrially and symbolically, Marseilles was one of the most important creations of mid-nineteenth-century France, and especially of the Second Empire (which took full credit for the work).[67] In 1830 it had been a straggling center of 100,000 around the narrow, silted Vieux Port, competing with Toulon, Nice, and Genoa in its immediate region. It had a tremendous potential advantage, however: it was linked to the industrial heart of northern Europe by the Rhone, which mounted to Lyon and led to canals to the Seine and Rhine basins. The possibility that Marseilles might become France's gateway to the Mediterranean had already inspired Louis XIV to develop the port and base a fleet there. This proved premature, but with the conquest of Algeria in the 1830s, the city's industrial and strategic importance began to manifest itself powerfully.

The exploitation of Marseilles came largely from outside, from the north where its significance as an outlet was understood. In 1829 the Limoges-born engineer and *polytechnicien* Paulin Talabot arrived in Nîmes to build the Aiges Mortes–Beaucaire canal.[68] He decided to realize the potential of the coal fields at Grand'Combe in the mountains behind Nîmes and in 1840 opened one of the first railroad lines in France, from there, past Nîmes, to Beaucaire. This success encouraged him to begin agitating for a rail line to Lyon in 1838. Working with the Saint-Simonian Didion, he persevered through all the lobbying that led up to the basic railroad legislation of June 11, 1842, the "Code des Chemins de Fer,"[69] and on July 24, 1843, obtained the concession for a line from Avignon to Marseilles, followed in 1845 by that for the line Avignon–Lyon (from which another company was building a line to Paris). The Gare Saint-Charles in Marseilles had been inaugurated and construction had almost reached Avignon when the economic crisis of 1848 stopped the work. On January 2, 1852, however, new laws returned Talabot's concessions with favorable clauses. The line reached Valence in 1854 and was pushed on to Lyon as the Crimean War broke out, the last section opening on April 16, 1855, in time for the returning troops to travel in relative comfort to Paris. Finally, in 1857 the Paris–Lyon company combined with Talabot's to create the famous Paris-Lyon-Méditerranée. In 1859, at the outbreak of the Piedmontese War against the Austrians in Italy, the line carried 227,669 men and 36,357 horses in eighty-six days to mount the first offensive and, incidentally, set the model that the German General Staff followed in August 1914.

Marseilles was the center of two sections of the system: the railroad to Lyon and Paris northward, and the shipping lines across the Mediterranean southward. In 1851 the Compagnie des Messageries Impériales was founded and by 1855 had forty-one ships providing service all over the sea.[70] In 1854 Talabot and the directors of the company founded the Compagnie des Docks et Entrepôts de Marseilles to erect the new port at La Jolliette, projected since 1844 north of the Vieux Port and at the foot of Vaudoyer's cathedral.[71] By January 1, 1861, this new port was in full use.

Talabot and his collaborators did not restrict their efforts to the French side of the Mediterranean. Talabot commenced work on the Algerian railroad system in 1862 and on steel mills there at Alokta-el-Hadid in 1865. In

1846 he had visited Egypt to survey a route for a canal to the Red Sea under the authority of the Saint-Simonian Société d'Etudes pour le Canal de Suez; in 1847 he published a report that in 1854 led to the great project of his friend Ferdinand de Lesseps.[72] On November 17, 1869, to the strains of Verdi's *Aïda* and in the presence of the Empress Eugénie, de Lesseps's Suez Canal was inaugurated, opening Marseilles to the Indian Ocean and to France's new colonial conquests in China (1860) and Indochina (1860–67).

This dramatic realization of its strategic and economic potential transformed Marseilles. Its population rose to 195,138 in 1851, then to 300,151 in 1866. The new port at La Jolliette, with its warehouses and shipping offices, rose on the shore, while the Gare Saint-Charles dominated the Canebière.[73] Fresh water was brought in by aqueduct to Longchamps, where in 1862–70 Espérandieu celebrated it with a massive cascade between the museums of fine arts and natural history. Boulevards of bourgeois *maisons de rapport* were cut, especially the rue Impériale, and a vast *cité ouvrière* was erected near La Jolliette by the builder Curtil. A new Prefecture (Auguste Martin, architect, 1861–67), a new Palais de Justice (Martin, 1858–62), a new Ecole des Beaux-Arts (Espérandieu, 1864–69), a great new barracks, the Caserne Saint-Charles (Guillamaud, 1865–68), all rose simultaneously to transform Marseilles into one of the great cities of the Second Empire. But first among all these monuments had been those begun in 1852 by Suleau: Pascal Coste's bourse and Vaudoyer's cathedral.

Impressive as all this is, it is only the material context of Vaudoyer's building. Marseilles also had symbolic force, particularly among the Saint-Simonians, who were frequently involved in the city's economic development. Michel Chevalier, in a series of articles in the *Globe* appearing between January 20 and February 12, 1832, outlined what he called the "système de la Méditerranée." Its basis was economic: he showed how the sea was the path from Europe to Asia and how its shore was articulated by a series of river valleys with ports at their mouths that would evolve into industrial elements in a whole system. Marseilles and the Rhone Valley were the most important of these, especially because when linked to Paris, they connected London to the Mediterranean. Beyond these economic facts, Chevalier's Saint-Simonian projection depicted a wonderful future when peace and harmony would be established as a result of the complete industrial integration of the nations of Europe and of all Europe with Asia. "The day when the *système de la Méditerranée* is sufficiently elaborated that one might envision its realization, peace will come to Europe as by enchantment, and it will remain forever."[74] In the next year, Enfantin led the initiated of the sect to Egypt to attempt to convince the Pasha, Mohammed Ali, to construct the Suez Canal.

The Saint-Simonians characteristically imagined a fusion of East and West in their "système de la Méditerranée," but another projection of

Marseilles's significance took the more popular form of the city as "la façade principale de la France sur la Méditerranée."[75] The idea that France was the carrier of civilization and enlightenment to the south had been the Romantic justification of the conquest of Algeria,[76] and in 1834 it was applied to the city itself by the local economist Jules Julliany in his important *Essai sur la commerce de Marseilles.*

France should possess a city that would be the capital of the Mediterranean shores. . . .

We have said that this is a question of general interest for France; it is more still, it is a question of civilization.

It is clear that the benefits of civilization can only spread over the Mediterranean coastline by means of Marseilles; it is the only important city around this sea controlled by a free people.

Thus we should try to cultivate at Marseilles the advances and the discoveries of civilization. . . .

This is not inspired by narrow local interest. It is in the interest, I dare say, of humanity as a whole that Marseilles should exercise over southern Europe, over northern Asia and Africa a progressive, civilizing, enlightening influence.[77]

All of this brings us back to Vaudoyer's transformation in 1855 of his design for the most prominent monument of the new Marseilles. One understands immediately his treatment of the facade as a monumental gate symbolic of the city's significance, as Charles Blanc pointed out. One also understands the references in its forms to various characteristic features of Mediterranean architecture: its Byzantine domes (rendered Turkish by the minaret-like corner turrets of the transepts) and the Tuscan green-and-white striping of its masonry. What had been in 1852 a project summarizing the history of Christian architecture became a project summarizing the Mediterranean tradition of building as well.

The elaborately inflected 1855 design nonetheless holds together. The essence of Vaudoyer's solution is making the cathedral a symbolic object set at this specific place in this specific landscape, the artistic equivalent of Chevalier's realization that Marseilles was a pressure point in a world economic system. The cathedral as redesigned in 1855 has a strong image from a distance, just as Marseilles was seen by Chevalier from the perspective of a man on the moon contemplating all Europe and the Mediterranean from outer space. (Jean Reynaud opened his *Terre et Ciel* of 1854 by presenting Earth through the eyes of a hypothetical astronomer on Jupiter.[78] Monsignor François Durand found the perfect image when in his history of the cathedral he compared it to "the miniature churches that the image-makers of the Middle Ages placed in the hands of holy builders"

—the brilliantly colored, reliquary-like church models that donors are holding in medieval representations like that in the apse of San Vitale in Ravenna.[79]

Vaudoyer's understanding of how the cathedral fit into its immediate context must have matured during his repeated visits to Marseilles after 1852. But to convert these abstract qualities into a single, inflected form he had to see them from a distance and in a landscape, something for which even his own work on the Conservatoire des Arts et Métiers would not have prepared him. In that earlier building his solution was to create framed, closed tableaux within a cityscape; here he had to arrange forms in a broad landscape, and his tools were scale, geometric shape, and color.

Vaudoyer's conception of the cathedral as an object in the landscape was refined in the design of the Marseilles pilgrimage chapel of Notre-Dame-de-la-Garde in 1853–54, made during the revision of the cathedral project (figure 55).[80] Vaudoyer himself was nominally the architect, as *architecte diocésain*, but in fact the designer was his twenty-five-year-old student and *inspecteur*, Espérandieu. Though young, Espérandieu was a Provençal and may have been much more than just a pencil in Vaudoyer's hand. Vaudoyer himself insisted upon Espérandieu's independence in conceiving the design.[81] The building tops a dramatic rock outcropping south of the Vieux Port and thus had to state its presence from a distance even more emphatically than the cathedral. Espérandieu's solution was to adopt the green-and-white banding simultaneously accepted by Vaudoyer and to give his structure the big, clearly defined geometric volumes of his master's projects—here a series of terraces supporting a tall, rectangular sanctuary topped by a dome and a tall, square tower. The most striking element of the composition and the key to its success is a colossal guilded statue of the Virgin topping the tower that changes the scale of the monument and makes it read from a distance as a sparkling reliquary. It was at this moment that the Marseilles sculptor Bartholdi posed the issue of colossal statuary, particularly with his project for a figural monument to mark the entrance of the Suez Canal (1867–69), the precursor of his statue of Liberty in New York harbor (1870–85).[82] Bartholdi claimed to have studied in Labrouste's atelier in Paris around 1850, and his Suez monument had precursors in a celebrated series of student projects for lighthouses of 1852 from the ateliers of Labrouste and his admirers Nicolle and Danjoy (figure 56).[83] In these as well as other projects, buildings were made in the form of colossal objects suggestive of their function and often brilliantly colored. In Bartholdi's case, the intention was to place these colossal markers at the pressure points of the new industrial world—Suez, New York, Marseilles—so that, in a sense, they would make it legible to an astronomer on Jupiter.

A basic component of the new sense of scale manifested in Notre-Dame-de-la-Garde and the cathedral, speaking to each other across the

55
Henri Espérandieu, Notre-Dame-de-le-Garde, Marseilles, 1854–64.

56
*Léopold-Amédée Hardy, Juste
Lisch, Emile Delangle, and Victor
Pertuisot, Lighthouses, projects
executed in the second class at the
Ecole des Beaux-Arts. From*
Revue générale de l'architecture
et des travaux publics *10 (1851):*
pl. *9.*

basin of Marseilles, was color, their green-and-white striping suggestive of Tuscany and Cairo but simultaneously harmonizing with the white cliffs and the green foliage of the immediate landscape. Polychromy had been an interest of the *pensionnaires* around 1830, but not this sort. Labrouste's conception of the coloring of the Basilica at Paestum and of his fantasy Agrigentum, both of 1828, was that it demonstrated the accretion of decorative clothing to the structural skeleton and was thus, in essence, painted or hung on and temporary. The polychromy of these Marseilles buildings is permanent, derived from their actual structural surfaces, and harmonious with the general chromatic tone of the region rather than expressive of specific events and ideas.

The conception of architectural polychromy had been evolving between 1830 and 1850.[84] In the 1820s German researchers studying the painting of the ancient Greek temples had already explained it as an effort to gain harmony with the brilliant chromatic Mediterranean environment, and the Cologne-born Hittorff offered this justification in his *Architecture antique de la Sicile* of 1827–30:

When one has visited old Sicily, when one has lived in this country, when one has admired the sky of this blessed land, when one has seen the sun spread its morning brightness over the whole surface of this Ile Verte *and enveloped it with its dying rays as with a net of gold; when one has observed the brilliant colors which in Sicily nuance the laurel, the palm, the aloe, the myrtle, the orange tree, in a word everything which the ground produces in the bosom of the desert as in the middle of a fertile field, one is convinced that the artist must take his inspiration from the beauties that surround him, place himself in harmony with them, and enrich the work of art with all the splendor of nature.*[85]

By the 1840s this conception had come to prevail over that of Labrouste and his admirers. The young scholar Emile Burnouf wrote in the *Revue des deux mondes* in 1847 that polychromy was intended to "soften the splendor" of the white marble temples when seen in the light and air of Athens, in the "transparent atmosphere which draws objects closer by making their contours distinct and which the vibrations of the heat render visible and almost palpable."[86] And this conception of architectural color embraced all the buildings of the Mediterranean, the glazed tilework of Spain and Asia as well as the striped masonry of Tuscany and Egypt or the painted temples of Greece and Sicily. In 1833–34 the English architecture student Owen Jones, in company with the French student Jules Goury, studied the Alhambra in Granada, which resulted in the monumental *Plans, Elevations, Sections and Details of the Alhambra* (1836–45) published in brilliant chromolithograph with essays on how the red, blue, and golden colors of the decoration would have blended and shimmered in the Spanish sun.[87] In Italy, beginning in 1822, the marble *placage* of Tuscan medieval architecture was revived with G. B. Silvestri's project to complete the facade of the Duomo.[88] Silvestri actually erected such a colored marble facade on the cathedral of Grosetto in 1833, while in 1837 Nicolas Matas suggested a similar treatment of Santa Croce in Florence (carried out 1857–63) and in 1843 of the Duomo. In 1851 the first volume of Ruskin's *Stones of Venice* appeared, and thus Italian polychromy became one of the ideals of nineteenth-century architecture.[89] Paralleling these developments was the revelation of the brilliant polychromy of the Islamic buildings of Cairo in the chromolithographed plates of *Architecture arabe* (1839) and *Monuments moderne de la Perse* (1867) by the Marseilles architect Pascal Coste. This documentation of the chromatic splendor of Eastern architecture was made even more striking by Félix Thomas's reconstructions of the Assyrian remains at Khorsabad shown in the Salon of 1858 and published in 1867.[90]

This new visualization of architectural polychromy formed part of a contemporary movement in taste sometimes called the Néo-Grec. It was not so much Greek as exotic, and its leitmotif was this Mediterranean sense of color. Its quintessential monument was Théophile Gautier's volume of exquisite, sensual, exotic poems, *Emaux et camées*, published in 1852. The Néo-Grec had burst upon the scene in 1843 with Gleyre's painting *Soir* at the Salon and Ponsard's play *Lucrèce*, with Rachel in the title role and piquantly archaic Pompeiian sets. It gave rise to a school of Néo-Grec painters around Gleyre and Gérôme: Boulanger, Hamon, Picou, and Moreau.[91] It coincided with a renewal of interest in polychromy among the Grand Prix winners, now spending their fourth year in Greece. Ballu sent his reconstruction of the Erechtheum in 1844–45, Paccard his of the Parthenon in 1845–46; Titeux his of the Propylea in 1846, and finally Garnier his remarkable visualization of the temple at Aegina in 1852.[92] The actress Rachel redid her dining room in this style; the Prince Napoleon built his Maison Pompéienne (1856–60).[93] Paris for a moment lived in a fantasy world somewhat Oriental, somewhat Etruscan and everywhere glittering with brilliant colors and precious materials.

Vaudoyer was an habitué of the *salon* of Gautier's friend, the Néo-Grec Arsène Houssaye,[94] he was a close friend of Pascal Coste,[95] and he possessed a copy of Matas's publication of his 1843 project for the facade of the Duomo.[96] Indeed, in this light his and Espérandieu's solutions for Notre-Dame-de-la-Garde and Marseilles Cathedral seem almost inevitable. This is important because, in fact, during the 1840s a number of churches had been erected in Germany clothed in striped polychrome brickwork and one might be tempted to see them as the principal source of Vaudoyer's design.[97] Clad in reds and browns, however, they had an earthy chromatic effect totally different from sparkling Néo-Grec coloration. Furthermore, to call the Marseilles buildings merely German would be to miss the manipulation of symbolism and scale which their polychromy subserves.

Nonetheless, this parallel introduces a basic fact of Vaudoyer's design: that it, like the Conservatoire des Arts et Métiers, is ultimately the correction and monumentalization of contemporary German architecture that Fortoul had proposed in 1842 in *De l'Art en Allemagne*. There, in volume one, as we noted earlier, he introduced the aesthetic ideal of an architecture that is rich and varied in its imagery, like that of von Klenze's Residenz or the whole Ludwigstrasse quarter in Munich. To him a palace or a cathedral should summarize the history of the architecture of its various parts, just as Vaudoyer's first project for the cathedral, in fact, does. Then, in volume two, Fortoul introduces the round-arched style as the basic vocabulary of Christian building and "capable of producing all impressions, from the simplest and most austere to the most complex and splendid: the round arch, the generative principle of these monuments, is treated in a thousand different fashions which should inspire the meditations of the artists of our age."[98] He especially praises the Byzantine over the Romanesque for the greater variety and expressiveness of its forms and holds that the strength of the Rhenish churches lies in their Byzantineness. Here he puts his finger on the great advance made by Vaudoyer, who already in his first project for the cathedral was using parts of the Byzantine vocabulary to escape the straitjacket of the simpler Romanesque style that Questel had introduced in his earlier attempt at a round-arched style, the church of Saint-Paul at Nîmes. Fortoul, as we have seen, called upon French designers to use their particular powers of composition and invention to transform German eclectic historicism and to make something monumental and exemplary in the round-arched vocabulary. This Vaudoyer accomplished at Marseilles. It is indeed "un des plus beaux et des plus curieux monuments dont la France puisse s'honorer," as Fortoul observed.

Elaborate as are Vaudoyer's gestures toward local character, one must note that his attitude is essentially cosmopolitan. The building recognizes commerce, France, and Asia, but not Provence. There was a Provençal architecture represented in Saint-Trophime at Arles, the cathedral at Avignon, and in the old cathedral of Sainte-Marie-Majeure on the site of Vaudoyer's new building. The local antiquary Casimir Bousquet could only note the complete distinction between the "roman" of the old cathedral and the "romano-byzantine" of Vaudoyer's new structure.[99] This disregard for the actual local tradition was made more pointed by Vaudoyer's plan to demolish the Sainte-Marie-Majeure (resisted and partially canceled by local partisans[100]); by the example of Questel's Saint-Paul, which honored the local style; by Revoil's studies of Provençal architecture published in 1867–73;[101] and finally by the founding in 1854 of the Félibrige, a circle of militant poets around Frédéric Mistral campaigning for the preservation and cultivation of Provençal literature and language.[102] These last achieved considerable fame (Mistral winning the Nobel Prize in 1904) writing in old Provençal and using the tight, elegant forms of the troubadours to express the courtly sentiments of piety and love set in smiling nature.

Marseilles was Babylon to the Félibrige; their Provence was that of Arles, Avignon, Aix, and the farm towns between. But they were unimportant to Marseilles, which was essentially a new creation, functioning as a link in the international "système de la Méditerranée." It is remarkable how little local influence was permitted or acknowledged in the development of the city at this time. Octave Teissier's propagandistic *Marseilles sous Napoléon III* gives all the credit to the Emperor and his appointed representative, Charlemagne-Emile de Maupas, who succeeded Suleau:

The renovating genius of Napoleon soared over Marseilles. The old Phoenician city awoke, broader ideas germinated in all minds, projects for enlargement were studied and submitted for the approval of the Prince, who France was about to proclaim Emperor.[103]

It is also striking that the local authorities were neither asked for nor expressed opinions about the designer or his artistic decisions. The only matters discussed in the *procès verbal* of the Département du Bouches du Rhône and the Conseil Municipal are financial. When Espérandieu, a Protestant, was named *inspecteur*, nothing more could be done than emit an ineffectual protest and require that Vaudoyer remain the architect of record of Notre-Dame-de-la-Garde.

In May 1869 an event of great importance took place in Marseilles: the election that sent the leftists Gambetta and Esquiros to the Chambre des Députés as the representative of the city.[104] Gambetta defeated Thiers, standing for the Opposition Liberale et Légitimiste, and Ferdinand de Lesseps, the official candidate, standing at the personal request of Napoleon III. In spite of the huge economic benefits bestowed upon Marseilles by the Second Empire, the hero of Suez could draw only 16.4 percent of the vote. We saw at the beginning of this chapter that the cathedral was initiated in large part to placate the Left, and we see that in 1869—despite the new port at its feet and all the other public works connected with it—it failed to do so. The election of 1869 points up the basic quality of all these projects, that they were *about* Marseilles, not *of* it. They all make Marseilles nothing more than a stopping place on the way to the East. The cathedral is but a marker for an administrator in Paris (or a Saint-Simonian astronomer on Jupiter), a glittering dollhouse church placed here by the Emperor like Ecclesius in the apse mosaic at San Vitale.

DUC'S PALAIS DE JUSTICE

That Marseilles Cathedral might be the statement of an imperial style is something of a revelation because the style of the Second Empire seems so indistinct—as indistinct, perhaps, as the Empire's own political nature. Napoleon III himself is supposed to have declared in a celebrated confidence, "The Empress is legitimist, my cousin [the Prince Napoleon] is Republican, Morny is Orléanist, I am a socialist; the only Bonapartist is Persigny and he is mad." In architecture the situation was no better. The Empress Eugénie was a partisan of Viollet-le-Duc's Gothic (which was secretly Republican); the Minister Fortoul helped conceive Vaudoyer's authoritarian Byzantine; the monument most widely accepted today as embodying the *style Napoléon III* was Garnier's *parvenu* Baroque Opera. And the structure awarded the Grand Prix de l'Empereur in 1869—an award of 100,000 francs for the greatest work of painting, sculpture, or architecture produced during the previous five years—was Duc's Palais de Justice, the style of which seemed so obscure that many contemporaries judged it mad.[1]

Viollet-le-Duc observed in the seventh volume of his *Dictionnaire raisonnée* (1864) that the palace is distinguished from the château by the fact that there the King renders justice.[2] What came to be called the Palais de Justice in Paris was the oldest continuously inhabited royal residence in the city, mentioned as having served Eudes (887–898), supposed to have served Childebert I (d. 558), and perhaps even first erected by the Romans.[3] By the end of the Middle Ages, when it achieved the form recorded in the *Très riches heures* of the Duc de Berri, the palace occupied the west end of the Ile de la Cité and consisted of a fortified *enceinte* bounding the *quais* and cutting across at the rue de la Barillerie (today the boulevard du Palais). It was a public building more than a residence: an open space dominated by the Sainte-Chapelle (erected 1246–48 to contain the Crown of Thorns), the Grand'Salle (the justice hall and ceremonial chamber), the Conciergerie (the residence and office of the *concierge* in charge of the structure), and the Grand'Chambre of the Parlement. Masses of tight wooden shops crowded the space today called the Cour de Mai and filled galleries beside the Grand'Salle, to the profit of the *concierge* in rents. This was one of the most intensely frequented corners of medieval Paris, the place of exotic shops, justice, parliamentary government, and public celebration.[4] Indeed, when the Seine inundated the palace in 1408, the King removed his residence, first to the Hôtel Saint-Pol, then to the Louvre. Victor Hugo opened *Notre-Dame de Paris* with an exciting and grotesque description of the public celebration of the Jour des Rois and the Fête des Fous in the Grand'Salle in 1482.

Shortly after 1500 the Cour des Comptes was erected west of the Sainte-Chapelle. In 1618 the Grand'Salle burned and Solomon de Brosse rebuilt it in 1619–38 from revenues from the sale of land cleared at Saint-Germain-des-Prés. The Grand'Chambre occupied by the Parlement was subsequently rebuilt by Libéral Bruant. In 1776 a serious fire destroyed the shops and the structures around the Cour de Mai (figure 57). A special tax was levied and a regular, monumental facade and court were erected by the architects Guillaume-Martin Couture, Pierre Desmaisons, and Jacques-Denis Antoine in 1781–83.

The terrible deliberations of the Tribunal Révolutionnaire took place here. During the Empire the law courts grew to occupy the whole of the structure except the Cour des Comptes, which became the Préfecture de Police, but no significant physical changes were made in the structures. With the regularization and reorganization of the French legal system and with the rapid growth of Paris, the building became utterly inadequate. Finally in 1835 the Conseil Général de la Seine named J.-N. Huyot to prepare plans for a modest rebuilding program to cost 1,100,000 francs. Huyot saw the grandure of the opportunity—the monumental composition of the principal, western end of the Ile de la Cité resting like a vast man-of-war in the Seine—and made a counterproposal which he estimated would cost 3,591,617.33 francs (figures 58, 59). As Vaudoyer would later do at the Conservatoire des Arts et Métiers, Huyot appropriated a large area for new construction by building over the back garden and placing the principal entrance here, on the west, enframed by a monumental facade of Baroque pavilions and columns.

After various modifications, this project was approved by the Conseil Général de la Seine, and a royal ordinance commanded work to proceed on May 26, 1840—sixty-eight days before Huyot's unexpected death on August 3. Huyot was immediately replaced by Louis Duc, assisted by Etienne-Théodore Dommey (1801–72); the latter was previously Huyot's *inspecteur* on the project and architect of the Palais de Justice at Lille.[5] They presented a modified project that was approved by the Conseil Général de la Seine on November 25, 1842, and construction was begun on the wings east and south of the Sainte-Chapelle for the Police Correctionnel. This,

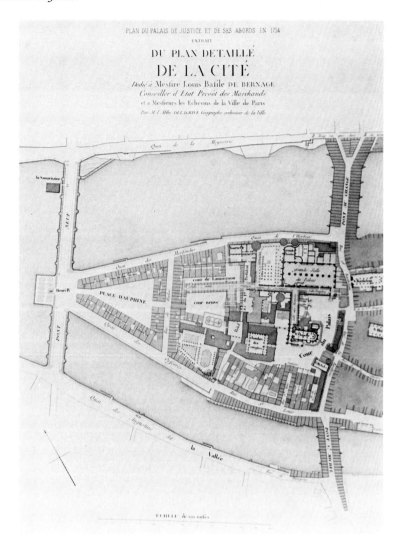

57

Palais de Justice, Paris, state of the buildings in 1754. From Documents relatifs au travaux du Palais de Justice de Paris, *1858, pl. 2.*

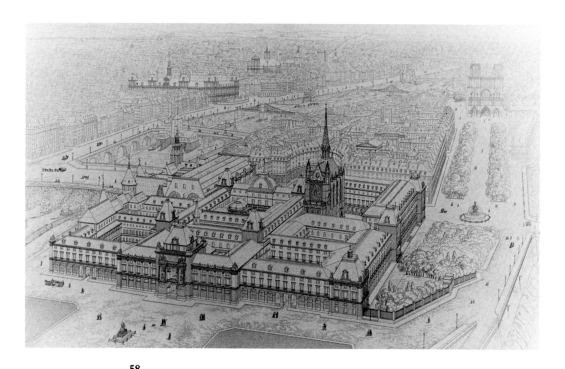

58
Jean-Nicolas Huyot, Palais de Jus-
tice, project for enlargement, 1838.
From Documents relatifs au
travaux du Palais de Justice de
Paris, *1858, pl. 9.*

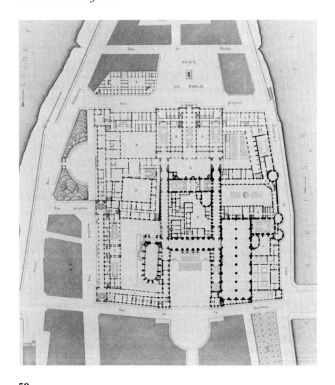

59
*Jean-Nicolas Huyot, Palais de Jus-
tice, project for enlargement, 1838.
From* Documents relatifs au
travaux du Palais de Justice de
Paris, *1858, pl. 10.*

however, inspired a vigorous protest and an order to stop work from the Commission des Monuments Historiques because it would hem in the Sainte-Chapelle excessively.[6] A new project was worked out and approved by the Conseil Général on November 14, 1846. The wing for the Police Correctionnel was to be completed by 1852 (figure 60). Construction was recommenced in 1847, and simultaneously a new project was submitted for the rest of the building, just in time to be postponed by the Revolution of February 1848, although it was examined and approved "en principe" by the Conseil des Bâtiments Civils on September 18, 1848 (figure 61).[7]

The Revolution resulted in the splitting of architectural authority. Gilbert and his son-in-law A.-S. Diet (1827–90) were put in charge of the Préfecture de Police; Louis Lenormand (1801–61) of the Cour de Cassation; Duc and Dommey of the law courts proper. The latter had retained the major part of the work, however, and added the Cour de Cassation to their charge when Lenormand died in 1861. In 1867 Dommey withdrew from the project and was replaced by Honoré Daumet (1826–1911), recently returned from the French Academy in Rome and the Macedonian archaeological expedition led by Léon Heuzey.[8]

In 1851 the site had been enlarged westward to the rue de Harlay just behind the Place Dauphine (figures 62, 63). New projects were prepared, especially by Duc for the west facade, which he made an even more dramatic centerpiece to the composition (figure 64). Duc also worked out a brilliant plan with the two great courtrooms of the Assizes suspended on iron columns above a large holding prison, linked back to the older parts by two straight corridors departing from the spacious Vestibule de Harlay (figure 65). The Place Dauphine was to be completely leveled to leave the western facade visible down the Seine to the Champs-Elysées and the Colline de Chaillot (figure 66). The cost of Duc's portion had now risen to 38,881,434 francs. The bill to fund it was sent to the Conseil Général de la Seine on January 31, 1856; construction was begun on January 1, 1857; and the grand Vestibule de Harlay opened to the public on October 30, 1868.[9] Two of the three sides of the Place Dauphine, however, remained standing, at first awaiting the completion of the Palais de Justice in all its parts and later as a result of public resistance to its destruction.

The Vestibule de Harlay and its monumental columned facade are clearly the centerpiece of Duc's composition and the accomplishments for which he was awarded the Grand Prix de l'Empereur. The classical Orders were ticklish things for the Romantic *pensionnaires,* but it is clear that Duc has handled his Orders quite uniquely, especially on the exterior. There is, first of all, the tall attic with its strange herms, and then the exotic capital type. Strange as well, and more important, is the relationship of the column shafts to the wall. These are precisely and geometrically half-

60
*Louis Duc, Palais de Justice, wing
for the Police Correctionnel, 1847–
52. (Photo: James Austin)*

61
*Louis Duc, Palais de Justice, view
from the northeast with the rebuilt
Conciergerie, c. 1860. (Photo: Service Photographique des Monuments Historiques)*

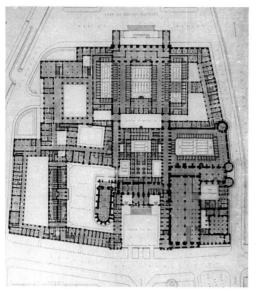
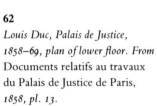
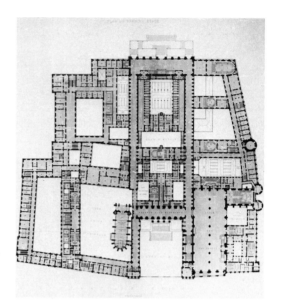

62
Louis Duc, Palais de Justice,
1858–69, plan of lower floor. From
Documents relatifs au travaux
du Palais de Justice de Paris,
1858, pl. 13.

63
Louis Duc, Palais de Justice, plan
of main floor. From Documents
relatifs au travaux du Palais de
Justice de Paris, *1858, pl. 17.*

64
*Louis Duc, Palais de Justice, west
facade on the rue de Harlay, 1857–
68. (Photo: James Austin)*

65
Louis Duc, Palais de Justice, interior of the Vestibule de Harlay, 1857–68. (Photo: James Austin)

66

Louis Duc, Palais de Justice, final project, before 1858. From Documents relatifs au travaux du Palais de Justice de Paris, *1858, pl. 33.*

columns, reduced to exact quarter-columns against the terminal antae.
Quatremère de Quincy in 1832 had specified that a "colonne adossée"
should be somewhat greater than half exposed, having either a third or
only a quarter of its circumference in the wall behind.[10] This was so the
column would clearly distinguish itself from the wall and cast a firm
shadow along the line of juncture (something Duc nevertheless achieves in
the Harlay facade by having his columns meet the wall in the middle of a
flute, a detail ancient architects avoided[11]). The reason for making this
sharp distinction between column and wall lay in the conception of the
former architectural element: it had entasis and often fluting and so was
distinct from a pilaster, which was a mere projection of the wall and thus
had neither.[12] Duc seems to have been trying to combine the qualities of
these two elements, pushing his columns into the wall and against the
antae, but retaining their fluting and entasis.

Quatremère's attitude reflects his belief in the complete separation of the
column—the embodiment of the sculptural ideal—and the inert structural
wall. He would have preferred that the two never touch at all and that the
Orders manifest themselves only as freestanding colonnades.[13] The academic Neoclassical model for the engaged colonnade was the Theatre of
Marcellus in Rome, where the capitals were conventional in detail and the
shafts were free for two-thirds of their circumference at all three levels.[14]
However, Duc had already challenged this paradigm in his fourth-year
envoi of 1829–31 (figure 67), in which he studied the simplification of the
Colosseum's capitals and proposed that they were merely reliefs cut in the
rough travertine of the whole structural surface.[15] Furthermore, his drawings showed that while the lowest of its four engaged Orders projected to
three-quarters of its circumference, this was steadily reduced as the tiers
rose so that the third, Corinthian, Order is precisely half exposed (like the
Corinthian Order of Duc's Harlay facade) and the fourth, Composite, Order is one merely of pilasters. That is to say, Duc demonstrated that the
applied Orders of the Colosseum actually served as buttresses, built into
the wall and progressively projecting as they approached the ground to
steady the mass behind them.[16] Quatremère had dismissed the Colosseum
as showing an "irrégularité" and "incertitude" in its detailing, which suggested "that one had not devoted much time or effort to the perfection of
these details."[17] Duc, in contrast, by submitting the building to close
scrutiny, makes clear that while these Orders might lack the sculptural
elaboration of those of the Theatre of Marcellus, they demonstrate a sensitivity to their actual structural function as elements in a continuous,
curving, arcuated wall.

One should extend this to analyze the relationship of Duc's Harlay
facade to the interior of the vestibule. Here the reason for the tall attic and
the precise half-columns of the facade becomes even clearer. The vestibule

67
Louis Duc, Restoration of the Colosseum, Rome. Fourth-year envoi,
*1829–31. Ecole des Beaux-Arts,
Paris. (Photo: Chevojon Frères)*

is roofed with an impressive stone-ribbed vault transmitting a diagonal outward thrust which the exterior columns, working as buttresses as in the Colosseum, carry to earth. To accomplish this they need only extend up to the springing of the vaults—leaving the high attic above them—and are firmly attached to the wall rather than set out from it as three-quarter columns. This also explains the broken entablature above the columns, for the shafts were not meant to appear to support a lintel but rather were intended to buttress a wall.

This enlightening and rather obvious explanation of the Harlay facade was already noted by Charles Clément in his critique of the Palais de Justice in the *Journal des Débats* of November 17, 1868 (although it is not mentioned by Paul Sédille in his necrology of 1879, the principal source for modern scholars). It is also why Viollet-le-Duc praised the Vestibule in the fifteenth of his *Entretiens* (1872), declaring, "the decoration adheres to the structure, even supports it."[18] But why would that be a virtue? Evidently because the classical analogy of the column with the human body is here made synonymous with that of the building's own structural dynamics—its movements and elasticity.

Duc's Harlay facade, with its deep, structurally expressive columnar decoration in relief, was not unique among the major works of the Romantic *pensionnaires*. Labrouste's Bibliothèque Sainte-Geneviève (figure 32), Vaudoyer's gallery wing at the Conservatoire des Arts et Métiers (figure 40), and Duban's quai Malaquais wing of the Ecole des Beaux-Arts, erected in 1858–62 (figure 68), all contain large interior spaces girdled by thick stone facades opened with broad bays and stabilized by buttresses. All were parallel solutions to the same problem, and comparison makes the brilliance of Duc's solution even clearer.

We have noted the depth of the thin piers that form the structural envelope of the Bibliothèque Sainte-Geneviève, holding the light iron interior frame in place and moderating the southern sunlight. Labrouste minimized the expression of these piers on the exterior by moving the window plane forward and by linking them with an arcade at the cornice. This, however, was one detail Vaudoyer was firm to dispute in his gallery wing at the Conservatoire des Arts et Métiers; instead, he exposed his girdling piers as clearly recognizable buttresses, which project further as they near the ground and are linked at the top by only the arching masonry of the wall itself. The buttresses are again exposed in Duban's quai Malaquais wing, which contains a broad, iron-roofed hall on each floor. But Duban was clearly disturbed by their disruption of the monumental surfaces of his mass, and he offered a subtle rendering of them: the facade plan is set alternately at the front and the rear of the eight bay-defining piers, giving the elevation an "indented trace," like a fortification. As a result the buttresses do not appear as projections but as the sides of

68
*Félix Duban, Ecole des Beaux-
Arts, Paris, 1858–62, wing facing
the quai Malaquais. (Photo: James
Austin)*

three advancing bays or pavilions that are carried up into powerful rounded dormers plugged with oeils-de-boeuf at the cornice. Exposed buttresses had always troubled nineteenth-century monumental architects (as they had eighteenth-century designers as well), and church designers—whether Vaudoyer at Marseilles or Viollet-le-Duc at Carcassonne—had tried to avoid them.[19] Duban avoids them in the quai Malaquais wing by making a virtue of necessity and integrating his buttresses into his mass composition to achieve a "Baroque" three-dimensionality in which the advancing bays themselves, not just the piers defining them, appear to hold the interior firm.

Duc's colonnade on the Harlay facade returns to Vaudoyer's solution, but avoids the pitfall of breaking the wall plane by seeming not to be buttresses at all, but rather decoration in a second plane in front of the wall, pressed back into it. And the satisfaction in Duc's solution extends a step further. All the facades we have been analyzing ornament the buttresses as columns in one way or another. Labrouste applies a sort of capital below the springing of the arcade; Vaudoyer carves Tuscan pilasters incongruously into the surfaces of the upper stage of his medieval buttresses; Duban marks his piers with meager pilasters whose cornice and pedestal moldings grid and control the proportions of the mass. None of them could accept a buttress in its pure, Gothic, structural form. Each tried to integrate it into their mass and dress it up as a classical column. But Duc was the most overt about it, and in the end the most effective. What was it about the classical column that in this, the most Gothic of all situations, it reasserted itself in the work of the Romantic *pensionnaires*?

We have seen how Hippolyte Fortoul set as his conceptual enterprise the formulation of an architecture organized by some means other than the Orders and how Reynaud and Vaudoyer pronounced Renaissance architecture to be in decline when, around 1500, the Orders became dominant and fixed. Vaudoyer deemphasized the Orders in the Conservatoire des Arts et Métiers and omitted them from Marseilles Cathedral, as Labrouste had done at the Bibliothèque Sainte-Geneviève. Quatremère's constant hammering on the importance of the colonnade in his writings and academic pronouncements had been answered. One of the pithiest refutations came from Fortoul's mentor Edgar Quinet at the beginning of his *Génie des religions* of 1842. He compares the idea (put forward by Laugier and carried on by Quatremère) that architecture has an ideal model in the primitive hut erected as an instinctual response by aboriginal man to Rousseau's conception of man as perfect in a state of nature. Quinet points out that this assumes that primitive man spontaneously thought like an eighteenth-century *philosophe,* although that had long since been proven just as wishful as it seems. Primitive man's first instincts were superstitious, not

rational, and his earliest architecture was magical and symbolic, not structurally logical. The origin of architecture is not in the hut but in the
spaceless Egyptian pyramid, Quinet concludes. The column and entablature have no claim to primordial, ideal sources.

In the face of this, one might well ask how Quatremère de Quincy—
and Duc too, as well as generations of architects after him—believed that
the column was the expressive element. The answer lies in the very fact
that the Harlay facade columns are actually buttresses, not forming part of
a lintelled colonnade of the sort Quatremère admired in the Bourse and
the "Palais d'Orsay" at all. That is, Duc has peeled off a residual
element in Quatremère's theory, the ideal of the primitive hut consisting
only of supports and lintels, and revealed the core that was still fecund: the
idea that architecture is sculptural, expressed by adjustments in the shape
of the metaphorical column.

One theme constantly reappearing in Quatremère's works is the analogy
between the sculpted column and the sculpted human form. In an essay
of 1805 he sought to prove that the proportions of the Greek Orders had
not become more elongated with the passage of time, as David Le Roy proposed,[20] but on the contrary varied constantly within fixed limits and were
thus expressive, not evolutionary.[21] In the entry "Architecture" in the
first volume of his *Architecture* of 1788 (part of the *Encyclopédie méthodique*),
after explaining the Orders' origin in the primitive hut, he asserts that
through a comparison of the column with the human body, the Greeks
transformed the model when they transposed it into stone.[22] Thus the column was shaped, as if bearing weight; related to the cornice by canonical
proportions; and divided into three Orders, each unified by a distinct expression: *force* (the Doric), *grace* (the Ionic), and *majesté* (the Corinthian).
He concludes:

*Nature gave to sculpture a fixed measure of relationships, a scale of proportions of
the human body . . . which functioned as a module for the figure: this controlled
the most subtle nuances of proportion by establishing a constant relationship of
parts. . . . Architecture created for itself something similar. . . . Henceforth, a
building became a sort of organized being controlled by constant laws whose principle and reason it found in itself. . . . The detailed study of the human body in all
of its variations made sculpture conscious of the differences of age and nature that
constituted the diverse modes Polycleitus defined in his treatise on the symmetries
and of which the visible rules are preserved in ancient statutes. Architecture created
a parallel in the invention of the Orders. These modes come down to three: one
expresses force, the other grace, the third, by the union of these two other qualities,
expresses the nobility and majesty that result.*[23]

Quatremère reiterated this idea in the entries "Ordre" and "Proportion" in the third volume of *Architecture* (1825), explaining that the column is the coincidence of the statue and the post, and through it the physical expression of building is raised to the moral expression of art.

There are two sides to Quatremère's analogy between the column and the human body. On the one hand, the column should be sculpted like a figural statue with infinite nuance of form and proportion. On the other, again like a classical statue, it must not step beyond the limits of its mode and type. It is here that the idea of the primitive hut became important: it enforced these limits. One might assume that, because of his sculptural analogies, for Quatremère the perfect column form would be the caryatid, but that would be to misunderstand the importance to him of these limits, which he raised to the level of a theory of "imitation." In his volume *Essai sur la nature, le but et les moyens de l'imitation dans les beaux-arts* (1823), Quatremère insists that the pleasure of art lies not in reproduction, but in transformation.[24] Two objects produced by the same mechanical process or two natural forms growing in the same way are not works of art in relation to each other because they do not activate in the viewer the "action de comparer." The same is true of *trompe l'oeil* in painting. Transformation itself, however, is accomplished by the careful management of "conventions," to which Quatremère devotes the last third of his volume. Reality must be translated into certain fictions, some necessitated by genre, others, like generalizations and metaphors, permitting the elevation of particularities to the plane of general expression. But what Quatremère insists must be avoided at all costs is the merely real and the merely agreeable. Thus in architecture the caryatid is artless because it is the literal transformation of the body into a column without the limits and conventions provided by the type of the hut.

The distinction between the concept of the primitive hut as the general type of architecture and that of the human body, manifested in the sculptural Orders, as its expressive element is important because it was by emphasizing the latter over the former that the classical ideal survived in French architecture and eventually prevailed after Quatremère's resignation as Secrétaire Perpétuel of the Académie in 1839.

Quatremère sincerely believed that the hut remained the type of modern architecture, that is, the simple one-storied, colonnaded volume. The dome to him was a pointless complication; the modern Christian church should be a colonnaded Roman basilica.[25] In 1846, seven years after his retirement, his chosen successor as Secrétaire Perpétuel, Désiré Raoul-Rochette, altered this stand in a document approved by the Académie. "Considérations sur la question de savoir s'il est convenable au XIXe siècle de bâtir des églises en style gothique" was a critique of the Prefect of the Seine's decision to erect the church of Sainte-Clothilde in the Gothic style.[26] Raoul-Rochette concluded that it was not appropriate to use that style, but no better to adopt that of Greco-Roman antiquity. Instead he made a new suggestion: adapt the Renaissance style. Christianity had not been static in its architectural expression, he wrote, but evolved constantly, although in Italy it never forswore what was universally valid in ancient architecture, its "éléments et règles" embodied in the Orders, understood abstractly by Raoul-Rochette, as a system of proportions and relationships applied to all parts of a structure, not just to its freestanding columns. He lists Alberti, Brunelleschi, Bramante, the San Gallos, Peruzzi, Palladio, and Vignola together with Bullant, Delorme, and Lescot as the modern architect's proper precursors. He demands that Notre-Dame and the Sainte-Chapelle not be valued at the expense of the Val-de-Grâce and the dome of the Invalides. "It is necessary," he ends, "to teach not to copy the Greeks and the Romans, but to imitate them, by taking, like them, from art and from nature what lends itself to the conventions of all societies and the needs of all periods."[27]

The concept of the Orders survived that of the primitive hut. It did so because Quatremère's idea of the expressive, sculptural column was based on a rudimentary form of aesthetic psychology and because aesthetic psychology emerged around 1850 as the mainstream of art theory. There is a continuous tradition of aesthetic investigation leading from Quatremère's first suggestions down to Violet Paget and Geoffrey Scott.[28] The first generation after Quatremère, that of the Monarchy of July, was dominated by Victor Cousin and his disciple Théodore Jouffroy, who, while accepting progress and evolution, depicted architectural aesthetics as essentially unchanging because based on the human body as reflected in the Orders. Cousin founded his "Eclecticism" on what he termed psychology, on the human mind that evolved and passed through a sequence of phases historically represented by different manners of conceptualization. Jouffroy studied this psychology further, producing his *Cours d'esthétique*, propounded in the 1820s to an audience that included Ludovic Vitet and Sainte-Beuve and published posthumously in 1842 by J.-P. Damiron. Here he develops the Cousinian idea that the beautiful lies in the response of the beholder, not in the object beheld, and goes on to explore the idea of sympathy, the psychological pleasure of seeing one's own form and expressions manifested in external objects. "Man loves himself," he says in the second lesson, "and the objects that demonstrate the triumph of his nature please him. . . . We love ourselves; there lies the origin of pleasure."[29] Through the influence of Cousin, Jouffroy, and Damiron—dominating the Conseil Royale de l'Instruction Publique, the Académie des Sciences Morales et Politiques, and the Ecole Normale Supérieure during the Monarchy of July —Eclecticism and its accompanying psychological aesthetic came to characterize French academic philosophy.

Raoul-Rochette in his 1846 restatement of academic classicism obviously reflects their ideas. As they wrote, however, a third generation was formulating its more dramatic extension of these concepts. On September 11, 1846, the establishment of the Ecole Française d'Athènes was authorized by the Chambre des Députés. It was to be a small institute (more political in origin than pedagogical) for the *architectes pensionnaires* and *normaliens* to perfect their knowledge of Greece.[30] Eleven French students were dispatched to Athens: the *pensionnaires* Philippe-Auguste Titeux, Théodore Ballu, and Alexis Paccard as well as eight *normaliens* including Emile Burnouf and Charles Lévêque. Among the *pensionnaires* who followed during the next few years was Charles Garnier, in 1851, and among the *normaliens* were Jules Girard (arriving December 19, 1848), Ernest Beulé (September 20, 1849), and Edmond About (December 1, 1851). They were all classicists, the architects mostly trained in the ateliers of Huyot and Lebas, the *normaliens* under the regime of Cousin (and, in the case of Lévêque, Jouffroy).[31] In Athens they were all profoundly struck by the details and particular beauty of the Greek environment and began to formulate what by 1872 Lévêque would call a "psychologie de l'architecture."[32] Its first manifestations were an essay by Burnouf, "Le Parthénon," published in the *Revue des deux mondes* on December 1, 1847, and a thesis by Lévêque, "Essai sur les causes physiques de la perfection de l'art dans la Grèce ancienne," begun in 1847 and partially published in the *Revue des deux mondes* of August 15, 1851.[33] Beulé's excavations on the Acropolis (1852–53) and his publications followed.[34]

Refinements in the Athenian temples—the curving of the stylobates and the inclination of the columns—had been discovered by the English architect Joseph Pennethorne in 1837 and had been confirmed by his countryman Francis Cranmer Penrose during the winter of 1846–47 as well as by the French *pensionnaires* Titeux, Ballu, and Paccard.[35] Beulé and Lévêque immediately perceived that not only were the columns animated by entasis (explained by Vitruvius) but the whole Greek temple pulsated with the curves and adjustments of a living organism. Quatremère was proved to be more correct than he had realized: his analogy with sculpture stood behind the Greek temple as a whole.[36] Burnouf asserted that the temple was analogous to an organic body not only in its curves and adjustments, but also in responding to the landscape surrounding it: "Greek art, born whole from nature and inspired by her at its origin, curved the steps and the pavement of the temples, the architraves, the friezes, and the pediments, as nature curved the sea, the horizons, and the rounded backs of the mountains."[37]

Beulé carried on their intense identification of Greek architecture with its human and natural context in his numerous and influential publications of the 1850s and 1860s. Lévêque made it part of a general theory of art in his *La Science du beau* of 1861. This last work the author presents as a continuation of the labors of Cousin and Jouffroy, that is, as a psychological theory of the ideal in art.[38] Like his precursors, Lévêque declares beauty to be independent of religion (and any other transitory influences) and to be based upon expression: the communication of a clear, worthy idea. But what, he asks, are the "expressive energies" in architecture? He then answers, "A certain power . . . the resistant force of inorganic matter."[39] A building becomes expressive through the display of its construction and most particularly through the metamorphosis of structural force into curves that render the architectural mass living: "Aggrandized in all ways by architecture, the powerful resistance of inorganic matter is always submitted by this art to a visible form which recalls in more than one way the form of the living body."[40] These expressive thrusts and counterthrusts bind the building together, from outside in, just as a living organism is bound together by thrusts and counterthrusts from inside out. "Deprived of this internal dynamism [of organic bodies], architecture imitates the effects as best it can. Incapable of achieving the relationship of the interior and the exterior by dilatation, it functions from outside inward by concentration."[41] Form is controlled by symmetry and proportion, yet is free to respond to climate by openness or enclosure and, most importantly, to function by the modulation of its ornamental dress. Lévêque's statements, he claimed in 1872, outlined a "psychologie de l'architecture."[42]

A parallel school of architectural theory was defining itself in Germany during these years. At the University of Berlin during the 1840s, Franz Kugler had formulated a definition of architecture not just as expressive structure (so simply manifested in the Greek temple) but as the expressive manipulation of space and had praised Renaissance design as the impressive manifestation of this *Raumschönheit*.[43] This was a bold confrontation of the rationalist and picturesque ideas of Schinkel (who died in 1841) and the Schinkelschule.[44] His students and assistants, Jakob Burkhardt and Wilhelm Lübke, followed his lead with enthusiasm, producing the former's *Cicerone* (1855, dedicated to Kugler) and the latter's *Reise nach Italien* (1858), coincident with Kugler's early death in 1858. Beginning in 1862 Burkhardt and Lübke together completed Kugler's *Geschichte der Architektur* by writing the volume on the Renaissance. Here the concepts of expressively proportioned mass and space—*Raumstil, Raumschönheit*—are fully developed. The "living" system of proportions of the Renaissance, they wrote, was based neither on copied Greek models nor on numerical ratios; it was an elastic and individual quality in Italian architecture hinted at in late-Roman vaulted construction and in medieval building but finding its purest expression in the Renaissance.[45]

There is a figure that serves as a bridge between these German writers and the French: Heinrich von Geymüller (1839–1909). He was a Swiss,

brought up in Vienna, trained as an engineer first in Switzerland, then at
the Ecole Centrale des Arts et Manufactures in Paris, and finally as an
architect, first at the Bauschule in Berlin, then at the Ecole des Beaux-Arts
in Paris as a student of Questel.[46] In Berlin he met Lübke and was introduced by him to French Renaissance architecture and to the problems
of reconstructing Bramante's original project for St. Peter's Cathedral,
which they realized was the greatest but the least understood monument
of Renaissance conception. This experience seems to have made Geymüller see the French tradition in a new light. In 1863 he returned to Paris and
in 1864 he traveled to Italy to search for documents of Bramante's project,
making the acquaintance of Burkhardt in Basel on the way. From this
there evolved a close friendship and Geymüller's great study of St. Peter's,
published fragmentally in 1868 and then definitively as a folio volume in
French and German in 1875.[47] He reconstructed Bramante's project in a
magnificent series of drawings and declared in his text that this proved
that it was not just the Pantheon placed on top of the Basilica of Constantine, but an organic whole unified by a system of proportions and by its
"majestueuse harmonie de l'espace." His compendius *Architektur des Renaissance in Toscana* followed in 1885–1908.

Geymüller lived in Paris, when not pursuing research in Italy, and became close friends with the Alsatian Eugène Müntz, librarian of the Ecole
des Beaux-Arts and a regular contributor to the *Gazette des Beaux-Arts,*
founded in 1859 by Charles Blanc. In the pages of that most prestigious art
journal, Müntz, Blanc, Beulé, and Geymüller, among others, published
numerous articles during the 1860s and 1870s expostulating their individual interpretations of classicism revived by psychology.[48] By 1870 Kugler's first suggestions of a *Raumschönheit* had become Geymüller's
evocation of "this mysterious impression" which one experiences only in
certain of the best Renaissance buildings in Italy: "The mind enjoys a real
pleasure in embracing these places; it seems that it dilates in the building
and occupies the entire space: it would not wish to experience it any larger
or any smaller. This charm comes from the harmony of the proportions of
the interior volume."[49] Back in Basel, Burkhardt's colleague Hermann
Siebeck elaborated this into a philosophy of art in his *Das Wesen der ästhe-
tischen Anschauung* (1876) and his brilliant pupil Heinrich Wölfflin devoted
his dissertation, "Prolegomena zu einer psychologie der Architektur"
(1886), to a definitive formulation of the idea.

During the years 1846–70 these men had transformed Quatremère's
statuesque conception of the Orders into a psychology of architecture—a
system of reading architecture as the projection of bodily states—that in
Germany, during the last decade of the century, became the science of
Einfühlung, empathy. This, in turn, produced the ideas of Bernard Berenson, Violet Paget, and Geoffrey Scott. In France its formulators went on

to posts of great importance: in 1862 Beulé was named Secrétaire Per-pétuel of the Académie des Beaux-Arts, succeeding Quatremère and Raoul-Rochette; in 1857 Lévêque succeeded Barthélemy Saint-Hilaire as Professor of History of Greek Philosophy at the Collège de France, while his *La Science du beau* was proclaimed by some the principal aesthetic treatise of mid-nineteenth-century France.[50]

If the Académie was moving to expand the old Neoclassical doctrine of the Orders, Duc was moving to meet them, declaring that one could not have order without Orders, defining the latter in broad, empathetic terms. In 1879 Paul Sédille published a letter written in 1856 by Duc to one of the other Romantic *pensionnaires*:

My esteem and admiration for the arch is no less great than that for the Order, but they are nevertheless of a completely different nature.

First, I pose as a principle that the one should not take the place of the other: the Order pertains to poetry, it is lyrical, it speaks nobly, it declaims and sings.

The arch pertains to prose, it is positive, it works, serves and carries.

The Order is noble, it is master and commands; the arch is plebian, servant and obeys.

The arch is nothing by itself as a term of art, it gains meaning only by a new element which is foreign to it and added, ornamentation. . . .

The arch by itself is incapable of constituting an architecture, the arch is only a method of building. . . .

If one asserts the equivalence of the Order and the arch, and not the supremacy of the first over the second, the logic of utility will present itself all the time, the terrain formerly shared will be appropriated exclusively by the arch so as to make the artistic law of the Order forgotten.[51]

Sédille also quotes Duc from an unidentified source:

Without the Order, what would our monuments be? Is it not the Order, with its proportions fixed by those of man, that becomes the unity and the measure of the buildings? . . .

Even in the Middle Ages, the Orders were incorporated into the pillars, at first on their principal faces, later in their angles and where there were loads to be supported. This was the organ of beauty in these monuments, despite the sacrifice of all proportion in the Orders. Without these last vestiges of poetic essence, there would be only masses of inert matter.

Fiction should occupy the primary place in architecture . . . it is its essence. Was not the Greek temple a legend in stone? All the members that composed it were so many natural objects which, by their transmutation into stone, not by imitation, but by translation, became so many fictions or nightmares. It is from this mysterious work of creation between nature and the human heart that art is born. It is this incorporation of nature into matter, an almost divine act, that is the whole dogma of architecture; the rest is earthy and remains only building.[52]

The empathetic theory of Greek and Renaissance architecture emerging in the 1850s and 1860s gave powerful new life to the idea of the columnar Orders. But it is still difficult to get from this generality to the explanation of the details of the facade of Duc's Vestibule de Harlay. His columns are not Greek, because they are engaged in the facade, nor Renaissance, because they are actually buttressing the thrusts of a ribbed vault inside. Burkhardt and Geymüller insisted categorically that the expressive deformations of Renaissance forms were disassociated from structural reality,[53] while Duc links the two, producing what Viollet-le-Duc praised as a decoration that adheres to the structure.

Duc's facade is constructed entirely of cut stone, the blocks elaborately keyed together (and bound with iron clamps) so that the structural pressure pushes them together and is carried to earth by the strongest, narrowest chain of support. The facade is thus almost entirely open in broad windows, and the buttress-columns are made of large stones built into the lighter masonry. This was a great tour-de-force of stereotomy, an art that had reached its peak in France in such eighteenth-century extravaganzas as Soufflot's Pantheon and that Duc prided himself upon having revived, first in the hanging stone staircase of the Police Correctionnel wing (1847–52) and then in the Vestibule de Harlay.[54] Stereotomy also is precisely what Viollet-le-Duc admired in Gothic construction. We mentioned in the last chapter that he saw the ribbed vault as a uniquely light and practical form of construction because of its principle of elasticity. In the first volume of his *Entretiens* (1863), he constantly compared the Greeks and the French Gothic builders of the twelfth century and pointed out that when the Greeks did have to build attached columns in their largest temple, that of Zeus at Agrigentum, they had made the shafts out of large pieces of stone keyed into the thinner wall-veil like a medieval construction of ribs and webbing. This he compared deprecatingly to the Roman practice of applying pilasters to their concrete constructions as mere decoration.[55]

In applying his theory of elastic construction, Viollet-le-Duc encountered two problems: first, that it was not expressed emphatically in Gothic design; second, that it did not function structurally the way he wished to believe it did.

Gothic buttresses, the principal elements of the hypothetical elastic system, were rarely ornamented in a manner expressive of this fact. Viollet-le-Duc accepted that the curves and refinements of Greek architecture were expressive of structural force and observed that they reflected a sensitivity to structure that would come to fruition in Gothic building, but he could point to no more decisive expression of this Gothic sensitivity than the use of colonettes enframing doorways, supporting vaults, and inserted at corners. In his own Neo-Gothic work such elements became more prominent than they had been historically: the buttresses supporting the vaults in his cloister at Vézelay (1850) and along the court facade at Pierrefonds (1859–70) are marked by large, thick, compressed columns that make their carrying function palpable (figure 69). Indeed Neo-Gothic architects throughout Europe and America similarly tried to envision the style as structurally expressive in the use of colonettes during the 1850s, 1860s, and 1870s.[56]

69
*Eugène-Emmanuel Viollet-le-Duc,
Cloister added in front of the Chapter House, Vézelay, c. 1850.*

A more basic fact is that Gothic construction was not, in fact, elastic. The celebrated instances during World War I where at Soissons shell damage to ribbed vaults caused the ribs to collapse and the webbing to remain intact indicated that, regardless of the help the skeletal system might have provided in construction, once the mortar had set, the vaults were monolithic.[57] The architect Pol Abraham in 1934 synthesized this evidence into a lengthy refutation of Viollet-le-Duc's elastic theory. The origin of Viollet-le-Duc's idea, however, was clear when he formulated it in the 1840s: not Gothic building at all, but the great French tradition of stereotomy in which stones were held together by their complex shape and structural arrangement without the help of mortar.[58] This actually was elastic. What made contemporary stereotomy unacceptable to Viollet-le-Duc was its complexity. He optimistically believed that in the Gothic ribbed vault he had found a more simple, practical, democratic version of this great French contribution to construction.

The two problems in Viollet-le-Duc's theory were solved in Duc's Vestibule de Harlay. Duc's column-buttresses are powerfully and decisively expressive of their structural function, more so than Vaudoyer's at the Conservatoire des Arts et Métiers, Duban's at the Ecole des Beaux-Arts, or Viollet-le-Duc's at Vézelay and Pierrefonds. Duc's structure furthermore is not Gothic but eighteenth century, that is, composed of complexly cut stones keyed together so that they are in elastic equilibrium. Indeed the Vestibule de Harlay makes one aware that what Viollet-le-Duc was doing was projecting the science of modern stereotomy back into the Gothic period to purify it with the naïveté and practicality of that simpler age. He was, like most of his contemporaries, working out the present by projection into the past. Duc, ready to accept the whole continuum of architectural history, including the recent past, was freer to manipulate his elements, and he came up with a solution as simple in its effect as it is multiple in its sources. "Here, everything holds together," Viollet-le-Duc wrote, "everything is linked by a lucid thought. The execution, as always happens, responds to the design; it is fine and pure. One senses an artist, a rare thing in our times, who respects his art and the public."[59]

The advantages of Duc's return to the Orders extend beyond this. The classical column includes a large capital that also can be manipulated expressively, but symbolically rather than empathetically. These capitals are the equivalent of the Gothic saints attached to the shafts of the Sainte-Chapelle or the kings of France topping the piers of the Gothic Grand'Salle once in the Palais de Justice itself, although in Duc's reconstituted classical system they are completely integrated into the unitary column form.

Neoclassicism, of course, had recognized the capital as the keynote of the expressive Order, as fixed in its forms as the shafts were in their proportions. The Order that Quatremère de Quincy proposed for a *palais de justice* (and that his friend L.-P. Baltard adopted in his magnificent law court in Lyon of 1832–35) was the Corinthian because it was the middle term between the Doric and Ionic and expressed "richesse et magnificence."[60] Yet Duc's capitals, like his shafts, are not conventional or of any immediately recognizable Order. Externally they display fluted bells emerging from two tiers of stubby acanthus leaves, a sort of elementary Corinthian resting on shafts whose proportions (1:8.5) are Roman Doric. He is trying to sharpen and focus the message of these forms by inflection and combination.

Duc's principal accomplishment before he was named architect of the Palais de Justice had been the redesigning of the Colonne de Juillet to make it more specifically expressive of the Revolution of July 1830 (figure 70).[61]

70

*Louis Duc, Colonne de Juillet,
Paris, 1834–39.*

In 1830 he had submitted a fifth-year *envoi* of a columnar monument to
the victims of the revolution, and it was appropriate that on July 31, 1832,
he had been named *sous-inspecteur* to Jean-Antoine Alavoine, commissioned to erect a columnar monument to the event in the middle of the
Place de la Bastille. Alavoine proposed a simple, conventional Doric shaft
in iron (his proposal of zinc having been coldly received) topped by a
winged statue, *Génie de la Liberté*, by the sculptor Augustin Dumont. Duc
referred to the design with disgust as a "stovepipe." When on November
14, 1834, Alavoine died, Duc was named *architecte-en-chef* and redesigned
the column to increase the force and specificity of its references. He divided the shaft into three broad bands and inscribed in gilt letters the
names of all those killed during the three days of the uprising. He decorated the base as a huge sarcophagus, garlanded and surmounted by
French cocks at the corners. He altered the profiles of the moldings to
acknowledge their execution in metal. Most importantly, Duc completely
reformulated the capital as a Corinthian type alive with unfamiliar symbolic details. Fortunately a description of its meaning was published in the
Magasin pittoresque in 1840 (just after Duc led the Fortoul–Vaudoyer
group, who were involved in that publication, on a visit to the column).[62]

*There is one part where M. Duc perceived that, even from afar, one might see
what is elegant and triumphant about his column: this part is the capital. The
Vendôme Column, all loaded with its rich sculptures, can do without this ornament; M. Duc, on the contrary, has put all the emphasis of his column on the
coiffure that he has designed for it. Among the ancients, when architecture began to
free itself from the austere forms of its origin, the capital became the part of the
decoration where they expressed by specific signs the idea attached to each of their
monuments. It was there that one engraved the mysterious symbols of art. As the
soul projects itself better on the face than on other parts of the body, so the idea of a
building made itself more clearly legible in the capital than elsewhere. M. Duc has
imitated this custom of the ancients; the composition of his capital is also the most
scholarly, the richest and the most interesting part of his design. The lower part of
the capital is ornamented with a ring of palm fronds that are like the last echo of a
mourning cry rising up to heaven; above this base commences a mélange of symbols
of victory. In the midst of a sprouting vegetation that will support the angle volutes, one sees the edges of the bell we had glimpsed in the lower parts of the
column; it is from the interior of this bell that the powerful thrusts which support
the abacus unfurl. But around this festive basket four* putti *with an audacious
allure dance an animated round, placing their feet on the funereal leaves, holding in*

their hands celebratory garlands, placing their heads below those of the lions, which are flanked by paired triumphal leaves comprising the finials. The balustrade that rests on top of the abacus is designed with a rare elegance so as to serve as a diadem.[63]

When Duc's friend and fellow *pensionnaire* Hector Berlioz wrote his *Symphonie funèbre et triomphale* for the inauguration ceremony of the monument, he similarly conceived it as a funeral march that by degrees becomes a hymn of triumph and celebration.[64] It was, in a word, the poetic content of Duc's capital expressed in another medium.

Duc's memorial column and its elaborately symbolic capital introduce a side of the work of the Romantic *pensionnaires* we have slighted until now. Certain of their circle believed that architecture could express very specific ideas, could constitute "poetry" itself, even to the point that structure, function, and material were actually impediments. This was a development of the idea by now familiar to us that architecture is "a method of communicating thought independent of all human convention" and "the true writing of peoples."[65] In Marseilles Cathedral this meant expression by configurations of architectural volumes, but Espérandieu in his contemporaneous Notre-Dame-de-la-Garde extended this to engender the overt symbolism of the gigantic Virgin on the tower top, which paralleled certain Néo-Grec projects produced at the Ecole des Beaux-Arts in 1852 while he had been a student there (figures 56, 71–76). The Néo-Grec was a branching of the Romantic *pensionnaires'* movement emanating from the ateliers of Labrouste and Constant-Dufeux. It coalesced during the 1840s and centered upon two particularly radical ateliers, those of the Duban student Joseph Nicolle (1810–87) and the Huyot and Labrouste student Léon Danjoy (1806–62). They gained a strong ally in Duban's student César Daly, whose important journal, the *Revue générale de l'architecture et des travaux publics*, pressed for the "poetic" rather than the purely architectural implementation of the Romantic *pensionnaires'* program.[66]

Earlier we noted that Labrouste simplified moldings in the Bibliothèque Sainte-Geneviève so that they became part of the wall itself and that he used inscriptions and symbols (the flaming lamps flanking the entrance) to make specific statements about the institution. In 1841 there had been a competition for the design of the tomb of Napoleon at the time of the repatriation of his remains, and Labrouste had submitted a design proposing a huge bronze shield held above the floor on the backs of four eagles to permit a view into a crypt containing the Emperor's sarcophagus and a mass of battle flags and memorabilia (figure 71).[67] The symbolism of the leader buried under his shield and the poignant immediacy of the objects piled in the crypt made César Daly single it out as a model and to praise it as both new and "poetic": "The poetry and novelty in a modern monument! Courage, artists! Art has not yet said its last word."[68]

71
Henri Labrouste, Competition project for the tomb of Napoleon under the dome of the Invalides, Paris. Signed and dated "1ᵉʳ octobre 1841." Cabinet des Dessins, Louvre, Paris.

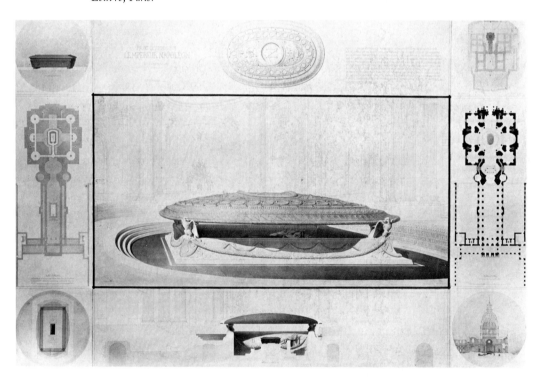

72

*Félix Duban, Competition project
for the tomb of Napoleon, 1840–41.
Sketch by Léon Vaudoyer. Archives Nationales, Paris.*

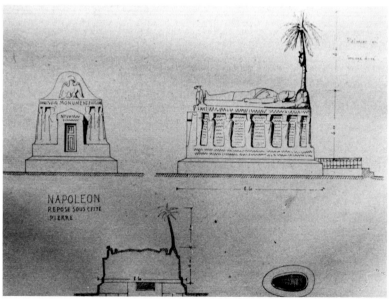

73

*Simon-Claude Constant-Dufeux,
Competition project for the tomb of
Napoleon, 1840–41. Redrawn
and published lithographically by
A. Joilly, Paris, 1872–75.*

Daly reproduced the project in the first volume of his journal along with
Duban's. The latter's seems less impressive until one knows the original
idea (preserved in a letter of Vaudoyer's, figure 72), which represents the
Emperor's sarcophagus surmounting the globe, half-buried in the pavement.[69] In his design, Constant-Dufeux suggested depicting Napoleon
in effigy on a bier shaded by an upright palm tree symbolizing his death
on distant Saint Helena (figure 73).[70] There were similar projects by
Duc, Nicolle, and Danjoy, which we know only from descriptions.
We read in *La Quotidienne*, for example, that Danjoy's was a "Byzantine"
sarcophagus surrounded by chroniclers writing the history of Napoleon's
reign and in the *Revue générale de l'architecture* that Nicolle's consisted
of an "Etruscan" sarcophagus ornamented with historical reliefs against
purple mosaic backgrounds. Surrounding this were scattered crowns
and personifications of the states created by the Emperor, girdled by a
barrier topped with "victories" driving miniature chariots.[71] What
distinguished this series of projects, Daly emphasized, was that each was
the elaboration of an original and specific conceit, immediate and
poignant rather than conventional and decorous. What also distinguished
them was the adoption of the "Byzantine" or "Etruscan" simplified
geometry of the Bibliothèque Sainte-Geneviève that was, by 1850,
to be the characteristic mark of this movement and the source
of its popular name, the Néo-Grec.

A conventional design by Charles Percier's student L.-T.-G. Visconti
was selected by the jury; Labrouste was asked to collaborate with him on
the design of the ceremony of translation.[72] A year later Constant-Dufeux
received the opportunity to design a similar memorial, erected in 1842–44
in the Cimetière Montparnasse, to Admiral Dumont d'Urville (figure
74).[73] The Admiral, after a distinguished career as an explorer, had been
burned to death with his wife and son in the first French railroad accident
on the Paris–Versailles line on May 8, 1842. Constant-Dufeux had been in
the accident himself, so the commission had particular immediacy. In 1849
Daly published the monument with the architect's explanation, pronounced at its inauguration on November 1, 1844, and a highly laudatory
introduction. Constant-Dufeux explained that it was his intention to express a complex sentiment combining both death and glorification. Death
is embodied in the solid sepulchral stone that forms the base; glorification
in the tall parabolic stone set on it, painted brilliant red. The stone's
profile, he explained, describes the line of a projectile fired into the air, the
line "the eye follows with the greatest pleasure." In its red robe—the color
"most noble and most proud"[74]—among the surrounding marble tombs,
it images the explorer standing in the polar regions he discovered. Finally,
it is the flame that killed the admiral: on one of its faces a flaming loco-
motive is inscribed in gold; above it three figures mount toward heaven.

74
Simon-Claude Constant-Dufeux,
Tomb of Admiral Dumont d'Ur-
ville, Montparnasse Cemetery,
Paris, 1842–44.

These two elements are not all: between them is a drum upon which the events of the Admiral's career are rendered in painted pictograms. At the front projects a ship's prow supporting his bust, colored realistically with black hair, blue eyes, and red lips.

The Dumont d'Urville tomb, with its narrative details and painting as well as its multiple scales, is obviously the precursor of the celebrated Ecole lighthouses of 1852 (figure 56). Again Daly is our guide in reading them. He published them at once in his *Revue* and praised their demonstration that one can make poetry in architecture.[75] He explained:

A lighthouse is [not simply a light-holder] placed on high so as to be seen from a distance and to be kept sheltered from the assaults of the sea. . . . To respect these factors is not much more than an effort of pure reason, an application of science to utility; feeling has hardly any part in it. . . . A lighthouse [is a] monument of solicitude and . . . interest, [a] monument of love and anxiety, [a] work born both of a need . . . and of a spiritual emotion, [a] work of UTILITY and of RELIGION.

Feeling, religion, [that is] . . . what constitutes the true artistic, architectural character monument.

Except for Juste Lisch's, each design is a huge sculpture to which the lantern is made to seem incidental. Léopold-Amédée Hardy's shows the Madonna and Child floating amid tiny angels below a glowing halo; Victor Pertuisot's an anxious colossus peering into the night with the aid of the light; Emile Delange's an angel holding the tree of life presenting the lamp as if a gift. Neil Levine has pointed out that each seems to embody one of the sentiments Daly listed in his critique: love, anxiety, and solicitude, respectively.

The project of Labrouste's student Lisch is not completely metaphorical like those of the students of Nicolle and Danjoy. What was seen as distinctive in their teaching was the complete denial of the functional in favor of the "poetic." Adolphe Lance, a more critical observer than Daly, summarized their doctrine in 1872:

Danjoy . . . pretended to free himself, necessarily, from all forms consecrated by science or tradition, and wished that feeling should dominate everything, even the material. Starting from there, he imagined a sort of imitative architecture (architecture imitative), which was like a poetic painting in relief of the objects of life, like a new art suspended between dream and reality.[76]

They and their students were designers more than architects. Nicolle worked principally as a ceramic designer for Sèvres, producing objects of remarkable color and wit (figure 75).[77] They were excellent draftsmen and

75
Joseph Nicolle, Vase Nicolle,
Manufacture de Sèvres, 1867.
(Photo: Philadelphia Museum of
Art)

sent striking architectural conceits to the Salons. One regrets not being able
to see Hardy's fountain of 1853, a composition of colored marble basins
made to resemble a parterre of flowers, or his scheme of 1855 that the
Moniteur des architectes described as the "translation d'une hallucination."[78]

But one can visit Père Lachaise cemetery to examine Danjoy's transformation of the tomb of Elizabeth Stroganoff Demidoff, executed sometime
in the 1850s (figure 76).[79] His design is actually only carved into the surface of an existing monument erected in 1818 by André-Marie Chatillon,
the sarcophagus and aedicula of which Danjoy retained unaltered. By re-
carving the base and adding four flaming lamps at the corners, Danjoy has
transformed it into a primitive funeral bier covered with a patterned
shroud, folded and blowing at the corners and held in place by a worked-
metal girdle with switching bands and ribbons. Here the Neoclassical of
Chatillon and the Néo-Grec of Danjoy are clearly distinguished. The Neoclassical is simple and conventional: a familiar ancient sarcophagus type
ensconced in a canonical Tuscan enframement. It is a conventional tomb
conventionally elaborated; nothing less and nothing more. The Néo-Grec
is Greek only in the expressive, stylized cutting of its surfaces—the exotic,
Romantic Greek of Gleyre and Gautier. The veil of conventions that
Quatremère de Quincy insisted should filter any sentiment has here been
torn away, revealing a vivid slice of reality: death as it was celebrated in
the deceased's Russian culture, with all its richness and strangeness. And
there is also a literary twist, a joke: were Danjoy's bier actually set aflame,
what would be consumed would be Chatillon's conventional sarcophagus
and aedicula. This is the tomb not only of Elizabeth Stroganoff Demidoff,
but also of Neoclassicism.

The final statement of the Néo-Grec metaphorical, "poetic" memorial is
César Daly's folio *Architecture funéraire* of 1871, which illustrates the Demidoff tomb as well as dozens of others. Daly categorizes the examples in his
volume by the ideas they express—*La Foi*, La Mort, *La Glorification*; and
by their combination of these ideas—*La Foi et la Mort*, *La Foi et la
Glorification*, *La Mort et la Glorification*; and finally all together—*La Foi, la
Mort et la Glorification*. (The Demidoff tomb he placed in this last category.) He makes it clear here, as he did in his analysis of the projects for
Napoleon's tomb in 1841, that to conceive or to read a Néo-Grec design,
one must determine its precise message, and that this is a matter of logic
rather than impressionism.

What, then, is the message of the capitals dominating the facade of the
Vestibule de Harlay? Contemporary critics are unhelpful because they—
unlike the writer for the *Magasin pittoresque* (Fortoul?)—seek satisfaction in
naming a historical source. Charles Clément says in the *Journal des Débats*
that Duc has reproduced the primitive Corinthian Order of the Temple of
the Winds in Athens, while Paul Sédille states that the capitals derive from

76

Léon Danjoy, Tomb of Elizabeth Stroganoff Demidoff, Père Lachaise Cemetery, Paris, c. 1855.
a. Engraving of Danjoy's plan from C. Daly, Architecture funéraire contemporaine, *1871, pl. 31.*
b. Detail of carved surface.

Stratonica, probably citing inaccurately the celebrated tomb near that site at Mylasa with similar "Carian" capitals.[80] But neither model is exact and the two critics do not suggest why Duc would have chosen them, leaving one to assume that it was mere aesthetic preference. A more helpful, if more distant, document is the Grand Prix design for a Cour de Cassation by François-Philippe Boitte premiated in 1859, the year after Duc's definitive design for his facade had been published (figure 77). It is a severe design fronted with a portico of four conventional Corinthian columns labeled on the entablature *Sagesse, Force, Vigilence,* and *Prudence.* They are thus the symbolic as well as the actual "pillars of justice," their inscriptions stating the specific qualities that Boitte hopes his conventional choice of Order might suggest and which a more subtle artist like Duc would seek to integrate into the form of his capitals.

More evidence lies in the decoration of the Palais de Justice itself. The theme was set in the Renaissance relief on the Tour de l'Horloge (attributed to Jean Pilon) representing *Justice* paired with *Force.* It was reiterated over the door of the old Cour de Cassation in a relief of *Justice* between two lions (representing *Force*) and stated more elaborately in the statues set over the four columns of the Cour de Mai facade in the 1780s: *Force, Justice, Abondance,* and *Prudence.*[81] The theme was clearly equity paired with firmness, the former expressed metaphorically as the books of the law, the latter as the lion. There might be added to this two-part quality prudence in the exercise of judgment, and authority and prosperity as their objective. This tradition was carried on in Boitte's inscription, where *Force* is doubled with *Vigilence* and equity divided into *Prudence* and *Sagesse.* It is continued and expanded in the six large reliefs in the lower part of Duc's Harlay facade expressing three qualities of equity and three of firmness: *Prudence, Vérité, Equité, Châtiment, Protection, Force.*[82]

There remains, however, one last step we must take in applying this long exploration of the Néo-Grec poetics first broached by Duc himself in the Colonne de Juillet to evaluate the Vestibule de Harlay: the analysis of how it is transformed when elaborated in a space-containing structure rather than applied to a freestanding memorial.

The radical movement centering on the work of Labrouste, Constant-Dufeux, Danjoy, and Nicolle received the definitive label Néo-Grec in place of more tentative appellations, particularly Etruscan, during the early 1850s because it was seen as part of the general rediscovery of Greece that coincided with the founding of the Ecole Française d'Athènes.[83] The links between the movement and the Ecole were loose but nonetheless multifarious. We noted one important parallel in Vaudoyer's adoption of polychromy. Of importance here is a second: the transformation of the vision of Greek architecture brought about by the detailed examination of

77

*François-Philippe Boitte, Design
for a* cour de cassation, *premiated
project for the Grand Prix de Rome,
1859. From Guerinet,* Les Grands
Prix de Rome d'architecture,
pl. 37.

the monuments of the Acropolis in the light of the Romantic idea that ancient architecture was specific in its meanings and highly inflected in its forms.

The *pensionnaires* and *normaliens* at the Ecole Française d'Athènes discovered that the buildings of the Acropolis were not simple renditions of conventional types but rather displayed infinite circumstantial inflection. Their confirmation of Pennethorne's discovery of refinements and of earlier researchers' projections of polychromatic decoration was only the beginning of their new visualization. We quoted Burnouf's 1847 essay on the Parthenon earlier in this chapter. In June 1848 he completed an essay on the Propylea (restored in 1846 by Titeux and Chaudet) that broached the puzzling question of its strange shape and mixture of Orders.[84] He concluded that it was not a temple (as Le Roy had supposed) but instead a gateway, which explained the intercolumniation widening toward the center, the lack of sculpture in the pediment, and finally the placement of heavy Doric shafts on the facades with more delicate Ionic columns inside. He noted how unity was nonetheless maintained by the rendering of the Ionic with Doric simplicity and the inflection of the form and proportions of the wings to balance each other and enframe the central mass. In a word, he demonstrated that the subtleties of the Orders were applied to complicated civil as well as simple religious types in Periclean Athens.

Interestingly, Burnouf's interpretation immediately inspired a more elaborate and more ingenious one from Beulé. He found the Propylea too carefully wrought to be a defensive gateway rather than just a "monument de décoration," and in 1852 he began excavations to find an outer defense shielding it, laying bare the Beulé Gate at the foot of the Acropolis steps.[85] This discovery not only proved his suspicion correct, but also gave the precise point from which the ancient visitor first glimpsed the Propylea and so demonstrated how subtly it had been designed to be seen in foreshortened perspective.[86] In 1853–54 Beulé published his influential *Acropole d'Athènes*, which emphasizes the Propylea because of its "originalité" and depicts the whole Acropolis as characterized by elaborate and essentially picturesque inflections of form and symbolism. "The Greeks," he concludes of the Erechtheum, "seem to have sought with particular care, in their great architectural ensembles, accidents, whether of construction or of perspective. This one notes everywhere, in the smallest Pompeiian house as in the largest buildings of Athens."[87] He insists that a single mind must have dominated and coordinated this picturesquely unified ensemble and that it must have been that of the sculptor Phidias.[88]

Duc's Vestibule de Harlay was likewise an inflected, picturesque vision of classical architecture. It was, first of all, symbolically inflected: the interior is feminine and the expression of *Justice;* the enclosing exterior masculine and a manifestation of *Force*. The inner wall of the Vestibule is dominated at its center by a columnar aedicule marking the public entry of the Assizes. Above this is a large relief by Jean-Joseph Perraud of *Justice* holding the attributes of equity (the tablets of the law) and firmness (the sceptre), flanked by caryatids. All the figures are female and the columns supporting them Ionic, the feminine Order. Around the Vestibule, supporting the ribs of the vault, are piers with strange capitals bracketed forward and sculpted into female heads crowned with rudimentary Ionic volutes. The separate elements of the aedicule—the female figures and the Ionic Order—are merged in these brackets and integrated into the structure of the room. We saw earlier that Duc had rendered the elements of the Vestibule "alive"; here we see that they live as the personification of *Justice*. But the interior is distinct in expression from the exterior: outside *Force* rather than *Justice* is the dominant quality, expressed most clearly in the lions flanking the central stairway and the shields with swords carved across the frieze, but also clearly expressed in the stark capitals whose Doric bells rise above a mere ruffle of Corinthian leaves.

It is important to note, finally, that this picturesque classicism justifies Duc's union of the Vestibule de Harlay with the rest of the Palais de Justice complex, which is medieval in some parts, Renaissance in others, and Baroque in still others. What unites these parts is not their various stylistic references: these are necessarily distinct because it is through them that the institution tells its history. What unites them is Duc's composition, his picturesque balancing of masses around the firm armature of the two east–west corridors. Also uniting them are a consistent scale and a consistent surface rendering in yellow Paris limestone. The ornamental motifs may be in one style or another, but they are all cut with the same expressive snap, so that the Gothic moldings are just a bit more Gothic, the Renaissance more Renaissance, and, of course, the nineteenth-century Greek more exquisite and subtle than Periclean Greek.

All of this raises a more basic and important question: what is the relationship of decorative sculpture to architecture? The key to the reading of Duc's rue de Harlay facade are the reliefs of *Prudence*, *Vérité*, *Equité*, *Châtiment*, *Protection*, and *Force* by the respected academic sculptors Dumont, François Jouffroy, and Jean-Louis Jaley. The foundation of its success is the manner in which they are both symbolically and formally integrated into the whole structure, lined up across the front like the columns they echo. This particularly complete harmony of decoration and architecture came to be characteristic of Second Empire government buildings and was a conscious objective of government patronage of the arts.

One of the most celebrated instances of a Second Empire architect obliging a respected sculptor to complement his building was Charles Garnier's instructions to Jean-Baptiste Carpeaux as he formulated *La Danse* for the facade of Garnier's Opera (figure 80).[89] We know that Garnier gave Carpeaux and the other sculptors commissioned to execute the facade groups their subjects, in the form of outline drawings of silhouettes to which they were to adhere, and that he had the authority to reject their proposals. The other artists conformed closely to Garnier's strictures, and their works complement the facade like the reliefs along Duc's rue de Harlay elevation. Carpeaux, however, resisted, and after much argument and revision, a more independent work resulted. Garnier, relating the story in his *Nouvel Opéra de Paris*, tellingly concluded: "Statuary sculpture forming part of the decoration of a building must accept several strictures of simple ornamental sculpture."[90]

This incident points up the fact that a Second Empire architect expected the work of even well-known artists to complement their structures like "la simple sculpture ornamentale." This attitude had bureaucratic sanction. During the Second Empire, a committee attached to the cabinet of the Prefect of the Seine, the Commission des Beaux-Arts, oversaw decorative projects. Its head was Victor Baltard, whose title was Inspecteur des Beaux-Arts, a much broader title than merely Inspecteur Général of architectural work. The committee named artists to specific projects, approved models, and settled disputes, consistently backing the architects' right to enforce harmony with their designs. Indeed, so little initiative seems to have been left to the sculptors that one wonders how they viewed these commissions.[91] The technical term for such commissions used in the government documents, "encouragement," is significant: it places such decorative jobs in the category of governmental charity in the support of artists. When the line for the support of artists first appeared in the budget of the Prefect of the Seine in 1816, it was just that, for the encouragement of artists by purchasing their existing works, which afterward would be hung in some government establishment. It was only at the end of the Monarchy of July and in the Second Empire that this system of "encouragements" became the commissioning of decorative works intended to be so tightly related to their architectural settings. It enriched the tools of the architects, but it restricted the freedom of the sculptors and, in the case of Carpeaux, was bitterly resented.

We noted at the beginning of this chapter that in 1869 Duc was awarded the Grand Prix de l'Empereur for his design of the Palais de Justice. This was a prize of 100,000 francs decreed on August 12, 1864, to be bestowed every five years on a work of painting, sculpture, or architecture that was "reconnue digne de cette récompense."[92] The jury was to be presided over by the Ministre d'Etat et de la Maison de l'Empereur, J.-P.-B. Vaillant, and was to have thirty members, ten from the Académie des Beaux-Arts. The Académie made the counterproposal that half the members be academicians, and that there be forty-two jurors, but the Minister rejected this and by *arrêté* of May 14, 1867, named the thirty jurors, ten in each field.

The Académie was represented by four painters, three sculptors, and three architects.[93] The architects were Duban, Lefuel, and Labrouste of the Académie and Ballu, Boeswillwald, Clerget, Garnier, Questel, Reynaud, and Viollet-le-Duc.[94] This was a liberal panel, especially if compared to that of the Opera competition of 1860–61. Lebas and Lesueur were passed over among the academicians (as well as Baltard, Gilbert, and Duc). Viollet-le-Duc and Boeswillwald were Gothic rationalists; Labrouste, Duban, Clerget, Questel, and Reynaud classicist rationalists; which left only Lefuel, Garnier, and Ballu to represent the Neoclassical tradition in their own watered-down manner.

The jury first met by sections and nominated works for consideration. The architects agreed upon three—Duc's Palais de Justice, Duban's restoration of the château at Blois, and Labrouste's Bibliothèque Nationale—plus four "complémentaires"—Viollet-le-Duc's restoration at Pierrefonds, Baltard's Halles Centrales, Ballu's La Trinité, and Garnier's Opera. The jury then met in plenary session and expanded the nominations from each section to ten; Lefuel's New Louvre, Questel's Asile Sainte-Anne, and Abadie's church of Saint-Ferdinand at Bordeaux were added to the architects' seven. These were then reduced to three in each medium: by vote, Duc's Palais de Justice, Lefuel's New Louvre (figures 78, 79), and Garnier's Opera (figures 80, 81) were now the architectural nominations. Since Lefuel and Garnier were members of the jury, they had to step down and were replaced by Vaudoyer and Charles Laisné, both rationalists.

The final voting of the plenary session is illuminating. Twenty-nine of the thirty jurors attended. The list of nominations included, besides the three buildings, Paul-Jacques-Aimé Baudry's ceilings at the hôtels Païva and Galliera, Alexandre Cabanel's *Paradis Perdu*, and Nicolas-Auguste Hesse's Chapel of Saint-Laurent at Saint-Gervais, as well as Jean-Baptiste Guillaume's group on the Opera facade, Charles Gumery's monument to Favart in Chambery, and Perraud's *Le Désespoir*. In the first round the Palais de Justice received nine votes; although the voting continued for thirteen rounds it never received less, and after the seventh round mounted steadily to the necessary majority of fifteen.[95] The building had already been proposed by the architectural section by near unanimity (nine votes), and after the withdrawal of Lefuel and Garnier from the jury there were nine rationalists on the panel. They had clearly made up their minds and refused to compromise even when, after six rounds of voting, they still had only one convert. The movement to a compromise candidate that might have been expected after the third or fourth round never took place (although in the fourth, fifth, and sixth rounds Baudry's work received support it had previously lacked, then lost it again).

Lefuel's New Louvre received seven or eight votes in each of the first seven rounds of voting but had never received more than a single vote

78
L.-T.-J. Visconti and Hector
Lefuel, New Louvre, Paris,
1852–57.

79

*Hector Lefuel, "Guichets" in the
Grande Galerie de Bord de l'Eau,
Louvre, Paris, 1862–69. (Photo:
N. D. Roger-Viollet)*

when the architects had met separately. It had to be added to their list of nominations at the beginning of the plenary session, we are told by the painters and sculptors whom Lefuel had so extensively employed on the project.[96] The same must have been true of Garnier's Opera, which received two or three votes each time up to the eighth round. The sculpture *Le Désespoir*, like the Palais de Justice, retained its support (three or four votes) until the twelfth round: the "swing votes" were obviously those going to the Opera and the New Louvre, and these votes went earlier to the Palais de Justice, especially after the seventh and eighth rounds when it became obvious that the support for Duc would not weaken.

This raises two questions: Why did the architects refuse to compromise when the painters and sculptors were suggesting the New Louvre and the Opera by their support; and why did the painters and sculptors resist so long when it became obvious that the Palais de Justice would eventually win? The answer to the first question must be that, given that the architects nominated the monument by nine out of a possible ten votes in the architectural section, the design must have profoundly satisfied a broad spectrum of the architectural profession. The answer to the second question must be that the Palais de Justice did not at all satisfy the painters and sculptors.

The telling point is that the New Louvre was added to the list of nominations by the painters and sculptors and supported in the voting over Labrouste's Bibliothèque Nationale and the restorations of Duban and Viollet-le-Duc. The painters and sculptors were agreeable to a building receiving the prize (except for the three or four who held out for Perraud's *Le Désespoir*), but it had to be a building of a particular sort. That sort seems to have been a highly decorated building, one with statues across its facade and allegorical ceilings interpreting its architectural statements. In this context one realizes how little ornament Duc permitted on and in his building and how thoroughly he had subordinated it to the architecture. The issue seems to have been the relationship between the arts and the executing artists. Lefuel had given the decorative artists free reign; Duc had controlled them tightly.[97]

In a word, the issue was the means by which a monument communicated an idea. We are thus led to ask two last questions of that solid nine-vote block that stole the Grand Prix de l'Empereur: Why were such a various collection of rationalists able to settle so firmly upon the Palais de Justice as their choice; and why did the government accept their decision (and indeed pack the jury to begin with)? The answer to these is circular: because it was the job of a government architect to make a public building speak and describe itself, so the building making the loudest and most unified declaration—that is, the Palais de Justice—would be simultaneously preferred by the profession and the administration.

We have described how the Palais de Justice speaks in all its parts, but we have not analyzed what it says in terms of its political context. From 1789 to 1875 France was governed under an evolving series of patterns of authority. Each pattern was the expression of the philosophy of the regime and its symbol. The regime of Louis-Philippe and Guizot was a "parliamentary" one, as we have seen, and its essential elements were the chief executive and the legislature: the Tuileries, the Chambre des Députés, and the Luxembourg (all three of which were rebuilt during the Monarchy of July). Napoleon III's Empire was the negation of this. What he outlined in his *Idées napoléoniennes* of 1839 and embodied in the constitution of January 14, 1852, was a system controlled by a chief executive answerable directly to the people and restrained by law. The cabinet was appointed by the chief executive and was not responsible to the legislature, which itself was only consultative. Thus there were three elements to this government: the ruler, the people, and the law. The Chambre des Députés and the Luxembourg were not significantly embellished during the Second Empire, but vast sums were expended upon the New Louvre, the public works of Paris (symbolized perhaps by the Halles Centrales and the Hôtel Dieu), and, finally, the Palais de Justice.

This characterization of Napoleon III's government is too general, however, because in precisely 1869, when the Grand Prix de l'Empereur was being awarded, its public image was being modified to emphasize its democratic rather than its authoritarian qualities. Napoleon III seemed to affirm the intimations that he was an opportunist prepared to modify his regime in response to pressure. When the clerical party weakened after 1860, he began to loosen the restraints on the press, political agitators, and the legislature. He set about wooing a Republican, Emile Ollivier, to lead his government. After the electoral campaign of May–June 1869, Ollivier negotiated the position of Prime Minister and a new constitution, taking power on January 2, 1870.[98] (Interestingly, Garnier and Ballu, sent to Marseilles and Bordeaux by the architectural section of the jury to examine buildings under consideration outside Paris, took time in their report to mention visiting Ollivier's new villa near Avignon and to praise its "qualités d'étude et de distinction." This is the only such side trip they permitted themselves and one wonders why they did so.[99])

In light of this, the clear lead in the voting established by the New Louvre and the Palais de Justice makes sense. These monuments from the start were the most worthy competitors for the Emperor's recognition. One might protest the whole situation—as those voting for Garnier's Opera or Perraud's *Le Désespoir* or casting blank ballots might have been doing —but the real choice was between the New Louvre and the Palais de Justice. The jury was a professional panel, both academic and non-academic. It selected, in the end, the more controlled, professional design.

Seven

LABROUSTE'S BIBLIOTHEQUE NATIONALE

In this volume we have repeatedly encountered the idea that a building should be an organism, mechanical in being fabricated from inert material, but also anthropomorphic in being shaped to appear to be experiencing elastic loads and thrusts in its structure like a human body. Duc's Vestibule de Harlay is only the most perfect manifestation of this idea, which we first encountered, tentatively and partially, in Labrouste's Paestum reconstructions of 1828–29. Cuvier's demonstration that all the parts of a biological organism are interrelated, so that the whole can be reconstructed from a single element, was accepted as a *typos* applicable to architecture by writers as different as Viollet-le-Duc and Beulé.[1] The ideal, in a word, was transparency, the situation where the whole work of architecture—its structure, its function, its philosophical nature—might be grasped by a glance at its exterior, as if one were conceptually seeing right through its walls. Léopold-Amédée Hardy even used the word in 1887 to characterize the approach of his *maître d'atelier*, Joseph Nicolle: "He sought to make the interior show through (*transparaître*) on the exterior of a building."[2] This is just the turn of phrase one wants to describe the Bibliothèque Sainte-Geneviève, Marseilles Cathedral, and the Vestibule de Harlay.[3]

In chapter two we saw how such an organic, "transparent" conception of architecture was possible at this time, especially in the circle producing the *Encyclopédie nouvelle*, but we have not explored why this idea was applied specifically to architecture. This is an important matter because until 1830 a work of architecture was not conceived as a self-sufficient object but as a setting. Its forms were determined by the social functions they enclosed rather than by their individual material nature. Architecture had been understood as an extension of clothing, furniture, and interior decoration. And, most importantly, it was the French above all who perfected the coordinated social setting: foreigners in the nineteenth century did not go to French designers for "transparency" in furniture or building but, on the contrary, for the most theatrical yet stylish and tasteful pretense.

Before the Revolution, French society was indistinguishable from the persons of the aristocracy and architecture was synonymous with the aristocratic habitation. The expression of the latter was the pretenses of the former; the aristocratic habitation was the statement of the rank and quality of the inhabitant.[4] Jacques-François Blondel does not enumerate building types in his compendious *Cours d'architecture* (1771–77, completed by Pierre Patte), and the chief specific examples he discusses are palaces. His other publications, *Architecture française* (1752–56) and *De la Distribution des maisons de plaisance* (1737–38), are mostly devoted to the topic of the expression of character. Among the things remarkable about Boullée's unpublished *Essai sur l'art* (c. 1785–93), Ledoux's *Architecture considerée . . .* (1804), and Durand's *Précis des leçons . . .* (1802 and 1805) is that they interpret the problem as one of distinguishing functional types rather than degrees of aristocratic rank and quality. During the 1830s in his lectures at the Ecole des Beaux-Arts, Huyot was extraordinary in developing the idea that building's origins were social, not formal, and in excoriating the concentration upon private architecture as a sign of decadence. "It was personal interest that . . . brought on the decadence of architecture," we read in his lecture notes, "and the sumptuous palaces built for simple, private individuals during the later times of the Great Empires sufficiently attest that the arts, in prostituting, so to speak, their works to the fashion and caprice of wealth, will perish themselves with the institutions to which they owe their origin."[5]

The links between these texts and the mentality of the Revolution (Huyot was a student of David in the 1790s) has been frequently noted.[6] Nevertheless the Empire and especially the Restoration revived many of the trappings of rank, and, appropriately, the leading architects of these two periods were palace designers, Charles Percier (1764–1838) and Pierre-François-Léonard Fontaine (1762–1853). All of their influential publications were of habitations or interior decoration, starting with their *Palais, maisons et autres édifices dessinés à Rome* (1798) and culminating in their *Plans de plusieurs châteaux, palais et résidences de souverains de France, d'Italie, d'Espagne et de Russie* of 1833, the last and most impressive volume devoted to royal architectural etiquette.[7] Percier's numerous students explored the genre further in a beautiful series of publications including Grandjean de Montigny and A.-P.-S.-M. Famin's *Architecture toscane* (1815), M.-P. Gauthier's *Plus beaux édifices de la ville de Gênes* (1818–30), L.-P. Haudebourt's *Palais Massimi à Rome* (1818), J.-B. Lesueur's *Architecture italienne* (with F. Callet, 1827), Jules Bouchet's *Villa Pia* (1837), and Paul-Marie Letarouilly's celebrated *Edifices de Rome moderne* (1840–57).

Percier and Fontaine in their 1833 volume quote Napoleon neatly rationalizing his needs at Malmaison by proposing three wings, two for his "habitation" and "travail," enframing a third, monumental block for his "représentation."[8] "Représentation," the 1835 edition of the dictionary of the Académie Française states, "denotes the rank (*état*) held by a person distinguished by his rank, by his dignity, etc. . . . It also denotes the good appearance (*bonne mine*), the imposing figure cut by a man who is tall and well proportioned."[9] It was an aristocratic, pre-Revolutionary term; Larousse in the 1860s just quotes the Académie's definition verbatim while Littré contemporaneously cites only seventeenth- and eighteenth-century examples of use. What is remarkable about Napoleon's conception of Malmaison is not that it centered on the sovereign's "représentation," but that his "habitation" and "travail" were given wings rather than space in the basement or the attic. What this points up is an important change that came with the Revolution: respect for the comfort and personality of the person being "represented." Before this what was being "represented" was rank. Etiquette, the *Encyclopédie des gens du monde* informs us in 1835, was originally merely the matter of precedence, deriving from the legal term "est hic quaestio" denoting the order of documents. Precedence is the subject of the great seventeenth- and eighteenth-century compendia of court etiquette, Théodore and Denys's *Cérémonial français* (1649) and Dumont's *Corps universel diplomatique* (1726–31). These consist of summaries of the order of processions and assemblies commencing (as far as documentation permits) with Charlemagne. The sumptuous publications of Napoleon's marriage ceremonies and *sacre* as well as the proposed publication of the *sacre* of Charles X were documents of precedence.[10] It was only in the nineteenth century, with the emergence of the dandy, that rank became less important than accomplishment, often expressed in calculated eccentricities.[11]

Louis XIV and his minister Colbert understood most clearly that a monarch's "représentation" lay in the adornment of his person, of the rooms he appeared in, of the palace containing these rooms, and of the grounds surrounding this palace—all equivalent in their splendor and hierarchy to the ceremonial assembly of his courtiers.[12] Versailles was the great manifestation of their vision. Just as they established firm, hieratic court etiquette, Louis XIV and Colbert organized the sartorial, decorative, and architectural setting—after reorganizing the royal finances and the French economy to support it all. In 1664 Colbert appointed himself Surintendant Général des Bâtiments du Roi, Arts et Manufactures, taking under his control royal building, the academies, the art manufactures (Beauvais, Gobelins, Sèvres), the royal fêtes, the Opera, the royal museums, and the royal library. To maintain Louis XIV's "représentation," a vast plant employing dozens of artists of the first rank and hundreds of craftsmen was created. Other monarchs trying to compete with the Sun King and his successors had to create similar plants, as the kings of Prussia did at Potsdam during the eighteenth century. But for all the emphasis upon excellence, manifested particularly in the deliberations of the academies, this was not an enterprise dedicated to disinterested professional quality: the object of it all was the "représentation" of the King and abstract ideals entered only insofar as the monarch saw himself as an ideal. It was the unqualified statement of the monarchic system, and Labrouste, for one, refused to visit Versailles because it was so completely at variance with his Liberal values.[13]

The plant created for the "représentation" of the last of the Bourbons continued after the Revolution, partly out of bureaucratic momentum, partly because components like Sèvres, Beauvais, and Gobelins were profitable, partly because the heads of the French state were still concerned about their "représentation."[14] The last monarch, Napoleon III, was the most concerned of all and the most profligate in his expenditures.

During the Second Empire the quality of "représentation" was extended to certain newly distinguished types producing a strange but influential hybrid, simultaneously palatial and institutional. The pattern was set in Napoleon III's creation of a Ministère d'Etat et de la Maison de l'Empereur, simultaneously a department of the bureaucracy and the Emperor's personal staff. The ministry's first great enterprise, the New Louvre, filled the pattern in: a building made to look palatial, like the Tuileries, but containing government offices, libraries, and museums instead. A second building from the second decade of the Empire raised that pattern to a paradigm: the new Opera, designed and erected from 1861 to 1875 by Charles Garnier (figures 80, 81).[15]

Duban had been appointed architect for the restoration of the Louvre voted by the Assemblée Constituante on May 24, 1848. The Prince-President, elected at the end of that year, finding Duban too difficult—having to treat with him "de puissance à puissance," we are told[16]—passed him over for the design of the New Louvre in favor of L.-J.-T. Visconti, an efficient and well-connected private and government architect, recommended perhaps by being the designer of Napoleon's tomb under the dome of the Invalides. Visconti died on December 23, 1853, however, and was replaced by a young Grand Prix winner and son of a successful building contractor in Versailles, Hector Lefuel, who was already in the administration of the Palais Impériaux and had done excellent work at Fontainebleau.[17] He proved a tremendous success with the Emperor, redesigning Visconti's facades and carrying the work to rapid completion in 1857.[18] He established himself close to the Emperor and especially the Empress Eugénie, redoing the private rooms at the Tuileries and Saint-Cloud, receiving commissions for houses and interiors from Fould, Nieuwerkerke (Directeur de Musées Impériaux), and the Princesse Mathilde, and drawing upon himself the venom of Viel-Castel.[19] We have

80
*Charles Garnier, Opera, Paris,
1862–75. (Photo: Giraudon)*

81
*Charles Garnier, Opera, grand
staircase. (Photo courtesy Northwestern University)*

already noted how in spite of this success the leaders of his profession resisted the consideration of his New Louvre for the Grand Prix de l'Empereur.

Garnier was a full generation younger than the Romantic *pensionnaires* and, as a student of Lebas, was not from their camp. He was only thirty-five when he was named architect of the Opera as the result of a two-part competition. The jury had been the architecture section of the Académie des Beaux-Arts and the members of the Conseil des Bâtiments Civils combined, a group of twelve in which Questel, Constant-Dufeux, Duban, and Gilbert were the only rationalists.[20] Garnier defeated Viollet-le-Duc on the first round and Duc (by default) on the second.

Napoleon III's lusty supporter Théophile Gautier received Garnier's design with great enthusiasm in the pages of the official *Moniteur universel* while it was still only a project or under construction.[21] At the display of the competition drawings on February 11, 1861, he wrote: "It is clearly the most individual project in the exhibition. It recalls no known monument."[22] When Garnier displayed a model at the Salon in 1863, Gautier waxed eloquent over the facade, which he compared to those of the Venetian palaces on the Grand Canal. "It reconciles the demands of architecture and those of life." Here he saw the grand staircase and used his literary talents to evoke the effect soon to be famous in actual fact:

A graciously curving ramp, the steps of which one hardly senses, leads to a landing from which two other ramps rise to the first floor by gentle slopes. The well of the staircase is supported by coupled Ionic columns in Seracolin marble upon which are posed immense arches and which unite, from floor to floor, the balconies with their richly ornamented balustrades where the curious can lean over as in a painting by Paolo Veronese, simultaneously spectators and spectacle, to watch at their leisure that marvel of modern civilization which one calls a sortie d'Opéra, *that is, this cascade of diamonds, of pearls, of feathers, of flowers, of white shoulders, of satins, of velvets, of moirés, of gauzes, of laces, which here foams on the white marble steps, to the sparkling of vivid lights, framed by a fairy architecture.*[23]

Finally on August 5, 1867, Gautier wrote with enthusiasm of the facade that would be revealed when the scaffolding was removed on the fifteenth of that month:

The Opera is the temple of modern civilization, it is the culmination of art, luxury, elegance, all the refinements of the haute vie. *The fortunate of society who frequent it are discerning and wish to find there the sumptuosities of their palaces and their* hôtels.

It must be both charming and grandiose, coy and pure, fashionable and classic;
the problem is not easy to solve. M. Garnier has succeeded in this almost impossi-
ble task.[24]

Unfortunately Gautier died before the building was completely finished
and inaugurated on January 5, 1875; one would like to have had his erup-
tions upon that occasion.

Duban, however, had been assigned to report on Garnier's project for
the Conseil des Bâtiments Civils. What he presented at their meeting on
July 16, 1861, was more critical. He thought the vehicle access too restricted, criticized the grand staircase, and particularly criticized the
lack of appropriate character in the facade. This he saw as based on the
palatial models of Perrault's Louvre and Gabriel's Place de la Concorde.

We express the opinion that if such a great show of architectural splendor must
indicate the function of the establishment, the elements should not be borrowed from
whatever building of diverse function, but on the contrary should indicate the spe-
cial function of the opera by displaying a definite character, a character which, in
our opinion, should embrace equally the beauty of external forms and the appear-
ance of internal comfort which good society seeks in the places that it frequents.[25]

He recommended further studies to clarify the character and to unify what
he saw as the incoherence of the arched system of the first story and the
trabeated one of the *piano nobile*.

Garnier made some modifications but answered most devastatingly in
the building itself and in a series of articles published in the *Moniteur uni-*
versel during the 1860s (republished as a book, *A travers les Arts*, in 1869),
in a theoretical treatise, *Le Théâtre* (1871), and finally in his monumental
Le nouvel Opéra de Paris (two volumes and atlas, 1878–81). In the building
as well as in his writings, Garnier insists that architecture is not a matter of
principles but of experiences. *Le Théâtre* is completely devoted to the description of the carefully paced path he has laid out from coach to box and
the changing but appropriate tableaux he arranges at each stage. The sub-
scribers—the class that managed the Opera and Garnier's principal
audience—arrived by coach at the east *porte-cochère* and entered the low,
circular *vestibule des abonnés* under the auditorium itself. This was provided
with mirrors and comfortable *poufs*; it was where the wealthy women of
the *haut monde* removed their wraps and prepared for their public appearance ascending the grand staircase. It was thus feminine and rococo in
decoration, preparatory to the most majestic piece of theater in the building, the Venetian grand staircase. Of this last Garnier wrote:

If the great central stairway is a place of luxury and movement, if ornament is
elegantly arranged, if the animation that rules the steps is an interesting and varied

spectacle, it will be an advantage from which everyone will profit. With the lateral walls of the staircase arranged to be left open, all the people circulating on each floor will be able to entertain themselves with the view of the great hall and with the incessant comings and goings of the crowd up and down the stairs. . . . Finally, by arranging fabrics and wall hangings, garlands, candelabra and chandeliers, as well as marble and flowers, color everywhere, one makes of this ensemble a brilliant and sumptuous composition that will recall in real life certain of the resplendant tableaux that Veronese fixed on his canvases. The sparkling lamps, the splendid gowns, the animated and smiling faces, the greetings exchanged, all have the air of festivity and pleasure, and without realizing what is owed to the architecture for the magical effect, everyone will enjoy it and everyone will, by their favorable impression, pay homage to this great art, so mighty in its manifestations, so noble in its effects.[26]

Garnier's Opera and the books he wrote in defense of it contrast sharply with the French architectural tradition studied in this volume. Vaudoyer, Reynaud, Fortoul, and Viollet-le-Duc insisted on historical and structural consistency in a work of architecture and also on a consistent, unifying chain of logic in the elaboration of the design and detailing. Yet Garnier praised the intuitive over the rational and precise:

Theories often have as their end the explanation of what has already been done; but they could sometimes be very dangerous if one were to listen to them before setting to work. From the first the artist has to compose and even execute without overly troubling himself with these axioms and dogmatic rationalizations. It is by intuition alone that they must penetrate into the spirit; it is by intuition alone that they must be manifested, and when they do so, they have more power, feeling being in harmony with reason. . . .

Sometimes when I take up my pencil to compose, I feel invaded by these theoretical ideas which rise before me like a schoolteacher confronting a child who has made a mistake; but I assure you that instead of trying to reason at such times with these learned visions, I chase them from me as best I can, until feelings alone, and nothing else, guide my eyes, my hand, and my thought.[27]

He insisted that in his broader social terms there *was* a consistency and distinctiveness to modern architecture in spite of "the instinctive impression of the masses, who would call the Bourse a Greek temple."[28] And his writings call to mind another genre, the literature on interior design exemplified in Henry Havard's *L'Art dans la maison* of 1883.[29] Like Garnier, Havard analyzes each space in the house in terms of the social activity it encloses. "He who says 'table' pronounces a weighty word," he opens his section on the dining room, and for sixteen pages he discourses on the shape of the table, the number of chairs, the placement of the windows, the lighting, the correct historical style, and the proper subjects for decorative paintings. "One should especially avoid posing an enigmatic composition, like a fatal question mark, before a decent man sitting down to dinner."[30] Also, like Garnier, Havard presumes that each room has a historical style particularly appropriate to its function: the Rococo for the bedroom; the Baroque for the vestibules and salons; the exotic styles for smoking rooms, and so on.

Garnier's accomplishment, in a word, was exactly what Duban had criticized when analyzing the project of 1861: he had made the Opera palatial, he had imposed on a public institution the concerns for social "représentation" particularly developed for domestic design. Such a development was not inexplicable at this moment. The Opera was not like a bank, a law court, or a library: it was (as Gautier insisted) a place of entertainment for the highest level of society—a perpetual *salon*, if you will—and was administered by a special commission in the Ministère d'Etat de la Maison de l'Empereur like the New Louvre. (Nevertheless Garnier never enjoyed Lefuel's access to the Emperor, in part, it is said, because the Empress Eugénie resented that her friend Viollet-le-Duc had been passed over for the commission.[31]) Furthermore, elaborateness and comfort in interior design advanced massively during the Second Empire, so much so that Siegfried Giedion could call the epoch that of the upholsterer.[32] In painting and literature the seventeenth and eighteenth centuries were rediscovered at this time and studied by Houssaye, the Goncourts, and even Cousin for the subtlety of that society's etiquette and social nuance.[33] Even in the work of Labrouste the hard, angular chairs of the Bibliothèque Sainte-Geneviève, opened in 1851, gave way to curving, expansive Louis XV *chaises* in the Bibliothèque Nationale when it opened in 1868.

Garnier's solution—the domestication of institutional architecture—was to become one of the most important threads of the French architectural tradition. He created in the Opera what by the end of the century emerged as the grand hotel, partially through the medium of his own casino at Monte Carlo (1878–82). He evolved something that was simultaneously comfortable and pretentious as well as indefinite in its references so that anyone and everyone could pretend it was home. He solved the problem César Daly signaled as the great one of the time in the introduction to his *Architecture privée sous Napoléon III* (1864–77): the introduction of intimacy in a modern architecture that no longer was the product of individual enterprise.[34] Garnier transformed and adapted the whole concept of "représentation." In the twentieth century, at the end of the tradition, this domestication of the institutional became one of architecture's most important elements, as for example in the work of Paul Philippe Cret, who conceived the Pan American Union building in Washington, D.C. (1907–13) as a place of meeting and so as a garden and a salon, and meant his museums, especially his Detroit Insitute of Arts (1919–29), to suggest palatial residences.[35]

So far we have been looking at only half of the matter broached at the beginning of this chapter. "Transparency," as Hardy remarked, characterized the work of Nicolle, one of the most radical followers of the Romantic *pensionnaries*. In 1853, as Hardy relates, "he made his students study a theater in which the auditorium and stage were visible on the exterior"[36]; and at the end of that decade Nicolle submitted a project in the competition for the Opera where indeed the interior volumes are evident externally. But more important, in that project the interior function symbolically shows through the masonry cladding in the depiction of the proscenium arch across the broad face of the flytower and in the festive tent form given the half-dome of the auditorium (figure 82).[37] "Transparency" to Nicolle was illusionistic and symbolic, not merely mechanical:

Stone, for him, was only a means for rendering an idea, to communicate a sentiment; it was the page of a book that one must read.

He sought to crystallize a memory, an idea, a form, an allusion.

He made us study a family tomb in the form of the paternal house, the tree which shaded it becoming itself the monument.[38]

Labrouste's daughter also wrote a poignant necrology of Nicolle under her pseudonym Léon Dassy: "Seeking the logic of forms in construction, but not in an absolute and exclusive manner, he attempted to elevate sentiments and forms to ideals, to the true external expression of the contents."[39]

Nicolle's example makes us realize that the "transparency" of Labrouste's Bibliothèque Sainte-Geneviève is more than practical and mechanical. We have noted Labrouste's explanation of the red-painted lists of names on the curtain walls as the manifestation of the bookshelves inside against them (figure 32). But these lists are more powerful than mere physical display: the names are not, in fact, those on the spines of the books beyond, but an abstract historical catalogue beginning with Moses and ending with the contemporary physicist Brezelius—the symbolic concentration of the meaning of a library and the knowledge it contains. Labrouste thus displays a very distinctive attitude toward the wall surface. Here it is neither a solid stone theater flat like the screen walls concealing

82
*Joseph Nicolle, Competition project
for the Opera, Paris, 1861. From*
Revue générale de l'architecture
et des travaux publics *19 (1861).*

the flying buttresses and domes of Soufflot's Pantheon across the street, nor is it a skin stretched over the structural skeleton and functional organs of the interior, as in Vaudoyer's Marseilles Cathedral. Labrouste's wall, on the contrary, is a kind of lens through which one appears to see into the building, but a lens that reveals the conceptual contents instead of the empty physical space.

"Transparency" to Nicolle and Labrouste meant the external manifestation of the spiritual contents of the architectural vessel. Their designs were not so much logical as cerebral. In analyzing them one is led from the facts of mechanical construction to the images and metaphors of the imaginative mind. The problem was the moment of passage—the entry from the real world into the cerebral illusion. Contemporaneous romantic literature often solved this problem with the simple tactic of the dream.[40] Labrouste, however, was given that of the door, and in the Bibliothèque Sainte-Geneviève he uses it to full advantage (figure 83).

Entering the door from the Place du Panthéon, one is abruptly confronted by a dark space into which intrude ranges of very solid, stone piers, without bases and with square, widely spaced flutes. These are repeated around the walls as pilasters, but the latter are interrupted and bound to the wall by leveling courses. The piers and pilasters terminate in a network of light iron trusses, the principals of Labrouste's iron floor system, which are strikingly lighter than their stone supports. Although a gesture of perfect honesty, this arrangement was very unsettling to an eye accustomed to the proportions of continuous masonry construction. In reviewing the building in *L'Artiste* in 1851, the young architect Achille Hermant wrote:

By the manner in which these two so different materials, stone and iron, are juxtaposed and united, the pier appears heavy and the arch fragile. There is something shocking in seeing so much strength expended in supporting so little. We are perfectly aware of the objections one might make about the comparative strength of the two materials; but is must not be forgotten that everything true is not always beautiful and that what is solid and sufficient materially might not satisfy the eyes. One sees and feels before one reasons and more quickly than one reasons. Thus it is necessary, after having calculated solidity mathematically, to calculate, with less precision, the impression the form might produce. This rule has not been sufficiently observed in the detail we have just cited.[41]

Hermant misses Labrouste's point, however, even though he reads the work and even notes the key when he calls the ceiling "the sky—the ceiling depicts nothing else."[42]

83

Henri Labrouste, Bibliothèque
Sainte-Geneviève, Paris, 1843–50,
vestibule. (Photo: James Austin)

Labrouste paints the ceiling away as a blue sky, which, to reinforce the conceit, he carries unbroken down the two side walls, where it becomes the background for two vistas of treetops (painted by Ingres's student Alexandre Desgoffe) suggesting a garden extending right and left.[43] The unexpected and seemingly impossible step from the massive stone piers to the ethereal iron trusses is thus made the entry point into an illusionistic fantasy. The fantasy itself is familiar from historical sources: walls thus painted away into garden vistas were a Pompeiian motif, while the particular rendering is familiar from Ghirlandaio's *Last Supper* in the Ognisanti.[44] The leveling courses of the lateral wall masonry that cut the pilasters also serve as bands across the wall surface that define the lower limit of the painted illusion and support a row of busts of French philosophers, scientists, and artists.[45] The foliage behind each bust, in fact, is an attribute. Labrouste himself explained in 1852:

I would very much have desired that a large space planted with big trees and decorated with statues were laid out in front of the building to shield it from the noise of the street outside and to prepare those who come there for meditation. A beautiful garden would undoubtedly have been an appropriate introduction to a building devoted to study, but the narrowness of the site did not permit such an arrangement and it had to be forgone. Thus the garden I would have loved to traverse in order to arrive at this monument I painted on the walls of the vestibule, the only intermediary space between the public square and the library. My painted garden is not so fine as the beautiful allées of chestnut and plane trees, but it has the advantage of offering trees always green and in bloom, even in the month of December; and more, without regard to the climate of Paris, I may, in the fertile earth of the imagination, plant trees of all localities, and place next to Saint Bernard the palms of the Orient, flowering orange trees next to Racine, the oak and the rose next to Fontaine, and myrtle and laurels next to Poussin.

The vestibule is a little dark, but the readers, in crossing it, perhaps will believe that this obscurity is only that of the shade of these trees which they glimpse and, if I may be pardonned, I hope they will.[46]

Thus the vestibule of the Bibliothèque Sainte-Geneviève is a historical grove of Academe occupied by the great minds of modern times, each in his own garden at the same time. "One sees upon entering," Labrouste remarked, "that here one is in good company."[47] But the illusion lasts only a moment: it is restricted to the two lateral sides of the space, while the facing wall opens to lead one's mind and feet up the stairs to the reading room.

Labrouste's last and greatest work was the Bibliothèque Nationale, and in its principal space, the Salle des Imprimés (1859–68), he repeated and refined the theme of the Bibliothèque Sainte-Geneviève's vestibule. The room's facade, facing north over a low vestibule into the entrance court, is skeletalized in three broad stone arches occupying the whole width of the otherwise unarticulated wall. In spite of this warning, upon entering the space through a low, unpretentious doorway, one is surprised and carried into an illusion, as in the much smaller vestibule of the Bibliothèque Sainte-Geneviève, but more profoundly (figure 84). Here, after the constriction of the entry space, there is a flood of light, but it is diffused and from concealed sources, for the walls on the three sides visible from the door are closed; there is the continuous arcuated structure signaled on the exterior, but now open and lightened to seemingly impossible proportions. The secret of the first impression is in part the broad north windows at the visitor's back, but it is due more to the nine white porcelain domes that cover the space, reflecting and diffusing the light admitted by their small central glazed oculi, like huge versions of the green porcelain lampshades at the desktops. Gas fixtures set in the pendentives of the domes function similarly by reflection and diffusion after dark. Labrouste's use of the new industrial materials of porcelain and glass to flood the reading room with light was unparalleled and extraordinarily successful, but it depended upon his utilization of a third material to open the space and lighten the roof: iron. We have noted how the stone vaulted ceiling of Duc's vestibule at the Palais de Justice answered to the nineteenth-century expectations of load and support (as enunciated by Viollet-le-Duc) and how Hermant criticized the Bibliothèque Sainte-Geneviève vestibule for not doing so in its iron trusses. The visual insecurity of iron construction was a common theme in the 1850s when Labrouste was conceiving the Salle des Imprimés. Charles Garnier, for example, had intoned in 1857:

The impression one should feel at the sight of a monument is the sentiment of grandeur, of nobility, of calm, and of confidence. . . .

The means one should employ to give architecture this character of nobility and security all derive from the same principle, specifically the harmony of the proportions and relationships in general between the masses and the voids. What is more opposed to these requirements than construction in iron? In fact, in this genre of construction, the supports are thin, elongated, and of less importance than the parts they support.

It is thus the inability of iron to provide masses and supports satisfying to the eye which necessitates its rejection for any artistic construction.[48]

84
*Henri Labrouste, Bibliothèque
Nationale, Paris, 1860–67, Salle
des Imprimés. (Photo: James
Austin)*

Labrouste in the Salle des Imprimés does precisely what Garnier proscribes: not only is the ceiling iron but the supports are as well, all in contrast to the solid masonry shell visible from the court and around the interior walls. But, precisely as in the Bibliothèque Sainte-Geneviève vestibule, the visual impossibility of the structure of the Salle des Imprimés is the trigger for an extended architectural illusion. The four central columns, which seem too thin to support the ceiling, and the ceiling itself, which in other hands might have been made to seem too heavy to be supported, are lightened as Labrouste arches the crossties and billows up the porcelain reflector domes as if they were cloth awnings in a gusting breeze. One seeks the source of the sustaining breeze and finds it in the lunettes along the east and west walls, painted away (again by Desgoffe) as vistas of treetops and blue sky. One seems to be in a garden tent. Labrouste ties the knot and brings the illusion back to reality behind the visitor, for the lunettes repeat the forms of the great north windows which from inside present similar vistas of blue sky and, during the nineteenth century when the courtyard was planted, treetops.[49] One becomes confused about what is real and what is fictive: what weighs down seems to billow up; the painted openings are in clearer, deeper perspective than the real ones; that which is solid—the domes—glows as if transparent. Nevertheless, the effect is unitary and unified, while the light and openness are precisely what the function of a reading room demands.

Labrouste had been appointed architect of the library (during the Second Empire called the Bibliothèque Imperiale) on February 16, 1854, after the death of Visconti, who had been in charge of the structure.[50] It had been housed in the seventeenth-century Palais Mazarin on the northeast corner of the rue de Richelieu and the rue des Petits-Champs, spilling over into the Hôtel Tarboeuf next door.[51] A general rebuilding of the structure had been projected for decades—indeed since 1785, when Boullée had proposed turning the court into a vast vaulted reading room[52]—and on December 19, 1857, a commission was named to produce an administrative and architectural program of reorganization with Labrouste's help. Meanwhile the architect restored the interiors of the Hôtel Tarboeuf, spending 50,000 francs in 1856; 110,000 francs in 1857; and 150,000 francs in 1858. The commission issued its report on August 20, 1858, and on April 7, 1859, Labrouste submitted a definitive project, to cost 9,000,000 francs.[53] It worked within the framework of the existing structures, retaining the Galerie Mazarine and the rococo library erected by Robert de Cotte, while placing a new stack structure and reading room where the *corps de logis* and garden of the old palace stood south of the *cour d'honneur*. The reading room, however, is a simple square with a coved iron ceiling pierced by a single, broad skylight; and the courtyard is shown opening into the Square Louvois through an arcade (which was omitted in execution at the request of the library authorities for security reasons). This project was approved with warm praise by the Conseil des Batîments Civils on April 27, 1859; approved by the Minister on May 7; and put under construction at the rotunda on the southwest corner on June 1.[54]

Sketches and preliminary projects indicate that Labrouste devoted a great deal of study and thought to the Salle des Imprimés after the approval of the initial project. The Conseil's one important criticism had been that the single mid-ceiling skylight might cast the shadow of the reader's heads on the desktops, and his system of domical reflectors would seem, in part, a response. Labrouste also added an exedra at the far end of the space and was experimenting with responding exedral forms on the court facade, creating an axis moving through the tableau of the room like that of the Bibliothèque Sainte-Geneviève vestibule. All the while construction progressed: the reading room's foundations were laid in 1860 and its masonry envelope erected in 1862–64. On March 8, 1864, the contract for the thin faïence plaques of the domes was signed with W. T. Copeland of Birmingham, and on May 31, 1865, Labrouste certified the arrival of the last of the consignment.[55] The Salle des Imprimés was decorated in 1865 and 1866: Desgoffe contracted for his paintings on May 9, 1864, and was paid on September 29, 1865; Perraud for his caryatids at the door of the stacks on March 27, 1864 and March 28, 1865.[56] The medallions in the embrasures of the arches were authorized on May 17, 1865, and the twenty iron heaters in Labrouste's design were contracted for with Donzel on November 4, 1865, and paid for on June 28, 1868. In 1867 construction moved on to the vestibule, and early in 1868 the room was open and being reviewed in the press.[57] Work continued elsewhere in the complex, most particularly in the wing along the rue de Richelieu, until Labrouste's death in 1875; after that it was carried on by J.-L. Pascal, culminating in the erection of his disappointing Salle des Périodiques in 1906.

There has always been a temptation to read conventional symbolic meaning into the Salle des Imprimés. Already in 1868 "Y," writing in the *Moniteur des architectes* mused, "It is the garden of Academe symbolized; the walkers may, in their thoughts, stroll under these trees."[58] Recently, the German scholar Christian Beutler has interpreted the apse on the south wall as the Aula of Athena and the part-fictive, part-real vistas of foliage in the lunettes as making the space a symbolic greenhouse for the nurture of knowledge: "The library as greenhouse of science, as incubator of knowledge, and the scholars as gardners—what a wonderful picture!"[59] Because of the room's Pompeiian style in its slim columns and fictive awning domes, I have proposed that Labrouste was referring to Pliny the Younger's study in his Laurentian villa, with its velaria and vistas on three sides.[60] Each reader would be a modern-day Pliny able to share the ancient Roman's comfort, now with 399 fellows, by the magic of paint, porcelain, iron, glass, and gas. I have also yielded to the temptation to see the repetitive, cellular arched space as a Piranesian fantasy.[61]

To thus conventionally read the space's illusion, however, is to miss Labrouste's whole point. He himself insisted that his intention in painting the lunettes was *not* to distract the readers with symbolic scenes. He wrote in 1867 to Félix Thorigny of *Le Monde illustré*, "The architect thought that these calm, refreshing paintings were more appropriate to decorate a room dedicated to study than historical subjects, which might have the disadvantage of distracting the readers."[62] This was repeated almost verbatim by Labrouste's son Léon in his booklet on the Bibliothèque Nationale of 1885.[63] Several contemporaneous critics, probably at the architect's suggestion, emphasized that here there were "no memories, no imitation."[64] The symbolic furniture of the space was as easy and unobtrusive as its shape or the access to it by a few steps across the vestibule from the courtyard.

Nonetheless, the tableau Labrouste creates in the Salle des Imprimés is so strong and unified that one struggles to place it and is gratified by the hint that Labrouste's student and friend, the architect A.-N.-L. Bailly, gives in his necrology of 1876. He remembers Labrouste reminiscing about the lunettes:

When I was in lycée, *before or after classes I would go and study in the Luxembourg Garden and especially in the Pépinière. There, where nothing disturbed me, my eyes as well as my mind would repose happily on the beautiful and luxuriant foliage that surrounded me. I thought that in a place of study the representation of what had had so much charm for me would be in a library a decoration without pretention, first of all, and also an occasion for rest for the minds of the readers occupying the room.*[65]

In 1866 the Pépinière of the Luxembourg Garden was destroyed and the space appropriated by the university buildings along the rue d'Assas, causing the students—who, like Labrouste, enjoyed its quiet *allées*—to assail the Emperor at the Odéon in protest.[66]

I have tried to interpret even this hint symbolically, as a reference to the Romantic theme of escape into a childhood fantasy of a garden past the mouth of a cave, as in Novalis's *Heinrich von Ofterdingen*.[67] One might propose that Labrouste was trying to make good his childhood refuge in the Pépinière, but its destruction was announced in 1866, well after the conception of the decoration of the Salle des Imprimés but just upon its completion. Labrouste's remark to Bailly seems an explanation offered after the fact. If that is so, however, Labrouste would have been proceeding precisely as he had in his Paestum *envoi* at the beginning of his career: the careful and elaborate interpretation of those remains was based on the identification of the three structures as a temple to Neptune, one to Ceres, and a basilica. Those initial identifications were merely a local tradition; there was no proof of their correctness. What was important to Labrouste was what they seemed to suggest and that these suggestions were a way of accepting the otherwise mute monuments.

One is not troubled by the lack of allegorical furnishings in the Salle des Imprimés because the architecture offers enough in itself. It creates a complete, pervading, embracing impression that a fresco of Plato musing in the Academy or a statue of Minerva would shatter. This impression imposes itself by Labrouste's use of a strange, intense light and of a simple repetitive domical geometry. These qualities so tightly link all the elements of the space that it seems very small, a bit primitive, and quite impossible.

We have noted the function of the domes to soften and diffuse the light from the skylights and gas fixtures. The most obvious result of this was that the domes thus glow, day and evening, as if they were a source of light themselves and transparent. In 1857 when Labrouste visited London to study the problems of library building, he visited both Smirke's reading room at the British Museum and the ferrovitreous Crystal Palace at Sydenham. He dined with Owen Jones, who had been partly responsible for the latter and had painted its interior in the primary colors red, yellow, and blue so as to intensify its effect of light and transparency.[68] One realizes that in the Salle des Imprimés Labrouste has combined lessons from both of these London buildings. He has achieved the pervasive glow Jones sought but controlled it and protected it from the weather by his fragile porcelain interior inserted in a masonry and ferrovitreous shell.

Labrouste's glowing porcelain domes thus achieve an intensity of hue that sets off their red patterning and the green ironwork supporting them, the beige masonry, the leaf green and sky blue of Desgoffe's lunettes, and the red buildings of the tiers of books. In our earlier discussion of Vaudoyer's and Espérandieu's adaption of colored exterior masonry for Marseilles Cathedral and Notre-Dame-de-la-Garde, we noted the transformation of the concept of ancient Greek polychromy into a vivid, harmonious, atmospheric vision dematerializing solid mass and making it blend with the landscape. Gottfried Semper, the refugee German architect and theorist of polychromy, recently settled in London after spending 1849–50 in Paris, presented one of the most evocative statements of this vision in 1851:

The prevailing colours of the [ancient Greek] temple burned with all the glowing beauty of the setting sun. The colour may be defined as of a yellow-red, very vapoury, ressembling that of the finest terra cotta. In fact, the general appear-

*ance of the temple would precisely resemble the appearance of a fine day in an
eastern climate.*[69]

We also saw how around 1850 this chromatic vision was applied to all the
epochs of Mediterranean architecture as if an inevitable response to that
luminous environment. Misty, cold Paris does not have the advantages of
that climate, but modern industry has placed glass, iron, porcelain, central
heating, and gas lighting at the architect's disposal so that now, during the
Second Empire, he can create a Mediterranean garden inside and improve
it by the suppression of seasons and times of day. The Salle des Imprimés
is thus a painted Greek temple or the Alhambra turned inside out. Labrouste has done with climate what he did with geography in the paintings in the vestibule of the Bibliothèque Sainte-Geneviève. One can say of
this space what César Daly did of an interior painted by Owen Jones: "We
have positively changed latitude: it seems as if the artist has reenacted the
miracle of Prometheus, that he has discovered how to bring down fire
from heaven to illuminate his work."[70]

Labrouste has concentrated the parts of his composition so that the effect is reminiscent of the wonderful innocent architecture of Pompeiian
and quattrocento paintings to which its specific motifs refer. His Italian
sketchbooks contain pages of architectural background extracted from
these paintings, reflecting his fascination with how architecture is transformed by a naive painter's mind when freed from the trammels of function and construction. In the Salle des Imprimés he manages to create
something like that, the quality Monsignor Durand recognized in Marseilles Cathedral when he compared it to a donor's model church in a
medieval mosaic.

Labrouste's Salle des Imprimés is a response to and a critique of the
series of solutions we have seen the Romantic *pensionnaires* offer in their
great monuments of the Second Empire. Vaudoyer, in Marseilles Cathedral, demonstrated how there might be order without Orders, a round-
arched vocabulary of spatial volumes that could refer to the whole history
of architecture in a single, symphonic composition. Duc, in his Vestibule
de Harlay, gave expressive emphasis to this eclectic ideal by returning to
the Orders, now reanimated with specific structural and symbolic meaning. Labrouste, in the Salle des Imprimés, played off Duc's emphasis on
the solidity of construction to create something seemingly structurally impossible and in so doing carries the viewer into a vision more timeless,
scaleless, and vivid than Vaudoyer's donor's church.

Labrouste's architecture was sufficient in itself. It made no compromises
with earth-borne spatial or structural forms used to express the history of
the Church or the ideas of *Justice* and *Force*. His Salle des Imprimés seems
pure fantasy unencumbered by any necessity to convey a specific message

at all. In the end, he produced a space that is utterly and unmistakably a reading room because here everything works to set the user's mind free, to allow it to wander conceptually rather than to labor logically.

Labrouste understood that architectural meaning had not just to be communicated, but to be embodied. Garnier embodied the meaning of his Opera in the most literal way: it is the representation, the setting, the cloak of its social function. But Labrouste's embodiment in the Salle des Imprimés is "transparent." It is not a setting for thought, it is thought itself.

CONCLUSION

There have been three questions underlying the narrative of this volume. First, what general objective, what embracing vision of architecture, had the Romantic *pensionnaires* formulated? Second, how was this manifested in specific architectural form? Third, under what circumstances and in what context did they execute their designs? I tried to answer the first two questions in my examination of the Romantic historicist ideal of the *pensionnaires* and its quite various manifestations in their first designs. In answering the third, I examined the distinct context of this work, its complete integration into the government architectural services. Finally, I analyzed the complex and impressive results in the great monuments of the Second Empire.

The Ecole des Beaux-Arts, the Bibliothèque Sainte-Geneviève, and the Conservatoire des Arts et Métiers, as well as the magisterial Cathedral of Marseilles, Palais de Justice, and Bibliothèque Nationale, constitute a series of impressive but puzzling creations. One comes to them knowing that they were considered the foundation monuments of the nineteenth-century French classical tradition, the Beaux-Arts. Yet they are not the predictable columniated machines Hasenauer and Ludwig Hoffmann, Blomfield and Baker, Burnham and McKim have made us expect. On the contrary, they are profound manifestations of the Romantic ideals of local historical projection, structural organicism, and (in the case of Labrouste) intuitive fantasy. Nevertheless, in the context of mid-nineteenth-century France, they are more accurate and incisive expressions of architectural thought than any Madeleine or Lincoln Memorial. They are firmly rooted in their time: the Ecole des Beaux-Arts is an alephlike summary in fragments of the modern artistic tradition; Marseilles Cathedral is a statement of historical and geographical colonialism; and Labrouste's two libraries are hallucinatory expressions of cerebral concentration.

These designs are manifestations not only of the mentality of a time but also of a social and professional circumstance. They were legible to the members of a certain class or circle. This was not the restricted circle of radical artists, nor the wide circle of the old nobility or the politicians or the general public. It was, instead, the circle of the administrative class—that peculiarly large, deathless, and in many ways unique segment of French society that observers from Alexis de Toqueville to Michel Crozier have felt its central phenomenon. This administrative world was the immediate context for the conception of these buildings and the factor informing and complicating their free and intuitive creation as works of art. The Romantic *pensionnaires*, working in the Bâtiments Civils or the

Edifices Diocésains, did not have to worry excessively about the Rothschilds or Louis-Philippe and Napoleon III, but they were beholden in myriad ways to the procedures, traditions, and mentality of their services—the procedures, traditions, and mentality as well of Labrouste's father and two brothers, of Vaudoyer's father, cousin, and son, of Duc's son-in-law, and so on.

In this context the Romantic rationalist and historicist ideals of the *pensionnaires* take on significant undertones. Marseilles Cathedral pretended to be an inflected history of the architectural culture of its site and time, yet in the end it was a remarkable statement of political and economic *power*: of France as the civilizing power of the Mediterranean world; of French art and scholarship as the unifying force in the history of culture. The Palais de Justice is only slightly less dramatic, especially if the Place Dauphine had been demolished to reveal the rue de Harlay facade astride the Ile de la Cité like the superstructure of a battleship. Its references are more complicated and concentrated: it is about order and authority in France itself, about a coordination of *Justice* and *Force* as perfect as that manifested in its balanced and responding half-columns and reliefs.

Here the Bibliothèque Nationale's Salle des Imprimés again stands out because it alone is speculative. Here the jingle of shibboleths—*Empire, Force, Justice*—is stilled. The lunettes, which might have been filled with symbolic turgidities, are mere illusionistic windows on treetops and sky. It is light, glowing, immaterial, where Marseilles Cathedral and the Palais de Justice had been resolutely solid and concrete. In a sense it is a protest, the quiet but firm protest of a man certain of his position and authority. Not a protest against modern industry, which provided the very materials that free his design to create illusions, nor against classicism as a tradition, which suffuses the tableau he created, but against the thoughtless repetition in iron and stone of the received ideas of mid-nineteenth-century culture. Yet it was the authority and relative freedom of his position as a government architect that gave him the opportunity to do this. He alone among the Romantic *pensionnaires* took full advantage of his position to produce in his glowing iron, glass, and porcelain box something as pointed as it was unexpected.

NOTES

INTRODUCTION

1

The only modern study of Duban was one begun by Mlle. Cristine Marmoz before her death. Otherwise: L. Vaudoyer, *Discours prononcé au funérailles de M. Duban* (Paris, 1871); V. Baltard, *Hommage à Félix Duban . . .* (Paris, 1871); C.-A. Questel, *Notice sur Duban* (Paris, 1872); E. Beulé, *Eloge de Duban* (Paris, 1872); C. Blanc, *Les Artistes de mon temps* (Paris, 1876). Three volumes of Duban's historical drawings from Rome survive in the library of the Ecole des Beaux-Arts, but otherwise his personal papers have not been located. Adolphe Lance provided illuminating critical entries for Duban and his friends in his *Dictionnaire des architectes français* (Paris, 1872). For Duban and his contemporaries, see also C. Bauchal, *Nouveau dictionnaire biographique et critique des architectes français* (Paris, 1887).

2

A seminal study of Labrouste exists in Neil Levine's dissertation, "Architectural Reasoning in the Age of Positivism: The Néo-Grec Idea of Henri Labrouste's Bibliothèque Sainte-Geneviève" (Yale University, 1975). See also: P. Saddy, *Henry Labrouste, architecte, 1801–1875* (Paris, 1977); R. Plouin, "Henry Labrouste, sa vie, son oeuvre, 1801–1875" (Thèse de troisième cycle, University of Paris, 1965); *Souvenirs d'Henri Labrouste, architecte, membre de l'Institut, notes recueillées et classées par ses enfants* (Paris, 1928); E. Millet, "Henry Labrouste, sa vie, ses oeuvres," *Bulletin de la société centrale des architectes* (1879–80); E. Bailly, *Notice sur M. Henri Labrouste* (Paris, 1876); H. Delaborde, *Notice sur la vie et les ouvrages de M. Henri Labrouste* (Paris, 1878). Labrouste's personal papers have been deposited in the Académie d'Architecture, Paris, and in the Cabinet des Estampes at the Bibliothèque Nationale.

3

There is no modern study of Duc beyond Katherine Taylor's current Harvard dissertation on the Palais de Justice. See: H. Delaborde, *Notice sur la vie et les ouvrages de M. Duc* (Paris, 1879), P. Sédille, *Joseph-Louis Duc, architecte (1802–1879)* (Paris, 1879); J.-L. Pascal, "M. Duc et son influence sur le mouvement architectural contemporain," *GBA* 2S, 19 (1879, pt. 1): 430–443; L. Cernesson, "Joseph-Louis Duc," *RGA* 37 (1880); cols. 75–79, 156–160. Duc's personal papers have not been located.

4

A monographic study of Vaudoyer is in process by Barry Bergdoll as a Columbia University dissertation. See also: G. Davioud, "Funérailles de M. Léon Vaudoyer," *Bulletin de la société centrale des architectes* (1872); A.-H. Revoil, "Léon Vaudoyer," *Le Messager du Midi,* February 14, 1872; T. Ballu, *Notice sur M. Léon Vaudoyer* (Paris, 1873); C. Blanc, *Les Artistes de mon temps,* pp. 225–248; E. Parrocel, *L'Art dans le Midi,* 4 vols. (Marseilles, 1881–84). Vaudoyer's papers survive in the possession of his descendants. An illuminating series of letters about Vaudoyer written to Charles Blanc by his assistant Henri Espérandieu survive in the Blanc papers at the Institut de France, ms. 1809.

5

"Comment désespérer maintenant de notre architecture, quand on songe que la connaissance des beaux modèles est toute récente et que la véritable Renaissance ne date pas de trente ans? Guidée par l'étude et par une critique lumineuse, armée de toutes pièces, notre école a devant elle aujourd'hui la plus illustre carrière." C. Blanc, *Grammaire des arts du dessin* (Paris, 1867), p. 305.

6

"La raison et la vérité pénètrent enfin dans la domaine réservé aux arts; on comprend que l'oeuvre ne dépend pas d'une formule vide, mais de l'expression rationelle d'une idée: une réforme artistique se prépare, et parmi les novateurs figurent au premier rang les élèves qui de 1821 à 1826 illustrent l'école de Rome, les Blouet, les Gilbert, les Duban, les Henri Labrouste, les Duc, les Vaudoyer." L. Magne, *L'Architecture française du siècle* (Paris, 1889), pp. 27–28.

7

"Au commencement du siècle, la seule esthétique était de concevoir *a priori* un édifice romain. . . . Un peu plus tard, une réaction violente substituait au romain *a priori* le moyen âge *a priori*, architecture d'une civilisation encore plus différente de la nôtre. . . . Heureusement, de fiers artistes—nos maîtres—ont vu et ont fait voir que l'indépendence ne consiste pas à changer de livrée, et notre art s'affranchi peu à peu de cette paléontologie. Tout n'a pas été également heureux, mais tous les efforts vers ce but ont été féconds, et aujourd'hui nous savons et nous proclamons que l'art a droit à la liberté, que seule la liberté peut lui assurer la vie et la fécondité, disons mieux, le salut!" J. Guadet, *Eléments et théorie de l'architecture*, 4 vols. (Paris, 1901–4), I, p. 85. He had started as a student of Labrouste but, when the atelier was closed in 1856, studied with the much more conservative André.

8
"Toute une pléïade d'artistes grandissait, dont les oeuvres devaient dominer le milieu du siècle et préparer l'avenement d'une architecture toute nouvelle, semblait-il en dépit de ses sources traditionelles, par la caractère, la variété, et la vie. La génération née avec le siècle, celle en somme qui avait l'âge des grands romantiques . . . devait éclairer des compositions de sa maturité les dix-huit années du règne de Louis-Philippe et soutenir, vingt ans encore, l'art architectural du second empire des exemples de l'autorité de sa vieillesse. Quatre artistes du premier ordre, dans une même période de quatre années, vont remporter successivement le grand prix: ce sont Gilbert en 1822, Duban en 1823, Labrouste en 1824, enfin Duc en 1825." G. Gromort, *Histoire générale de l'art français de la Révolution à nos jours*, 3 vols. (Paris, 1922), II (architecture and sculpture), p. 43.

9
See his treatment of Labrouste in *Space, Time and Architecture*, 5th edition (Cambridge, Mass., 1967), pp. 218–228.

10
See the publications of the archaeological *envois* by the Ecole des Beaux-Arts: *Pompéi: travaux et envois des architectes français au XIXe siècle* (1981); *Paris . Rome . Athènes: le voyage en Grèce des architectes français au XIXe et XXe siècles* (1982); and *Roma antiqua: envois des architectes français (1788–1924). Forum, Colisée, Palatin* (1985). Exhibitions of the work of Victor Laloux and Charles Garnier are slated at the Musée d'Orsay.

11
P. Saddy, *Henry Labrouste*; D. Rabreau, et al., *Gabriel Davioud, architecte (1824–1881)* (Paris, 1981); B. Foucart, et al., *Paul Abadie, architecte, 1812–1884* (Angoulême, 1984); Uwe Westfehling, et al., *Hittorff: un architecte du XIXe siècle* (Paris, 1986).

One

THE STUDENT WORK

1
This moment is studied in Neil Levine's essay, "The Romantic Idea of Architectural Legibility: Henri Labrouste and the Néo-Grec," *EBA*, pp. 325–416; in D. Van Zanten, "The Beginnings of French Romantic Architecture and Félix Duban's Temple Protestant," *In Search of Modern Architecture*, ed. Helen Searing (New York and Cambridge, Mass., 1982), pp. 64–84; as well as in Levine's dissertation, previously cited, and D. Van Zanten, "The Architectural Polychromy of the 1830's," (Ph.D. dissertation, Harvard University, 1970; published under that title by the Garland Publishing Company, New York, 1976). On the Grand Prix competitions: *EBA*; D. D. Egbert, *The Beaux-Arts Tradition in French Architecture*, ed. D. Van Zanten (Princeton, 1980); Neil Levine, "The Competition for the Grand Prix in 1824," *The Beaux-Arts*, ed. Robin Middleton (London, 1982), pp. 66–123.

2

Réglements pour les travaux des pensionnaires à l'Académie de France à Rome, ordonnance of January 26, 1821. Neil Levine has kindly provided me with a photocopy of this. The Director of the Academy in Rome, Horace Vernet, protested the restriction of exploration to Rome in a letter of June 6, 1829 (in the Institut de France archives), but was overruled by the Académie.

3

Léon Vaudoyer maintained a regular correspondence with his father, who was a respected *maître d'atelier*, Secrétaire-Archiviste of the Ecole des Beaux-Arts, and, from 1823, member of the Académie. These letters have been preserved by their descendants and permit a remarkable glimpse into one of the Romantic *pensionnaire*'s minds.

Of Siena: "La cathédrale m'a fait un plaisir infini. Il y règne une harmonie entre l'extérieur et l'intérieur et tout cela est décoré de marbres de couleurs, de peintures, etc. . . . et ressemble en rien à nos églises blanches et froides de Paris."

Of the Pitti Palace: "dont le caractère je trouve ne convient pas à une habitation de prince."

Of the Duomo and the Baptistry: "de choses dont on [ne] peut se faire une idée quand on ne les a pas vues."

Of San Miniato: "Comme Labrouste me l'avait écrit est une bien jolie chose."

Of Florence: "Je serais bien heureux quand je retournerai pour y travailler."

4

"Nous sommes extremement unis, on nous trouve fiers je ne sais [pas] pouquoi; . . . Labrouste et Duc m'ont conduit voir toutes les antiquités."

5

Cf. Letter, Léon Vaudoyer to his father, February 16, 1827.

6

Decraëne became a successful architect in Tournai in his native Belgium. His drawings, including those made in Rome, are preserved in the Musée des Beaux-Arts there.

7

Léon Vaudoyer, letters of June 13 and 22, 1827.

8

C. Blanc, *Les Artistes de mon temps*, (Paris, 1876), p. 16.

9

Léon Vaudoyer, letter of June 9, 1828.

10

Letter of August 3, 1828.

11

Letters of September 10, October 30, November 18, 1828. Kubly became a successful architect in St. Gall. See Benno Schubiger, *Felix Wilhelm Kubly, 1802–1872* (St. Gall, 1984). Dr. Schubiger has been very kind in sharing his research with me. See also: G. Germann, *Der protestantische Kirchenbau in der Schweiz* (Zurich, 1963), pp. 133–135.

12

"L'aspect de cette belle antiquité m'a ravi. C'est une des choses qui m'ait fait le plus d'effet." Letter of November 18, 1828.

13

Letter of April 23, 1829.

14

Ibid.

15

Letter of September 16, 1829.

16

Letter of November 3, 1829.

17

A very sketchy journal of that trip survives in the possession of the Vaudoyer family.

18

"En général ici nous renions ce que nous avons produit à Paris et comptons par nos productions à venir effacer les erreurs du passé."

19

Letter of January 22, 1827: "Toutes les villa [sic] que je vois me prouvent le charlatanisme de l'ouvrage de Mr. Percier."

Letter of February 16, 1827: "Les dessins de Mr. Thibault prouvent que de son temps on faisait quelque chose de rien[. C]ette mode est passé et l'on pense plus sérieusement; on ne passe pas son temps . . . à faire des croquis à boisseaux."

Letter of April 4, 1827: "Est-ce que avec une chambre-claire que sont fait les entablements et les chapitaux qu'on vous envoye chaque année? J'ai mésuré celui de Jupiter Stator et j'ai été à même juger toute la peine que cela donne, à mésurer, à restaurer, à rapporter, et mettre au net. Est-ce que à la chambre-claire que Duc et Labrouste ont fait leur voyage de Pompéia dont ils ont rapporté non pas des croquis et des vues pittoresques, mais des plans et des coupes levées et rapportées; on ne fait plus de minutes comme autrefois que l'on ne rapportais jamais et qui restent au portefeuille sans être jamais consultées. On arrive à Paris aujourd'hui avec un voyage complet, tant sur l'antique que sur le moderne et dont on peut jouir immédiatement; notre manière de travailler, aujourd'hui, n'est pas un mode; elle est positive et incontestablement supérieur à celle de nos prédecesseurs."

20

EBA, pp. 144–145. Cf. Labrouste's laudatory remarks: "Ecole des Beaux-Arts," *RGA* 1 (1840): cols. 546–547. Katherine Fisher Taylor is working on Huyot as part of her Harvard dissertation on the Palais de Justice.

21

"N'ayant rien fait, étant resté un jour à Pompéia." Letters of July 26 and April 30, 1827.

22

His first-year *envoi* had been details of what were thought to be the temple of Marcus Aurelius and that of the Sun.

23

Letter of July 20, 1829: "J'ai cherché par mon étude de 2ème année à diriger mes vues sur une architecture plus primitive, sur cette architecture simple qui ne doit sa beauté qu'à ses formes et à ses proportions sans que l'attention se fixe sur une frise ou un raye de coeur plus ou moins bien fait."

Letter of March 22, 1830: "Les modernes ont dénaturé cet ordre [at Cori] faute d'en avoir étudie les principes[. C]'est ainsi que l'on a vu mettre des bases attiques à des colonnes doriques. . . . Je n'ai pas cherché à faire une belle porte [for the temple of Fortuna Virilis], mais à faire une porte dans le caractère du reste du monument ce qui m'a obligé d'employer des moulures un peu grossières. . . . Je n'ai pas fait de ce qu'on appelle de beaux dessins c'est-à-dire de ces détails à ornements frises, etc. . . . mais je crois [avoir] fait de bonnes études."

24

The original reports on the *envois* are in the archives of the French Academy in Rome and are in the process of publication.

25

See letters of April 28 and August 8, 1830.

26

"Je cherche à faire comprendre que je n'ai pas voulu faire une étude comparative mais bien des études isolées dans des monuments cependant qui ont quelque analogie de forme et de construction c'est-à-dire l'architecture d'arcades et de voûtes." Letter of April 28, 1830.

27

Letter of July 10, 1831.

28

Letter of September 10, 1828.

29

"Les idées ont changé [sic]; est arrivé le système constitutionnel qui nous a apporté l'esprit d'examen, de raisonnement et d'économie. On a commencé, dès lors, à penser qu'il ne suffisait pas d'avoir un excellent goût d'arrangement, d'ajuster parfaitement des ornements, de les dessiner dans la perfection, de surcharger les monuments de figures, de bas reliefs, etc. pour faire de l'architecture. . . . On est arrivé à comprendre que nos institutions politiques et sociales veulent une architecture sage, raisonnée, d'une éxécution facile, simple et économique. Je ne me charge pas de décider si c'est un bien ou un mal, mais je crois, cependant, qu'il y a autant de mérite dans les monuments de la [Roman] République que dans ceux du temps de Trajan; que ce n'est pas la richesse des matériaux ni l'immensité des monuments qui constituent la véritable beauté, mais bien une juste idée des convenances, des besoins de l'époque et enfin la noblesse des formes et une expression du caractère appropriée à chaque chose. Le Temple de la Paix, de brique et de stuc, est un chef d'oeuvre qui ne cède en rien aux plus riches monuments de marbres. Je crois donc que pour arriver à satisfaire aux besoins de notre époque, il faut de préférence étudier l'architecture radicale des anciens, c'est-à-dire celle qui eut à satisfaire des usages primitifs et non encore corrompue par le luxe. C'est dans cette architecture première qu'on retrouve davantage la raison des formes[,] le *squelette* enfin qui, plus tard, se dérobe sous les habits bordés. C'est pour pouvoir dépouiller ces riches monuments de l'Empire de toutes leurs parures et y retrouver le nud qu'il faut passer par l'étude de ces monuments républicains on grecs qui n'ont pour ornements que la pureté de leurs formes et leur simplicité. . . . Or, quelle est donc cette architecture qu'on appele Romantique, je ne sais trop pourquoi, c'est une architecture qui veut remonter aux vrais principes, qui veut que toute forme soit donnée par la raison et le besoin[,] qui veut se soumettre à la nature des matériaux, qui veut enfin, mettre cet art en harmonie avec le siècle."

30

"Après une longue discussion architectonique . . . ils se sont séparés en disant: que lui, Duc, était partisan de ce qui était donné par la raison et le besoin et que lui, Huyot, était partisan de ce qui plaisait d'abord aux yeux en dépit de ces deux considérations. . . . Voilà donc deux systèmes tout à fait incompatibles et sans qu'ils ait aucun espoir de les voir jamais changés."

31

On Labrouste's Paestum *envoi*: published—*Temples de Paestum par architectes élèves pensionnaires de France à Rome* (Paris, 1877); L. Dassy [pseud.], *Compte rendu sur la restauration de Paestum exécutée en 1829 par Henri Labrouste* (Paris, 1879); analyzed—Neil Levine, *EBA*, pp. 325–416, and "Architectural Reasoning . . . ," ch. 7, pt. 3. On the reaction to the *envoi*: E.-E. Viollet-le-Duc, "Lettres extra-parlementaires," *Le XIXᵉ Siècle*, January 29, 1877, ff., especially March 21; H. Van Brunt, "Greek Lines," *The Atlantic Monthly* 7 (1861): 654–667. The original drawings are preserved in the library of the Ecole des Beaux-Arts.

32

C.-M. Delagardette (or de Lagardette), *Les Ruines de Poestum ou de Posidonia mésurées et desinnées sur les lieux* (Paris, An. VII).

33

See the correspondence between the Director and the Académie in the Institut archives, especially Vernet's letter of March 29, 1830.

34

H. Delaborde, *Notice sur la vie et les ouvrages de M. Henri Labrouste* (Paris, 1878).

35

Cf. Quatremère de Quincy, *Mémoire sur la manière dont les temples des grecs et romains étaient éclairés*, read in 1805 at the Institut.

36

Published in the colored plates of Hittorff's *Architecture antique de la Sicile* (Paris, 1827–30). See also my doctoral dissertation, cited above, and the catalogue *Paris . Rome . Athènes* (Paris, 1982).

37

JD, September 24, 1829.

38

This Labrouste explains in the essay he sent with his drawings, published in edited form with them in 1877.

39

See Thierry's reminiscences in his *Lettres sur l'histoire de France* (Paris, 1827).

40

Hector d'Espouy, *Fragments d'architecture antique*, 2 vols. (Paris, n.d.), I, pl. 24; II, pls. 6, 7.

41

Léon Vaudoyer, letter of December 4, 1830. Labrouste's project is reproduced in *EBA*, 396–397.

42

"Quelque chose . . . qui fut fait pour la France mais paraît inspiré par les voyages et les études de l'Antiquité." "Ecole des Beaux-Arts," *RGA* 1 (1840): cols. 543–547.

43

See Levine, *EBA*, p. 400.

44

See E. Quinet, *Le Génie des religions* (Paris, 1842), ch. 2, and his concept of the "révélation de la nature." Also: G. Monod, *La Vie et la pensée de Jules Michelet* (Paris, 1923), ch. 14.

45

"Lord Byron, et non Biron n'a jamais été admiral, mais poëte très distingué et défenseur de la liberté des grecs. . . . Pour avoir une idée de son caractère il faut lire le dernier chant du Pèlerinage du Chil Harolde [sic] par Mr. A. de Lamartine[.] C'est un chef d'oeuvre de poésie française." Letter of June 22, 1827.

46

"Il ne s'agit pas pour cela d'aller chez Merlin librairie rococo qui ne sait pas seulement de ce que c'est que Lamartine; mais chez Gosselin." Letter of October 12, 1827.

47

F.-R. de Chateaubriand, *Mémoires d'outre-tombe* (Paris, 1849); J.-O.-B.-C. Comte d'Haussonville, "L'Ambassade de M. de Chateaubriand (1828)," *RDM* 3S, 69 (June 1, 1885): 481–504; E. Beau de Lomenie, *La Carrière politique de Chateaubriand de 1814 à 1830*, 2 vols. (Paris, 1929).

48

"On parle d'art." Letter of December 9, 1828.

49

"Je persiste dans mon opinion il ne nous faut plus de mithologie[;] nous sommes dans le siècle du positif; je n'ai pas blamé les vièrges de Raphaël[;] au contraire je les cite comme un peintre qui a representé les idées de son siècle[.Q]uant aux sujets modernes je soutiens qu'on peut les traiter très bien je ne veux pas d'autres exemples que la Peste de Jaffa les Batailles d'Aboukir et d'Eylau de Mr. Gros le Sacre de David le Sermant de jeu de paume la bataille d'Austerlitz de Gérard son Henry quatre et pour bien vous faire sentir mon idée je vous dirai que la famille malheureuse de Mr. Prud'hon me fait plus d'effet que tous les narcisses du monde[. C]'est ce que j'appele une scène morale[. J]e n'exclue pas les sujets grecs ni romains ni l'allegorie mais il est temps . . . de peindre notre histoire. . . . On ne veut plus de mithologie[. C]'est fini dans les arts comme dans le théâtre comme en litérature." Letter of January 6, 1830.

50

"Je n'ai pas le talent de me faire comprendre. . . . La Guerre dont je parle n'est pas dangereuse[. I]l ne s'agit ici que de goût[. O]r vous savez qu'en fait de gout il est difficile de prouver qu'est-ce qui a raison[;] ainsi cette guerre en architecture n'est autre chose que celle qui existe en littérature entre les Victor Hugo et les classiques et de même en peinture[. P]ourquoi l'architecture ne ferait-elle ainsi sa petite révolution[? C]ela est tout naturel[;] C'est la force des choses qui l'amène là[. L]'architecture d'un peuple doit emprunter son caractère 1. des institutions 2. des moeurs 3. du climat 4. de la nature des matériaux etc. . . . Ainsi donc l'architecture de 1830 ne peut être celle de 1680 ou on batissait Versailles en faisant mourir le peuple de faim et de misère[. L]e luxe d'un despot est superbe étourdissant mais le bonheur d'une nation entière gouvernée sagement est bien plus satisfaisant[. A]insi donc c'est une extrême sagesse qui nous porte aujourd'hui à ramener l'architecture à une expression plus vrai et plus en harmonie avec les idées du siècle." Letter of March 22, 1830.

51

See Van Zanten, "The Beginnings of French Romantic Architecture." Lecointe's sketches are in the "Carnets Hittorff" in the library of the Ecole des Beaux-Arts; Labrouste's are among his notebooks in the Académie d'Architecture.

52

On Stier's project: K. E. O. Fritsch, et al., *Der Kirchenbau des Protestantismus* (Berlin, 1893), pp. 192–193. See also Berlin, Technisches Universität, Plansammlung, II.M.89.

53

"Cet édifice n'admettant ni sculpture, ni peinture, ni richesse d'ornement, on regrette que M. Duban . . . n'a pas pu trouver, dans la simplicité obligé du sujet qu'il a choisie pour sa composition, les moyens d'y faire l'application de ses précédentes études." *Compte rendu de la séance annuelle publique* . . . .

54

Germann, *Der protestanische Kirchenbau*, pp. 131–135.

55

See G. Germann, "Melchior Berris Rathausentwurf für Bern (1833)," *Baseler Zeitschrift für Geschichte und Alterthümskunde* (1969), pp. 239–319. Berri was brother-in-law of the historian Jakob Burckhardt.

56

In a letter to the Académie of August 22, 1829, Duban mentions visiting Geneva (Institut de France, archives); but Petrus Borel notes that "Duban avait fait en Suisse et en Allemagne une étude sérieuse et minutieuse des temples protestants" ("Du Mouvement en architecture," *L'Artiste* 2 (1833): 74–78, especially p. 75). See Schubiger, *Felix Wilhelm Kubly*, pp. 99–100.

57

G. de Bertier de Sauvigny, *La Restauration* (Paris, 1955), p. 325.

58

"Subordonna l'Etat à l'Eglise . . . la société civile à la société réligieuse, et prépara dans Genève une croyance et un gouvernement à tous ceux en Europe qui rejetteraient la croyance et s'insurgeraient contre le gouvernement de leur pays. C'est ce qui arriva en France sous la minorité de Charles IX; en Escosse, sous le règne troublé de Marie Stuart; dans les Pays-Bas, lors de la révolte des Provinces Unis; et en Angleterre sous Charles Ier. . . . Ce système, qui devait s'étendre dans une grande partie de l'Europe, qui préparait le protestantisme de l'insurrection contre les princes, comme le système de Luther avait préparé le protestantisme de l'insurrection contre les papes; qui mettait un gouvernement écclésiastique à la disposition de tous les pays où le pouvoir politique n'en établissait pas un lui-même; qui devait agiter soixante ans la France, servir à l'opérer la réformation d'Escosse, contribuer à l'émancipation de la Hollande, présider à la révolution d'Angleterre, qui devait donner son empreint à Coligny, au prince d'Orange, à Cromwell, Calvin l'introduisit d'abord dans Genève." F. Mignet, "Etablissement de la réforme à Genève," *Mémoires historiques* (Paris, 1854), pp. 347–348. See also: Y. Knibiehles, *Naissance des sciences humaines: Mignet et l'histoire philosophique au XIXe siècle* (Paris, 1973), especially pp. 354ff.

59

Cf. E. Quinet, *Le Christianisme et la révolution française* (Paris, 1845).

60

"Romantisme c'est le protestantisme dans les arts." L. Vitet, "De l'indépendence en matière du goût," *Le Globe* 89 (April 2, 1825). M. Parturier, ed., *Lettres de Mérimée à Ludovic Vitet* (Paris, 1934), biographical introduction. Also: F. Guizot, "M. Vitet, sa vie et ses oeuvres," *RDM* 3S, 2 (March 1, 1874): 33–65; Sainte-Beuve, *Portraits littéraires* (Paris, revised ed., 1862–64), III, pp. 412–423.

61

C. Jullian, *Extraits des historiens français du XIXe siècle* (Bordeaux, 1879); L. Halphen, *L'Histoire en France depuis cent ans* (Paris, 1914); Moreau, *L'Histoire en France au XIXe siècle* (Paris, 1935); G. P. Gooch, *History and Historians in the Nineteenth Century* (London, 1913).

62

"Ce temple parfaitement composé, soigneusement pensé, d'un bel et inaccoutumé aspect, fit jeter les hauts cris à MM les académiques; cette composition, pour le moins aussi hérétique que les réligionnaires à l'usage desquels elle était destinée, fut traitée comme on traitait les huguenots, et peu s'en fallut qu'on n'en fît un auto-da-fé, ou, pour parler un langage plus enharmonique, un holocoste au *Dieu de bon goût*. . . . A ce premier et terrible manifeste, la belle au bois dormant, c'est-à-dire l'Académie, s'éveilla toute en alarmes et protesta de toutes ses forces contre le temple bafouant le légitimité de son architecture de droit divin; car il est aussi des légitimités et des droits divins à l'Académie; car il est un art légitime et un art illégitime, car il est un art révélé et un art apocryphe non reconnus tels par le concile de Nicée ou de Trente, mais par le concile Fontaine et Guénepin." Borel, *"Du Mouvement,"* p. 75. Borel's title, "Du Mouvement en architecture," seems to refer to the Liberal Republican "mouvement" that emerged with the Revolution of July.

63

Monod, *Michelet*, ch. 12.

64

"Ont rapporté de Rome, avec un sentiment vrai et nouveau des monuments antiques, le besoin de reprendre la tradition architecturale au point où elle était en France au commencement du XVIIe siècle." Fourtoul, *De l'Art en Allemagne*, 2 vol. (Paris, 1842), I, p. 170.

65

F. Guizot, *Histoire de la révolution d'Angleterre* (Paris, 1826–27); Mignet, "Etablissement de la réforme à Genève"; Quinet, *Christianisme et la révolution française*, chs. 9 and 10.

66

Germann, *Der protestantische Kirchenbau*, p. 55.

67

MP 13 (1845): 77–78.

68

Léon Vaudoyer, letters to his father of August 3 and September 10, 1828.

69

The subjects are given, with short critiques in the publications of the Académie's annual *séances publiques*.

70

Seen so by the Republican critic Théophile Thoré in *Le Siècle*, August 25, 1836.

71

"Vous allez je crois me blâmer le peu d'importance de ce projet." "Qu'on peut faire quelque chose de très monumental et d'un grand caractère."

72

"Je t'avoue que ce choix m'a singulierement étonné. Est-ce que là, me suis-je dis, un motif de faire l'application (suivant le but, l'institution de ce dernier envoi) de toutes les hautes et bonnes études que tu as fait pendant tes quatres premières années? Y-a-t-il là aucune invention de plan? Une occasion de disposition et proportions architecturales et monumentales? . . . Ne crains-tu pas qu'on ne dise de ton Beffroi ce qu'on a dit . . . de la prêche de M. Duban, du pont de M. Labrouste, et enfin du petit monument de Juillet de cette année en une demie feuille du simple trait sans plan ni coupe par M. Duc?"

73

"Voilà ton coup de tonerre . . . tache qu'il soit éclatant!"

74

"Je ne transige jamais avec mes doctrines et . . . je ne sacrifie aucune de mes idées à l'envie de plaire un moment. [J]e ne ferai point de pétard[. J]e n'en ai ni le temps ni les moyens ni le désir[. S]i on me demande demain un projet comme j'entends[,] un projet vaste[,] doit être fait, je réponderais je ne suis pas architecte[,] mes études ne sont pas terminées[,] et cela parce que les arts ne sont pas enseignés en France comme ils de-vraient être."

75

"Qu'au lieu de retomber dans l'enfance de l'art, tu recuilleras dans les siècles des lumières les monuments qui datent des beaux siècles de l'architecture."

76

"Comment peut-on faire de l'architecture comme Venus et Roma avec lec idées[,] les besoins[,] les matériaux d'aujourd'hui? Voilà bien la vielle école de l'antique quand même . . . et cela produit la Madeleine, monument sans caractère local[,] puis en face la Chambre des Députés[,] qui est un autre temple antique[,] puis la Bourse[,] puis enfin le portique du Panthéon avec ses infames plates-bandes[. V]oilà comme depuis longtemps notre architecture est sans caractère[;] voilà pour mieux dire nous n'avons pas d'ar-chitecture. . . . Pauvre France!!! Ce que je désire le plus c'est d'avoir un mauvais rapport sur mon projet parce qu'alors je pourrais croire qu'il n'est pas mal."

77

"S'etant renfermé dans un sujet si peu considérable, il s'est lui-même privé de tous ses moyens." *Séance annuelle publique . . . ,* 1832.

78

"Tour ou clocher, d'où l'on fait le guet, d'où il y a une cloche pour sonner l'alarme." *Dictionnaire de l'Académie française (Paris,* 1835).

79

"C'est, dans les villes de guerre ou dans les places où la portée de l'ennemi, une tour, un clocher, ou quelque lieu élevé, dans lequel est une cloche qui sonne lorsqu'on aperçoit l'ennemi ou quel'on veut assembler les troupes." *D d'A,* 1832, "Beffroi."

80

"Le beffroi et l'hôtel de ville sont souvent pris l'un pour l'autre, et dans les chartes et franchises on accordait à une ville le droit de beffroi comme signe d'immunité." *MP* (1841): 231. The issue was an important one in the 1820s; see Simonde de Sismondi's "Histoire critique du pouvoir municipal," *Revue encyclopédique* 41 (March 1829): 643–666; A.-G.-P.-B. de Baraute, *Des Communes et de l'aristocratie* (Paris, 1829).

81

E.-E. Viollet-le-Duc, *Histoire d'un hôtel de ville et d'une cathédrale* (Paris, 1878).

82

"La première et la plus grosse pour la convocation des assemblées; la deuxième pour signaler les incendies, attaques, émotions; la troisième pour sonner l'heure du travail des ateliers et le couvre-feu." Ibid., p. 48.

83

"Souvent, la nuit, on entendait sonner la cloche du beffroi, annonçant l'attaque d'une troupe sortie de l'évêché contre les plus riches maisons." Ibid., p. 52.

84

"On publia par la ville l'abolition de la commune et l'injonction à tous magistrats de la cité d'avoir à cesser leurs fonctions, de déposer le sceau et la bannière de la commune à l'évêché, de descendre sand délai les cloches du beffroi et de cesser toute réunion." Ibid., p. 55.

85

"Supposé en face d'un hôtel de ville qui comprenderait l'espace occupé par la place Dauphine et les rues et bâtiments qui l'environnent." Letter of August 27, 1831.

86

These events were closely followed in the weekly *Journal des artistes*. Documents relating to the Commission des Beaux-Arts are in the Académie archives filed under the years 1829–32.

87

"Si l'Institut continue à marcher dans la voie absurde où elle aujourd'hui je me déclare en opposition ouverte avec lui . . . et cette opposition se grossira tellement qu'elle parviendra à renverser ce corps si le ne veut pas céder comme l'opposition libérale a renversé Charles X." Letter of August 27, 1831.

88

"Il n'a pas fait sa révolution, le pauvre diable, il faut qu'il la fasse, il la fera, je n'en doute pas, . . . mais nous ne verrons probablement pas la vienne dans cette ère . . . il nous faut un 1792." Letter to E. Millet, February 4, 1862, in *Lettres inédites de Viollet-le-Duc, receuillées et annotées par son fils* (Paris, 1902).

89

"La magnificance romaine, que l'on aimerait à voir. *Séance annuelle publique* . . . , 1834.

90

Cf. catalogue *The Second Empire 1852–1870: Art in France Under Napoleon III* (Philadelphia and Paris, 1979), entry I-9.

91

The original drawings are lost, but the design was published in a lithographic reproduction of his work by his students (A. Joilly, Paris, 1872–75). On Constant-Dufeux: P.

Féraud, "Constant-Dufeux," *RGA* 29 (1872): cols. 81–91, 132–137, 251–255; A. Lance, *Dictionnaire des architectes français* (Paris, 1872); F. Canlowicz, "M. Constant-Dufeux," *Moniteur des architectes* (1871): cols. 252–256.

92

P. Féraud, "Constant-Dufeux," cols. 81–91.

93

It was being rebuilt in 1828–33 under the supervision of Jules de Joly (1788–1865).

94

Constant-Dufeux's self-imposed program is transliterated in Joilly's plates.

95

"Il nous semble que les habitudes d'un gouvernement fondé sur la représentation nationale, sur la discussion publique de certaines questions et l'élection des magistrats, donneront lieu à un création d'un édifice nouveau dont l'emploi pourrait avoir quelque rapport avec ceuli de la basilique antique." *EN*, II, p. 470.

96

"Aujourd'hui où toute capitale, toute ville, et jusqu'au moindre village, doivent avoir leurs *salles d'assemblées*, pourquoi ne cherche-t-on pas là le motif d'une nouvelle architecture? Pourquoi ne fait-on pas de ces édifices un objet particulier d'études et de recherches, pour constituer un type nouveau, puisqu'ils sont maintenant au premier rang et qu'eux aussi sont nouveaux? . . . Serons-nous impuissants pour constituer une *architecture représentative?*" *RGA* 7 (1846–47): cols. 296–299, specifically col. 298.

97

"Ayons plus de confiance dans nos institutions et dans notre avenir, et surtout ayons plus de confiance en nous-mêmes. Pensons que pour arriver à faire de bonne architecture, il faut d'abord imaginer les distributions des espaces et les moyens de construction, *sans aucune précoccupation de style*, et n'avoir en vue que de *satisfaire aux besoins matériels et moraux*, aussi largement que le permet *une sage économie des moyens mis à notre disposition*. Cette première opération de l'esprit que nous appelons l'ART DE BATIR doit être suivie de celle qui constitue ce que nous appelons L'ART DE SCULPTER, c'est-à-dire l'art de concevoir et de donner à l'oeuvre la forme la plus appropriée et la plus heureusement expressive, afin qu'elle puisse à son tour recevoir de L'ART DE PEINDRE, le complément indispensable au perfectionnement de l'ouvrage pour qu'il soit digne d'être appelé monument d'art."

98

This tradition of the ideal Republican assembly hall culminated in that described by Charles Chipiez and Emile Trélat in their *Sitellarium* (Paris, n.d.), a program given to their students at the Ecole Spéciale d'Architecture in January 1870.

Two

THE FORMULATION OF THE APPROACH

1

F. Dartien, *M. Léonce Reynaud: sa vie et ses oeuvres par l'un de ses élèves* (Paris, 1885).

2

D. A. Griffiths, *Jean Reynaud: encyclopédiste de l'époque romantique d'après sa correspondence inédite* (Paris, 1965).

3

P. Raphael and M. Goutard, *Hippolyte Fortoul, 1851–1856: un ministre de l'Instruction Publique sous l'Empire autoritaire* (Paris, 1975). His papers survive in the Archives Nationales, 246 A.P. His journal, which is part of that material, has been partially published: G. Massa-Gille, *Journal d'Hippolyte Fortoul* (Geneva, 1979 ff.).

4

See Vaudoyer's letters to Fortoul: AN 246 A.P. 14. The Marseilles architect Pascal Coste, visiting Fortoul in October 1852, found Vaudoyer, Duc, Lassus, and Gourlier in his antechamber *(Mémoires d'un artiste: notes et souvenirs de voyage (1817–1877)*, 2 vols. [Marseilles, 1878], I, p. 519).

5

G.-A. Lefevre-Pontalis, *Notice sur M. Hippolyte Carnot* (Paris, 1891). Also, G. Weill, *L'Ecole saint-simonienne* (Paris, 1896).

6

Griffiths, *Jean Reynaud*, ch. 3.

7

Cf. H. Fortoul, "L'Arc de Triomphe de l'Etoile," *La France littéraire* 26 (1839): 67–82.

8

Letters from Vaudoyer, AN 246 A.P. 14.

9

Letters from Edouard Charton, AN 246 A.P. 14.

10

"Demain mercredi nous dinons avec Duban Duc Reynaud et une de nos amis Boullée qui est à Paris maintenant. Il serait très aimable à vous joindre à nous ainsi que Fortoul. . . . C'est un pique-nique. . . .

"J'oublie de vous dire que demain nous allez visiter la colonne de Duc le rendez vous est à 2 hrs 2 1/2 hrs chez lui rue du Marché St. Honoré 4."

11

It is mentioned in Vaudoyer's subsequent letters to Fortoul (AN 246 A.P. 14) and a sketchy journal of it survives in Vaudoyer's papers. Fortoul cites it in the *avertissement* of his *De l'Art en Allemagne* (1842), p. ii.

12

AN 246 A.P. 14.

13

"Plus de bonnes dissertations du matin au milieu de la fumée bleuâtre de cigaretto! plus d'espoir de se trouver réunis autour d'un flacon de curaçao."

14

"Duban continue sa Sainte Chapelle et va commencer son château de Blois, Duc va commencer cette année son palais de justice et Reynaud vient de finir sa gare du chemin de fer du nord."

15

"Je ne comprends plus un voyage sans vous. Voyons nous souvent pour mûrir nos idées communes sur l'art en général et l'architecture en particulier." Letter of September 18, 1839.

16

"Vous ne devez pas douter en combien d'occasions j'ai été appelé à défendre des doctrines que je partage." Letter of April 18, 1842, apropos the appearance of Fortoul's book *De l'Art en Allemagne*.

17

"Il en a paru . . . sur la Renaissance dans laquelle vous trouvez un grand nombre de ces idées qui nous sont communes mais exprimées malheureusement dans une forme beaucoup plus vulgaire." Letter of August 18, 1842.

18

"Quand vous revenez à Paris et quand reprendrons nous la question des ordres entramée [?] sur la place de Bamberg?" Letter of July 31, 1843.

19

Griffiths, *Jean Reynaud*, ch. 3.

20

EN, I (1834), p. 770.

21

"L'art de bâtir suivant des proportions et des règles determinées et fixées par la Nature et le goût." Quatremère de Quincy's well-known 1832 *Dictionnaire historique d'architecture* was a revision of this earlier three-volume contribution to Pancoucke's *Encyclopédie méthodique*.

22

"N'en doutons point: c'est par cette heurseuse tromperie que l'homme jouit dans l'*architecture* d'un plaisir d'imitation, qui sans cela, n'y auroit lieu, de ce plaisir qui accompagne tous les arts & en est le charme, de ce plaisir d'être à demi trompé, qui lui fait cherir les fictions & la poésie, lut fait préférer la vérité déguisée à la vérité nue."

23

EN, III (1836–37), pp. 686–688.

24

"De même que, dans le corps humain, rien d'inutile ou de capricieux ne vient frapper nos regards, de même dans leurs constructions, et surtout dans leurs colonnes, ils n'ont rien admis qui ne se puisse légitimer aux yeux de la raison ou qui ne portât au moins un cachet d'utilité." *EN*, III, p. 688.

25

"Si l'art doit puiser ses effets dans des imitations de formes, ou s'il doit les trouver dans l'observation des conditions diverses qui lui sont imposées par ses moyens de réalisation et par les convenances auxquelles il faut satisfaire; en un mot, si l'art doit demander à la création un modèle matériel ou des principes." *EN*, III, p. 686.

26

EN, I, pp. 770–778.

27

"Nous avons établi dans tout cet ouvrage, que notre architecture est celle des anciens Grecs et Romains, en un mot, l'architecture antique."

28

The basic texts are Reynaud's entry "Architecture," Vaudoyer's "Etudes d'architecture en France" in *MP* (1839–54), and Fortoul's *De l'Art en Allemagne.*

29

"Il faut établir une distinction entre la *forme ogivale* et le *style ogival*, c'est-à-dire entre l'ogive considerée comme forme isolée, et l'ogive constituant tout un système d'architecture." "Etudes d'architecture en France," *MP* 7 (1839): 334–336, specifically 334.

30

J.-I. Hittorff and L. Zanth, *Architecture moderne de la Sicile* (Paris, 1835).

31

Fortoul's coinage, *De l'Art en Allemagne*, II, ch. 20.

32

"Vraiement le type primordial de l'architecture chrétienne en France." Vaudoyer in J. Aicard, *Patria*, 2 vols. (Paris, 1846), II, col. 2138.

33

"Jamais monumens réligieux n'avaient reçu un caractère plus complet et plus convenable, n'avaient été plus identifiés avec les sentiments dont ils devaient témoigner, n'avaient mieux résumé et mieux fait comprendre tout la poésie de leur époque; et jamais aussi salles plus vastes et plus élevées n'avaient été exécutées avec des points d'appui tellement rares et légers. L'art et la science avaient marché ensemble; ils s'étaient prêté un mutuel secours; et le savant et l'artiste devaient être également satisfaits à la vue de ces admirables créations." *EN*, I, p. 777.

34

"Nous attachons la plus grande importance à cette définition: *affranchissement de l'arcade*: car c'est par là que l'on peut, selon nous, expliquer tout naturellement la formation de l'art byzantin, de l'art arabe, de l'art roman et de l'art gothique, et par suite déduire enfin les principes au nom desquels ont commencé les protestations de la renaissance.

"En copiant la basilique antique pour en faire leurs premiers temples, les chrétiens n'en ont pas copié l'ordonnance. Soit qu'ils aient puisé dans les constructions de Bas-Empire l'example d'un système nouveau, ainsi qu'on pourrait le supposer quand on voit les restes du palais de Spalatro; soit qu'ils y aient été conduits matériellement par un mode différent de construction; soit qu'il y ait eu en eux l'instinct d'une nouvelle forme propre à donner une physionomie distincte au temple chrétien, il est constant qu'ils se servirent habituellement de colonnes pour en faire le point d'appui et de retombée des arcades qu'ils substituèrent aux plates-bandes monolithes de l'antiquité païenne. Ces colonnes furent d'abord celles qui provenaient des monuments antiques, et telles qu'elles avaient été composées pour porter des architraves; seulement on accordait la préference à celles de l'ordre corinthien; mais bientôt on sentit le besoin d'en modifier les proportions et d'y substituer des chapitaux d'une nouvelle forme mieux appropriée à leur nouvelle fonction; plus tard enfin, ce système de construction en arcades qui n'avait été appliqué dans le principe qu'à la réunion des points d'appui isolés, fut généralisé, et donna naissance à un système général des voûtes. C'est ainsi que fut engendré l'art byzantin, pendant que l'Italie conservait encore fidèlement ses premières basiliques latines, dont elle devait plus tard transmettre à l'Occident.

"Il semble que dans cette architecture, ainsi constituée à l'aide d'éléments tout nouveaux, on aurait dû de prime abord coordonner ces éléments et les ériger en principes, de manière à établir des rhythmes totalement différents des rhythmes païens; mais il n'en fut rien, et en adoptant cette architecture comme appelée à devenir l'expression du spiritualisme chrétien, les artistes du moyen âge paraissent avoir eu peu de souci de tout ce qui aurait pu passer pour une consécration de la forme matérielle; ils s'en tinrent simplement aux conditions nécessaires à la stabilité de leurs oeuvres." "Etudes d'architecture en France," *MP* 11 (1842): 122.

35

"Ses édifices rappelaient encore les édifices gothiques; ils avaient les mêmes dispositions et les mêmes proportions générales; toutes les exigences qui les avaient commandés étaient franchement exprimées, toutes les convenances sagement satisfaites. C'étaient encore les édifices gothiques, mais avec des formes plus harmonieuses, des contours plus purs et plus gracieux, et recouvert, en quelque sorte, d'une voile étranger, voile riche et diaphane qui décorait sans rien dissimuler."*EN*, I, p. 777.

36

"Dans sa manière de voir, la forme devait être une conséquence naturelle des nécessités de la construction; le beau ne pouvait être que la manifestation du bien." "Brunelleschi," *EN*, III, pp. 96–99, specifically p. 98.

37

"C'était donc un principe nouveau pour son époque que Brunelleschi se sentait appelé à proclamer; c'était, en architecture, faire une plus large part à l'intelligence, et réhabiliter les lois impresciptibles de la nature." Ibid., p. 97.

38

"L'oeuvre capital de l'architecture de la renaissance, nous serions presque tentés de dire, de l'architecture des temps modernes." Ibid., p. 99.

39

"Brunelleschi," *D d'A*, 1832.

40

"Après avoir emprunté aux monumens de l'antiquité quelques formes de détail, on cherche à imiter les rapports et les dispositions de ces détails, et on finit par considérer ces monumens comme des types absolus de beauté. . . . L'architecture devint quelque chose de mystérieux et de fatal, qui avait des règles et des préceptes immuables, et les imposait fixement. . . . C'est ainsi qu'on vit s'introduire chez nous les portiques ouverts, les terrasses, les petites fenêtres, à la place des portiques fermés, des troits élancés et des grandes ouvertures du moyen âge. . . . Enfin, dans ces dernières années, nous avons vu revêtir de la forme des temples antiques nos églises, nos bourses, nos théâtres, nos barrières et jusqu'à nos corps-de-garde. Chose étrange, ce fut précisément au moment où l'on enleva ainsi à l'architecture tout caractère, toute vérité, toute expression, c'est-à-dire tout ce qui en fait un art, ce fut à ce moment qu'on ne voulut plus y voir qu'un art d'imagination, et qu'on repoussa avec le plus de force toute influence scientifique ou industrielle. . . . Ainsi nos édifices modernes ne présentent ni l'expression qui appartient à l'art, ni les dispositions réclamées par nos usages et notre climat, ni la solidité que notre science permettaient d'obtenir. Loin de représenter notre société sous toutes ses faces, ils ne la représentent sous aucune."*EN*, I, pp. 777–778.

41

AN 246 A.P. 2.

42

S. Boisserée, *Histoire et description de la cathédrale de Cologne* (Paris and Stuttgart, 1822–33). See also P. Moissy, *Les Séjours en France de Sulpice Boisserée (1820–1825)* (Lyon and Paris, 1956).

43

"J'ai souvent rêvé à une nouvelle architecture qui serait une réalisation plus vaste, plus divine des formes terrestres. . . . Ce rêve ne serait-il pas impie, et ne tendrait-il pas à faire retrograder les idées et les arts?"

44

"Les constructions de l'Asie et de l'Egypte imitaient les formes terrestres et s'incorporaient quelquefois avec lui."

45

"N'est-ce pas là ce qui fait son caractère éminemment social, général, civilisateur; elle devient l'enveloppe de l'homme, au lieu d'être celle des forces de la nature. Les temples grecs ne sont que la maison des dieux, et non pas leur image."

46

"L'architecture gothique me semble avoir fait un progrès en refaisissant l'univers. L'architecture orientale, c'est l'abri de l'Homme écrasé par la nature; l'architecture grecque c'est la toute [?] de l'homme posé sur le sommet de la nature; l'architecture gothique c'est la nature elle-même—transfigurée par la pensée de l'homme; c'est l'univers où . . . les végétaux, les figures sculpturales, les chants, les images et les parfums de l'homme, la voûte du ciel lui-même proclament d'une seule voix la présence de Dieu."

47

"Quelle compromis pourrait produit l'alliance de l'art grecque et de l'art du moyen-âge? . . . Faudra-t-il une nouvelle barbarie pour les assouplir d'une façon inattendue? Il me semble que c'est dans le sentiment moderne de la nature que se peut trouver la source de leur transformation."

48

"Edgar Quinet remarque dans les monumens bizantins de la Morée la fusion de tous les élémens antérieurs et l'annonce de l'architecture gothique qui va être une nouvelle transformation de tous les élémens historiques."

49

"Les peuples, comme les individus, sont des instruments qui servent à l'accomplissement du plan général de la création; c'est ce plan qu'un esprit sérieux doit se proposer d'étudier." *De l'Art en Allemagne*, II, p. 317.

50

"L'architecture est de tous les arts celui qu'on peut le moins deviner, parce que c'est un art postérieur, qui présuppose l'existence de quelque chose à satisfaire et à envelopper. Or, si pareille chose existait de nos jours, nul doute que l'architecture prêtât son vêtement. Si on peut prévoir l'esprit de cette chose, on saurait en prévoir la forme." AN 246 A.P. 2.

51

"Sa gloire et les immenses progrès qu'il fit faire à la peinture consiste donc en ce qu'il détermina, dans le péninsule, le passage de l'époque *dorienne* a l'époque *ionienne*, et qu'il composa le principe de celle-ci par la fusion de l'élément ogival, avec un moindre part de l'élément antique qui devait prévaloir peu à peu en Italia, et y amener insensiblement une révolution dernière." *De l'Art en Allemagne*, II, p. 226.

52

It was precisely at this moment that Cologne was being grudgingly acknowledged as of French derivation; see G. Germann, *The Gothic Revival in Europe and Britain* (Cambridge, Mass., 1972), pp. 151–152.

53

"La mission de l'art contemporain est de commencer la recherche des rhythmes curvilignes. Si cette tentative, sur laquelle la critique n'a rien à préjuger, pouvait jamais réussir, le plein cintre et l'ogive, rapprochés par des rapports certains, et mésurés par des ordres qui nous demeurent inconnus, deviendraient, dans la main de nos architectes, ce que le dorique et l'ionique étaient pour les architectes de la dernière époque grecque, des modulations susceptibles d'être fondues dans une modulation complexe et suprême. Alors aussi de rapports nouveaux et régulièrement déterminés naîtrait forcément un style analogue, qui rendrait à la sculpture et à la peinture leur majesté perdue, et qui, de proche en proche, répandrait le sentiment de l'ordre et de la beauté dans toutes les productions de notre société, livrée à l'anarchie de mauvais gout. Voilà ce que nos architectes doivent méditer, et ce qu'eux seules peuvent accomplir." *De l'Art en Allemagne*, II, p. 560.

54

"Quelle resultante pourrait produire l'alliance de l'art grec et de l'art du moyen-âge?" AN 246 A.P.2.

55

"On peut, dans un sens profond, comparer les monumens humains à ces coquilles formées par des animaux qui y mettent l'empreinte de leurs corps et en font leur logis: les méthodes naturelles ne séparent point la description du test de la description des mollasques." *EN*, I. p. 773.

56

E. Quinet, *Le Génie des religions* (Paris, 1842).

57

T. Cahn, *La vie et l'oeuvre d'Etienne Geoffroy Saint-Hilaire* (Paris, 1962), chs. 20–22, with bibliography. See also: I. Geoffroy Saint-Hilaire, *Vie, travaux et doctrine scientifique d'Etienne Geoffroy Saint-Hilaire par son fils* (Paris, 1847), ch. 11.

58

Especially the entries "Zoologie" and "Teratologie," VIII (1841), and "Organogénie," VII (1839).

59

G. Cuvier, "Sur le squelette fossile d'un *reptile volant* des environs d'*Aichstedt*, que quelque naturalistes ont pris pour un oiseau et dont nous formons un genre de *sauriens* sous le non de *pterodactyl*," *Annales du musée de l'histoire naturelle* XIII (1809), reprinted in his *Recherches sur les ossemens fossiles de quadrupèdes* (Paris, 1812) and rewritten in the third edition of that work, 1825, vol. V, pt. 2, pp. 258–283, pl. 23. Cuvier was actually correcting the extrapolations of his predecessors Collini and Hermann, pointing out that the pterodactyl was a reptile and therefore scaled, with large eyes for nocturnal habits. The remains known in Cuvier's time gave no hint of the beast's sometimes huge size.

60

Typical is A. Conan Doyle, *The Five Orange Pips* (London, 1891): "The ideal reasoner . . . would, when he had once been shown a single fact in all its bearings, deduce from it not only the chain of events which led up to it but also the results which would follow from it. As Cuvier could correctly describe a whole animal by the contemplation of a single bone, so the observer who has thoroughly understood one link in a series of incidents should be able to accurately state all the other ones, both before and after." Poe cites Cuvier in his *Murders in the rue Morgue* (1843). See T. Narcejac, *Une Machine à lire: le roman policier* (Paris, 1975); R. Messac, *Le Detective Novel et l'influence de la pensée scientifique* (Paris, 1929); T. A. Sebeok and J. Uniker-Sebeok, *You Know my Method: A Juxtaposition of Charles S. Pierce and Sherlock Holmes* (Bloomington, Ind., 1980).

61

For example, E. Beulé, *Histoire de l'art grec avant Périclès* (Paris, 1868), p. 33.

62

L. Reynaud, *Traité d'architecture*, 2 vols. (Paris, 1850 and 1858), II, pp. 532–536.

63

"Je me représente un emplacement convenablement choisi, les rues, les jardins, les places publiques bien tracés, le lieu de chaque édifice marqué, les maisons s'élèvant au gré de chacun, et l'on sent, à les voir, qu'elles sont toutes de la même famille. . . . Chaque rue est une harmonie dont les maisons variées qui la composent sont les termes, et dont la convenance réciproque des habitans réunis dans le même voisinage est le principe. Chaque quartier, par la convenance analogue de toutes les rues qu'il contient, forme une autre harmonie d'un ordre plus élevé. Enfin, la ville elle-même, par la composition de toutes ces harmonies entre elles et avec les édifices publics, en forme une dernière qui peut, ou frapper d'ensemble, et à plusieurs points de vue, ou se diviser en élémens détachés, semblables aux phrases variées mais toujours connexes d'une mélodie bien conduite, et frappant, l'un à l'autre, l'oeil qui se promène dans l'intérieur de la cité. Et ce grand monument d'architecture, qui, avec tant d'unité dans son ensemble, se laisse pourtant partager sans résistance en une multitude de monumens différens, n'est que la figure symbolique de la société qu'il contient, et dont il n'est pour ainsi dire que le vêtement. . . .

   "On peut donc considérer chaque ville comme une inscription, marquant sur la terre, en termes ardus mais positifs, l'histoire du monde dans le point où elle s'élève. Et je remarque même que, comme le goût, l'esprit, les moeurs, les institutions politiques et religieuses varient d'un lieu à l'autre selon les lois du climat et de la dissémination primitive des peuples, les villes, qui sont proprement la figure de toutes ces choses, varient naturellement sur la terre dans le même ordre. De sorte que, différant les uns des autres par le caractère de leurs constructions, suivant un système de variation strictement identique avec celui des groupes divers dont le genre humain se compose, elles constituent par leur ensemble comme une seule ville, qui, enveloppant tout le globe et s'y harmonisant chaque jour davantage, fait resplendir parmi les astres l'expression symbolique du genre humain lui-même." "Ville," *EN*, VIII (1841), pp. 676–684, specifically 682 and 684. Cf. Fortoul, *De l'Art en Allemagne*, I, p. 113.

64

G. Monod, *La Vie et la pensée de Jules Michelet* (Paris, 1923).

65

Frank Bowman explores Hegel's reception in France in a forthcoming volume.

66

H. Carnot, et al., *Exposition de la doctrine Saint-Simonienne*, 2 vols. (Paris, 1829–30), II, p. 161, note 47.

67

V. Cousin, *Cours d'histoire de philosophie: cours de 1829*, 2 vols. (Paris, 1829); *Cours de philosophie professé à la faculté des lettres pendant l'année 1818*, edited by A. Garnier (Paris, 1836).

68

Quinet, *Le Génie des religions*, ch. 6.

69

For visual sources there were the inevitable re-editions of Vignola (for example, that of 1815 by Lebas and Debret) and a mass of publications of Renaissance palatial architecture by Charles Percier and his students Grandjean de Montigny, Haudebourt, Suys, Gauthier, Bouchet, and Letarouilly. One should examine the auction catalogue of Huyot's library made upon his death in 1840.

70

L.-P. Baltard, *Discours d'ouverture du cours de Théorie d'Architecture* (Paris, n.d.); *Aperçu ou essai sur le bon goût dans les ouvrages d'art et architecture de l'année* (Paris, 1841); *Introduction au cours de Théorie d'architecture de l'année 1839* (Paris, 1839).

71

For all the respect it elicited from Vaudoyer, expressed in his letters to his father, and from Labrouste ("Ecole des Beaux-Arts," *RGA* 1 [1840]: cols. 487–488 and 546–547), Huyot's doctrine was conservative, at least as far as we know it from the manuscripts of his lectures (University of Paris, Institut d'Art et d'Archéologie, Fondation Doucet, MS 15).

72

On Durand: W. Szambien, *Jean-Nicolas Louis Durand, 1760–1834: de l'imitation à la norme* (Paris, 1984), with complete bibliography. Henry-Russell Hitchcock, in his influential volume in the Pelican History of Art series, subsumes the whole of the early nineteenth century in Continental architecture under the heading "The Doctrine of Durand." This has come to seem questionable. The examples in Durand's *Précis des Leçons . . .* (Paris, 1802 and 1805) seem so familiar because they were based on projects from the Grand Prix competitions at the Ecole des Beaux-Arts, as Szambien has shown ("Durand and the Continuity of Tradition," *The Beaux-Arts*, pp. 18–33). What was new in that volume was his abstract compositional method, which would enable his engineering students at the Ecole Polytechnique to learn some architecture in the thirty or so hours permitted in the curriculum. (One should consult the *Registre de l'Instruction* preserved at the Ecole Polytechnique, which records each of his lectures.) Durand was the butt of vigorous criticism: A. Lance, *Notice sur la vie et les travaux de M. Achille Leclère* (Paris, 1854); Gottfried Semper, *Vorläüfige Bemerkunge über die bemalte Architektur und Plastik bei den Alten* (Altona, 1834), p. 2. Durand's strength was that he simplified the Percieresque, and on this level his work enjoyed some popularity in Germany (Engelhard, "Schinkels Architekturschule in Norddeutschland," *Allgemeine Bauzeitung* 1 [1836]: 271–282). And one must note that the *pensionnaires'* predecessor, Emile Gilbert, had studied with Durand, as perhaps had Léonce Reynaud.

73

The Ecole courses on history and theory were not required and were notoriously lightly attended.

74

L. Clément de Ris, *Portraits à la plume* (Paris, 1853), pp. 143ff.; T. Gautier, *Histoire de romantisme* (Paris, 1872); R. Jazinski, *Les Années romantiques de Théophile Gautier* (Paris, 1929).

75

P. Dufournet, et al., *Hector Horeau, 1801–1872* (Paris, 1979).

76

A. Lorenz Van Zanten, "César Daly and the *Revue Générale d'Architecture*" (Ph.D. dissertation, Harvard University, 1981), pp. 12–72. See also her "Form and Society," *Oppositions* 8 (Spring 1977): 137–145; "The Palace and the Temple: Two Utopian Architectural Visions of the 1830's," *Art History* 2, no. 2 (June 1979): 179–200. Further work is in progress by Hélène Lipstadt and Richard Becherer.

77

Victor Hugo raconté par un témoin de sa vie, 2 vols. (Paris, n.d.), ch. 53, "Hernani."

78

The claque, the anonymous author of *Hugo raconté* states, was recruited from these two ateliers and that of Garnaud, Borel's own. Since neither atelier had yet been formally founded, we must assume that the students were the secessionists from A.-L.-T. Vaudoyer's studio who later presented themselves to Labrouste and the Blouet students Duban taught in 1829 before setting up on his own.

79

Charles Questel, *Notice sur Duban* (Paris, 1872). Questel was in Blouet's atelier at the time. Also in the atelier at that time was Adolphe Lance, who left a short reminiscence in his *Dictionnaire des architectes français* as a note to his entry about Léon Feuchère.

80

L. Labrouste, *Esthétique monumentale* (Paris, 1902), pp. 214–215, a reminiscence of these events by Labrouste's son.

81

Ibid., and A.-L.-T. Vaudoyer's letter to his son of July 23, 1830.

82

E. Delaire, et al., *Les Architectes élèves de l'Ecole des Beaux Arts*, 2nd ed. (Paris, 1907), p. 121. Delaire's dates for ateliers are often incorrect.

83

L. Batissier, "Notice sur Aimé Chenavard," in the second edition of Chenavard's *Album de l'ornameniste* (Paris, 1845). Chenavard originally published this in 1832, followed by his *Nouveau recueil de décorations intérieures* (Paris, 1833–35).

84

P. Borel, "Du Mouvement en architecture," *L'Artiste* 2 (1833); C. Robert, *Essai d'une philosophie d'art* (Paris, 1836), p. 179.

85

On Pommier: Lance, *Dictionnaire; RGA* 1 (1840): col. 444.

86

B. Galbaccio, *Le dernier Jour de Paris: panorama fantastique* (Paris, 1831). On him: J. Gigoux, *Causeries sur les artistes de mon temps*, 3rd ed. (Paris, 1885), pp. 59–60. On the Casino Paganini: T. Thoré, "Ouverture du Casino Paganini," *Le Siècle*, November 28, 1837; H. d'Almeras, *La vie parisienne sous Louis-Philippe* (Paris, n.d.), p. 115. I owe this last reference to the kindness of Charles Millard, who brought it to my attention because of Galbaccio's friendship with the sculptor Préault.

87

"Ce Galbaccio avait bien la conversation la plus intéressante et la plus variée du monde, sauf qu'il concluait toujours par la négation de toute chose." Gigoux, *Causeries sur les artistes de mon temps*, pp. 59–60.

88

"En avril, il vint des désordres assez graves. . . . Nous dîmes que ceux qui ne se croient pas satisfaire à nos intentions étaient libres de ne pas continuer à suivre nos leçons, et que, pour reprimer les désordres arrivés, l'atelier serait suspendu pendant deux jours.

"L'un des meneurs, car il y en a partout, convoquer les élèves dans un café ou ailleurs, et fit signer ceux qui comme lui voulaient déserter l'atelier. Il obtint 7 a 8 signatures des moutons qui, depuis ce tems, n'ont pas reparu. . . .

"Perdant leurs temps, depuis trois mois, ils ont pensé que M. Labrouste arrivant pourrait les reçevoir, ils s'y présente avec une petition.

"M. Labrouste les a refusé d'abord; leur disant qu'il nous soumettre cette demande qui lui paraissait trop sérieuse à notre égard. . . .

"Flattés de cette démarche, loin de nous opposer au succès de cette proposition qui peut lui être utile, . . . nous avons encouragé Monsieur Labrouste à accepter le noyau d'atelier."

89

L. Labrouste, *Esthétique monumentale*, pp. 214–215.

90

"Je travaille énormément et, ce qui est plus difficile, je fais travailler mes élèves." Letter to his brother Théodore of November 20, 1830, published in *Souvenirs d'Henri Labrouste, architecte, membre de l'Institut, notes recueillées et classées par ses enfants* (Paris, 1928), p. 24.

91

A. Pommier, "Des Ouvrages d'architecture envoyés par les élèves de l'Ecole de Rome," *La Liberté* 4 (September 1832): 58–64; 5 (September 1832): 65–71.

92

"Comment Pommier a été reçu le second je n'y comprend rien." Letter to his father of December 9, 1828.

93

"Sont-ils en progrès? Non, puisqu'ils retournent aux Etrusques et à Pompéia. Sont-ils en relatifs? Oui, parce qu-ils ont de meilleurs intentions que leurs devanciers et qu'ils sont plus habilles." "Du mouvement," p. 77.

94

[P. Borel], "Les Artistes penseurs et les artistes creux," *L'Artiste* 5 (1833, pt. 1): 253–259.

95

Revue encyclopédique 59 (1833): 107–153, especially p. 109. See A. Cassagne, *La Théorie de l'art pour l'art en France* (Paris, 1895), pp. 47–48.

96

"C'est le mot d'ordre auquel les affiliés de certaines coteries se reconnaissent." "De l'Art actuel," p. 109.

97

"La poésie c'est la glorieuse fantasie d'un homme." Ibid.

98

This is strange since Fortoul cites the work, ibid., pp. 128ff.

99

Neil Levine has worked at length on the implications for and the influence on architecture of Hugo's *Notre-Dame de Paris*. See his "The Book and the Building: Hugo's Theory of Architecture and Labrouste's Bibliothèque Sainte-Geneviève," *The Beaux-Arts,* edited by Robin Middleton (London, 1982), pp. 138–173. Also: J. Mallion, *Victor Hugo et l'art architectural* (Paris, 1962).

100

On the *phalanestère*, see A. Lorenz Van Zanten, "The Palace and the Temple," with further bibliography.

101

"M. Hugo, M. Hugo! qui a construit je ne sais quel ridicule théorie, qui a sué sang et eau durant trois ou quatre chapitres, pour établir en phrases pompeuses que l'humanité a fait jadis de l'architecture dans le but *unique* et *simpliste* de faire de la poésie. . . .

"Donc, artistes, croyez plutôt au génie de l'humanité qu'à la voix du faux prophètes. . . . L'Architecture, qu'ils nous disent morte et enterrée, a encore à grandir de bien des coudées, vraiment, pour atteindre se taille!—l'avenir est large, l'homme est puissant. Les apôtres de l'étroit et de la faiblesse, de pauvre et du mesquin, ne puisent pas leurs inspirations en sources vives et ce n'est pas eux qu'il faut écouter." V. Considérant, *Considérations sociales sur l'architectonique* (Paris, 1834), pp. 532–533.

102

The history of the founding of the Commission des Monuments Historiques has been written several times, for example: P. Léon, *La Vie des monuments français* (Paris, 1951); P. Verdier, "Le Sérvice des Monuments Historiques: son histoire, organization, administration, législation (1830–1834)," *Congrès archéologique* (1934), pp. 53–246; F. Bercé, *Les premiers travaux de la commission des monuments historiques, 1837–1848* (Paris, 1979), with bibliography.

103

De l'Art en Allemagne, I, p. 170.

104

T. Thoré, "L'Ecole des Beaux-Arts," *L'Artiste* 2S, 1 (1838): 220–222, 305–307.

105

"Il y a longtemps déjà que la théorie songe à révolutionner l'architecture." Ibid., p. 220.

106

"Pourquoi n'a-t-il pas osé prendre l'initiative d'une réforme radicale, et attacher ainsi son nom à l'histoire de l'art, comme firent en leurs temps les grands réformateurs de la Renaissance, Bullant, Philibert et Lescot?" Ibid.

107

"Quand on aura fait un peu cette architecture mélangée et en quelque sorte anarchique, il ne sera possible de revenir à la vieille orthodoxie." Ibid, p. 221.

108

"Il faudra bien que nous arrivons à créer un art en harmonie avec les conditions de notre temps et de notre pays; car ce sont lá les deux éléments relatifs et variables qui se combinent dans une merveilleuse unité avec la poésie, cette faculté divine, immuable et absolue comme la vérité." Ibid.

109

E. Beulé, *Eloge de Duban*. Duban executed the commemorative monument to Ingres erected in the Ecole des Beaux-Arts in 1871 (*RGA* 33 [1876]: cols. 207–209, pl. 49). Busts of Ingres and Duban now flank the door to the Institut de France.

110

See A. Blouet, "Avertissement," *Expédition scientifique de la Morée*, vol. III (Paris, 1838).

Three

THE FIRST BUILDINGS

1

On the Ecole buildings: AN N III Seine 1128, F^{13}1115–1119, F^{21}1420, F^{21}779, F^{21}614, Versement d'Architecture, albums 48 and 49. The records of the Ecole as an institution are deposited in the series Aj52. Further drawings survive in the library of the Ecole. Recent studies: C. Marmoz, "Félix Duban et l'Arc de Gaillon à l'Ecole des Beaux-Arts," *Bulletin de la société de l'histoire de l'art français* (1977): 217–223; C. Marmoz, "The Buildings of the Ecole des Beaux-Arts," *The Beaux-Arts*, ed. by Robin Middleton (London, 1982), pp. 124–137; D. Van Zanten, "Félix Duban and the Buildings of the Ecole des Beaux-Arts," *Journal of the Society of Architectural Historians* 37, no. 3 (October 1978): 161–174. Older histories: E. Müntz, *Guide de l'Ecole Nationale des Beaux-Arts* (Paris, 1889); J. Formigé, "L'Ecole des Beaux Arts," *L'Architecture* (1920): 16–24. Critiques: T. Thoré, "L'Ecole des Beaux-Arts," *L'Artiste* 2S, 1 (1838): 220–222, 305–307; L. Peisse, "L'Ecole des Beaux-Arts," *RDM* 24 (October 15, 1841): 232–245.

2

The young, active politician Adolphe Thiers seems to have been behind this. On Thiers's support for Romanticism in the arts: H. Malo, "M. Thiers et les artistes de son temps," *Revue de Paris* 31 (July 1, 1924): 140–159.

3

H. Fortoul, *De l'Art en Allemagne* (Paris, 1842), I, p. 170.

4

"As-tu vu les nouvelles constructions de l'Ecole des Beaux-Arts? . . . Les uns disent: c'est admirable! Les autres: c'est absurde!—je ne me permettais pas de juger d'une manière aussi absolue, mais s'il faut te donner mon avis, je t'avouerai que je ne comprends pas cette architecture là; les uns disent que c'est de la Renaissance, les autres du bas-Empire, quelques uns de l'Etrusque." Letter to his father of November 28, 1836, published by Geneviève Viollet le Duc, *E. Viollet-le-Duc: Lettres d'Italie. 1836–1837, addressées à sa famille* (Paris, 1971), p. 200.

5

A. Lenoir, *Description historique et chronologique des monuments de sculpture réunis au musée des monuments français* (Paris, An V), with numerous subsequent editions. Lenoir's journal was published by L. Courajod, *Alexandre Lenoir: son journal et le musée des monuments français*, 3 vols. (Paris, 1878–87). Also: A. Erlande-Brandenburg, "Alexandre Lenoir et le Musée des Monuments Français," *Le Gothique retrouvé avant Viollet-le-Duc* (Paris, 1979), pp. 75–84.

6

AN F^{13}1117.

7

"Chargé par le Ministre de la rédaction définitive du Projet d'achèvement de l'Ecole des Beaux-Arts, j'ai dû avant tout, me rendre compte par un examen approfondi de l'Etat des localités." This document is marked "Lu au conseil des B.C. le 21 juin 1833."

8

"Sa position au Sud-Est si favorable à l'aspect des formes légeres et gracieuses qui le composent, son parallélisme avec la rue qui permet à l'oeil d'en saisir de suite tout le développement, ses formes découpées à jour qui laissent la vue pénétrer jusqu'au Palais qu'il précède, qu'il annonce pour ainsi dire, la limite qu'il pose en quelque sorte, entre cette première cour composée des formes des siècles passés et celle du musée des Etudes, les sujets d'examen et de comparaison qu'il offre à la méditation, tout en un mot, tout m'a fait une loi d'en faire la plus bel ornament de ce nouvel Etablissement.

"Les fragments amorcelés dans les cours de l'Ecole, les assises numérotés et prêtes à reprendre leurs formes premières dont l'Opinion publique reproche depuis si longtemps à l'administration l'abondon et les dégradations qui en résultant, m'avaient donné l'idée de relever deux légers portiques à jour qui en consolidant le monument principal réaliseraient une pensée conçue, il y a 30 ans, par l'illustre Maître de tous nos Maîtres de former une cour où la jeunesse viendrait, sinon chercher des modèles, au moins admirer ce que les siècles passés ont produit. Les étrangers envier [sic] nos richesses nationales, et tous, artistes, gens de lettres, antiquaires rendre grace à l'Administration qui conserve, qui protège le dépôt des arts qui lui est confié.

"Au delà, deux demi-cercles ou seraient incrustés tous les fragmens qui n'auraient pu entrer comme matériaux dans la composition de ces Edifices, laisseraient la vue pénétrer et découvrir la plus grand développement possible du Palais. Au sortir du Musée des Etudes, cette forme amphithéâtrale offrirait une surface immense de fragments disposés avec art, interrompu par les protiques à jour qui enceindraient cet espèce de musée découvert."

9

"Je dois dire que translation est ici synonime de destruction.

"Personne ne contestera que des parties d'édifice de la légerté et de la délicatesse de celle dont il est question, ne supportent pas impunément une double démolition, une double reconstruction." AN F^{13}1117.

10

"Eh bien, si l'architecte d'un Edifice peut élever la voix en faveur non de son oeuvre, mais de l'oeuvre des grands maîtres dont il demande la conservation, je disai ici que la façade de l'Edifice du fond a été conçu de manière à être non pas masquée, mais précédée de cet Elégant Portique, de cet Enseigne (si j'ose dire ainsi) de l'Etablissement qu'il avait à restaurer, que le saillie de ses différentes détails a été combinée pour former de toutes ces parties un ensemble agréable à la vue, pittoresque sans désorde, à faire ressortir par la contraste des formes du bâtiment du fond, l'élegante légerté de ce portique découpé à jour qui masque l'Edifice comme l'arc de triomphe du Carrousel les Tuileries, comme l'aiguette de Luxor la chambre des députés, comme toutes les basiliques étaient masquées par les portiques à jour qui les précédaient, comme les Temples Egyptians par les Pylons, comme tous les Edifices de tous les temps, dont la beauté s'est toujours accrue de l'agglomération pittoresque des Edifices qui les précédaient ou qui les accompagnaient.

"Mais ce qui a été pour nombre d'édifices une simple beauté pittoresque est ici, j'ose le dire, une beauté de convenance. Si ce portique n'existait pas, l'architecte aurait proposé un équivalent. En effet que l'on se pénétre de la division de l'Etablissement, en avant, dans la cour d'entrée à droite, Etudes quotidiennes, agglomération d'Etudiants se pressant à chaque heure du Jour, aux cours de l'Ecole, allées et venues continuelles des Employés: au delà, tout est silence et recueillement: un musée, une bibliothèque, des salles d'exposition, tous lieux ou l'on se rend un à un dans un but d'étude et d'examen. Une destination si différente exige une limite, *une grille selon l'avis du Conseil*; Eh bien, cette grille existe, elle est de pierre, elle existe, c'est un chef d'oeuvre du temps passés, c'est un admirable fragment d'architecture et de sculpture, c'est un souvenir de Joconde, de Louis XII, de Georges d'Amboise, elle existe là, dans une Ecole des beaux-arts, là où le Gouvernement devait l'élever si elle n'y était pas, elle forme avec le portique d'Anet et les fragmens de l'art Gothique qui seraient déposée en face un admirable résumé de notre architecture nationale, et un Conseil composé des premiers architectes de france en médite la translation, c'est à dire la ruine!" AN F^{13}1117.

11

"Peut-être faudrait-il eviter, dans le musée d'une Ecole des Beaux-Arts, de mettre trop en évidence des ouvrages d'art dont la composition et le goût pourraient ne pas être entièrement en harmonie avec les principes de l'architecture antique."

12

"Avant de se créer un nouveau système d'architecture . . . avaient dû examiner ceux qu'avaient suivis nos pères pour en vérifier la valeur et en étudier les lois." *EN*, I, p. 778.

13

"Cette proposition a pour objet d'offrir à l'admiration et à l'étude dans la cour principale: sur la facade à gauche les fragments de l'art Gothique, au fond les formes de l'architecture du siècle de Louis XII et à droite celles du règne de Henri II, resumé de notre architecture nationale." AN F^{13}1117.

14

"Elle occuperait la place qu'il destinait à un portrail du XIII siècle, en face du fragment d'Anet." F. Bercé, *Les premiers travaux de la commission des monuments historiques, 1837–1848* (Paris, 1979), p. 278.

15

See N. Ziff, "Paul Delaroche: A Study in Nineteenth-Century French History Painting" (Ph.D. dissertation, New York University Institute of Fine Arts, 1974), pp. 167ff. See also: H. Delaborde, *L'Oeuvre de Paul Delaroche . . . accompagné d'une notice historique sur la vie et les ouvrages de Paul Delaroche* (Paris, 1858); H. Lemonnier, "La Peinture murale de Paul Delaroche à l'hemicycle de l'Ecole des Beaux-Arts," *GBA* 4S, 13 (1917): 173–182.

16

"La destination du lieu indique en quelque sorte le choix du sujet." A. Fillioux, "Peintures murales de la Salle des Cours à l'Ecole des Beaux-Arts par M. Paul Delaroche," *RGA* 2 (1841): col. 570.

17

"Comme le chaînon qui relie la partie antique et tout idéale du tableau avec sa partie moderne et presque vivante." L. Vitet, "Paul Delaroche: la Salle des Prix a l'Ecole des Beaux-Arts," *RDM* 28 (December 15, 1841): 937–954, republished in his *Etudes sur les beaux-arts*, 2 vols. (Paris, 1846), I, pp. 289–309, especially p. 290.

18

"M. Delaroche, par la trempe de son esprit, par le direction de ses études, est historien plus encore que poëte: ses idées se plaisent peu dans le champ des abstractions symboliques, elle revêtent plus volontiers le costume d'un pays ou d'une époque, elles s'attachent à un lieu, à une date, elles se spécialisent et se personifient. Où d'autres verraient l'art, il aperçoit l'artiste: la sculpture, pour lui, e'est le sculpteur." Vitet, *Etudes*, I, p. 286.

19

"On croit entendre tant il y a de justesse, de fine intention, de la clarté dans son action, dans sa pantomime." C. Blanc, "L'Hémicycle de Paul Delaroche gravé par Henriquel-Dupont," *GBA* 8 (December 15, 1860): 354.

20

"L'écoute, mais d'un air un peu distrait; on voit qu'il pense encore à sa coupole." Vitet, *Etudes*, I, p. 293.

21

"Avec la pétulence d'un Français, s'avance pour écouter le vieux Florentin, et s'appuie familièrement sur l'épaule de Bramente." Ibid.

22

"Pourront alors parcourir avec nous les salles et les galeries . . . et voir de leurs yeux et toucher de leurs mains cette *histoire figurée* de l'art que M. Delaroche aura aussi alors achevé de peindre symboliquement sur le mur de l'amphithéâtre." L. Peisse, "L'Ecole des Beaux-Arts," p. 245.

23

Documents: AN N III Seine 1135, F^{21}1362, and in Labrouste's personal papers deposited in the Académie d'Architecture, Paris, and the Cabinet des Estampes, Bibliothèque

Nationale. Recent studies: N. Levine, "Architectural Reasoning in the Age of Positivism: The Néo-Grec Idea of Henri Labrouste's Bibliothèque Sainte-Geneviève" (Ph.D. Dissertation, Yale University, 1975); N. Levine, "The Romantic Idea of Architectural Legibility: Henri Labrouste and the Néo-Grec," *The Architecture of the Ecole des Beaux-Arts* (New York, 1977); N. Levine, "The Book and the Building: Hugo's Theory of Architecture and the Bibliothèque Sainte-Geneviève," *The Beaux-Arts* (London, 1982). Contemporary reviews: C. Daly, "Bibliothèque Sainte-Geneviève," *RGA* 10 (1852): cols. 379–384; H. Trianon, "La nouvelle Bibliothèque Sainte-Geneviève," *L'Illustration* (1852): 29–30; A. Hermant, "La Bibliothèque Sainte-Geneviève," *L'Artiste* 5S, 7 (December 1, 1851): 129–131; T. de Banville, et al., *Paris-guide* (Paris, 1867), republished by A. Boinet and F. Calot as *Le Quartier Latin et la Bibliothèque Sainte-Geneviève* (Paris, n.d.).

24

This simple but fundamental observation I owe to Neil Levine, who in turn cites Colin Rowe as his source.

25

One should compare it to the reticent treatment Alavoine gave his projected archives building in Napolean's scheme to rebuild the Champs de Mars. See *Htcr*, V, pp. 185–188.

26

On the library as a type: N. Pevsner, *A History of Building Types* (Princeton, 1976); H. M. Crass, *Bibliothekbauten des 19 Jahrhunderts im Deutschland* (Munich, 1976).

27

AN F^{21}1362.

28

Such a statement must be carefully qualified. Earlier unmonumental buildings, like the Marché de la Madeleine in Paris of 1824, had utilized exposed iron skeletons. Monumental buildings, like John Nash's Regent Street Quadrant (1819–20), had iron elements, but they were carefully disguised to appear like stone. At least one monumental building, Heinrich Hubsch's Trinkhalle at Baden-Baden (1839–41) had exposed iron elements used frankly, but in very small pieces, as stiffeners for a masonry ceiling.

29

"Ce catalogue monumental est la principale décoration de la facade, comme les livres eux-mêmes sont le plus bel ornament de l'intérieur." In a letter reproduced in César Daly's critique of the structure, *RGA* 10 (1852): cols. 381–382.

30

Trianon, "La nouvelle Bibliothèque Sainte-Geneviève."

31

This fact about the structure was kindly pointed out to me by Mark Thompson, an architect in Philadelphia.

32

Cf. Levine, "Architectural Reasoning," ch. 2.

33

This basic observation seems to have been made in print only by the architect Pascal Coste when his journals were published. See entry for June 17, 1867, in *Mémoires d'un artiste: notes et souvenirs de voyage (1817–1877)*, 2 vols. (Marseilles, 1878): "Ces voussures, en forme de coupoles plates, revêtues des carreaux de faïence blancs, reflètent un jour égal sur toute la surface de la salle éclairée par le haut des ces voussures."

34

Documents: AN N III Seine 1130, F²¹766, F²¹1388, Versement d'Architecture 86. More preliminary drawings survive in the hands of the family and in the archives of the Commission des Monuments Historiques. See F. Pigeory, *Les Monuments de Paris: histoire de l'architecture civile, politique et religieuse sous le règne de Louis Philippe* (Paris, 1847), pp. 421ff. An illuminating critique of the structure by Léon Labrouste is in the Labrouste papers at the Académie d'Architecture. On the institution: A.-J. Morin, *Catalogue des collections de la conservatoire des arts et métiers* (Paris, 1851, with numerous augmented editions); *Recueil des lois, decrets, ordonnances, arrêtés, décisions et rapports relatives à l'origine, à l'institution, à l'organization et à la direction du conservatoire des arts et métiers* (Paris, 1889). Also: L. Lasalle, et al., *Cent cinquième anniversaire du conservatoire nationale des arts et métiers* (Paris, 1952).

35

"Notice historique sur l'ancien prieure de Saint-Martin-des-Champs," *Catalogue des collections*; also published as a separate pamphlet in 1882.

36

AN N III Seine 1130, F²¹1388.

37

Vaudoyer's student and close friend Gabriel Davioud laid out the square in his capacity as director of the Service Municipal des Promenades et Plantations. See the catalogue *Gabriel Davioud, architecte (1824–1881)* (Paris, 1981), p. 41.

38

AN F²¹1388; F. Bercé, *Les premiers travaux de la commission des monuments historiques, 1837–1848* (Paris, 1979), pp. 70–71, 83.

39

"La Chambre des Députés m'a proclamé architecte . . . à 43 ans . . . je vais donc enfin mettre quelque chose au soleil." Letter of June 18, 1846, AN 246 A.P. 14.

40

AN Versement d'architecture 86.

41

In the family's possession.

42

"Caraytids d'un grand caractère font partie de l'appareil de la construction." Manuscript among Henri Labrouste's papers, Académie d'Architecture.

43

"Un jour que je passais dans la rue au moment où un jeune sculpteur, M. Elias Robert, travaillait à ces figures, je remarquai avec quelque surprise que, loin de dissimuler les joints, il s'étudiait à laisser évidente la superposition des assises, de facon que la statue, coupée par les grandes horizontales de l'appareil, parût être non pas un ornement additionel apporté par la sculpture, pour tenir lieu de colonne, mais une évolution de la pierre elle-même, un relief énergique de la construction, et, pour ainsi dire, une partuition de l'édifice. Ne sachant alors de l'architecture que ce que tout le monde en sait ou croit en savoir, c'est-à-dire ne sachant rien, je fus frappé comme d'un trait de lumière, et dans ma naïveté profonde, je crus avoir découvert, à moi tout seul, un des grands principes de l'architecture, c'est-à-dire que la décoration doit être engendrée par la construction." C. Blanc, *Les Artistes de mon temps* (Paris, 1876), pp. 225–226.

44

"Très érudit dans les monuments de la Renaissance." V. Calliat, *Hôtel de Ville de Paris . . .* , 2 vols. (Paris, 1844–56).

45

One should compare this to Alphonse de Gisors's later and similar enlargement of the Luxembourg. See A. de Gisors, *Le Palais du Luxembourg* (Paris, 1847).

46

"Appliquant ainsi aux productions du Moyen-Age une routine qu'ils ne sauraient appuyer sur aucun exemple de la saine Antiquité." *De L'Art en Allemagne*, I, p. 108.

47

"Grand Dieu! que diraient ces gens-là du palais du roi de Bavière? . . . Le palais du roi Louis est comme un livre dont les quatre parties, composées dans quatres siècles différents, embrassent l'histoire de l'art et du monde." Ibid.

48

"Dans aucun pays il ne serait possible de rencontrer cette variété de systèmes et ce luxe de reminiscences que l'on trouve dans les constructions de la capitale de la Bavière. . . . Animée par les passions politiques et réligieuses de ce pays-ci, elle est parvenue à réaliser à sa surface une histoire vivante et à peu pres complète de l'architecture." Ibid.

49

"En France on convient généralement que l'art consiste surtout dans l'invention; mais ce grand principe, qui encourage souvent l'ignorance, ne préserve ni de la monotonie, ni du mauvais goût. En Bavière on pratique l'art comme si on s'accordait à le faire surtout résider dans la mémoire; mais en déployant plus de savoir que de génie, les architectes de ce pays fournissent un champ curieux aux études de la critique et préparent peut-être une époque nouvelle, dans laquelle, selon la loi ordinaire, viendront se fondre, avec les réserves faites par le caractère particulier de chaque peuple, les formes transfigurées des époques antérieures." Ibid., I, pp. 179–180.

50

"J'ai vu le public, épris pour ce palais d'une passion toute mystérieuse, s'étonner de trouver tant de plaisir dans un art qui l'a si long-temps enuyé, et tant d'invention dans ce qui ne lui avait paru, jusqu'à présent, que la science d'élever des pierres les unes sur les autres." Ibid., I, pp. 170–171.

51

"Le monument élevé dans le 19^E siècle ne devait pas être denué des moyens que l'état actuel de l'art nous donne pour caractériser notre époque." AN F^{21}117.

Four

THE ORGANIZATION OF THE ARCHITECTURAL PROFESSION

1

The mechanics of the professional life of the nineteenth-century French architect was explored by Hautecoeur and more recently has become part of monographic studies, especially R. Middleton, "Viollet-le-Duc" (Ph.D. dissertation, Cambridge University, 1959); W. Szambien, *Jean-Nicolas-Louis Durand, 1760–1834: de l'imitation à la norme* (Paris, 1984); J.-M. Leniaud, *Jean-Baptiste Lassus (1807–1857), où le temps retrouvé des cathédrales* (Geneva, 1980). A corner of the institutional framework itself is studied by F. Wacquet, *Les Fêtes royales sous le Restauration, ou l'ancien régime retrouvé* (Geneva, 1981). See also: P. Verdier, "Le Service des Monuments historiques," *Congrès archéologique de France* 2S, 1 (1934): 53–261; F. Bercé, *Les premiers travaux de la commission des monuments historiques, 1837–1848* (Paris, 1979). Also: G. Teyssot, "Planning and Building in Towns: The System of the Bâtiments Civils in France, 1795–1848," *The Beaux-Arts*, edited by R. Middleton (London, 1982), pp. 34–49. The history of governmental administration in France has been the subject of active research during the past two decades. See these collections of documents and essays: P. Legendre, *L'Administation de 1750 à nos jours* (Paris, 1968); Institut Français des Sciences Administratives, *Histoire de l'administration* (Paris, 1972, with extensive bibliography); Centre de Recherches d'Histoire et de Philologie, *Histoire de l'administration français depuis 1800: problèmes et méthodes* (Geneva, 1975). G. Thuillier has published basic volumes in this field, especially his *Témoins de l'administration de St. Just à Marx* (Paris, 1967) and *La Vie quotidienne des ministères au XIXe siècle* (Paris, 1976). An important study is O. Pirotte, *Alexandre-François-Auguste Vivien de Goubert (1799–1854)* (Paris, 1972), focused on one of the first theorists of administration. Also: A. Jacques, *La Carrière de l'architecte au XIXe siècle* (Paris, 1986).

2

Beulé in his *Eloge de Duban* (Paris, 1872) asks where is his Marseilles Cathedral? his Palais de Justice? and bewails the fact that he never designed more than what Beulé considers fragments.

3

M.-L. Biver, *Pierre Fontaine: Premier Architecte de l'Empereur* (Paris, 1964).

4

Visconti, Second Grand Prix in 1814, inherited great advantage from the eminence of his father, the antiquary Ennio Tullio Visconti (1751–1818), and built extensively for the nobility as well as, in his governmental capacities, the tomb of Napoleon, four large city fountains and finally—immediately before his death on December 29, 1853—the New Louvre. Adolphe Lance in his *Dictionnaire des architectes, français*, however, sharply criticized his ignorance of and impatience with practical matters and cited rumors of his dependence upon a series of brilliant assistants: Constant-Dufeux, who in the late 1820s supervised the construction of the Fontaine Gaillon (P. Féraud, "Constant -Dufeux," *RGA* 29 [1872]: col. 81), Louis-Pierre Haudebourt (1788–1849), and Jules Bouchet (1799–1849). The latter two were both students of Percier, like their employer, and Bouchet was Visconti's successor as architect of the tomb of Napoleon. See: H. Barbet de Jouy, "Jules-Frédéric Bouchet: architecte, dessinateur, graveur," *GBA* 1S, 6 (1860): 168–173; A. Lance, "Jules Bouchet, architecte: notice sur sa vie et ses travaux," *E d'A* (February 1860): cols. 17–22, where he denies rumors that Bouchet was the actual author of Visconti's Napoleon project. M.-C.-E. Tiran also claimed to be an *inspecteur privé* for Visconti in documents of 1855 (AN 64 Aj 186).

5

"Duc entrevoyait des horizons magnifiques; présentait une rénovation de l'architecture, et il s'abandonnait aux illusions du bel âge. Vaudoyer, homme de sens critique et de sens pratique, gauloise spirituel et aisé, pour n'être pas d'ailleurs du même avis que son ami Duc, Vaudoyer se raillait de lui et traitait de chimère ses aspirations. Il prévoyait qu'à la poésie du rêve succederait la prose des réalitiés, et qu'il faudrait beintôt descendre du portique d'Octavie au mur mitoyen." C. Blanc, *Les Artistes de mon temps* (Paris, 1876), p. 16.

6

"Quand je pense au sort qui m'attend à Paris, il me prend de moments de découragement dont je ne suis pas le maître. Il paraît que ce sera de même, nous apprenons ici que nos prèdecesseurs sont sans place, que celle de Labrouste a été donné à un écrivain de la direction. . . . L'Institut admet le zèle des architectes mais quelle est notre recompense?"

7

A printed prospectus entitled *Société des architectes* preserved in the library of the successor organization, the Académie d'Architecture, Paris.

8

H. Malo, "M. Thiers et les artistes de son temps," *Revue de Paris* 31 (July 1, 1924): 140–159; L. Clément de Ris, *Portraits à la plume* (Paris, 1853).

9

AN F^{21}6697: the decree of July 22, 1832. "Ils ne pourraient jamais être chargés . . . des travaux dans leurs attributions ordinaires que d'une seule grande construction, et, dans ce cas, ils ne recevront qu'une seule allocation fixe."

10

The foundation documents were published in the first volumes of the *Bulletin de la société centrale des architectes* (1843ff.).

11

The commission is listed as Huyot, president; Blouet; Cousin; Durand; Constant-Dufeux; E. Gilbert; A. Lenoir, secretary; Goulier, *rapporteur*.

12

"Aussitôt apres leur sortie des écoles, les ingénieurs sont immédiatement admis dans les grades inferiéures où ils acquaierent en même temps l'expérience pratique qui peut leur manquer, et les droits tout à des grades supérieures qu'à une retraite honorable. A la vérité les avantages pécuniaires attachées à cette carrière ne sont pas considérables; mais, en général, la position des ingénieurs est honorable et sûr; . . . Membre d'un corps fortement constitué, ils jouissent de la considération publique qui y est attaché, en même temps que celle que chacun peut mériter personellement." *Bulletin de la société centrale des architectes* 1 (1843): 11.

13

The members were Blouet, F.-A. Cendrier, Chatillon, Constant-Dufeux, Léon Danjoy, Dejoly [sic], Duc, Garnaud, Gilbert ainé, Gourlier, Jean-Louis Grillon, Albert Lenoir, Renié, Léon Vaudoyer.

14

H. H. Saylor, "The A. I. A.'s First Hundred Years," *Journal of the American Institute of Architects* (May 1957): 1–84, where the objectives of these early societies are discussed.

15

Bulletin de la société centrale des architectes (1844).

16

They are listed on the menu of the annual dinner of the railroad administration employees of 1847, a copy of which is preserved among Detlef Lienau's papers in the Avery Library, Columbia University. Cendrier was *architecte-en-chef* and the named men on his staff were B.-H. Sirodot (student of Guénepin), Jacques-Jean Clerget (student of Baltard), Lienau, Queyron, and Langlois. The last three were all students of Labrouste.

17

Htcr, V, pp. 143ff., citing the scattered but clear testimony on this point.

18

See the essay on the profession of the architect written by Léon Vaudoyer for Charton's *Guide pour le choix d'un état, ou dictionnaire des professions* (Paris, 1842), pp. 16–27, with numerous subsequent editions. He lists five careers: *dessinateur,* contractor's architect, consulting architect, government architect in the Bâtiments Civils, and finally "architecte-artiste," a member of the Institut and master of an atelier.

19

Forty-eight percent of the names listed as architects in the *Bottin* of 1859 also appear in E. Delaire, *Les Architectes élèves de l'Ecole des Beaux-Arts* (Paris, 1895).

20

A mysterious but influential group chiefly documented today in the collections of the Musée des Arts Décoratifs, Paris, especially among their *dessins originaux.*

21

Leroux de Lincy, *MU*, February 22, 1852.

22

The family's architectural papers are now deposited in the Canadian Centre for Architecture, Montreal.

23

"Je suis resté étranger aux entreprises de construction particulières qui sont la seule chance de fortune offerte aux architectes." Among the Labrouste papers, Académie d'Architecture, Paris.

24

See the catalogue *Colbert, 1619–1683* (Paris, 1983), with extensive bibliographies.

25

This administration was recorded annually in the *Bottin*, as it and that of the Palais Royaux, the Bâtiments Civils, and the Edifices Diocésaines were in the *Almanach royal*.

26

P. Sédille, "Victor Baltard," *GBA* 2S, 11 (1874, pt. 2): 485–496, specifically p. 487.

27

C. Gourlier, *Notice historique sur le service des travaux et sur le conseil générale des bâtiments civils* (Paris, 1848), with updated editions in 1886 and 1895.

28

AN 64 Aj series, especially 64 Aj 65.

29

Girard was made *inspecteur de la seconde classe* in 1854; *inspecteur de la première classe* in February 1856. Crépinet was *agent* in 1852; *inspecteur de la troisième classe* in May 1860.

30

As is noted in his sketchbooks from these trips preserved among his papers in the American Institute of Architects, Washington, D.C.

31

In the mid-1840s the Inspecteur Général, Mérimée, wrote a memorandum on the necessity of creating a "profession" in this branch with job security and opportunities for advancement. (The specific reference here, a document my wife, Ann, found and copied out for me at the Archives Nationales, was lost in Goldenberg's restaurant on August 9, 1982). See P. Léon, *La vie des monuments français* (Paris, 1951); Bercé, *Monuments historiques*; and Verdier, *Le Service des Monuments Historiques*.

32

Documented in the AN F^{19} series especially $F^{19}4561$, and in Fortoul's ministerial papers, AN 246 A.P. 22. See J.-M. Leniaud, "Viollet-le-Duc et le Service des Edifices Diocésains," *Actes du colloque international Viollet-le-Duc* (Paris, 1982), pp. 153–164.

33

"L'examen de ce projet amène la commission à se demander si, dans le cas où un department ne renfermerait pas d'architecte capable de composer un project de grand édifice, ne devrait pas en charger de jeunes architectes de Paris dont le talent serait bonnes [sic] et qui dirigeraient aussi l'exécution des travaux. Si ce système était adopté, il serait indesponsable que ces architectes fussent nomées par le M^{tre}: car l'infériorité des architectes de department est dûe surtout à leur position précaire révocables au gré des Préfets, il n'y à guère de sujets remarquables qui veuillent accepter une situation pareille. Il faudrait donc donner à ceux que l'adm.^{on} emploierait toute leur liberté d'action en ne les faisant dépendre directement et absoluement que de l'adm.^{on} centrale. Leur nombre pourrait être élevé à vingt: la France serait partagée en un égal nombre de circonscriptions établies d'après l'importance des différentes diocèses." AN $F^{19}4544$.

34

AN $F^{19}7739$.

35

Labrouste's, at 4 rue des Beaux-Arts, was a hundred yards from the Ecole's gate on the rue Bonaparte.

36

AN $Aj^{52}9$.

37

AN $F^{21}1385$, $F^{21}3572$, and Versement d'architecture album 56.

38

AN $F^{21}1362$, including letters from the Minister asking Labrouste to hurry up.

39

The calculation is my own. Cf. the figures in J. Singer-Kerel, *Le Coût de la vie à Paris de 1840 à 1845* (Paris, 1961). Vaudoyer, in Charton, *Guide pour le choix d'un état,* projects average salaries.

40

See Carol Ockman, "The Restoration of the Château of Dampierre: Ingres, the Duc de Luynes and an Unrealized Vision of History" (Ph.D. dissertation, Yale University, 1982).

41

Bercé, *Monuments historiques*; AN $F^{21}2542^9$.

42

Commission des Monuments Historiques, archives, dossier 645.

43

Bercé, *Monuments historiques*, pp. 127, 142, 153, 188, 212, 253, 280.

44

AN $F^{19}7739$. A *vacation* was three hours in length and there were supposed to be four in a working day; see *Le Semaine des constructeurs* 2, 16 (October 20, 1877).

45

AN $F^{19}7741$.

46

AN $F^{19}6393$.

47

This is recorded in Labrouste's notebooks in the Académie d'Architecture, Paris.

48

Beulé, *Eloge de Duban.*

49

RGA 32 (1875): cols. 269–274, pls. 54–61; 33 (1876): cols. 242–243, pls. 53–55.

50

AN $F^{19}1439$ and $F^{21}6393$.

51

Noted in Labrouste's account books, Académie d'Architecture, Paris.

52

AN $F^{19}7741$. Mme. Charles Garnier was tremendously conscious of her husband's finances and in a biographical sketch noted his earnings at each stage of his career (*L'Architecture* 38, no. 21 [1925]: 377–390). In his first position after his return from Rome, *sous-inspecteur* at the Tour Saint-Jacques, he received 1500 francs per annum, plus 300 francs per annum as *auditeur* for the Conseil des Bâtiments Civils. Later he received 2000 francs per annum as *inspecteur* at the Ecole des Mines, supplemented by a 3000-franc fee for helping design a building on the Boulevard de Sébastapol. Relative security came when he was named Architecte de la Ville de Paris for the fifth and sixth *arrondissements* with a salary of 8000 francs per annum, but an interdiction of any private work. The Opera cost 34,000,000 francs, but Mme. Garnier was incensed that Garnier was not awarded a three-percent fee (which would have brought Garnier almost a million francs spread over the fourteen years of construction), but instead two percent and sometimes only one-and-a-half percent. (Labrouste made a total of 591,443.36 francs during the last fourteen years of his career.)

53

On the *fonctionnaire*: G. Jèze, *Cours de Droit public: le statut des fonctionnaires publics* (Paris, 1928). Also the administrative encyclopedias: M. Block, *Dictionnaire de l'administration française* (Paris, 1856, with later editions); L. Bequet, *Répertoire du Droit administratif*, 24 vols. (Paris, 1885–1911). See the recent studies: G. Thuillier, *Bureaucratie et Bureaucrats en France au XIXe siècle* (Geneva, 1980); C. Charle, *Les hauts Fonctionnaires en France au XIXe siècle* (Paris, 1980); A. Brunot and R. Coquand, *Le Corps des ponts et chaussées* (Paris, 1982).

54

A. Vivien, "Etudes administratives," *RDM* (October 15, November 15, 1841; December 1, 1842; May 1, 1844; and especially October 15, 1845); published separately as a book under that title in 1845.

55

T. Gaehtgens, "Napoleon's Arc de Triomphe," *Abhandlungen der Akademie der Wissenschaft in Göttingen, Philogosich-historische Klasse* 3S, 42 (1974).

56

The most detailed and famous of these exposés: Jules Ferry, *Les Comptes fantastiques d'Haussmann* (Paris, 1868). See also: D. H. Pinkney, *Napoleon III and the Rebuilding of Paris* (Princeton, 1958).

57

M. Block, *Dictionnaire de l'administration française*, 3rd ed. (1891), p. 256.

58

C. Gourlier, L.-M.-D. Biet, E.-J.-L. Grillon and J.-J. Tardieu, *Choix d'édifices projetés et construits en France depuis le commencement du XIX siècle*, 3 vols. (Paris, 1825–50); *Paris dans sa splendeur* (Paris, 1861); F. Narjoux, *Architecture communale . . .* , 3 vols. (Paris, 1870–80).

59

J.-L. Pascal, *Les Bibliothèques et les facultés de médecines en Angleterre* (Paris, 1884).

60

A. Blouet and M. Demets, *Rapport à M. le Comte de Montalivet . . . sur les pénitenciers des Etats Unis* (Paris, 1837).

61

Cf. P.-P. Cret in his article on libraries for the twelfth edition of the *Encyclopedia Brittanica*.

62

C.-P. Marie Haas, *Administration de la France*, 4 vols. (2nd ed., Paris, 1861), IV, pp. 698–703.

63

"Préfère la liberté; mais elle s'accommode parfaitement d'un bon despotisme." Ibid., p. 1699.

64

"Il songeait à l'éducation, non au châtiment, du genre humain." Ibid., p. 1703.

65

P. Leroux, *Réfutation de l'eclectisme* (Paris, 1839); H. Taine, *Les Philosophes français du XIXᵉ siècle en France* (Paris, 1857).

66

Vaudoyer's visits are chronicled in the journals of Pascal Coste, *Memoires d'un artiste: notes et souvenirs de voyage (1817–1877)*, 2 vols. (Marseilles, 1878).

67

Published in E. Parrocel, *L'Art dans le Midi*, 4 vols. (Marseilles, 1881–84), III.

68

See, for example, *L'Artiste* 4 (1833, 1): 85: "L'un des concurrants [for the Grand Prix], c'est M. Guénepin, neveu de M. Guénepin, professeur de l'Académie, son oncle, son maître, et son juge; l'autre, c'est M. Baltard, fils de M. Baltard, professeur de l'Académie, son père, son maître, et son juge; l'autre c'est un cousin de M. Vaudoyer [Chargrasse]; l'autre c'est un filleul de M. Huyot [Noleau? Lefuel?]; etc.; etc.; etc.; élèves, professeurs, juges sont tous parens, alliés, et cousins: le génie est héréditaire!"

69

On Labrouste's father: *MU*, August 9, 1835, after he was killed riding near Louis-Philippe in the *Attentat de Fieschi*.

70

G. Picot, "Le comte de Montalivet," *Notices historiques* (Paris, 1907), pp. 193–284; de Montalivet, *Fragments et souvenirs*, 2 vols. (Paris, 1899). Also: Duc d'Anmale, *Notice sur le comte de Cardaillac* (Paris, 1880).

71

At least by Mme. Garnier in her biographical reminiscence, cited in note 52.

72

In chapter five I discuss the small contribution made by local authorities in the design of Marseilles Cathedral. Among the papers relating to Labrouste's work at the Bibliothèque Nationale is a letter of October 30, 1858, addressed by the architect to the Ministre d'Etat (Fould) complaining about a lack of cooperation from the library authorities, who had been instructed to send him a program for the new building. He also makes it clear that he feels them to have very restricted authority: "Je ne dois pas vous dissimuler, Monsieur le Ministre, que la pièce transmise par Monsieur le Ministre de l'Instruction publique n'est point le programme que j'attends depuis longtemps et qu'aurait pu m'être utile; ce n'est point une programme, mais une longue critique de tout ce que j'ai fait jusqu'à présent et même de ce que j'ai l'intention de faire. Je n'ai présenté cependant que vos ordres et si Monsieur l'administrateur a cru devoir les critiquer il aurait dû le faire d'une manière moins désobligeante pour moi." AN F^{21}1360.

73

"J'oubliais de vous parler des différents ministres qui se sont succédé dans la direction des travaux du gouvernement.

"M. de Montalivet, qui a demandé et fait étudier ce projet.

"M. Teste, qui a présenté le projet de loi.

"M. Dumon, qui a posé la première pierre de l'édifice.

"MM. Jayr, Trélat, Recurt, Vivien, Lacrosse, Bineau, Magne.
"En tout, onze ministres; mais il n'y a eu qu'un architecte."
RGA 10(1852): col. 384.

Five

MARSEILLES CATHEDRAL

1

Documents: AN F^{19}7737–7745; Commission des Monuments Historiques; Archives des Bouches-du-Rhône, Marseilles, 62.V.1–12; Archives Communales, Marseilles, 52.M.11, 52.M.35; Archives Diocésains, Marseilles, dossier "La Major"; Bibliothèque Municipale, Marseilles, Fonds Spéciaux, no. 1969; drawings in the possession of the family. Modern studies: *The Second Empire, 1852–1870: Art in France Under Napoleon III* (Philadelphia, 1979), entries I.23–I.27; Barry Bergdoll, work in progress. Older histories: C. Bosquet, *La Major: cathédrale de Marseilles* (Marseilles, 1857); A. Fabre, *Les Rues de Marseilles* 4 vols. (Marseilles, 1867–68), pp. 350–366; F. Durand, *La nouvelle cathédrale de Marseilles* (Nîmes, n.d.); E. Rougier, *La Cathédrale de Marseilles* (Marseilles, 1894). Also: E. Parrocel, *L'Art dans le Midi*, 4 vols. (Marseilles, 1881–84). On Bishop de Mazenod: Msgr. Jeancard, *Oraison funèbre de Msgr. Charles Eugène de Mazenod* (Marseilles, 1861); Msgr. Ricard, *Msgr. de Mazenod, évêque de Marseilles* (Paris, 1892); J. Leflon, *Eugène de Mazenod (1782–1861)*, 3 vols. (Paris, 1957–65).

2

His voluminous correspondence on the topic: AN F^{19}7739–7741.

3

"Il sera à craindre qu'un plus long mécompte dans les espérances données à cette population si religieuse, ne nuisît un peu à l'idée qu'elle s'en formée des bonnes dispositions du gouvernement à l'égard de tous ce qui rattache au culte. Dans le moment actuel où tous les passions s'agitent pour semer des alarmes sur ce point (alarmes que certes je reconnais tout à fait dénuées de fondement) un fait sans réplique comme l'encouragement de construire une cathédrale, rendrait vaine à Marseilles cette tentative de l'esprit de parti, et rattacherai peut-être au gouvernement du Roi bien des personnes que n'ont pu toucher encore les autres bienfaits que notre ville a reçue depuis 1830." NA F^{19}7739, letter of July 22, 1844.

4

He had been appointed to that task in a letter of March 14. AN F^{19}7739.

5

These survive bound with some other projects in a volume inscribed *Cathédrale de Marseilles, 1845* in the Marseilles Bibliothèque Municipale, Fonds Spéciaux, no. 1969.

6

At the meeting of the Conseil Municipal of October 16, 1846.

7

"La construction d'une nouvelle cathédrale à Marseilles n'est point réclamée par des besoins impérieux d'utilité publique. C'est un projet purement d'intérêt local dont la dépense doit en première ligne et presque exclusivement tomber à la charge des populations destinées à en profiter." AN F^{19}7739.

8

P. Coste, *Mémoires d'un artiste: notes et souvenirs de voyage (1817–1877)* (Marseilles, 1878); *MU*, September 28, 1851.

9

AN F^{19}7740.

10

AN F^{19}4548.

11

Photographs of this model survive among Vaudoyer's papers.

12

AN F^{19}7744. These documents make it clear that the decorative carving was executed after Vaudoyer's death, principally during the tenure of Revoil.

13

AN F^{19}7741.

14

"Il va falloir aborder le fameux probléme du type catholique en 1845. Hélas, ce n'est pas facile et je tremble." AN 246 A.P. 14.

15

In the same archive, letters to Fortoul of August 16 and 21, 1845.

16

"Je suis allé voir chez Vaudoyer le plan de la cathédrale de Marseilles. J'ai encore fait quelques observations mais je trouve le plan assez amélioré pour produire un des plus beaux et des plus curieux monuments dont la France puisse s'honorer. C'est l'oeuvre dont je serai le plus fier. Je crois avoir beaucoup contribué même à la conception." G. Massa-Gille, *Le Journal d'Hippolyte Fortoul* (Geneva, 1979), entry for May 23, 1855.

17

AN F^{19}7739.

18

AN 246 A.P. 14, letter to Fortoul of May 15, 1845.

19

AN F^{19}7741.

20

"La disposition de la cathédrale procède à la fois des salles des thermes romains et des églises byzantines (surtout de St. Marc de Venise)." Institut de France, library, MS 1809: two informative letters of February 15 and 19, 1875, addressed to Charles Blanc to help him in preparing his profile of Vaudoyer in his *Les Artistes de mon temps*.

21

Leflon, *Eugène de Mazenod*, III.

22

"Éprouvant . . . le besoin de renouer la chaîne entière de sa tradition."

23

Several cross sections in watercolor showing this decorative scheme survive in the possession of the family; an additional one was sold at the Hôtel Druot in 1986.

24

H. Fortoul, *De l'Art en Allemagne* (Paris, 1842), I, p. 107.

25

As is proven by the sketchy journal of the trip kept by Vaudoyer and preserved by the family.

26

De l'Art en Allemagne, II, p. 381.

27

"Ce n'est pas la première fois que l'antiquité m'apparaît vivante encore presque à la vieille du siècle qui a prétendu la tirer, après mille ans, du tombeau. Dans toutes les directions qu'embrasse le développement de l'esprit humain, elle avait conservé son empire presque absolu jusque dans le XIIᵉ siècle; au XIIIᵉ elle fut un instant vaincu par le mouvement qui enfanta du même coup les langues modernes et l'art ogival; mais déjà au XVᵉ elle avait repris toute son autorité en Italie, et elle était sur le point de s'imposer à l'Europe entière plus fortement que jamais." Ibid., II, p. 429.

28

"Nous croyons que, pour y parvenir, le programme pourrait être ainsi formulé:—pour la disposition, application de tous les avantages que peut fournir la science de la construction en voûte; adoption du style vertical et de l'arcade libre et affranchie des ordres antiques; introduction du dôme sans exclusion des clochers. Quant au style, prendre pour point de départ les grands principes de l'architecture antique, tout en faisant la part de ceux qui appartiennent à l'art chrétien, et se proposer en somme de créer un monument qui soit de notre temps, de notre pays, et qui soit de la même famille que ceux dont nos différents besoins peuvent motiver la construction dans le même lieu." *MP* 14 (April 1846): 111.

29

The Commission's minutes: AN F¹⁹4544. Viollet-le-Duc's report: AN F¹⁹7740.

30

"Qui, par ses proportions ainsi bien que par sa situation dans une des plus belles et des plus riches villes de France, doit attirer l'attention de tous les hommes éclairés en Europe."

31

"Il y a vait deux partis à prendre: ou, projeter un monument dans les données completement neuves, et qui résument le goût particulier à notre époque, ou suivre les traditions, et s'inspirer des types anciens."

32

"Car quel est celui d'entre nous qui peut définir l'architecture de notre temps?"

33

"Prendre pour guide nos grandes cathédrales gothiques, c'était élever un monument en désaccord avec l'architecture méridionale, avec les éléments et les habitudes de ces contrées."

34

"S'inspirer de nos édifices de la Renaissance, c'était tenter de reproduire une architecture bâtarde, c'était risquer de tomber dans les écarts si fréquents dans cette architecture."

35

"Mr. Vaudoyer me paraît s'être trop occupé, dans l'ensemble de sa composition, de l'accusation banale *d'imitation*. Il semble vouloir prouver, qu'on peut allier dans une même édifice des formes appartennant à des âges et à des peuples différents. Certes, si quelqu'un est en état de surmonter cette difficulté, c'est Mr. Vaudoyer qui a longement etudié les styles qu'il veut réunir; mais si l'on peut louer ici les efforts du savant, admirer son adresse à fondre ensemble des formes d'origines diverses, l'artiste regrettera toujours ces efforts qui détruisent l'unité sans ajouter à l'effet. Mr. Vaudoyer sait mieux que nous, qu'une architecture n'est le produit du hasard; quand donc on se décide (et comment faire autrement aujourd'hui) à adopter un style, pourquoi ne pas le prendre tel qu'il est à sa source la plus pure? Pourquoi chercher à composer une langue *macronique*, quand on a sous la main un beau et simple langage?"

36

L. Vitet, *Monographie de l'église Notre-Dame-de-Noyon* (Paris, 1845).

37

"Où voyons-nous les grandes cathédrales s'élever à la fin du XIIᵉ siècle et au commencement du XIIIᵉ? C'est dans les villes telles que Noyon, Soissons, Laon, Reims, Amiens, qui toutes avaient, les premières, donné le signal de l'affranchissement des communes. . . .

"Au commencement du XIIᵉ siècle, le régime féodal était constitué; il enserrait la France dans un réseau dont toutes les mailles, fortement nouées, semblaient ne devoir jamais permettre à la nation de se développer. Le clergé régulier et séculier n'avait pas protesté contre ce régime; il s'y était associé. . . . Il n'en était pas de même des évêques; ceux-ci n'avaient pas profité de la position exceptionnelle que leur donnait le pouvoir spirituel; ils venaient se ranger, comme les seigneurs laïques, sous la bannière de leurs suzerains. . . . C'est alors que, soutenus par le pouvoir monarchique déjà puissant, forts des sympathies des populations qui se tournaient repidement vers les issues qui leur faisaient entrevoir une espérance d'affranchissement, les évêques voulurent donner une forme visible à un pouvoir qui leur semblait désormais appuyé sur des bases inébranlables; ils réunirent des sommes énormes, et jetant bas les vieilles cathédrales devenues trop petites, ils les employèrent sans délai à la construction de monuments immenses faits pour réunir à tout jamais autour de leur siège épiscopal ces populations désireuses de s'affranchir du joug féodal." *DR*, II (1856), pp. 281–282.

38

Ent, VI.

39

Ibid., I, p. 241.

40

"Au moyen âge en France, la plus modeste maison, la plus pauvre église, appartenaient à l'art aussi bien que le château seigneurial et la cathédrale de l'évêque. . . . L'art de l'architecture s'est peu à peu retiré des extrémités, pour ne plus vivifier que les centres de population; et autant dans les grandes cités il accumule des ressources immenses, il se fait fastueux, autant il est misérable partout ailleurs. . . .

"Or, l'architecture se trouve aujourd'hui soumise à une sorte de gouvernement intellectuel, plus étroit encore que n'était celui établi par Louis XIV; elle n'a pas fait sa révolution de 1789." Ibid., I, pp. 385–387.

41

"Chacun d'eux est basé sur un système général de construction conçu en raison des dimensions de l'édifice et de la nature des matériaux; c'est ainsi qu'une petite église n'est pas la réduction d'une grande et que le caractère architectural varie suivant les provinces." A. de Baudot, *Eglises de bourgs et villages*, 2 vols. (Paris, 1867), I, p. 5.

42

Ibid., I, with six plates and explanatory text. See L. MacClintock, "Monumentality versus Suitability: Viollet-le-Duc's Saint-Gimer at Carcassonne," *Journal of the Society of Architectural Historians* 40, no. 3 (October 1981): 218–235; B. Foucart, "Viollet-le-duc et la construction des églises," *Viollet-le-Duc* (Paris, 1980), pp. 178–181. Neil Levine first brought this to public consciousness in 1978 in a lecture at the Architectural Association in London.

43

"Avec le système des voûtes en arcs d'ogive, plus le comble des bas côtés est plat, plus il est facile de restreindre la hauteur de la vôute principale, par suite celle de l'édifice, et par conséquent d'éviter les arcs-butants; or la tuile creuse n'exigeant qu'une très-faible pente, l'architecte a profité de cet avantage pour placer aussi bas que possible la naissance des voûtes hautes, tout en laissant au-dessus du comble des collatéraux, des roses occupant toute la largeur de chaque travée, et donnant un grand jour à l'intérieur."

44

The basic summation of the topic: A. Kingsly Porter, *Lombard Architecture*, 3 vols. (New Haven, 1917), especially ch. 1, "Bibliographic Foreword."

45

"Des principautés indépendents, des communautés, des républiques commencèrent à se constituter de toutes parts, et un principe de vie fut rendu à cette contrée longtemps ensevelie dans un sommeil léthargique." J.-C.-L. Sismondi, *Histoire des républiques italiennes du moyen-âge*, 2nd French edition (Paris, 1832), I, p. 29.

46

Vol. I, 119–121.

47

Cordero di San Quintino. *Dell'italiana Architettura durante la dominazione longobarda* (Brescia, 1829).

48

L. Vitet, "De l'Architecture lombarde," *Oeuvres complètes de L. Vitet*, 4 vols. (Paris, 1868), II, pp. 291–315.

49

Ent, I, p. 197. Also: Rivoira, *Le Origine della architettura lombarda e delle sue principali derivazioni nei paesi d'oltr'Alpo*, 2 vols. (Rome, 1901–7); Porter, *Lombard Architecture*.

50

D. and G. Sacchi, *Della Condizione economica, morale e politica degli Italiani nei bassi tempi* (Milan, 1828).

51

L. Reynaud, *Traité d'architecture*, 2 vols. (Paris, 1850, 1858), II, pp. 214–218.

52

"Ces deux choses: les pied-droits cantonnés de colonnes, et les colonnes alongées et montant du sont fondamentales dans l'histoire de l'art. Elles constituent l'élément le plus caractéristique, la base la plus essentielle de toute l'architecture du moyen âge; elles sont de bien plus grande importance que l'ogive. Ce sont elles qui ont permis les voûtes, les proportions élancées et la prédominance des lignes verticales, qui ont assuré, en un mot, un art spécial au christianisme de l'Occident. Leur invention est un titre de gloire qu'on a vainement voulu contester à la Lombardie." Ibid., pp. 217–218.

53

See the lengthy biographical essay by F. Dartien, *M. Léonce Reynaud: sa vie et ses oeuvres par l'un de ses élèves* (Paris, 1885).

54

A. Lenoir, *RGA* I (1840): cols. 7–17, 65–76, 257–263, 321–327, 449–456, 585–590.

55

DR, IV (1859), pp. 352–354; *Ent*, I, p. 203.

56

AN F^{19}7813. See B. Foucart, et al., *Paul Abadie, architecte, 1812–1884* (Angoulême, 1984).

57

Lombard Architecture, I, pp. 443–483.

58

C. Clericetti, *Richerche sull'architettura lombarda* (Milan, 1869); R. Cattaneo, *L'Architettura in Italia dal secolo VI al mille circa* (Venice, 1888).

59

Ent, I, p. 197.

60

De l'Art en Allemagne, I, p. 229; II, pp. 330–332, 413–416.

61

VII (1839), pp. 359, 398–399; VIII (1840), p. 59; XII (1844), pp. 259–262. Also, *Patria*, col. 2159.

62

Traité d'architecture, II, p. 271, also pp. 255–259.

63

"Les Mandarins à Paris," *GBA* I (1859): 90–97, specifically attacking the Académie's praise of Reynaud's *Traité* published in the *Moniteur universel,* December 14, 1858.

64

DR, IV (1859), pp. 352–354.

65

"Il a été amené à donner à la nef plus de largeur, aux alentours de la coupole centrale et du sanctuaire des dispositions plus simples et en rapport avec les pesanteurs et poussées, à ses élévations et coups un caractère d'unité qui manquait au premier projet. Ce système d'architecture admis (et il convient parfaitement au climat et aux matériaux de Marseilles) on ne pouvait en faire une application plus sage et plus heureuse." AN F^{19}7740.

66

C. Blanc, *Les Artistes de mon temps* (Paris, 1870).

67

Dramatically documented in a publication of photographs by O. Teissier, *Marseilles sous Napoléon III* (Marseilles, 1866). Also: Chambre de Commerce et de l'Industrie de Marseilles, *Marseilles sous le Second Empire* (Marseilles, 1961); G. Rambert, *Marseilles: la formation d'une grande cité moderne* (Marseilles, 1934).

68

A.-A. Ernouf, *Paulin Talabot, sa vie et son oeuvre (1799–1885)* (Paris, 1866). Also:
L. Girard, *La Politique des travaux publics du Second Empire* (Paris, 1951), and especially, "Le Politique des grands travaux à Marseilles sous le Second Empire," *Marseilles sous le Second Empire*, pp. 75–88.

69

A. Picard, *Les Chemins de fer français*, 6 vols. (Paris, 1884–85), I, pp. 21–23, 239–317, 321, 410ff.

70

Ernouf, *Paulin Talabot*; Bousquet and T. Sapet, *Etude sur la navigation et l'industrie de Marseilles* (Marseilles, 1858), especially pp. 249ff.

71

J. Drujon, *Etude sur les Docks de Marseilles* (Paris, 1913).

72

J. Charles-Roux, *L'Isthme et le canal de Suez*, 2 vols. (Paris, 1901). Also, of course, F. de Lesseps, *Histoire du canal de Suez* (Paris, 1870).

73

The transformation is impressively documented in Teissier's photographs.

74

"Du jour où ce système de la Méditerranée aura été assez élaboré pourqu'on puisse en entramer la réalization, la paix reviendra en Europe comme par enchantement, et elle y reviendra à tout jamais." M. Chevalier, *Religion Saint-Simonien. Politique industrielle. Système de la Méditerranée* (Paris, 1832), p. 28. This is but the most visionary of a large literature inspired by the conquest of Algeria in 1830; for example, François Mignet's articles in *Le National*, March 1 and 4, May 23, July 16, 1830.

75

Bousquet and Sapet, *Etude sur la navigation et l'industrée de Marseilles*, p. 286.

76

See E. Said, *Orientalism* (New York, 1978), who cites numerous primary sources.

77

"La France doit tenir à posséder une ville qui soit la capitale des bords de la Mediterranée. . . .

"Nous avons dit que c'est une question d'intérêt général pour la France; c'est plus encore, c'est une question de civilisation.

"Il est évident que les bienfaits de la civilisation ne peuvent se répondre sur le littorale de la Mediterranée que par Marseilles; c'est la seule ville importante qui, dans cette mer, appartient a un peuple libre.

"Attachons donc à favoriser à Marseilles les progrès des lumières et de la civilisation. . . .

"Ceci n'est pas inspiré par un étroit intérêt de localité. Il est de l'intérêt, j'ose dire de l'humanité tout entière, que Marseilles exerce sur le Midi de l'Europe, sur le Nord de l'Asie et de l'Afrique une influence de progrès, de civilisation, de lumière." J. Julliany, *Essai sur la commerce de Marseilles* (Marseilles, 1834,) p. 559.

78

J. Reynaud, *Terre et Ciel* (Paris, 1854), pp. 28–29.

79

"Des réductions d'églises que les *imagiers* du moyen âge placaient entre les mains des saints batisseurs." F. Durand, *La nouvelle cathédrale de Marseilles.*

80

On Notre-Dame-de-la-Garde: Espérandieu's papers survive in the archives of the Bouches-du-Rhône, Marseilles. Mlle. Nadine Pointel is working on a dissertation on Espérandieu for the University of Aix. The church was examined at length in *RGA* 24 (1866): cols. 32–37. Espérandieu appears frequently in Coste's journals and in Parrocel, *L'Art dans le Midi*, III.

81

Parrocel, ibid., III, pp. 306–307. Vaudoyer had a letter printed in the *Gazette du Midi*, December 22, 1857, stating without qualification that Espérandieu was architect of the structure.

82

M. Trachtenberg, *The Statue of Liberty* (New York, 1976), pp. 49–57.

83

J. Betz, *Bartholdi* (Paris, 1954), pp. 24–25. See also: E. Lesbazilles, *Les Colosses anciens et modernes* (Paris, 1876).

84

See the fourth chapter of D. Van Zanten "The Architectural Polychromy of the 1830's" (Ph.D. dissertation, Harvard University, 1970).

85

"Lorsqu'on a visité l'antique *Triancrie*, qu'on a veçu dans le pays, qu'on a pu admirer le ciel de cette terre fortunée; quand on a vu le soleil répondre sa clerté matinale sur toute la surface de *l'Ile-Verte*, et l'envelopper de ses dernieres rayons comme d'un réseau d'or; quand on a observé les brillantes couleurs qui nuancent, en Sicile, le laurier, le palmier, l'aloès, le myrte, l'oranger, en un mot, tout ce que le sol produit au sien du désert comme au milieu du champ cultivé, on demeure convaincu que l'artiste devait puiser ses inspirations dans les beautés qui l'entouraient, se mettre en rapport avec elles, et enrichir l'oeuvre d'art de tout l'éclat de la nature." J.-I. Hittorff and L. Zanth, *Architecture antique de la Sicile* (Paris, 1827–30), prospectus, signed "Hittorff."

86

"Adoucir l'éclat." "Atmosphère transparante qui rapproche les objets, en arrête les contours, et que les vibrations de la chaleur rendent visible et comme palpable." E. Burnouf, "Le Parthénon," *RDM* 5S, 20 (December 1, 1847): 835–853, specifically p. 849.

87

O. Jones and J. Goury, *Plans, Elevations, Sections and Details of the Alhambra*, 3 vols. (London, 1836–45). Also: D. Van Zanten, "The Architectural Polychromy of the

1830's," ch. 3; M. Darby, "Owen Jones and the Eastern Ideal" (Ph.D. dissertation, Reading University, 1974); D. Van Zanten, "Architectural Polychromy: The Life in Architecture," *The Beaux-Arts*, edited by R. Middleton (London, 1982), pp. 196–215; M. Darby, *The Islamic Perspective* (London, 1983).

88
Van Zanten, "The Architectural Polychromy of the 1830's,"pp. 312–317. Also: L. Beltrami, *Storia della facciata di Santa Maria del Fiore* (Milan, 1900).

89
H.-R. Hitchcock, *Early Victorian Architecture*, 2 vols. (New Haven, 1954), ch. 17.

90
V. Place, *Ninève et l'Assyrie*, 3 vols. (Paris, 1867).

91
See John Whiteley's dissertation, "The Revival in Painting of Themes Inspired by Antiquity in the Mid-Nineteenth Century" (Oxford University, 1972). Also: Pierre Petroz, *L'Art et la critique en France depuis 1822* (Paris, 1875), pp. 147–166; H. Peyre, *Bibliographie critique de l'héllenisme en France de 1843 à 1870* (New Haven, 1932).

92
Paris . Rome . Athènes, (Paris, 1982), catalogue of an exhibition of the polychromed *envois*.

93
T. Gautier, A. Houssaye, C. Coligny, *Le Palais pompéien* (Paris, 1866); Musée des Arts Décoratifs, *La Maison pompéienne du Prince Napoléon, 1856* (Paris, 1979).

94
J. Salmson, *Entre deux Coups de ciseau* (Paris, 1892), ch. 38.

95
As is clear in numerous references in Coste's journal.

96
N. Matas, *Dimonstrazione de progetto . . . per compiere calla facciata insigne basilica Santa Maria del Fiore . . .* (Florence, 1843), and now in the family's possession.

97
E. Börsch-Suppan, *Berliner Architektur nach Schinkel 1840–1870* (Munich, 1977); G. Graundmann, *August Soller, 1805–1853: ein Berliner Architekt im Geiste Schinkels* (Munich, 1973), for his Michaelskirche in Berlin of 1845–61.

98
"Propre à produire toutes les impressions, depuis les plus simples et le plus austères, jusqu'aux plus mêlées et plus fastueuses: le plein ceintre, qui est le principe de ces monuments, y est traité de mille façons diverses qui devraient provoquer les méditations des artistes de notre temps." *De l'Art en Allemagne*, II, p. 413; cf. ch. 20 of that volume, "De l'Architecture curviligne," especially pp. 323–333.

99
C. Bousquet, *La Major*, pp. 117ff.

100
Fragmentary documents surviving in the archives of the diocese show the resistance starting as early as 1853, after Vaudoyer's first project was displayed.

101

M.-G. Raulin, *Charles-Auguste Questel* (Paris, 1888). A.-H. Revoil, *Architecture romane du Midi de la France*, 3 vols. (Paris, 1867–73). Revoil exhibited his studies of Provençal Romanesque monuments in the Salon regularly from 1846, while still a student of Caristie at the Ecole des Beaux-Arts. In 1852 he was appointed *architecte diocésain* of Montpellier, Nîmes, and Fréjus (AN F^{19}7233). In response to Fortoul's circular of 1853 requesting designs for model parish churches of various scale, Revoil submitted a series of polished Provençal Romanesque adaptions (AN F^{19}4681).

102

F. Mistral, *Mes Origines: mémoires et récits* (Paris, 1945) (translation of the original volume of 1906); M.-C. Rostaing, "La Vie littéraire dialectale à Marseilles sous le Second Empire," *Marseilles sous le Second Empire*, pp. 195–236. A complication is that Fortoul, a southerner, had also studied Provençal literature while at Toulouse, providing, for example, the *avertissement* to C.-H.-B.-A. Moquin-Tandon, *Carya Magalonensis ou Noyer de Magnelonne* (1844) and as Minister had sent Adolphe Dumas to Provence to collect material (although in a letter of February 25, 1856, Dumas refers to Fortoul as "Cet idiot de Fortoul"; see F. Mistral, *Un poète bilingue: Adolphe Dumas* (Paris, 1927), p. 151.

103

"Le génie rénovateur de Napoléon plane sur Marseilles. La vieille cité phocéene se réveille, des idées plus larges germent dans tous les esprits, des projets d'agrandissement sont étudiés et sounises à la haute sanction du Prince que la France vient de proclamer Empereur," O. Teissier, *Marseilles sous Napoléon III.*

104

L. Girard, *Les Elections de 1869* (Paris, 1960).

Six

PALAIS DE JUSTICE

1

Documents: AN F^{13}1106, F^{21}3399, F^{21}2370, Commission des Monuments Historiques (F. Bercé, *Les premiers travaux de la commission des monuments historiques (1837–1948)* (Paris, 1979), pp. 91–93, 233–235, 237–239, 243, 245, 279, 313–315). A mass of drawings survive in the office of the architect of the building and are being studied by Katherine Fisher Taylor in her Harvard doctoral dissertation. Older studies: F. Pigeory, *Les Monuments de Paris* (Paris, 1847), pp. 345–360; F. Narjoux, *Monuments élevés par la Ville, 1850–1880*, 4 vols. (Paris, 1881–83), I; H. Stein, *Le Palais de Justice et la Sainte-Chapelle de Paris* (Paris, 1912). The basic documents and projects are the subject of a remarkable contemporary publication: *Documents relatifs aux travaux du Palais de Justice de Paris . . .* (Paris, 1858). I reproduce Napoleon III's famous confidence from T. Zeldin, *The Political System of Napoleon III* (London, 1958), p. 46.

2

"Palais," pp. 1–36, specifically p. 1, "C'est la maison royale ou suzeraine, le lieu où le suzerain rend la justice."

3

On the archaeology of the monument: L. Duc and E.-T. Dommey, *Rapport sur . . . les antiquités romaines* (Paris, 1846); J.-P. Schmit and B. Sauvan, *Histoire et description pitto-*

resque du Palais de Justice, de la Conciergerie et de la Sainte-Chapelle de Paris (Paris, 1825);
F. Gebelin, *La Sainte-Chapelle et la Conciergerie* (Paris, 1931).

4

As this setting it held an important place in literature, for example, in Corneille's comedy *La Galérie du Palais* of 1633.

5

While Dommey appeared to share the post with Duc, contemporaries gave all the credit for the design to the latter. Dommey's position remains a mystery, Katherine Fisher Taylor has kindly informed me.

6

The matter was discussed by the Commission des Monuments Historiques in its meetings of January 20 and 23, February 3, 10, 13, and 24, and March 10 and 17, 1843; January 19 and May 17 and 24, 1844 (Bercé, *Monuments historiques*, pp. 233–235, 237–239, 243, 245, 279, 313–315).

7

Cf. the review of that decision by the Conseil on July 25, 1853: AN $F^{21}2542^{16}$.

8

On Daumet: "Honoré Daumet, 1826–1911, sa vie et ses oeuvres," *L'Architecture* 27 (February 1914): 49–55. See L. Heuzey, *Mission archéologique de Macédoine*, 2 vols. (Paris, 1876).

9

The building was severely damaged during the Commune in 1871 but rebuilt by Duc and Daumet.

10

D d'A, "Colonne."

11

As, for example, in the Monument of Lysicrates in Athens.

12

D d'A, "Pilastre."

13

See Quatremère de Quincy, "Notice sur la vie et les ouvrages de M. Hurtault," *Recueil des notices lues dans les séances publiques de l'Académie royale des Beaux-Arts* (Paris, 1834). This particular declaration on Quatremère's part occasioned a violent protest from the students present (*MU*, October 9, 1826).

14

A.-L.-T. Vaudoyer studied the Theatre of Marcellus for his archaeological *envoi* of 1788 and published it as a model for the applied Order: *Description du théâtre de Marcellus à Rome . . .* (Paris, 1812).

15

His friend Reynaud cited the Colosseum as an example of such adaption in his entry "Amphithéâtre" in the *Encyclopédie nouvelle*, I, (1834), p. 480.

16

Cf. Duc's explanatory essay preserved with his drawings in the library of the Ecole des Beaux-Arts. See *Roma antiqua* (Paris, 1985), pp. 258–291, where it is analyzed by M. L. Conforto and S. Panella.

17

"Qu'on n'a pas apporté beaucoup de temps ni de soin à la perfection de ces détails."
D d'A, "Amphithéâtre."

18

"La décoration tient à la structure, l'appuie même." *Ent*, II, p. 209, note.

19

Neil Levine discusses this point illuminatingly in his dissertation "Architectural Reasoning in the Age of Positivism: The Néo-Grec Idea of Henri Labrouste's Bibliothèque Sainte-Geneviève" (Yale University, 1975), ch. 2, pt. 10.

20

J.-D. Leroy, *Les Ruines des plus beaux monuments de la Grèce* (Paris, 1758).

21

Quatremère de Quincy, "Sur la Restitution du temple de Jupiter olympien à Agrigente," *MU*, May 6, 1805; reprinted as a pamphlet.

22

Encyclopédie méthodique, I, pp. 118–119.

23

"La nature avoit donné à la sculpture une mesure déterminée de rapports, une échelle de proportions du corps humain. . . . qui servoit de modulê à la figure: elle régloit les nuances les plus légères de proportions en établissant un accord constant des parties. . . . *L'architecture*, à son instar, s'en créa un semblable. . . . Dès lors, un édifice devint une espèce d'être organisé, subordonné à les lois constantes dont il trouvoit en lui le principe et la raison . . . L'étude approfondie du corps humain dans toutes ses variétés, avoit fait apercevoir à la sculpture ces différences d'âge et de Nature qui formèrent les divers modes que Polyclete avoit fixés dans son traité des symétries, et dont les statues antiques nous ont conservé les règles visibles. *L'architecture* s'en forma de pareils dans l'invention des ordres. Ces modes se réduisent à trois: l'un exprime la force, l'autre la grâce, le troisième, par la réunion des deux autres qualités, exprime la noblesse et la majesté qui en résultent." Ibid., I, p. 119.

24

Section I, para. 1.

25

See *D d'A*, "Coupole," "Basilique," "Eglise."

26

Académie Royale des Beaux-Arts, "Considérations sur la question de savoir s'il est convenable au XIXᵉ siècle de bâtir des églises en style gothique," printed in *RGA* 6 (1845–46): cols. 316ff. There followed an important series of responses: J.-B. Lassus, "Réaction de l'Académie des Beaux-Arts contre l'art gothique," *Moniteur des arts* 24 and 25 (July 12 and 19, 1846), also published as a pamphlet; E.-E. Viollet-le-Duc, "Du Style gothique au XIXᵉ siècle," *Annales archéologiques* 4 (1846): 325–353; C. Daly, "Opinion de l'Académie royale des beaux-arts sur l'architecture gothique," *RGA* 6 (1845–46): cols. 313–316; G. Laviron, "De l'architecture contemporaine et de la convenance de l'application du style gothique aux constructions religieuses du XIXᵉ siècle," *Revue nouvelle* (October 1846), also printed separately; A. Morin, "De la Construction d'une église gothique au XIXᵉ siècle," *Moniteur des arts*, 13 (April 26, 1846): 99–100.

27

"Il faudrait enfin . . . enseigne, non pas à copier les Grecs et les Romains, mais à les imiter, en prenant, comme eux, dans l'art et dans la nature tout ce qui se prête aux covenances de toutes les sociétés et aux besoins de tous les temps."

28

G. Scott, *The Architecture of Humanism* (London, 1914); B. Berenson, "A Word on Renaissance Churches," *The Study and Criticism of Italian Art* (London, 1902), pp. 62–76; Vernon Lee (pseudonym of Violet Paget) and C. Anstruther-Thomson, *Beauty and Ugliness* (London, 1912), the last with extensive bibliographical references to precursors. See also their more scientific precursors: H. Siebeck, *Das Wesen asthetischen Anschauung* (Berlin, 1875); H. Wölfflin, *Prolegomena zu einer Psychologie der Architektur* (Basel, 1886); T. Lipps, *Raumästhetik und geometrisch optisch Tauschungen* (Munich, 1897).

29

"L'homme s'aime, et les objets qui font triompher sa nature lui plaisent. . . . Nous nous aimons, voilà l'origine de tout plaisir."

30

The extensive bibliography on this institution is summarized in G. Radet, *L'Histoire et l'oeuvre de l'Ecole française d'Athènes* (Paris, 1901) and updated in the catalogue *Paris . Rome . Athènes* (Paris, 1982). Also: H. Peyre, *Bibliographie critique de l'héllenisme en France de 1843 à 1870* (New Haven, 1932); R. Canat, *L'Hellénisme des romantiques*, 3 vols. (Paris, 1951–55).

31

The architects and their *maîtres d'ateliers* in chronological order: Théodore Ballu (Lebas), 1844–45; Alexis Paccard (Huyot and Lebas), 1845–46; Philippe Titeux (Blouet and Debret), 1846; Jacques Tétaz (Huyot and Lebas), 1847–48; Prosper Debuisson (Leclère), 1848; Louis-Jules André (Huyot and Lebas), 1851; Charles Garnier (Lebas), 1852; Louis-Victor Louvet (Huyot, Leveil, and Lebas), 1855.

32

C. Lévêque, *La Science du beau* (Paris, 1861; 2nd ed., 1872), II, p. 29, note.

33

Radet, *L'Ecole française d'Athènes*, p. 51, lists the publications of the students at the Ecole.

34

Especially his *Acropole d'Athènes*, 2 vols. (Paris, 1853–54), and *Etudes sur la Pelopenèse* (Paris, 1855). See also his reminiscences of his thinking in these years: *Fouilles et découvertes*, 2 vols. (Paris, 1873). His notes survive in the Cabinet des Manuscrits of the Bibliothèque Nationale.

35

F. C. Penrose, *An Investigation of the Principles of Athenian Architecture* (London, 1851); A. Paccard, *Mémoire explicative de la restauration du Parthénon . . .* (1845), Ecole des Beaux-Arts, MS 241, published with Paccard's drawings in the catalogue *Paris . Rome . Athènes*, pp. 351–368.

36

E. Burnouf, "Les Propylées," *Archives des missions scientifiques et littéraires*, 1 (1850): 22.

37

"L'art grec, né tout entier de la nature et inspiré par elle dès son origine, courba les degrés et le pavé des temples, les architraves, les frises, la base des frontons, comme la nature a courba la mer, les horizons, et les dos arrondis des montagnes." E. Burnouf, "Le Parthénon," *RDM*, 5S 20 (December 1, 1847): 842.

38

Lévêque, *La Science du beau*, introduction, as did his brilliant and prolific contemporaries at the Ecole Normale Supérieure, for example, J.-A. Girard, in his *Le Sentiment religieux en Grèce d'Homère à Eschyle* (Paris, 1868).

39

"Energies expressives. Une certaine puissance . . . la force résistante de la matière inorganique." Ibid., 2nd ed., II, p. 20.

40

"Agrandie de toutes façons par l'architecture, la puissante résistance le la matière inorganique est, en même temps, soumise par cet art à un ordre visible qui ne laisse pas que de rappeler à plus d'un égard l'ordre animé des corps vivants." Ibid., II, p. 23.

41

"Privée de ce dynamisme interne, l'architecture en imite de son mieux les effets. Impuisante à réaliser l'unité de dedans en dehors par la dilatation, elle l'opère du dehors en dedans par la concentration." Ibid., II, pp. 23–24.

42

Ibid., II, p. 29, note.

43

We glimpse this in Burckhardt's notes from Kugler's lectures of 1839–40 published by W. Kaegi, *Jakob Burckhardt: eine Biographie* (Basel, 1950), II, pp. 32–35. See F. Kugler, "Architekturbriefe," *Zeitschrift für bildende Kunst, Baukunst und Kunstgewerbe* 7, no. 48 (November 27, 1856) to no. 51 (December 18, 1856).

44

Cf. the introduction of C. Neumann, *Jakob Burckhardt: Briefwechsel mit Heinrich von Geymüller* (Munich, 1914), pp. 8ff.

45

J. Burckhardt and W. Lubke, *Geschichte der Neueren Baukunst* (Stuttgart, 1878), I, especially para. 57, for example.

46

On Geymüller: Neumann, *Jakob Burckhardt*, pp. 3–15.

47

H. von Geymüller, *Die ursprunglichen Entwürfe für Sankt Peter in Rom von Bramante, Raphael Santi, Fra Giocondo, den San Gallo, u. a. . . .* (Paris, 1875).

48

Most particularly Blanc's articles on architecture of 1861–64 that were to form part of his *Grammaire des arts du dessin* (Paris, 1867).

49

"Cette impression mystérieuse"; "L'âme jouit d'un vrai bonheur à séjourner dans ces lieux; il semble qu'elle se dilate dans l'édifice et en occupe exactement tout l'espace: elle ne voudrait le sentir ni plus grand ni plus petit. Ce charme provient de l'harmonie des proportions du volume intérieure." "Trois Dessins inedits de Raphael," *GBA* 2S, 3 (1870, 2): 79–91, specifically p. 87.

50
E. Saisset, "Un nouvel essai d'esthétique," *RDM* (November 15, 1861): 405–432.

51
"Mon estime et mon admiration pour l'arc ne sont pas moins vives que pour l'ordre, elles sont seulement d'une nature tout différente.

"D'abord je pose en principe que l'un ne doit pas prendre la place de l'autre: l'ordre appartient à la poésie, il est lyrique, parle noblement, déclame et chante.

"L'arc appartient à la prose, il est positif, travaille, sert et porte.

"L'ordre est noble, il est maître et commande; l'arc est plébien, serviteur et obéit.

"L'arc n'est rien par lui-même comme terme d'art, il ne compte que par un nouvel élément qui lui est étranger et superposé, l'ornementation. . . .

"L'arc seul est impuissant à constituer une architecture, l'arc n'est qu'un moyen de construction. . . .

"Si on admettait l'équivalence de l'ordre et de l'arc, et non la suprématie du premier sur le second, la raison d'utilité se présentant à chaque instant, l'empire d'abord partagé passerait exclusivement à l'arc pour faire oublier la la loi artistique de l'ordre." P. Sédille, *Joseph-Louis Duc, architecte (1802–1879)* (Paris, 1879), p. 10.

52
"Sans l'ordre, que pouvaient être nos monuments? N'était-ce pas l'ordre qui, par ses proportions réglées sur celle de l'homme, devenait l'unité et la mesure des édifices? . . .

"Au moyen âge même, les ordres étaient incorporés aux piliers, d'abord sur leurs faces principales, puis sur les angles et aux points qui indiquaient un effort de portée. C'était la condition de beauté de ces monuments, malgré les sacrifices de toutes proportions dans les ordres. Sans ces derniers vestiges d'essence poétique il ne pouvait rester que des masses de matière inerte.

"La fiction devait occuper la première place dans l'architecture . . . elle en était l'essence. Le temple grec n'était-il pas une légende de pierre? Tous les membres qui le composaient étaient autant d'objets naturels qui, par leur transmutation en pierre, non par imitation, mais bien par traduction, devenaient autant de fictions ou de mensonges. C'est de cette opération mystérieuse de création entre la nature et le coeur de l'homme que l'art était né. C'est cette incorporation de la nature avec la matière, oeuvre presque divine, qui était tout le dogme de l'architecture; le reste appartenait à la terre, le reste n'était que de la construction." Ibid., p. 7.

53
Geymüller, *Die ursprunglichen Entwürfe für Sankt Peter*, p. 5, for example.

54
Sédille, *Duc*, p. 6.

55
Ent, VI, pp. 212ff.

56
Neil Levine's master's thesis for Yale is a brilliant elucidation of this in the context of American architecture: "The Idea of Frank Furness' Buildings" (1967).

57

Pol Abraham, *Viollet-le-Duc et le rationalisme médiévale* (Paris, 1934). See more recently J. Fitchen, *The Construction of Gothic Cathedrals* (Oxford, 1961), and Robert Mark's structural studies of Gothic cathedrals, especially (with William W. Clark) "The First Flying Buttresses: a New Reconstruction of the Nave of Notre Dame de Paris," *Art Bulletin* 66, no. 1 (March 1984): 47–65, and his volume *Experiments in Gothic Structure* (Cambridge, Mass., 1982).

58

Recently thoroughly studied by Pérouse de Montclos in his *L'Architecture à la française* (Paris, 1982).

59

"Là, tout se tient, tout est lié par une pensée claire. L'exécution, comme il arrive toujours, répond à la composition; elle est belle et pure. On sent l'artiste, chose rare dans notre temps, qui respecte son art et le public." *Ent*, II, p. 209, note.

60

D d'A, "Ordre."

61

AN F^{13}1244, N III Seine 1152. Cf. *L'Artiste* 3 (1832): 176–177, an attack on the inexpressiveness of Alavoine's project. Also: C. Daly, "Monument de Juillet élevé sur la Place de la Bastille," *RGA* 1 (1840): cols. 406–419, 665–690, 746–759.

62

AN 246 A.P. 14: a note announcing the visit, set for May 20, 1838.

63

"Il y a une partie dans laquelle M. Duc a vu que, même de loin, on pût voir ce qu'il y avait d'élégant et de triomphal dans sa colonne; cette partie c'est le chapiteau. La colonne de Vendôme, toute chargée de ses riches sculptures, a pu se passer de cet ornament; M. Duc a mis au contraire tout le luxe de sa colonne dans la coiffure que lui a dessinée. Chez les anciens, quand l'architecture commença a s'émanciper des formes austères de l'origine, le chapiteau devint la partie de la décoration où ils experimèrent par des signes particuliers le souvenir attaché à chacun de leurs monuments. C'était là qu'on gravait les symboles mystérieux de l'art. Comme l'âme se peint mieux sur le visage que dans les autres parties du corps, de même la pensée de l'édifice se lisait dans le chapiteau plus clairement que partout ailleurs. M. Duc a imité cette habitude des anciens; aussi la composition de son chapiteau est la partie la plus savante, la plus riche et la plus intéressante de son dessin. La partie inférieure du chapiteau est ornée d'un rang de palmes qui sont comme le dernier echo de la plainte lugubre qui s'élève vers le ciel; au-dessus de cette base commence le mélange des symboles de la victoire. Au milieu d'un végétation élancée qui s'en va porter appui aux volutes des angles, on voit passer les extremités du panier dont nous avons aperçu l'indication dans les régions inférieures de la colonne; c'est de l'intérieur de ce panier que se déploient les jets puissants qui supportent le tailloir. Mais autour de la corbeille de fête quatres enfants d'une allure audacieuse forment une ronde animée, tenant leurs pieds posés sur les feuilles funéraires, portant dans leurs mains la guilande des réjouissance, appuyant leurs têtes au-dessus de celles du lion, lesquelles escortées de deux hautes feuilles triomphales, comprenant les fleurons. La balustrade qui repose sur le tailloir a été dessinée avec une rare élégance, de manière à lui servir de diadème." "La Colonne de Juillet," *MP* 8 (1840): 209–211.

64

Although very rarely played, Berlioz's composition has been recorded by the Paris Police Band under the direction of Désiré Dondeyne for Nonsuch (H-71368).

65

"Un mode de transmission de la pensée indépéndant de toute convention humaine." (Reynaud, 1834); "la véritable écriture des peuples" (Fortoul, 1842).

66

Defining the term Néo-Grec is a thorny matter, and I refer the reader to Levine's dissertation or its summation in *EBA*.

67

The presentation drawing survives in the Cabinet des Dessins at the Louvre (G. Monnier, *Dessins d'architecture du XVe au XIXe siècle* (Paris, 1972), entry 75, p. 36), and other drawings are preserved in the Labrouste material in the Académie d'Architecture (P. Saddy, *Henry Labrouste, architecte, 1801–1875* (Paris, 1977), pp. 22–24). See *RGA* 2 (1841): cols. 613–614; pl. 32; *L'Artiste* 2S, 8 (1841): 273–276, 289–293.

68

RGA 1 (1840): cols. 614.

69

AN 246 A.P. 14.

70

Published in the folio of loose lithographs of his work by A. Joilly.

71

La Quotidienne, November 11, 1841; *RGA* 1 (1840): cols. 595–596.

72

The ceremony is described in *L'Illustration* 9 (February 1841): 41–48. See J. Boison, *Le Retour des cendres* (Paris, 1973), with bibliography. Labrouste's drawings survive in the Académie d'Architecture, Paris.

73

The tomb was thoroughly treated in *RGA* 8 (1849): cols. 437–445. See also, *Journal des artistes* (1844): 388–389; *Le Constitutionel*, November 12, 1844.

74

"Que l'oeil suit avec le plus de plaisir . . . le plus noble et le plus fier."

75

RGA 10 (1852): cols. 42–43, pl. 9. See Levine, *EBA*, pp. 408–411.

76

"Danjoy . . . prétandait s'affranchir, au besoin, de toute forme consacrée par la science ou par la tradition, et voulait le sentiment dominât tout, même la matière. Partant de là, il avait imaginé une sorte d'architecture imitative, qui eut été comme une poétique peinture en relief des choses de la vie, comme un art nouveau tenant le milieu entre le rêve et la réalité." A. Lance, *Dictionnaire des architectes français* (Paris, 1872) notes to his entries "Danjoy" and "Constant-Defeux."

77

The Second Empire 1852–1870: Art in France Under Napoleon III (Philadelphia, 1979), IV-10, pp. 181–182.

78

E d'A, III (July 1853): col. 93. *Moniteur des architects* (November 15, 1855), p. 317. The Salon reviews of these years regularly described these extravagances. At the end of the Second Empire, François Thierry-Ladrange edited a short-lived journal of radical projects under the title *Architecture* (1869–71).

79

Published in C. Daly, *Architecture funéraire contemporaine* (Paris, 1871), II, D, pl. 12. Because it is a reworking of an existing monument, I have not been able to date it firmly.

80

C. Clément, *JD*, November 17, 1868. The Mylasa tomb was repeatedly illustrated, for example, in M.-G.-F.-A. de Choiseul-Gouffier, *Voyage pittoresque de la Grèce*, 3 vols. (Paris, 1782–1822), I (1782), pls. 85–89. Other, similar capitals: C. Texier, *Description de l'Asie Mineur*, 3 vols. (Paris, 1839–49), III, pls. 185–187, 189.

81

See F. Pigeory, *Les Monuments de Paris*, pp. 345–360.

82

The iconography is summarized by Clément, *JD*, November 17, 1868. From left to right: *Prudence* and *Vérité* (by Dumont); *Châtiment* and *Protection* (by Jouffroy); *Force* and *Equité* (By Jaley). In the center of the inner wall of the Vestibule de Harlay is *Justice* by Perraud and *Loi* by Duret.

83

Cf. Henri Peyre, *Bibliographie critique de l'héllenisme en France*.

84

Dated June 1848 and published as "Les Propylées" in the *Archives des missions scientifiques et littéraires* I (1850): 8–38. Titeux and Chaudet's reconstruction is published in the catalogue *Paris . Rome . Athènes*, pp. 172–177.

85

Beulé published the journal he kept during the excavations: *Fouilles et découvertes*, (Paris, 1873), II.

86

E. Beulé, *Acropole d'Athènes*, pp. 58–59.

87

"Les Grecs semblent avoir recherché avec un soin particulier, dans leurs grands ensembles d'architecture, les accidents, soit de construction, soit de perspective. C'est ce que l'on remarque partout, dans la moindre maison de Pompéi, comme dans les plus grands édifices d'Athènes." Ibid., p. 366.

88

Ibid., p. 23.

89

C. Garnier, *Le Nouvel Opéra de Paris*, 2 vols. (Paris, 1878–81), I, pp. 423ff; II, pp. 109ff, 272ff.

90

"La sculpture statuaire faisant partie de la décoration d'un édifice, doit emprunter quelques données à la simple sculpture ornamentale." Ibid., II, p. 424.

91

In two cases recorded in the minutes of the Commission des Beaux-Arts, artists insisted that the members chose between projects made to their ideas and models made following the directions of the architects, but in both the Commission supported the architects.

92

The proclamation is reproduced in *RGA* 22 (1864): cols. 214–215.

93

RGA 27 (1869): cols. 183–184. Charles Garnier's papers at the library of the Ecole des Beaux-Arts include the minutes of the jury meetings and the voting, carton 545, II. Professor Christopher Mead has kindly pointed this material out to me.

94

The painters: Couder, Robert-Fleury, Cabanel, Gérôme, Amaury-Duval, Barrias, Baudry, Jalabert, Larivière, Lenepveu; the sculptors: Dumont, Guillaume, Bayre, J.-A. Barre, Cabet, Carpeaux, Crauk, Gumery, G.-J. Thomas, Triqueti.

95

The voting, as recorded in Garnier's papers:

Round	1	2	3	4	5	6	7	8	9	10	11	12	13
Duc	9	9	10	9	10	10	11	12	13	13	13	12	15
Lefuel	7	7	8	8	8	8	7	6	4	4	3	3	2
Garnier	3	3	3	2	2	3	3	2	1	1			1
Baudry			1	1	1								
Hesse													
Cabanel													
Guillaume													
Gumery													
Perraud	3	4	3	3	3	3	4	3	3	3	4	3	1
blank	7	6	4	6	6	5	4	6	8	8	9	11	9

96

C. Daly, "Le Prix de cent mille francs," *RGA* 27 (1869): cols. 177–183.

97

Charles Millard's research into Préault's sculptures for Lefuel at the Louvre, which he has kindly shared with me, indicate that the artists were given relatively loose rein there.

98

T. Zeldin, *Emile Ollivier and the Liberal Empire of Napoleon III* (Oxford, 1963). See also his *Political System of Napoleon III*, cited above.

99

Garnier papers, Ecole des Beaux-Arts carton, 545, II.

Seven

BIBLIOTHEQUE NATIONALE

1

DR, "Restauration," VIII (1866), pp. 14–34; E. Beulé, *Histoire de l'art grec avant Périclès*, (Paris 1868), p. 33.

2

"Il cherchait à faire transparaître à l'extérieur d'un édifice ce qui était à l'intérieur." L.-A. Hardy, *RGA* 43 (1887): col. 244.

3

"Transparency" after 1750 was an ideal of great power but also of various definition. This was the term most often (but also most casually) used to express the congruence of meaning and form in philosophy, for example by Lessing and later Emerson (David Welberry, *Lessing's Laocoon: Semiotics and Aesthetics in the Age of Reason*, Cambridge, 1984). "Transparent" was the opposite of conventional, the arbitrary signification of one thing by another. The term was also used to express the incisiveness sought in scientific langauge as it developed during these years (Barbara Stafford, *Voyage into Substance: Art, Science, Nature and the Illustrated Travel Account, 1760–1840*, Cambridge, Mass., 1984). By the early nineteenth century it had also taken on a moral connotation when applied to personal deportment: it stood for an ideal of natural openness in contrast to artificial posing (Karen Halttunen, *Confidence Men and Painted Women*, New Haven, 1982).

4

Louis XIV and Versailles are the most celebrated demonstrations of this assumption. See Nicolas le Camus de Mézières, *Le Génie de l'architecture, ou l'analogie de cet art avec nos sensations* (Paris, 1780).

5

"Ce fut l'intérêt personnel, qui . . . amena la décadence de l'architecture; et ces palais somptueux construits pour que de simples particuliers dans les derniers temps des Grands Empires, attestent assez que les arts, en prostituant, pour ainsi dire, leurs oeuvres à la mode et aux caprices de la fortune, périrent eux-mêmes avec les institutions auxquelles ils devaient leurs origines."

The manuscripts of Huyot's lectures survive in the library of the Institut d'Art et d'Archéologie, Paris. Katherine Fisher Taylor is exploring Huyot's ideas in her doctoral dissertation on the Palais de Justice.

6

For example, A. Pérez-Gómez, *Architecture and the Crisis of Modern Science* (Cambridge, Mass., 1983). On Huyot in David's atelier: E. Delécluze, *Louis David: son école et son temps* (Paris, 1855), p. 93.

7

Fontaine's diaries, now in the library of the Ecole des Beaux-Arts, and just published by that institution (1987), document his project under Louis-Philippe to produce a volume of plans and descriptions of all the royal residences of France for the personal use of the King. Manuscripts of historical notices on these buildings by A.-L.-T. Vaudoyer, now mostly deposited in the Musée des Arts Décoratifs, might form part of this project.

8

C. Percier and P.-F. L. Fontaine, *Plans de plusieurs châteaux, palais et residences des souverains de France, d'Italie, d'Espagne et de Russie* (Paris, 1833), p. 342.

9

"Se dit de l'état qui tient une personne distinguée par son rang, par son dignité, etc. . . .
Il se dit encore de la bonne mine, de la figure imposante d'un homme grand et bien
fait."

10

Percier and Fontaine, *Sacre de S. M. l'Empereur Napoléon dans l'église metropolitaine de
Paris, le xi frémaire, an 13* (Paris, n.d.); *Recueil des décorations exécutées dans l'église Notre-
Dame de Paris pour la cérémonie de 11 décembre, 1804, et pour la fête de la distribution des aigles
au Champs de Mars, du 5 décembre, 1804* (Paris, 1804); *Marriage de Napoléon Ier avec Marie
Louise . . .* (Paris, 1810). The publication of Charles X's *sacre* would have been magnifi-
cent, but it was never completed: Ann Martin, "Charles Nodier, historiographe du
Sacre de Charles X," *GBA* 6S, 72 (November, 1968): 265–270.

11

See J. Barbey d'Aurevilly, *Du Dandysme et de G. Brummel* (Paris, 1844).

12

Recently surveyed in two Paris exhibitions with compendious (if necessarily summary)
catalogues: *Colbert, 1619–1683* (Paris, 1983); *Collections de Louis XIV: dessins, albums,
manuscrits* (Paris, 1977). The classic study in English: W. H. Lewis, *The Splendid Century*
(New York, 1954), especially chs. 1 and 2.

13

H. Delaborde, *Notice sur la vie et les ouvrages de M. Henri Labrouste* (Paris, 1878).

14

It is informative to examine the bureaucratic management of this plant in the nineteenth
century. Colbert's *surintendance* was finally dissolved by a decree of June 15, 1791; and
after the disestablishment of the Monarchy, its components placed in the Ministry of
the Interior. (The history of the services are outlined in Bequet, *Répertoire du Droit
administratif,* 24 vols. Paris, 1885–1911.) One element, the Bâtiments Civils, was carefully reorganized and made a self-sufficient administration under the Conseil des
Bâtiments Civils with a clear identity regardless of its shifts to the Ministère des
Travaux Publics (May 19, 1830), the Ministry of Commerce (March 31, 1831), back to
the Ministry of the Interior (1834), then back to the Ministère des Travaux Publics
(February 19, 1839), and finally to the Ministry of the Interior (February 11, 1852)
before being placed in the Ministère d'Etat (February 14, 1853; renamed the Ministère
d'Etat et de la Maison du Roi, June 23, 1863), where it remained until the creation of
Ollivier's Ministère des Beaux-Arts (January 2, 1870) and its transformation into his
Ministère des Lettres, Sciences et Arts (May 15, 1870). The sovereign had lost control
over the Bâtiments Civils (even when under Napoleon III it was part of his personal
Ministère d'Etat), but a closer bureaucratic relationship was maintained over the Manufactures Nationaux, the Opera, the administration of the fine arts (Salons, awards,
schools), and most particularly over the Palais Nationaux. (The administration was
outlined annually in the *Almanach impérial.* See also AN O^{5}40.) This last was a corps of
fountain engineers, gardeners, and architects in charge of maintaining the royal residences; and it remained part of the sovereign's household until the Third Republic,
when it was combined with the Bâtiments Civils to create the Direction des Bâtiments
Civils et Palais Nationaux, which exists to this day. Under Napoleon, in 1813, there
were ten architects in this administration (led by Pierre Fontaine, in charge of the
Louvre, the Tuileries, and the "bâtiments impériaux à Paris") overseeing fifteen palaces
under the direction of a Comité Consultatif des Bâtiments de la Couronne (*Almanach
impérial,* 1813, p. 60).

Under the Restoration a rejuvenated and expanded administration of the Fêtes et Cérémonies—from 1818 to 1830 under the artistic direction of the architects Hittorff and Joseph Lecointe—attempted to revive the theatrical "représentation" of the monarch as well, as Françoise Waquet has recently documented in *Les Fêtes royales sous la Restauration, ou l'ancien régime retrouvé* (Geneva, 1981). Not unexpectedly, however, Louis-Philippe's bureaucratic regime was simultaneously the heyday of the independant Bâtiments Civils and the nadir of the Palais Royaux. The *Almanach royal* in 1847 shows no Comité Consultatif and lists only three architects in the Service des Palais, Maisons et Résidences Royales, the faithful Fontaine being in charge of the Louvre, the Tuileries, the Elysée, and the Palais Royal. This situation changed radically with the proclamation of the Second Empire, however, when Napoleon III created the Ministère d'Etat under Achille Fould, housed in the New Louvre and administering all the state's art activities (including the Bâtiments Civils) under the Emperor's eye. The Ministry records show that already in 1853 there were ten palaces each with an *architecte-en-chef* (paid 6000 francs per annum) and a staff of *inspecteurs* (up to five, as in the cases of Versailles and the Elysée, where work was in progress) as well as staffs for the *eaux* at Versailles and Marly with architects; forty-four designers in all (AN O^{5}40). When work was begun on the New Louvre, a separate administation was created within the Ministère d'Etat, supervised by Visconti and then Lefuel (the latter given the title Architecte de l'Empereur in 1855 and an astronomical salary; see AN series 64 Aj, and especially the pay books, 64 Aj 65–68), as well as a Commission de Controle des Travaux du Louvre consisting of engineers and administrators.

15

M. Steinhauser, *Die Architektur der Pariser Oper . . .* (Munich, 1969). Also: C. Garnier, *A travers les Arts* (Paris, 1867); *Le Théâtre* (Paris, 1871); *Le nouvel Opéra de Paris*, 2 vols. and atlas (Paris, 1878–81). Detailed studies of Garnier and his Opera are currently underway by Professor Christopher Mead of the University of New Mexico and by Henri Loyrette of the Musée d'Orsay. Garnier's papers are divided among several Parisian institutions, most importantly the Bibliothèque de l'Opéra and the Ecole des Beaux-Arts. See the biographical manuscript left by his wife, published in *L'Architecture* 38 (1920): 377–390.

16

J.-L. Pascal, "H. Lefuel," *RGA* 38 (1881): col. 263.

17

See ibid. and H. Delaborde, "M. Lefuel, architecte, sa vie et ses oeuvres," *E d'A*, 39 (1882), pp. 83–88; as well as the shorter, ceremonial eulogies of Questel Ginain and Alfred Normand, "Lefuel, architecte, membre de l'Institut," *Bulletin de la société centrale des architectes* 8 (June 1881).

18

For a comparison of the two men's conceptions see the catalogue *The Second Empire 1852–1870: Art in France Under Napoleon III* (Philadelphia, 1979), entries I-19, I-20 and I-33. See also: L. Vitet, "Le Louvre," *Revue contemporaine*, September 15, 1852; L. Vitet, "Le Nouveau Louvre, *RDM* 2S, 64 (July 1, 1866): 57–93; L. Hautecoeur, *Histoire du Louvre . . .* (Paris, 1928); C. Aulanier, *Le Louvre sous Napoléon III* (Paris, 1953).

19

Mémoires du Comte Horace de Viel-Castel, edited by L. Léonzon le Duc, 6 vols. (Paris, 1883–84), III, p. 250; IV, pp. 59, 65, 74, 147, 287.

20

The other jurors were Lebas, Hittorff, de Gisors, Lefuel, Lesueur, Lenormand, Caristie, and the Comte de Cardaillac, See C. Daly, "Concours pour le grand Opéra de Paris," *RGA* 19 (1861): cols. 14–51, 76–134. Viollet-le-Duc's project has been frequently reproduced and has been discussed most recently and definitively in the catalogue *Viollet-le-Duc*, (Paris, 1984), pp. 200–207.

21

MU, February 11, 1861; May 13, 1863; May 20, 1863; August 5, 1867.

22

"C'est, à coup sûr, le projet le plus individuel de toute l'exposition. Il ne rapelle aucun monument connu."

23

"Elle concilie les exigences de l'architecture et celles de la vie." "Une rampe gracieusement évasée et dont les marches sont presque insensibles conduit à un palier d'où partent deux autres rampes atteignant le premier étage par des pentes douces. Le cage de l'escalier a pour supports des colonnes accouplées d'ordre ionique, en marbre sérancolin, sur lesquelles s'appuient d'immenses arcades et que relient d'étage en étage des balcons à balustrades richement ornés où les curieux pourront s'accouder comme dans une toile de Paul Véronèse, spectateurs et spectacle en même temps, pour voir à leur aise cette merveille de la civilization moderne qu'on appelle une sortie d'Opéra, c'est-à-dire cette cascade de diamants, de perles, de plumes, de fleurs, d'épaules blanches, de satin, de velours, moirés, de gauzes, de dentelles, que cette fois écumera sur des degrés de marbre blanc, au scintillement des plus vives lumières, encaisée par une architecture féerique." *MU*, May 20, 1863.

24

"L'Opéra, c'est le temple de la civilization moderne, c'est là qu'aboutissent l'art, le luxe, l'élégance, tous les raffinements de *la haute vie*. Les heureux du monde qui le fréquentent sont difficiles et veulent y retrouver les somptuosités de leurs palais ou de leurs hôtels.

"Il faut être à la fois charmant et grandiose, coquet et pur, à la mode et classique; le problème n'est pas aisé à résoudre. M. Garnier a réussi dans cette tâche presque impossible."

25

"Nous exprimons l'opinion que un si grand developpement de splendeur architecturale doit indiquer la destination du lieu, les éléments n'en doivent pas être emprunté à tel autre édifice de destaination divers, mais indiquer au contraire la destination spéciale de l'opéra par un caractère déterminé, caractère qui, selon nous, doit participer également de la beauté des formes extérieures et de l'apparance de bien-être intérieur que recherche la bonne compagnie dans les lieux qu'elle fréquente." AN F^{21}830.

26

"Si le grand escalier central est un endroit somptueux et mouvementé, si l'ordonnance décorative est élégante, si l'animation qui règne sur les emmarchements est un spectacle interessant et varié, il y aura avantage à ce que chacun profite. Si l'on dispose alors les murs latéraux de la cage de telle sorte qu'ils soient largement ouverts, tous les personnages circulant à chaque étage pourront à leur gré se distraire par la vue du grand vaisseau et par la circulation incessante de la foule, qui gravit les rampes ou les descend.
. . . Enfin en disposant des étoffes ou draperies tombantes, des girandoles, des candé-

labres ou des lustres, puis des marbres et des fleurs, de la couleur partout, on fera de tout cet ensemble une composition somptueuse et brillante qui rappellera en nature quelques unes des splendides dispositions que Véronèse a fixés sur ses toiles. La lumière qui étincellera, les toilettes qui resplendiront, les figures qui seront animées et souriiantes, les rencontres qui se produiront, tout aura un air de fête et de plaisir, et sans se rendre compte de la part qui doit revenir à l'architecture dans cet effet magnifique, tout le monde le jouira et tout le monde rende ainsi, par son impression heureuse, hommage à cet grand art, si puissant dans ses manifestations, si élevé dans ses résultats." *Le Théâtre*, pp. 85–86.

27

"Les théories ont surtout pour but l'explication de ce qui a été fait; mais elles seraient parfois bien dangereuses si l'on les écoutait avant de produire. De prime dabord, l'artiste doit composer et exécuter même, sur se préoccuper outre mesure de ces axiomes et de ces raisons dogmatiques. C'est par l'intuition seulement qu'elles doivent pénétrer dans l'esprit; c'est par intuition qu'elles doivent se manifester, et lorsqu'il en est ainsi, elles n'en ont que plus de force, le sentiment étant d'accord avec la logique. . . .

"Lorsque je prenais le crayon pour composer, je me sentais parfois envahi par ces idées théoriques qui se dressaient devant moi comme un pédagogue se dresse devant un enfant qui fait une faute; mais je vous assure qu'au lieu de chercher à raisonner en ces moments-là avec ces sages visions, je les chassais de mon mieux, jusqu'au moment où le sentiment seul, et tout seul, avait guidé mes yeux, ma main et ma pensée." *Le nouvel Opéra*, I, pp. 121–122.

28

"L'impression instinctive de la foule, qui appelle la Bourse un temple grec." *L'Habitation humaine* (with A. Ammann) (Paris, 1892), p. 809.

29

Appearing in several editions of different degrees of splendor between that year and 1887. Cf. C. Blanc, *Grammaire des arts décoratifs* (Paris, 1882).

30

"Qui dit: 'table' prononce un grand mot." "Envitons, surtout, qu'une composition énigmatique se dresse, comme un point d'interrogation fatal, devant un honnête homme qui dîne." Harvard, *L'Art dans la maison* (Paris, 1883), pp. 324, 335.

31

Bibliothèque de l'Opéra, *Charles Garnier et l'Opéra* (Paris, 1961), p. 11.

32

S. Giedion, "The Reign of the Upholsterer," in *Mechanization Takes Command* (Oxford, 1948), pp. 364–388.

33

A. Houssaye, *Histoire de l'art français au dix-huitième siècle* (Paris, 1860), and especially the product of the Goncourt brothers' efforts to sketch a "histoire de la société française au dix-huitième siècle," their *Portraits intimes du dix-huitième siècle*, 2 vols. (Paris, 1857 and 1858) and *La Femme au dix-huitième siècle* (Paris, 1862).

34

"But de ce livre," I, pp. 16–19.

35

Professor Elizabeth Grossman at the Rhode Island School of Design, working on Cret, has developed this theme, especially in her "Paul Cret and the Pan American Union Competition," *Modulus* 1 (1982): 30–39.

36

"Il faisait étudier par un de ses élèves un théâtre dont la salle et la scène étaient visibles à l'extérieure." L.-A. Hardy, *RGA* 43 (1887): col. 244.

37

RGA 19 (1861): pl. 35.

38

"La pierre, pour lui, n'était qu'un moyen de rendre une idée, de transmettre un sentiment; c'était la page d'un livre où l'on doit lire. . . .

"Il cherchait à cristalliser un souvenir, une idée, une forme, une allusion. . . .

"Il nous a fait étudier un tombeau de famille sous forme de la maison paternelle, l'arbre qui l'ombrage devenant lui-même monument." *RGA* 43 (1887): col. 244.

39

"Cherchant la raison des formes dans la construction, mais non pas d'une manière absolue et exclusive, il tenta d'amener à l'idéalization des sentiments et des formes, à la verité de l'expression extérieure du contenu." L. Dassy, *Forum artistique* (February 1888).

40

For example, Gérard de Nerval in his story "Isis" in his collection *Les Filles de feu* (1854) or Gautier in his story "Arria Marcella" and his novel *Le Roman de la Momie* (1856). See Jacques Bousquet, *Les Thèmes du rêve dans la litérature romantique* (Paris, 1964).

41

"Par la manière dont sont rapprochés et réunies ces deux matières si différentes, la pierre et la fonte, le pilier paraît lourd et l'arc maigre. Il y a quelque chose de choquante a voir tant de force dépensée pour supporter si peu. Nous savons parfaitement tout ce qu'on peut nous objecter sur la puissance comparée de chacun de ces matériaux; mais il ne faut pas oublier que tout ce qui est vrai n'est pas toujours beau, et que ce qui est solide et suffisant, matériallement, peut bien ne pas satisfaire nos yeux. On voit et on sent avant de raisonner et plus vite qu'on ne raissonne. Il faut donc, de toute nécessité, apres avoir calculer mathématiquement la solidité, calculer, avec moins d'exactitude, l'impression que la forme doit produire. Cette règle n'a pas été suffisamment observée dans le détail que nous venons de signaler." A. Hermant, "La Bibliothèque Sainte-Geneviève," *L'Artiste* 5S, 7 (December 1, 1851): 129–131, specifically p. 130.

42

"Le ciel—le plafond, ne représente pas autre chose." Ibid., p. 130.

43

The ceiling has been repainted white, evidently about 1965.

44

See the material gathered in E. Börsch-Suppan, *Garten- Landschafts- und Paradiesmotive im Innenraum: ein ikonographische Untersuchung* (Berlin, 1967). She mentions the Salle des Imprimés only in passing, and the Bibliothèque Sainte-Geneviève not at all.

45

The subjects, at the left, from front to back: Saint Bernard, l'Hôpital, Montaigne, Descartes, Pascal, Poussin, Molière, Corneille, La Fontaine, Racine; at the right: Bossuet, Fénelon, Masillon, Montesquieu, Voltaire, Rousseau, Buffon, Mirabeau, Laplace, Cuvier.

46

"J'aurais bien désiré qu'un vaste espace planté de grands arbres et décoré de statues fût disposé en avant de l'édifice, pour l'éloigner du bruit de la voie publique, et préparer au recueillement les personnes qui le fréquentent. Un beau jardin eût été sans doute une introduction convenable à un monument consacré à l'étude; mais l'exiguïté du terrain ne permettait pas une semblable disposition, il fallait y renoncer. Alors le jardin que j'aurais aimé à traverser pour arriver au monument, je l'ai fait peindre sur les murs du vestibule, seul intermédiaire entre la place publique et la bibliothèque. Mon jardin en peinture ne vaut pas sans doute de belles allées de marronniers et de platanes; mais il a l'avantage de présenter des arbres toujours verts et toujours en fleurs, même au mois de décembre; et puis, sans avoir égard au climat de Paris, je pouvais, dans cette terre fertile de l'imagination, planter des arbres de tous les pays, et placer auprès de saint Bernard des palmiers d'Orient, auprès de Racine des orangers en fleurs, auprès de la Fontaine un chêne et un roseau, et des myrtes et des lauriers auprès de Poussin.

"Le Vestibule est un peu sombre; mais les lecteurs, en le traversant croiront peut-être un instant que cette obscurité n'est autre chose que l'ombrage des arbres qui frappent les regards, et l'on me pardonnera, je l'espère." *RGA* 10 (1852): col. 382.

47

"On voit on entrant qu'ici on est en bonne compagnie." Ibid.

48

"L'impression que l'on doit ressentir à la vue d'un monument, c'est un sentiment de grandeur, de noblesse, de calme et de confiance. . . .

"Les moyens que l'on doit employer pour donner à l'architecture ce caractère de noblesse et de sécurité, découlent tous d'un grand principe, c'est-à-dire de l'harmonie des proportions et des rapports bien entendus des pleins et des vides. Or quoi de plus oppose à ces données que les constructions en fer? En effet, dans ce genre de construction, les points d'appui sont maigres, élancés, et ont moins d'importance que les parties qu'ils supportaient.

"C'est donc l'impuissance du fer à donner des masses et des points d'appui suffisants pour les yeux, qui force à rejetter de toute construction artistique." C. Garnier, "Architecture en fer," *Le Musée des sciences* 41 (February 11, 1857), pp. 321–322. I am indebted to Christopher Mead for the reference.

49

This analysis was originally suggested to me in 1973 by the architect Michael Graves, to whom I remain profoundly indebted here.

50

Labrouste's son Léon published a short history of the construction: *La Bibliothèque Nationale: ses bâtiments et ses constructions* (Paris, 1885). Also: AN F^{13}1246, F^{21}750, F^{21}1355–1361, F^{21}2915. See also: P. Mérimée, *Correspondence générale*, edited by M. Parturier (Paris, 1941ff.), VII, p. 112; VIII, p. 396; IX, p. 181; XVI, pp. 360–361.

51

G. Guilleminot, "La Bibliothèque du Roi," *Colbert*, pp. 379–381, with bibliography.

52

Published as *Mémoire sur les moyens de procurer à la Bibliothèque du Roi les avantages que ce monument exige* (Paris, 1785), with engraved plates illustrating the project. Neil Levine informs me that a copy of the plates survives in Labrouste's library.

53

The drawings accompanying this project are in the Labrouste papers in the Cabinet des Estampes at the Bibliothèque Nationale, and are partially published in P. Saddy, *Henry Labrouste, architecte, 1801–1875* (Paris, 1977), p. 77, and *The Second Empire*, entry I-14.

54

The members of the Conseil at the time were Duban, Caristie, and de Gisors with the *members temporaires* Gilbert, Paccard, Duc, and Grisart.

55

AN F^{21}1361.

56

AN F^{21}1361.

57

Reviews appeared immediately in the *Moniteur des architectes* (1868), pp. 92–95; *L'Illustration,* May 30, 1868, pp. 341–346; and *MU*, June 12, 1868, p. 825.

58

"C'est le jardin d'Académus symbolisé; les peripatéticiens peuvent, par la pensée, lire en se promenant sous ces ombrages." *Moniteur des architectes*, 1868, p. 95.

59

"Die Bibliothek als Gewächshaus der Wissenschaft, als Triebhaus des Weisheit, und die Gelehrter als ihre Gärtner—welch trosliches Bild!" C. Beutler, "St.-Eugène und die Bibliothèque Nationale," *Miscellanea pro arte: Festschrift für Hermann Schnitzler* (Dusseldorf, n.d.), pp. 321–324.

60

D. Van Zanten, "The Architectural Polychromy of the 1830's" (Ph.D. dissertation, Harvard University, 1970), pp. 44–45.

61

The Second Empire, p. 38.

62

"L'architecte a pensée que ces peintures calmes et fraîches convenaient mieux pour décorer une salle destiné à l'étude que des sujets historiques qui auraient peut-être l'inconvénient de distraire les lecteurs." Labrouste papers, Académie d'architecture, Paris.

63

La Bibliothèque Nationale, pp. 63–66.

64

"Pas de souvenir, pas d'imitation." (Henri Crozic, *L'Illustration*, May 30, 1868, p. 343). Cf. H. Lacroix, *MU*, June 12, 1868, using the same words.

65

"Lorsque j'ai été au lycée, après ou avant les classes, j'allais étudier au jardin du Luxembourg, et surtout dans la pépinière. Là, je n'étais distrait par rien, mon regard ainsi que mon esprit reposaient avec bonheur sur la belle et luxuriante verdure qui m'entourait. J'ai pensé que dans un lieu d'étude la représentation de ce qui avait eu pour moi tant de charmé serait à la Bibliothèque une sans prétention d'abord et aussi comme une occasion de repos pour l'esprit des lecteurs occupant la salle." E. Bailly, *Notice sur M. Henri Labrouste* (Paris, 1876).

66

L. Halevy, *Carnets* (Paris, 1935), I, pp. 90–91 (March 17, 1866); H. Dabot, *Souvenirs et impressions d'un bourgois du Quartier Latin de Mai, 1854, à Mai, 1869* (Paris, 1899), p. 195 (March 18, 1866).

67

In an untitled essay in the *Chicago Architectural Club Journal* 2 (1982): 156–157.

68

See M. Darby and D. Van Zanten, "Owen Jones's Iron and Glass Buildings of the 1850's," *Architectura* (1974): 53–75.

69

G. Semper, "On the Study of Polychromy and Its Revival," *Museum of Classical Antiquities* 1 (1851): 228–255.

70

"Nous avions positivement changé de latitude: il semblait que l'artiste avait renouvelé le miracle de Promethée, et que lui aussi avait su dérober le feu du ciel pour illuminer son oeuver." C. Daly, *RGA* 6 (1845): col. 12. He was remembering a visit to London in 1839.

BIBLIOGRAPHY

Abraham, P. *Viollet-le-Duc et le rationalisme médiévale*. Paris: Vincent, Fréal, 1934.

Académie des Beaux-Arts, Paris. *Compte rendu de la séance annuelle publique*. . . . Paris: Firmin-Didot.

Académie des Beaux-Arts, Paris. *Considérations sur la question de savoir s'il est convenable au XIXe siècle de bâtir des églises en style gothique*. Paris: Firmin-Didot, 1846.

Actes du colloque international Viollet-le-Duc. Brussels: Pierre Mardaga, 1982.

Aicard, J. *Patria*. 2 vols. Paris: Dubochet, Le Chevalier, 1846.

Aulanier, C. *Le Louvre sous Napoléon III*. Paris: Musées Nationaux, 1953.

Auzas, P.-M. *Eugène Viollet-le-Duc, 1814–1879*. Paris: Caisse Nationale des Monuments Historiques et des Sites, 1965.

Bailly, E. *Notice sur M. Henri Labrouste*. Paris, 1876.

Baltard, L.-P. *Discours d'ouverture du cours de Théorie d'Architecture*. Paris: Crapelet, n.d.

Baltard, L.-P. *Introduction au cours de Théorie d'Architecture de l'année 1839*. Paris: Crapelet, 1839.

Baltard, L.-P. *Aperçu ou essai sur le bon goût dans les ouvrages d'art et architecture de l'année*. Paris: Didot, 1841.

Baltard, V. *Hommage à Félix Duban*. . . . Paris, 1871.

de Balzac, H. *Les Employés* (published originally as *La Femme supérieure*). Paris: Werdet, 1838.

Ballu, T. *Notice sur M. Léon Vaudoyer. Paris,* 1873.

de Baudot, A. *Eglises de bourgs et villages*. 2 vols. Paris: Morel, 1867.

Becherer, R. J. "Between Science and Sentiment: César Daly and the Formulation of Modern Architectural Theory." Doctoral dissertation, Cornell University, 1980.

Bequet, L. (continued by E. Laferrière). *Répertoire du Droit administratif*. 24 vols. Paris: P. Dupont, 1885–1911.

Bercé, F. *Les premiers travaux de la commission des monuments historiques, 1837–1848*. Paris: Picard, 1979.

de Bertier de Sauvigny, G. *La Restauration*. Paris: Flammarion, 1955.

Betz, J. *Bartholdi*. Paris: Minuit, 1954.

Beulé, C.-E. *Acropole d'Athènes*. 2 vols. Paris: Didot, 1853 and 1854.

Beulé, C.-E. *Etudes sur la Pelopenèse*. Paris: Didot, 1855.

Beulé, C.-E. *Histoire de l'art grec avant Périclès*. Paris: Didier, 1868.

Beulé, C.-E. *Fouilles et découvertes: résumées et discutées en vue de l'histoire de l'art.* 2 vols. Paris: Didier, 1873.

Beutler, C. "St.-Eugène und die Bibliothèque Nationale," *Miscellanea pro arte: Festschrift für Hermann Schnitzler.* Dusseldorf, n.d.

Biver, M.-L. *Pierre Fontaine: Premier Architecte de l'Empereur.* Paris: Plon, 1964.

Blanc, C. *Grammaire des arts du dessin.* Paris: Renouard, 1867.

Blanc, C. *Les Artistes de mon temps.* Paris: Didot, 1876.

Block, M. *Dictionnaire de l'administration française.* Paris-Strasbourg: Berger-Levrault, 1856, with augmented later editions.

Boime, A. "The Teaching Reform of 1863 and the Origins of Modernism in France." *Art Quarterly* NS1 (1977): 1–39.

Boime, A. *Thomas Couture.* New Haven: Yale University Press, 1980.

Boison, J. *Le Retour des cendres.* Paris, 1973.

Boisserée, S. *Histoire et description de la cathédrale de Cologne.* Stuttgart: Cotta; Paris: Didot, 1822–33.

Borel, P. "Du Mouvement en architecture." *L'Artiste* 2 (1833): 74–78.

Borel, P. "Les Artistes penseurs et les artistes creux." *L'Artiste* 5 (1833): 253–259.

Börsch-Suppan, E. *Berliner Architektur nach Schinkel 1840–1870.* Munich: Prestel, 1977.

Börsch-Suppan, E. *Garten- Landschafts- und Paradiesmotive im Innenraum: eine ikono-graphische Untersuchung.* Berlin: Hessling, 1967.

Bosquet, C. *La Major: cathédrale de Marseilles.* Marseilles, 1857.

Boullée, C.-E. *Mémoire sur les moyens de procurer à la Bibliothèque du Roi les advantages que ce monument exige.* Paris, 1785.

Brunot, A., and R. Coquand. *Le Corps des ponts et chaussées.* Paris: C. N. R. S., 1982.

Burnouf, E. "Le Parthénon." *Revue des deux mondes* 5S, 20 (December 1, 1847): 835–853.

Burnouf, E. "Les Propylées." *Archives des missions scientifiques et littéraires* 1 (1850): 8–38.

Caisse Nationale des Monuments Historiques et des Sites. *Le "Gothique" retrouvé avant Viollet-le-Duc.* Paris, 1979.

Canat, R. *L'Hellénisme des romantiques.* 3 vols. Paris: Didier, 1951–55.

Canlowicz, F. "M. Constant-Dufeux." *Moniteur des architectes* (1871): cols. 252–256.

Carnot, H. *Exposition de la doctrine Saint-Simonienne.* 2 vols. Paris: Le Globe, 1829–30.

Cassagne, A. *La Théorie de l'art pour l'art en France.* Paris: Hachette, 1895.

Cernesson, L. "Joseph-Louis Duc." *Revue générale de l'architecture et des travaux publics* 37 (1880): cols. 75–79, 156–160.

Charle, C. *Les hauts Fonctionnaires en France au XIXe siècle.* Paris: Gallimard, 1980.

Charles-Roux, J. *L'Isthme et le canal de Suez.* 2 vols. Paris: Hachette, 1901.

Charton, E.-T. *Guide pour le choix d'un état, ou dictionnaire des professions.* Paris, 1842, with editions in 1851 and 1880.

de Chateaubriand, F.-R. *Mémoires d'outre-tombe.* 12 vols. Paris: Penaud, 1849.

Chenavard, A. *Nouveau recueil de décorations intérieures.* Paris: Leconte, 1833–35.

Chenavard, A. *Album de l'ornameniste.* Edited by L. Batissier. Paris: Lenoir, 1845.

de Chennevieres, P. *Souvenirs d'un Directeur des Beaux-Arts.* 5 vols. Paris: L'Artiste, 1883–89.

Chevalier, M. *Religion Saint-Simonien. Politique industrielle. Système de la Méditerranée.* Paris: Le Globe, 1832.

de Choiseul-Gouffier, M.-G.-F.-A. *Voyage pittoresque de la Grèce.* 3 vols. Paris: Blaise, 1782–1822.

Clément de Ris, L. *Portraits à la plume.* Paris: Didier, 1853.

Considérant, V. *Considérations sociales sur l'architectonique.* Paris: Librairies du Palais-Royal, 1834.

Cordero di San Quintino. *Dell'italiana architettura durante la dominazione longobardo.* Brescia: N. Bettoni, 1829.

Coste, P.-X. *Mémoires d'un artiste: notes et souvenirs de voyage (1817–1877).* 2 vols. Marseilles: de Cayes, 1878.

Courajod, L. *Alexandre Lenoir: son journal et le musée des monuments français.* 3 vols. Paris: Champion, 1878–87.

Cousin, V. *Cours d'histoire de philosophie: cours de 1829.* 2 vols. Paris: Pichon & Didier, 1829.

Cousin, V. *Cours de philosophie professé à la faculté des lettres pendant l'année 1818.* Edited by A. Garnier. Paris: Hachette, 1836.

Cuvier, G. *Recherches sur les ossemens fossiles des quadrupèdes.* 4 vols. Paris: Deterville, 1812.

Daly, C. "Opinion de l'Académie royale des beaux-arts sur l'architecture gothique." *Revue générale de l'architecture et des travaux publics* 6 (1845–46): cols. 313–316.

Daly, C. "Bibliothèque Sainte-Geneviève." *Revue générale de l'architecture et des travaux publics* 10 (1852): cols. 379–384.

Daly, C. *L'Architecture privée au XIXme siècle sous Napoléon III.* 6 vols. Paris: Morel, 1864–77.

Daly, C. *Architecture funéraire contemporaine.* Paris: Ducher, 1871.

Daly, C. "Le Prix de cent milles francs." *Revue générale de l'architecture et des travaux publics* 27 (1869): cols. 177–183.

Darby, M. "Owen Jones and the Eastern Ideal." Doctoral dissertation, Reading University, 1974.

Darby, M. *The Islamic Perspective.* London: World of Islam Festival Trust, 1983.

Dartien, F. *Etudes sur l'architecture lombarde.* 2 vols. with atlas. Paris: Dunod, 1865–82.

Dartien, F. *M. Léonce Reynaud: sa vie et ses oeuvres par l'un de ses élèves.* Paris, 1885.

Dassy, L. *Compte rendu sur la restauration de Paestum exécutée en 1829 par Henri Labrouste.* Paris: Baur, 1879.

Davioud, G.-J.-A. "Funérailles de M. Léon Vaudoyer." *Bulletin de la société centrale des architectes* (1872).

Delaborde, H. *L'Oeuvre de Paul Delaroche . . . accompagné d'un notice historique sur la vie et les ouvrages de Paul Delaroche.* Paris: Goupil, 1858.

Delaborde, H. *Notice sur la vie et les ouvrages de M. Henri Labrouste.* Paris: Firmin-Didot, 1878.

Delaborde, H. *Notice sur la vie et les ouvrages de M. Duc.* Paris: Firmin-Didot, 1879.

Delagardette, C.-M. *Les Ruines de Paestum ou Posidonia.* Paris, An. VII.

Delaire, E., et al. *Les Architectes élèves de l'Ecole des Beaux-Arts.* Paris: de Chaix, 1895; second, augmented edition 1907.

Delécluze, E. *Louis David: son école et son temps.* Paris: Didier, 1855.

Documents relatifs aux travaux du Palais de Justice de Paris. . . . Paris: Préfecture de la Seine, 1858.

Drexler, A., et al. *The Architecture of the Ecole des Beaux-Arts.* New York and Cambridge, Mass.: Museum of Modern Art and The MIT Press, 1977.

Dufournet, P., et al. *Hector Horeau, 1801–1872.* Paris, 1979.

Durand, F. *La nouvelle cathédrale de Marseilles.* Nîmes, n.d.

Durand, J.-N.-L. *Précis des leçons d'architecture données à l'école polytechnique. . . .* 2 vols. Paris: author, 1802 and 1805, with later editions and additions.

Durand, J.-N.-L. *Recueil et parallèle des édifices de tout genre, anciens et modernes.* Paris, 1801.

Egbert, D. D. *The Beaux-Arts Tradition in French Architecture.* Princeton: Princeton University Press, 1980.

Ernouf, A.-A. *Paulin Talabot, sa vie et son oeuvre (1799–1885).* Paris: Plon, Nourrit & Cie, 1886.

d'Espouy, H. *Fragments d'architecture antique.* 2 vols. Paris: Schmid, n.d.

Fabre, A. *Les Rues de Marseilles.* 4 vols. Marseilles: Camouin, 1867–68.

Féraud, P. "Constant-Dufeux." *Revue générale de l'architecture et des travaux publics* 29 (1872): cols. 81–91, 132–137, 251–255.

Ferry, J. *Les Comptes fantastiques d'Haussmann.* Paris: Le Chevalier, 1868.

Formigé, J. "L'Ecole des Beaux-Arts." *L'Architecture* (1920): 16–24.

Fortoul, H.-N.-H. "De l'Art actuel." *Revue encyclopédique* 59 (1833): 108–153.

Fortoul, H.-N.-H. "L'Arc de Triomphe de l'Etoile." *La France littéraire* 26 (1839): 67–82.

Fortoul, H.-N.-H. *De l'Art en Allemagne*. 2 vols. Paris: Jules Labitte, 1842.

Foucart, B., et al. *Viollet-le-Duc*. Paris: Réunion des Musées Nationaux, 1980.

Foucart, B., et al. *Paul Abadie, architecte, 1812–1884: entre archéologie et modernité*. Angoulême: Musée d'Angoulême, 1984.

Fritsch, K. E. O., et al. *Der Kirchenbau des Protestantismus*. Berlin, 1893.

Garnier, C "Architecture en fer." *Le Musée des sciences* 41 (February 11, 1857).

Garnier, C. *A travers les Arts: causeries et mélanges*. Paris: Hachette, 1869.

Garnier, C. *Le Théâtre*. Paris: Hachette, 1871.

Garnier, C. *Le nouvel Opéra de Paris*. 2 vols. and atlas. Paris: Ducher, 1878–81.

Garnier, C., and A. Amann. *L'Habitation humaine*. Paris: Hachette, 1892.

Gautier, T., et al. *Le Palais pompéien*. Paris: "Au Palais pompéien," 1866.

Gautier, T. *Histoire de romantisme*. Paris: "bien publique," 1872.

Gebelin, F. *La Sainte-Chapelle et la Concièrgerie*. Paris: H. Laurens, 1931.

Geoffroy Saint-Hilaire, I. *Vie, travaux et doctrine scientifique d'Etienne Geoffroy Saint-Hilaire par son fils*. Paris: Bertrand, 1847.

Germann, G. *Der protestantische Kirchenbau in der Schweiz*. Zurich: Orell Fussli, 1963.

Germann, G. "Melchior Berris Rathausentwurf für Bern (1833)." *Baseler Zeitschrift für Geschichte und Alterthümskunde*. 1969, pp. 239–319.

Germann, G. *The Gothic Revival in Europe and Britain*. Cambridge, Mass.: The MIT Press, 1972.

Girard, L. *La Politique des travaux publics du Second Empire*. Paris: Colin, 1952.

de Gisors, A. *Le Palais du Luxembourg*. Paris: Plon Frères, 1847.

Gooch, G. P. *History and Historians in the Nineteenth Century*. London: Longmans Green, 1913.

Gourlier, C., et al. *Choix d'édifices projetés et construits en France depuis le commencement du XIXᵉ siècle*. 3 vols. Paris: Colas, 1825–50.

Gourlier, C. *Notice historique sur le service des travaux des Bâtiments Civils*. Paris: Cloas, 1848–49, with augmented editions in 1886 and 1895.

Graundmann, G. *August Soller, 1805–1853: ein Berliner Architekt im Geiste Schinkels*. Munich: Prestel, 1973.

Griffiths, D. A. *Jean Reynaud: encyclopédiste de l'époque romantique d'après sa correspondance inédite*. Paris, 1965.

Gromort, G. *Architecture*. Vol. 2 of *Histoire générale de l'art français de la Révolution à nos jours*. Paris: Librairie de France, 1922.

Guadet, J. *Eléments et théorie de l'architecture.* 4 vols. Paris: Librairie de la Construction Moderne, 1901–4.

Guizot, F. *Histoire de la révolution d'Angleterre.* 2 vols. Paris: Chantpie, 1826–27.

Haas, C.-P.-M. *Administration de la France.* 4 vols. Paris: Cosse & Marchal, 1861.

Halphen, L. *L'Histoire en France depuis cent ans.* Paris: A. Colin, 1914.

Hautecoeur, L. *Histoire de l'architecture classique en France.* 7 vols. Paris: Picard, 1943–57.

Hautecoeur, L. *Histoire du Louvre.* Paris: L'Illustration, 1928.

Hermant, A. "La Bibliothèque Sainte-Geneviève." *L'Artiste* 5S, 7 (December 1, 1851): 129–131.

Hitchcock, H. R. *Early Victorian Architecture.* 2 vols. New Haven: Yale University Press, 1954.

Hitchcock, H. R. *Architecture: Nineteenth and Twentieth Centuries.* Hammondsworth: Pelican, 1958.

Hittorff, J.-I., and L. Zanth. *Architecture antique de la Sicile.* Paris: Renouard, 1827–30.

Hittorff, J.-I., and L. Zanth. *Architecture moderne de la Sicile.* Paris: Renouard, 1835.

Hittorff, J.-I. *Restitution du temple d'Empédocle à Selinonte, ou l'Architecture polychrome chez les grecs.* Paris: Firmin-Didot, 1851.

"Honoré Daumet, 1826–1911, sa vie et ses oeuvres." *L'Architecture* 27 (1914): 49–55.

Hugo, V. *Notre-Dame de Paris, 1482.* Paris: Gosselin, 1831.

Jones, O., and J. Goury. *Plans, Elevations, Sections and Details of the Alhambra.* 3 vols. London, 1836–45.

Jullian, C. *Extraits des historiens français du XIXe siècle.* Bordeaux: Feret & fils, 1879.

Knibiehles, Y. *Naissance des sciences humaines: Mignet et l'histoire philosophique au XIXe siècle.* Paris: Flammarion, 1973.

Labrouste, H. *Temples de Paestum, Restaurations des monuments antiques par les architectes pensionnaires de l'Académie de France à Rome.* Paris: Firmin-Didot, 1877.

Labrouste, L. *La Bibliothèque Nationale: ses bâtiments et ses constructions.* Paris: Lutier, 1885.

Labrouste, L. *Esthétique monumentale.* Paris: Charles Schmid, 1902.

Lampue, P. *Programmes des concours d'architecture pour le Grand Prix de Rome.* Paris: Derenne, 1881.

Lance, A. *Dictionnaire des architectes français.* Paris: Morel, 1872.

Lassus, J.-B. "Réaction de l'Académie des Beaux-Arts contre l'art gothique." *Moniteur des arts* 24 and 25 (1846).

Laviron, G. "De l'architecture contemporaine et de la convenance de l'application du style gothique aux constructions religieuses du XIXe siècle." *Revue nouvelle* (October 1846).

Leflon, J. *Eugène de Mazenod (1782–1861).* 3 vols. Paris: Plon, 1957–65.

Legendre, P. *Histoire de l'administration de 1750 à nos jours.* Paris: P. U. F., 1968.

Leniaud, J.-M. *Jean-Baptiste Lassus (1807–1857), ou le temps retrouvé des cathédrales.* Geneva: Droz, 1980.

Lemonnier, H. "La Peinture murale de Paul Delaroche à l'hémicycle de l'Ecole des Beaux-Arts." *Gazette des Beaux-Arts* 4S, 13 (1917): 173–182.

Lenoir, Albert. "De l'Architecture byzantine." *Revue générale de l'architecture et des travaux publics* 1 (1840): cols. 7–17, 65–76, 257–263, 321–327, 449–456, 585–590.

Lenoir, Alexandre. *Description historique et chronologique des monuments de sculpture réunis au musée des monuments français.* Paris: Au Musée, An V, with numerous later editions.

Léon P. *La Vie des monuments français.* Paris: Picard, 1951.

Leroux, P. *Réfutation de l'eclectisme.* Paris: Gosselin, 1839.

Lesbazilles, E. *Les Colosses anciens et modernes.* Paris: Hachette, 1876.

de Lesseps, F. *Histoire du canal de Suez.* Paris: Pichon-Lamy & Dewez, 1870.

Lévêque, C. *La Science du beau.* Paris: Durand, 1861.

Levine, N. A. "The Idea of Frank Furness' Buildings." Master's thesis, Yale University, 1967.

Levine, N. A. "The Competition for the Grand Prix in 1824" and "The Book and the Building: Hugo's Theory of Architecture and the Bibliothèque Sainte-Geneviève." *The Beaux-Arts.* Edited by Robin Middleton. London: Thames and Hudson, 1982, 66–123 and 138–173.

Levine, N. A. "Architectural Reasoning in the Age of Positivism: the Néo-Grec Idea of Henri Labrouste's Bibliothèque Sainte-Geneviève." Doctoral dissertation, Yale University, 1975.

MacClintock, L. "Monumentality versus Suitability: Viollet-le-Duc's Saint-Gimer at Carcassonne." *Journal of the Society of Architectural Historians* 40, no. 3 (October 1981): 218–235.

Magne, L. *L'Architecture française du siècle.* Paris: Firmin-Didot, 1889.

Mallion, J. *Victor Hugo et l'art architectural.* Paris: Presses Universitaires de France, 1962.

Malo, H. "M. Thiers et les artistes de son temps." *Revue de Paris* 31 (July 1, 1924): 140–159.

Marmoz, C. "Félix Duban et l'Arc de Gaillon à l'Ecole des Beaux-Arts." *Bulletin de la société de l'histoire de l'art français.* (1977): 217–223.

Marmoz, C. "The Buildings of the Ecole des Beaux-Arts." *The Beaux-Arts.* Edited by Robin Middleton. London: Thames and Hudson, 1982, 124–137.

Massa-Gille, G. *Le Journal d'Hippolyte Fortoul*. Geneva: Droz, 1979.

Matas, N. *Dimonstrazione del progetto . . . per compiere la facciata insigne basilica Santa Maria del Fiore. . . .* Florence: M. Cellini, 1843.

Mérimée, P. *Correspondance générale.* Edited by M. Parturier. Toulouse: E. Privat; Paris: Le Divan, 1941ff.

Middleton, R. "Viollet-le-Duc." Doctoral dissertation, Cambridge University, 1959.

Middleton, R., and D. Watkin. *Neoclassicism and Nineteenth-Century Architecture.* New York: Abrams, 1980.

Middleton, R., editor. *The Beaux-Arts.* London: Thames and Hudson, 1982.

Mignet, F. "Etablissement de la réforme à Genève." *Mémoires historiques.* Paris: Charpentier, 1854.

Millet, E. "Henry Labrouste, sa vie, ses oeuvres." *Bulletin de la société centrale des architectes* (1879–80).

Mistral, F. *Un poète bilingue: Adolphe Dumas.* Paris: "Les Belles Lettres," 1927.

Mistral, F. *Mes Origines: mémoires et récits.* Paris: Plon-Nourrit, 1945.

Moissy, P. *Les Séjours en France de Sulpice Boisserée (1820–1825).* Lyon and Paris, 1956.

Monod, G. *La Vie et la pensée de Jules Michelet.* 2 vols. Paris: Champion, 1923.

Morin, A.-J. *Catalogue des collections de la conservatoire des arts et métiers.* Paris: Guiraudet & Jouaust, 1851 (with later augmented editions).

Müntz, E. *Guide de l'Ecole Nationale des Beaux-Arts.* Paris: Quantin, 1889.

Narjoux, F. *Monuments élevés par la Ville, 1850–1880.* 4 vols. Paris: Morel, 1881–83.

d'Ocagne, M. *Auguste Choisy et l'art de bâtir chez les anciens.* Vannes: Lafolye & La Marzelle, 1930.

Paris dans sa splendeur. Paris: Charpentier, 1861.

Parrocel, E. *L'Art dans le Midi.* 4 vols. Marseilles: Chatagnier, 1881–84.

Paris · Rome · Athènes: le voyage en Grèce des architectes français au XIXe et XXe siècles. Paris: Ecole des Beaux-Arts, 1982.

Percier, C., and P.-F.-L. Fontaine. *Plans de plusieurs châteaux, palais et résidences des souverains de France, d'Italie, d'Espagne et de Russie.* Paris: Marguerie, 1833.

Perouse de Montclos, J.-M. *L'Architecture à la française.* Paris: Picard, 1982.

Parturier, M., editor. *Lettres de Merrimée à Ludovic Vitet.* Paris: Plon, 1934.

Pascal, J.-L. "M. Duc et son influence sur le mouvement architectural contemporain." *Gazette des Beaux-Arts* 2S, 19 (1879, pt. 1): 430–443.

Pascal, J.-L. "H. Lefuel." *Revue générale de l'architecture et des travaux publics* 38 (1881): cols. 259–266.

Peisse, L. "L'Ecole des Beaux-Arts." *Revue des deux mondes* 24 (October 15, 1941): 232–245.

Penrose, F. C. *An Investigation of the Principles of Athenian Architecture*. London: Society of Dilettanti, 1851.

Petroz, P. *L'Art et la critique en France depuis 1822*. Paris: Germer Baillière, 1875.

Pevsner, N. *A History of Building Types*. Princeton: Princeton University Press, 1976.

Peyre, H. *Bibliographie critique de l'hellénisme en France de 1843 à 1870*. New Haven: Yale University Press, 1932.

Picard, A. *Les Chemins de fer français*. 6 vols. Paris: J. Rothschild, 1884–85.

Pigeory, F. *Les Monuments de Paris: histoire de l'architecture civile, politique et religieuse sous le règne de Louis Philippe*. Paris: Hermitte, 1847.

Pinkney, D. H. *Napoleon III and the Rebuilding of Paris*. Princeton: Princeton University Press, 1958.

Pirotte, O. *Alexandre-François-Auguste Vivien de Goubert (1799–1854)*. Paris: Librairie générale de droit et de jurisprudence, 1972.

Plouin, R. "Henry Labrouste, sa vie, son oeuvre, 1801–1875." Thèse du troisième cycle, University of Paris, 1965.

Porter, A. K. *Lombard Architecture*. 3 vols. New Haven: Yale University Press, 1917.

Questel, C.-A. *Notice sur Duban*. Paris: Firmin-Didot, 1872.

Quatremère de Quincy, A.-C. *Architecture* in the *Encyclopédie méthodique*. 3 vols. Paris: Panckoucke, 1788–1835.

Quatremère de Quincy, A.-C. "Mémoire sur la manière dont les temples des grecs et romains étaient éclairés." *Académie des inscriptions et belles lettres: mémoires* 3 (1818): 166–284.

Quatremère de Quincy, A.-C. *Dictionnaire historique d'architecture*. 2 vols. Paris: Leclère, 1832.

Quatremère de Quincy, A.-C. *Recueil des notices lués dans les séances publiques de l'Académie royale des Beaux-Arts*. Paris: Leclère, 1834.

Quinet, E. *Le Génie des religions*. Paris: Charpentier, 1842.

Quinet, E. *Le Christianisme et la révolution française*. Paris: Comon, 1845.

Rabreau, D., et al. *Gabriel Davioud, architecte (1824–1881)*. Paris: Délégation à l'Action Artistique de la Ville de Paris, 1981.

Radet, G. *L'Histoire et l'oeuvre de l'Ecole française d'Athènes*. Paris: Fontemoing, 1901.

Rambert, G. *Marseilles: la formation d'une grande cité moderne*. Marseilles: "Sémaphor." 1934.

Raphael, P., and M. Goutard. *Hippolyte Fortoul, 1851–1856: un ministre de l'Instruction Publique sous l'Empire autoritaire*. Paris: P. U. F., 1975.

Raulin, M.-G. *Charles-August Questel*. Paris: Firmin-Didot, 1888.

Revoil, A.-H. *Architecture romane du Midi de la France*. 3 vols. Paris: Morel, 1867–73.

Revoil, A.-H. "Léon Vaudoyer." *Le Messager du Midi*, February 14, 1872.

Reynaud, J., editor, with P. Leroux. *Encyclopédie nouvelle*. 8 vols. Paris: Gosselin, 1834–41.

Reynaud, J. *Terre et Ciel*. Paris: Furne et Cie, 1854.

Reynaud, L. "Architecture," "Bramante," "Brunelleschi," "Colonne." *Encyclopédie nouvelle*. 8 vols. Paris: Gosselin, 1834–41.

Reynaud, L. *Traité d'architecture*. 2 vols. with atlas. Paris: Carlian-Goeury & Dalmont, 1850 and 1858.

Rivoira, G. T. *Le Origine della architettura lombarda e delle sue principali derivazioni nei paesi d'oltr'Alpo*. 2 vols. Rome: Loescher, 1901–7.

Rougier, E. *La Cathédrale de Marseilles*. Marseilles, 1894.

Saddy, P. *Henry Labrouste, architecte, 1801–1875*. Paris: Caisse Nationale des Monuments Historiques et des Sites, 1977.

Said, E. *Orientalism*. New York: Pantheon, 1978.

Schmit, J.-P. and B. Sauvan, *Histoire et description pittoresque du Palais de Justice, de la Conciergerie et de la Sainte-Chapelle de Paris*. Paris: Engelmann, 1825.

Schubiger, B. *Felix Wilhelm Kubly, 1802–1872*. St. Gall: Staats-und Stiftsarchiv St. Gallen, 1984.

The Second Empire 1852–1870: Art in France Under Napoleon III. Philadelphia and Paris: Philadelphia Museum of Art and the Réunion des Musées Nationaux, 1979.

Sédille, P. "Victor Baltard." *Gazette des Beaux-Arts* 2S, 11 (1874): 485–496.

Sédille, P. *Joseph-Louis Duc, architecte (1802–1879)*. Paris: Morel, 1879.

Semper, G. "On the Study of Polychromy and its Revival." *Museum of Classical Antiquities* 1 (1851): 228–255.

Singer-Kerel, J. *Le Coût de la vie à Paris de 1840 à 1845*. Paris, 1961.

Simonde de Sismondi, J. C. L. *Histoire des républiques italiennes du moyen-âge*. 11 vols. Paris: Treuttel & Wurtz, 1815–18.

Souvenirs d'Henri Labrouste, architecte, membre de l'Institut, notes receuillées et classées par ses enfants. Paris, 1928.

Stein, H. *Le Palais de Justice et la Sainte-Chapelle de Paris*. Paris: Longuet, 1912.

Steinhauser, M. *Die Architektur der Pariser Oper*. Munich: Prestel, 1969.

Szambien, W. *Jean-Nicolas-Louis Durand. 1760–1834: de l'imitation à la norme*. Paris: Picard, 1984.

Taine, H. *Les Philosophes français du XIXe siècle*. Paris: Hachette, 1857.

Teissier, O. *Marseilles sous Napoléon III*. Marseilles: A. Gueidon, 1866.

Texier, C.-F.-M. *Description de l'Asie Mineur*. 3 vols. Paris: Firmin-Didot, 1839–49.

Teyssot, G. "Planning and Building in Towns: The System of the Bâtiments Civils in France, 1795–1848." *The Beaux-Arts*. Edited by Robin Middleton. London: Thames and Hudson, 1982, 34–49.

Thierry, A. *Lettres sur l'histoire de France*. Paris: Sautelet, 1827.

Thoré, T. "L'Ecole des Beaux-Arts." *L'Artiste* 2S, 1 (1838): 220–222, 305–307.

Thuillier, G. *Témoins de l'administration de St. Just à Marx*. Paris: Berger-Levrault, 1967.

Thuillier, G. *La Vie quotidienne des ministères au XIXe siècle*. Paris: Hachette, 1976.

Thuillier, G. *Bureaucratie et Bureaucrates en France au XIXe siècle*. Geneva: Droz, 1980.

Thuillier, G. *Histoire de l'administration française*. Paris: P. U. F., 1984.

Trachtenberg, M. *The Statue of Liberty*. New York: Viking, 1976.

Trianon, H. "La nouvelle Biblothèque Sainte-Geneviève." *L'Illustration* (1852): 29–30.

Van Brunt, H. "Greek Lines." *The Atlantic Monthly* 7 (1861): 654–667 (republished in his *Greek Lines and Other Architectural Essays*. Boston: Houghton Mifflin, 1893).

Van Zanten, A. L. "Form and Society." *Oppositions* 8 (Spring 1977): 137–145.

Van Zanten, A. L. "The Palace and the Temple: Two Utopian Architectural Visions of the 1830's." *Art History* 2 (June 1979): 179–200.

Van Zanten, A. L. "César Daly and the *Revue Générale de l'Architecture*." Doctoral dissertation, Harvard University, 1981.

Van Zanten, D. T. "The Architectural Polychromy of the 1830's." Doctoral dissertation, Harvard University, 1970 (published by the Garland Publishing Company, 1976).

Van Zanten, D. T. "Félix Duban and the Buildings of the Ecole des Beaux-Arts." *Journal of the Society of Architectural Historians* 37, no. 3 (October 1978): 161–174.

Van Zanten, D. T. "The Beginnings of French Romantic Architecture and Félix Duban's Temple Protestant." *In Search of Modern Architecture*. Edited by Helen Searing. Cambridge, Mass.: The MIT Press, 1982, 64–84.

Van Zanten, D. T. "Architectural Polychromy: The Life in Architecture." *The Beaux-Arts*. Edited by Robin Middleton. London: Thames and Hudson, 1982, 196–215.

Vaudoyer, A.-L.-T. *Description du théâtre de Marcellus à Rome. . . .* Paris: Dusillon, 1812.

Vaudoyer, L. "Etudes d'architecture en France." *Magasin pittoresque* 7–21 (1839–53).

Vaudoyer, L. "Histoire de l'architecture en France." *Patria*. Edited by J. Aicard. Paris: Dubochet, Le Chevalier, 1846.

Vaudoyer, L. *Discours pronouncé au funérailles de M. Duban*. Paris: Firmin-Didot, 1871.

Verdier, P. "Le Service des Monuments Historiques: son histoire, organization, administration, législation (1830–1834)." *Congrès archéologique de France* 2S, 1 (1934): 53–246.

Victor Hugo raconté par un témoin de sa vie. 2 vols. Paris: Nelson, n.d.

de Viel Castel, H. *Mémoires sur le règne de Napoléon III.* Edited by Léonzon le Duc. 4 vols. Paris: Chez Tous les Librairies, 1883–84.

Viollet-le-Duc, E.-E. "Du Style gothique au XIXe siècle." *Annales archéologiques* 4 (1846): 325–353.

Viollet-le-Duc, E.-E. "Les Mandarins à Paris." *Gazette des Beaux-Arts* 1 (1859): 90–97.

Viollet-le-Duc, E.-E. *Dictionnaire raisonné de l'architecture française du XIe au XVIe siècle.* 10 vols. Paris: Morel, 1854–68.

Viollet-le-Duc, E.-E. *Entretiens sur l'architecture.* 2 vols. and atlas. Paris: Morel, 1863 and 1872.

Viollet-le-Duc, E.-E. "Lettres extra-parlementaires." *Le XIXe Siècle,* January 29, 1877, ff.

Viollet-le-Duc, E.-E. *Histoire d'un hôtel de ville et d'une cathédrale.* Paris: Hetzel, 1878.

Viollet-le-Duc, E.-L. *Lettres inédites de Viollet-le-Duc, recueillées et annotées par son fils.* Paris: Libraries-Imprimeries Réunies, 1902.

Viollet le Duc, G., editor. *E. Viollet-le-Duc: Lettres d'Italie, 1836–1837, addressées à sa famille.* Paris: Laget, 1971.

Vitet, L. "De l'Indépendance en matière du goût." *Le Globe* 89 (April 2, 1825).

Vitet, L. "Paul Delaroche: la Salle des Prix à l'Ecole des Beaux-Arts." *Revue des deux mondes* 28 (December 15, 1841): 937–954.

Vitet, L. *Monographie de l'église de Notre Dame-de-Noyon.* Paris: Imprimerie Royale, 1845.

Vitet, L. *Etudes sur les beaux-arts.* 2 vols. Paris: Charpentier, 1846.

Vitet, L. "Le Louvre." *Revue contemporaine* (September 15, 1852).

Vitet, L. "Le Nouveau Louvre." *Revue des deux mondes* 2S, 64 (July 1, 1866): 57–93.

Vivien, A.-F.-A. "Etudes administratives." *Revue des deux mondes* 32ff. (1842–45), published as a book under that title, Paris: Guillaumin, 1845.

Wacquet, F. *Les Fêtes royales sous la Restauration, ou l'ancien régime retrouvé.* Geneva: Droz, 1981.

Weill, G. *L'Ecole Saint-Simonienne.* Paris: Alcan, 1896.

Whiteley, J. "The Revival in Painting of Themes Inspired by Antiquity in the Mid-Nineteenth Century." Doctoral dissertation, Oxford University, 1972.

Ziff, N. "Paul Delaroche: A Study in Nineteenth-Century French History Painting." Doctoral dissertation, New York University Institute of Fine Arts, 1974.

INDEX